Macroeconomic Foundations of Macroeconomics

Contrary to common belief, macroeconomics is not merely a theory of aggregates, and cannot be constructed from individual behaviour. Both nationally and internationally, there are economic laws that are logically independent of economic agents' behaviour. These are the macroeconomic foundations of macroeconomics.

Presenting cutting-edge material, Alvaro Cencini explores these foundations, and shows that the introduction of money entails economics being interpreted conceptually not mathematically. His innovative book provides the elements for a new approach by applying the most recent results of monetary analysis to the study of national and international economics. It covers recent progress in monetary theory, provides the reader with a greater understanding of the subject, and will be essential reading for economic students as well as a valuable resource for economists.

Alvaro Cencini is Professor of Monetary Economics at the University of Lugano, and director of the Laboratory of Research in Monetary Economics at the Centre for Banking Studies, Lugano, Switzerland.

Routledge frontiers of political economy

Macroeconomic Foundations
of Macroeconomics

Alvaro Cencini

LONDON AND NEW YORK

First published 2005
by Routledge
2 Park Square, Milton Park, Abingdon, Oxon, OX14 4RN

Simultaneously published in the USA and Canada
by Routledge
270 Madison Ave, New York NY 10016

Routledge is an imprint of the Taylor & Francis Group

Transferred to Digital Printing 2007

© 2005 Alvaro Cencini

Typeset in Baskerville by Wearset Ltd, Boldon, Tyne and Wear

British Library Cataloguing in Publication Data
A catalogue record for this book is available from the British Library

Library of Congress Cataloging in Publication Data
A catalog record for this book has been requested

ISBN10: 0-415-31265-5 (hbk)
ISBN10: 0-415-45929-X (pbk)

ISBN13: 978-0-415-31265-3 (hbk)
ISBN13: 978-0-415-45929-7 (pbk)

To Ginevra, Marco, and Massimo

This means, on the one hand, that an economic writer requires from his reader much goodwill and intelligence and a large measure of co-operation; and, on the other hand, that there are a thousand futile, yet verbally legitimate, objections which an objector can raise. In economics you cannot *convict* your opponent of error; you can only *convince* him, if there is a defect in your own powers of persuasion and exposition or if his head is already so filled with contrary notions that he cannot catch the clues to your thought which you are trying to throw to him.

(Keynes 1973b: 470)

Contents

Figures

Tables

Acknowledgements

My work, and indeed this book, have greatly benefited from the support of my colleague and friend Bernard Schmitt. I know no worthier way of thanking him but to say that his ideas pervade the analysis expounded in this book. In a different way I am also much indebted to Niklas Damiris, a physicist, whose interest in economics and whose grasp of the subject go beyond any reasonable expectation. He combed through the whole manuscript, critically, and helped to refine it conceptually and linguistically. My thanks also go to Sergio Rossi, who trained his sharp eye on both the manuscript and the proofs, spotting even errors invisible to others. My research assistant Igor Franchini plotted all the figures and tables and, together with Nicole Martinez, provided bibliographical assistance. They deserve warmest thanks. An affectionate mention is due to Simona Cain, who has once again proved to be the guardian angel and *arbiter* of English style. Finally, I would like to thank Rob Langham and Taiba Batool – senior editor and editorial assistant at Routledge – as well as their team, for their very professional guidance and advice.

Introduction

In their contribution to Harcourt's book on the microeconomic foundations of macroeconomics (Harcourt 1977), Malinvaud and Younès start by
admitting that, although '[i]t is by now widely accepted that the general
competitive equilibrium does not provide the appropriate foundation for
the macroeconomic theory [...] we have no alternative accepted microeconomic model that would provide such a foundation' (Malinvaud and
Younès 1977: 62). Then, they set at work to provide a new formalization
capable to account 'both for the competitive equilibrium of the Walrasian
economy and for the underemployment equilibrium of the Keynesian
economy' (ibid.: 62). Finally, they admit that their effort aims at 'finding a
fundamental model that helps to unify various lines of theoretical development and may be used for subsequent research in mathematical economics' (ibid.: 62). In just a few lines of their introductive section,
Malinvaud and Younès emphasize four important features of the conventional mainstream approach to macroeconomics: (1) that macroeconomics must be founded on microeconomics; (2) that the
microeconomic foundations of macroeconomics are derived from general
equilibrium analysis; (3) that Keynesian economics may be essentially
represented as an equilibrium model; and (4) that the *core* of economics is
mathematical. The aim of our study is to show that each of these four
claims is wrong. In particular, we shall attempt to show that macroeconomics has its own foundations, which are by no means microeconomic, and that the introduction of money requires economics to be
interpreted conceptually and not mathematically.

Later on, in his 1991 book on macroeconomic research, Malinvaud was
to ask himself whether or not macroeconomic events can be understood
independently of microeconomic events. His answer was that this is obviously not the case, since economists must necessarily derive data from
their direct experience of microeconomic occurrences. '[Macroeco-
nomic] models' purpose is to specify what we already know about factors
liable to determine macroeconomic events and about the relations
between these factors; but our previous knowledge derives from the
microeconomic level, since it concerns the conditions in which economic

agents act as well as the decisions they take' (Malinvaud 1991: 24, our translation). Malinvaud has always been well aware of the difficulty to move from reality to its intellectual representation when this is done through economic modelling. As he claims: 'the [mathematical] modelling of behaviour has not yet been achieved' (ibid.: 120, our translation). Yet, this does not discourage him from arguing that the lack of rational behaviour can successfully be accounted for if we are able 'to introduce into our reasoning a new dimension of complexity without making every theory, every induction and every application impossible' (ibid.: 120, our translation). The French economist never seems to doubt the general validity of mathematical modelling. He believes it to be the only way to transform economics into a scientific discipline, even though he recognizes that if too much complexity is introduced into models, they become totally useless, too complicated to provide any solution and incapable of handling even by the most sophisticated mathematical tools.

Now, it is in Walras's formalization of general equilibrium that mathematical economics finds its modern foundations. Strongly influenced by classical mechanics and by the desire to transform economics into an exact science, Walras was the first to provide a full mathematical model aiming at reproducing the workings of a real economy. As he claimed in a paper titled 'Economie et mécanique' published in the *Bulletin de la Société Vaudoise de Sciences Naturelles* (1909), his starting point was the belief that economics is a psychico-mathematical science whose objects of inquiry are essentially 'intimate' facts. In his attempt to establish a close analogy between economics, mechanics, and astronomy, Walras claims that, in the same way as in physics '*forces* would be the causes of *the traverse of space, masses* the causes of *time elapsed* during the traverse, [in economics] the *utilities* and the *raretés* would be the causes of *supply* and *demand*, from which would result the *value in exchange*' (Walras 1909/1990: 213). Even though utility and rarity cannot be measured, their effect, that is, 'the value of exchange or the characteristic contained in those things constituting the social wealth which enables them to be exchanged in certain quantifiably determined proportions, [is enough to make of] pure economics [...] a mathematical science' (ibid.: 207). The logical chain of events is therefore supposed to go from utility and rarity to the value in exchange. Were it to be possible to determine relative value through direct exchange, utility and rarity could be conceived of as the causes of supply and demand and, through their interplay, of the quantitative relationship between real goods.

In a letter to Walras, the great French mathematician Poincaré pointed out some of the difficulties faced by Walras's general equilibrium analysis, in particular concerning the need to get rid of the arbitrary functions introduced to deal with the fact that human satisfaction is not a measurable magnitude, so that 'there are no means to compare satisfactions felt by different individuals' (Poincaré in Walras 1909/1990: 324, our translation). Poincaré's reservations as to the use of mathematic formalism in economics are currently shared by numerous economists. For example, in a letter to *Science* Leontief did not hesitate to state that

> Year after year economic theorists continue to produce scores of mathematical models and to explore in great detail their formal properties; and the econometricians fit algebraic functions of all possible shapes to essentially the same sets of data without being able to advance, in any perceptible way, a systematic understanding of the structure and the operations of a real economic system.
>
> (Leontief 1982: 104)

Another example is given by Lawson who, in the preface to his highly praised volume on economics and reality, states: '[h]aving come to economics by way of first studying mathematics I was immediately impressed by, as I saw it, the widespread and rather uncritical application of formalistic methods and systems to conditions for which they were obviously quite unsuited' (Lawson 1997: xiii).

Despite numerous criticisms addressed to mathematical formalization in the realm of economics, Walras's neoclassical paradigm has never been rejected. In fact, the great majority of economists has long since replaced economic conceptualization with mathematical modelling. Another clear sign of the influence exerted by the Walrasian approach to economic thinking is the widely shared belief in the microeconomic foundations of macroeconomics. Opinions differ among economists about the kind of microeconomics best suited to provide a consistent foundation for macroeconomics. While Keynesian economists privilege non-Walrasian choice theories, to a neoclassical economist the 'study of the microfoundations of macroeconomics is coextensive with general equilibrium analysis' (Weintraub 1979: 10). Although the majority of Keynesians and the totality of post-Keynesian economists would disagree with Weintraub's claim, it is a fact that the majority of them share his belief in the need for microfoundations. For example, it is well known that '[n]ew Keynesians fully endorse the call, initiated by Lucas, that macroeconomic models should be based on coherent microfoundations' (Snowdon and Vane 1997a: 439). As confirmed by Mankiw when interviewed by Snowdon and Vane, there seems to be little doubt that 'all macrophenomena are the aggregate of many microphenomena; [so that] in that sense macroeconomics is inevitably founded on microeconomics' (Mankiw 1997: 456).

Neoclassical and Keynesian economists part company when it comes to defining the autonomy of macroeconomics with respect to microeconomics. Can macroeconomics 'provide any significant insight that was *logically* unattainable from a mere rigorous disaggregative approach' (Weintraub 1979: 7), or is it entirely dependent on microeconomics? The position shared by neoclassical economists is clear: microeconomics is prior to and independent of macroeconomics. 'There should be little argument about the proposition that some sort of revivified, reconstituted general equilibrium theory is the only logically possible general link between microeconomics and macroeconomics' (ibid.: 161). In their attempt to show the logical priority of microeconomics and general equilibrium analysis (GEA), neoclassical theorists go as far as to reject the traditional distinction between micro and macroeconomics. Thus, Weintraub maintains that micro and macroeconomics are best distinguished by referring to the specific problems each approach is best suited for, instead of emphasizing now the individual now the aggregate aspects of the two analyses. According to mainstream (neoclassical) economists, macroeconomics is not a distinct body of knowledge, but a particular way of applying a neo-Walrasian synthesis in cases when 'practical answers to practical questions require the analyst to suppress the complexity of interaction to gain the richness of specificity' (ibid.: 71). The choice between one approach and another is thus a question of emphasis and of degree of complexity within a theoretical framework essentially based on the neo-Walrasian GEA. The upshot: whether defined as the result of aggregation or generalization, macroeconomics remains entirely dependent on microeconomics. '[T]he ADM [Arrow–Debreu model] structure is a metatheory, or an investigative logic which, since it is used to construct all economic theories, must necessarily be used to examine "microfoundations of macroeconomics" models' (ibid.: 73).

Most Keynesian economists do not accept Weintraub's claim that 'general equilibrium theory, the kind of general systems theory that economists have developed, is the appropriate logic to investigate the compatibility between microeconomics and macroeconomics' (ibid.: 73). Even those most in tune with neoclassical analysis admit that they are not 'sure that all macroeconomics necessarily has to start off with microeconomic building blocks' (Mankiw 1997: 456), and are not prepared to endorse all the main tenets of GEA. Their own positions, however, are far from coherent, and vary from alternative versions of non-Walrasian equilibrium analysis to attempts to do away with any form of neoclassical analysis. For example, according to Leijonhufvud, the central questions in macroeconomics regard the way 'the market system "automatically" co-ordinates economic activities' (Leijonhufvud 1992: 29). Hence, the emphasis is put on the capacity of the free market to co-ordinate the activity of individual agents, 'when people have not succeeded from the outset in setting these general equilibrium prices that would have co-ordinated all activity' (ibid.: 29–30). Since assumptions about rational expectations, rational choices, and market clearing are not enough to guarantee perfect co-ordination as in the case of asymmetric information or in the presence of externalities, the question asked by Leijonhufvud is whether it is still possible to consider macroeconomics as the study of system co-ordination, that is, how the system as a whole can deal with equilibria outside the general equilibrium condition.

By and large, most Keynesian economists would probably accept Romer's claim that 'uniting microeconomics and macroeconomics may not be [a realistic goal]: the simplifications that are useful in understanding most microeconomic phenomena may be fatal to efforts to understand macroeconomic fluctuations' (Romer 1993: 20). It is also generally agreed that 'perhaps the most obvious and fundamental [avenue of research], is to examine the macroeconomic evidence concerning the effects of monetary and other aggregate demand disturbances' (ibid.: 20). In fact, Weintraub admits that monetary analysis is best developed through a macroeconomic approach. 'One should not infer arrogance among general equilibrium theorists: their understanding of money, bonds, and intertemporal choice in a monetary economy will be shaped almost totally by the more sophisticated, although more aggregated understanding of macro-monetary theorists' (Weintraub 1979: 8). As maintained by an increasing number of theorists, monetary economics is not satisfactorily dealt with by traditional GEA. Recent developments in neoclassical analysis show that concepts such as that of the Walrasian 'auctioneer' or the 'tâtonnement' (groping) process fail to account for changes in transaction structures, expectations, information, monetary and financial institutions. In order to deal with the problems of a decentralized monetary economy, a new series of models has been proposed, ranging from non-Walrasian models of general equilibrium based on game theory to the monetary models of an Edgeworthian-type disequilibrium *à la* Ostroy and Starr. As innovative as these attempts may appear, however, they still rely on an old-fashioned conception of money. In particular, they seem unable or unwilling to recognize the totally immaterial nature of bank money. In fact, the reason for their anachronistic choice of commodity money is that it pares away the risk to be forced to abandon the safe harbour of the neoclassical paradigm of general equilibrium. Yet, the hope of safeguarding the principles of the axiomatic approach, as advocated by Walras and his followers, is jeopardized by the actual working of our economies. From prices to profits, from capital to interest, from saving to investment, economic concepts and magnitudes are clearly of a monetary nature. Moreover – as bankers well know – money does certainly not pertain directly to the world of real goods and services, so that any attempt at explaining economics in pure real terms is doomed to failure. Unless one uncritically accepts Debreu's axiom that real goods *are* numbers, one has to admit that Walras's relative exchange is unsuited to solving the problem for which it was conceived: the determination of numerical prices. It is only money – conceived of as a purely numerical form – that can allow for the solution to this key problem. But this implies a radical change affecting the whole body of theoretical economics, and, in particular, the relationship between micro- and macroeconomics.

The central role played by mathematical formalization within the neoclassical framework has led a great number of economists to believe microeconomics to be more rigorous than, and logically prior to, macroeconomics. '[M]icroeconomics was codified and given a well-articulated mathematical structure when macroeconomics was just emerging from its pre-analytical stage' (Howitt 1992: 633). Let us observe that, while it is true that microeconomics was given a mathematical structure from the outset, it seems exaggerated to claim that authors such as Smith, Ricardo, and Marx belong to the pre-analytical stage of economic theory. In fact, it would be far more correct to acknowledge that the mathematical tools used by Walras were extremely simplistic and that his economic analysis was far less articulated than the Classics. The success of Walras's microeconomic approach stems from a peculiar state of affairs: on the one hand, the use of mathematics gave his analysis a scientific imprimatur, on the other, the limited level of economic conceptualization increased its appeal to economists of a more pragmatic bend than the Classics. This is not to say, however, that Walras's analysis did not mark a progress with respect to that of his predecessors. In particular, it is he who definitively abandoned the metaphysical conception of incorporated value defended by the Classics, replacing it with his idea that value results from an exchange and not from a materialization of labour time. Now, the real point at stake is whether Walras's microeconomic approach is the analytically necessary foundation of economics or just a step towards a new theory that will ultimately encompass both classical and neoclassical analyses. The aim of this book is to show that it is the second alternative that holds.

As can easily be shown, the classical economists of the past developed their theories in macroeconomic terms, and it can be legitimately maintained that even Quesnay worked out his *Tableau économique* from a macroeconomic point of view. Physiocrats apart, it is hard to deny that from Smith to Marx economics has mainly been seen as the science studying the laws governing the economic system as a whole. The classical analyses of value, wealth, distribution, capital accumulation, and economic crises are essentially macroeconomic. The market and equilibrium approaches to economics are certainly not essential in classical analysis, which considers prices to be absolute and derived from production. Of course, when Keynes published his *Treatise on Money* (1930), Walras's *Elements of Pure Economics* was already a successful book, and the neoclassical view was well accepted. Yet, Keynes's thought remained closely related to the Classics, whose influence is strong and evident in several passages in the *Treatise* as well as in the *General Theory*. Obviously, this is not to deny the merits and the originality of Keynes's own contribution, but to emphasize the fact that macroeconomics has preoccupied economic theories since the beginnings of our discipline. Keynes took over the Classics' point of view precisely to the extent that he privileged, as they did, the analysis of production over that of exchange. The great step forward made by Keynes consisted in his choice of money as the numerical standard of value. His attempt clearly consisted in working out a monetary theory of production. And in this sense it can indeed be claimed that Keynes's work marks the beginning of *modern* macroeconomics.

The microeconomic approach advocated by Walras was antithetical to the macroeconomic analysis developed by the Classics. To the extent that it provided a valid alternative to the physicalist conception of value, it represented a necessary step towards a better understanding of economics. Yet, as always happens in a dialectical process, the neoclassical antithesis cannot be considered the final stage of economic theorizing, but will itself have to be replaced by a theory combining the best elements of the two approaches. This is what Keynes's theory was intended to do: provide a synthesis between classical and neoclassical analyses transcending the traditional opposition of micro and macroeconomics. As economists know, this aim has been scorned and neglected given the attempt by general equilibrium theorists to subsume Keynes's contribution under a neoclassical synthesis and also because of Keynes's own inability to found macroeconomics on consistent and autonomous macroeconomic principles.

Walras's main contribution to economic analysis is his discovery of the numerical nature of value as opposed to the dimensional conception of the Classics. Against the belief of his predecessors as well as against the opinion of most mathematicians of his time, Walras consistently maintained that economic value is not part of the physical dimension of goods and that a standard of economic value is therefore also dimensionless. In its essence, Walras's *numéraire* is nothing other than a purely numerical standard. Now, Walras missed an important part of the implications of his seminal discovery. In particular, he did not integrate it correctly with his conceptions of money and production, thus missing the opportunity to discover the very foundations of macroeconomics. Keynes's analysis did not quite succeed either. Emphasis now shifted from relative exchange to production, and money was made to play a central role; yet the influence of general equilibrium analysis was strong enough to force Keynes to look for a compromise permitting the incorporation of microeconomic principles into his macroeconomic approach. Keynesians tried to push further in this direction, thus legitimating a neoclassical interpretation of Keynes's theory. In the process, both Walras's and Keynes's central insights got lost in the search for microeconomic foundations of macroeconomics.

A true synthesis between Walras on one side and Keynes and the Classics on the other requires the application of Walras's concept of *numéraire* to the monetary analysis of production and the working out of coherent macroeconomic foundations. It is symptomatic that even a non-Walrasian general equilibrium theorist like Fitoussi stands for the autonomy of macroeconomics. 'If a macroeconomic logic partially independent of that which determines individual behaviour exists [...] perhaps that logic deserves to be analysed in itself. That it has only rarely been analysed does not represent an impossibility theorem. My conviction is that macroeconomics has its own dimension which must be considered and not just alluded to' (Fitoussi 1983: 27–8). Fitoussi's is still a minority point of view, as is that of Hoover, who maintains that macroeconomics is independent of individual behaviour and that 'the arguments for microfoundations for macroeconomics are unsound, resting on equivocations and false analogies' (Hoover 2001: 285); and he does not hesitate to claim that '[t]he representative-agent model is an implicit concession, a capitulation, to the impossible goal of the microfoundational program' (ibid.: 285). In this book we have endeavoured to contribute to the effort of building up the macroeconomic foundations for macroeconomics while allowing for the dialectical synthesis of the classical, neoclassical, and Keynesian analyses into a new monetary theory of production and circulation.

The book is structured into four parts. Part I considers the latest state of the art concerning the distinction between micro and macroeconomics, and contrasts the traditional microeconomic approach of mainstream economics to a new, macroeconomic approach based on a reappraisal of Keynes's fundamental identities. Chapter 1 is concerned with a brief survey of neoclassical, new classical, and real business cycle economics. As clearly stated by Gerrard, all these approaches stem from the same theoretical background and presuppose macroeconomics to be based on microeconomic foundations. 'The defining character of mainstream macroeconomics is the presupposition that the macro economy should be interpreted as the aggregate outcome of optimizing choices by rational agents seeking to allocate scarce resources between competing ends in a set of markets regulated by the price mechanism' (Gerrard 1996: 65). Seriously challenged in the 1960s by Keynesian macroeconometric models, general equilibrium analysis experienced a landslide comeback promoted by Lucas's new classical approach to macroeconomics. Based on the GEA principles of price flexibility and competitive market clearing, new classical economics is a sophisticated attempt to account for temporary disequilibrium due to uncorrelated random errors, while reaffirming the centrality of GEA. Economic agents are supposed to act according to the rational expectations hypothesis. When the economy is subjected to random exogenous shocks, voluntary responses to misperceived price signals may lead to output and employment fluctuations. Yet, in conformity with the rational expectations hypothesis, economic agents will soon become aware of their mistake and modify their behaviour so as to restore equilibrium at a level compatible with the evolution of relative prices. Unlike new classical economists, real business cycle theorists strongly reaffirm the neoclassical homogeneity postulate and reject the idea that monetary shocks can be the main cause of business cycles. Consistent with the GEA conception of money neutrality, they believe money to play no essential role, economic fluctuations being mainly due to real shocks such as large random variations in the rate of technological change. Now, both the rational expectations hypothesis of new classical economics and the homogeneity postulate of real business cycle theories are highly unsatisfactory assumptions, not just because of their unrealistic character but because they rest on two erroneous axioms; namely, that (relative) prices can be determined through direct exchange and that money is essentially a commodity. The validity of GEA – in its traditional, new classical, or real business cycle form – is subordinated to the validity of these two axioms, and so is that of the microeconomic foundations of macroeconomics.

In Chapter 2 analysis shifts to Keynesian economics. In particular it is shown that, despite their important differences, orthodox Keynesian, new Keynesian, and post-Keynesian economists share the common goal to base macroeconomics on coherent microfoundations. This can easily be established for the Keynesian and the new Keynesian approaches. Strongly influenced by the desire to reinterpret Keynes's theory according to the principles of general equilibrium analysis, Keynesian economists are unanimous in believing that macroeconomics deals with aggregates that can be constructed from individual behaviour. A clear example of this dual characteristic of Keynesian economics – namely, its emphasis on the notion of equilibrium and its need for microfoundations – is given by the general acceptance of Hicks's *IS–LM* interpretation of Keynes's *General Theory*. Admittedly neoclassical, Hicks's interpretation has also been taken over by new Keynesian economists, whose main goal is 'the search for rigorous and convincing models of wage and/or price stickiness based on maximizing behaviour and rational expectations' (Gordon 1990: 501–2). It is thus possible to interpret new Keynesian economics as an attempt to come to terms with the success of new classical economics by incorporating its key assumptions into a Keynesian framework, thus reconciling the need for monetary and fiscal policies with the neoclassical principle of utility and profit maximization as well as with Lucas's rational expectations hypothesis. Post-Keynesian economics differs substantially from Keynesian and new Keynesian economics. It rejects the market-clearing definition of equilibrium as well as the rational expectations hypothesis, and emphasizes the role played by money, effective demand, technical conditions of production, and market structures. Yet, even though post-Keynesian analysis is not explicitly grounded in individual behaviour, microfoundations are not altogether rejected. 'The first principle of microfoundations within [the post-Keynesian] paradigm is that macroeconomics refers to the aggregation of the outcomes of individual action, and thus should not be logically inconsistent with the analysis of individual behaviour' (Dow 1996: 98). Finally, none of the three main schools laying claims on Keynes's heritage has provided so far any clear indication on how to free macroeconomics from its microeconomic fetters.

Chapter 3 shows how the distinction between micro- and macroeconomic foundations is closely related to that between equilibrium and identity. Neoclassical and Keynesian theories of whatever type are essentially based on equilibrium analysis, and this is precisely why none of them has ever been capable to provide macroeconomics with macroeconomic foundations. The central idea of equilibrium analysis is that economic causality can be translated into a series of functional relationships and that '[f]ormal models are a requirement of all schools of economics, as they bring a form of rigour and may illuminate comprehension' (Lavoie 1992: 19). Whether equilibrium analysis pertains to the determination of relative prices in a neoclassical setting or to the determination of national income in a Keynesian framework, its general features remain unaltered. While the various theories differ as to the choice of the variables and the specific relationships that are supposed to exist between them, they all rely on the mathematical solution of a model attempting to reproduce the state of an economy that induces individual agents or aggregates to behave coherently in order to achieve a given result – usually equilibrium between individuals or aggregate supply and demand. A set of independent equations is the most common form of general model proposed by the various theories, and exogeneity is the criterion usually adopted to determine a causal relationship between variables. Yet, when equilibrium models are truly general, all economic variables are 'endogenized' and causality has to be replaced by 'functional relationships', which means that it is the model that decides which variables have to be taken as exogenous and how they are predetermined. Now, the axiomatic and mathematical equilibrium models proposed by neoclassical and Keynesian economics can be seriously challenged only by an economic theory based on strict causality. This is precisely what Keynes's logical identities allow us to do. Generally misperceived as tautologies or 'simplifying assumptions of doubtful validity' (Vercelli 1991: 225), Keynes's identities are in reality the cornerstone of modern macroeconomics, the very reason of its macrofoundations. In Hicks's interpretation of Keynes's theory, the identities between Y and $C + I$ and between S and I are transformed into conditions of equilibrium. Keynesian economists do the same, thus implicitly agreeing to incorporate Keynes's contribution into the theoretical framework of equilibrium analysis. Does this mean that the originality of Keynes's message has entirely been lost and that there is no room left for a reappraisal of his logical identities?

Chapter 4 attempts to give an answer to this question. Through the analysis of Keynes's principle of effective demand it is shown that a macroeconomic approach to macroeconomics is indeed possible once effective demand is connected to Keynes's identities and a perfect symmetry is established between supply and demand. The principle of effective demand was introduced by Keynes in order to show that the equality between global supply and global demand obtains irrespective of the level of employment. It can be interpreted to mean (a) 'the present value of the expected sale proceeds' (Keynes 1973b: 425), or (b) the actual amount of global demand for each level of produced output. In the first case, effective demand relates to the *ex ante* relationship between planned production and expected sales. Supply and demand are therefore also 'expected', purely virtual magnitudes, and no functional relationship can be established between them. Before production takes place, no positive demand can truly be exerted, since no income is available to this effect. Thus interpreted, the principle of effective demand amounts to the common sense notion that entrepreneurs' decisions are influenced by their expectations. The second interpretation of Keynes's principle is more far-reaching, for it refers to actual or realized magnitudes. Since current income is generated by current production, and since demand is determined by the amount of current income, *ex post* the principle of effective demand establishes the necessary equality of supply and demand. A unique event engenders both current output (supply) and current income (demand). As the twin outcomes of production, supply and demand co-determine its dual identity: 'the income derived in the aggregate by all the elements in the community concerned in a productive activity necessarily has a value exactly equal to the *value* of the output' (Keynes 1936/1973a: 20). Keynes's statement could not be clearer: the macroeconomic identity between supply and demand is the unavoidable result of current production and expresses the fact that production generates the amount of income necessary and sufficient for the final purchase of current output. Properly understood, the identity $Y \equiv C + I$ means that, whatever the expectations of entrepreneurs and whatever the decisions taken by consumers and investors, actual supply (produced output) cannot differ from actual demand (current income). This result is further corroborated by Keynes's second identity: $S \equiv I$. Repeated efforts to transform this relationship into a condition of equilibrium and interpret it according to microeconomic principles make it difficult to recover its original meaning. As we will see, Schmitt's quantum monetary analysis provides the conceptual framework required to understand that S and I are always equal, whatever the level of income actually produced, and that their identity is a positive macroeconomic law and not a mere definitional tautology.

Part II of the book deals explicitly with the macroeconomic analysis of national economics and aims to provide a new insight into the macroeconomic nature of some key concepts concerning the logical and pathological working of national economics.

In the first chapter of the second part, Chapter 5, we show how, conceptually and factually, money differs from income. After a short introductory survey of the way monetary economics has greatly been influenced by the tenets of equilibrium analysis, we ask whether money can be considered as an asset. According to monetarism, money is indeed a positive asset allowing barter to be split into a sale and a subsequent purchase. Money is thus conceived of as a stock and the money supply is seen as the quantity of this stock determined, directly or indirectly, by monetary authorities. Yet, if money is identified with a positive asset, then banks are bound to benefit from the extraordinary power to create riches out of nothing, as it were, which is plain nonsense. In reality, banks act as monetary intermediaries, which means that money is issued as a flow any time banks carry out a payment on behalf of their clients. Every payment is a tripolar transaction involving a bank and two of its clients, in which each of the three agents involved is simultaneously a purchaser and a seller on the labour, commodity, and financial markets. As a purely numerical form money never enters a net sale or a net purchase and must therefore be clearly distinguished from bank deposits, net assets and liabilities entered as stocks in the bank's balance sheet, and that can only result from the association between money proper and real output established by production. Knapp's idea that money is essentially state money is thus contradicted by the fact that, like any other economic agent, the state cannot finance its spending through money creation, that is, by issuing its own acknowledgement of debt. In a logical (as opposed to pathological) system, public spending is constrained by the amount of income the government can obtain through taxation, private loans, and the sale of public goods and services, which simply means that, again like any other agent, the state can finance its purchases only by simultaneous and equivalent sales on the commodity and financial markets. What lies behind the confusion between money and income is the concept of credit money and the wrong belief that when banks create money they grant a positive credit to the economy. This is particularly clear in the monetary analysis of production proposed by the advocates of the so-called 'theory of the circuit'. Apparently unaware of the absurdity implicit in maintaining that banks can create positive financial assets out of nothing, these economists claim that production is *financed* by newly created credit money that firms spend to cover their costs. Their misunderstanding of the very peculiar nature of bank money leads them to believe that 'having access to bank credit, firms benefit from an almost unlimited purchasing power' (Graziani 1996: 12, our translation). What has been entirely missed by the theorists of the circuit is the 'vehicular' nature of money. Its understanding requires entering the world of purely numerical magnitudes and of double-entry book-keeping. What 'circuitists' and post-Keynesian economists have clearly seen is that money is bank money. What they have failed to see is that banks create a purely numerical magnitude that is simultaneously positive and negative, and that this magnitude exists only instantaneously, as a circular flow. Furthermore, most of these authors miss the particular nature of labour and end up sharing the neoclassical view that labour is nothing but a factor of production among others. In reality, as the Classics and Keynes knew well, labour is the only macroeconomic factor of production, and it is through the payment of wages that physical output is given its numerical form and that a positive income first appears. Income is thus a stock (a bank deposit) whose value is positive because it defines money's real content – produced output – expressed in wage units.

Chapter 6 deals with production and consumption, and aims to show that both these events are of a macroeconomic nature. With the notable exception of Keynes's monetary approach, production has mostly been analysed as a linear process (sequential Austrian models), as the result of a simultaneous adjustment (general equilibrium models), or as a circular process (input–output models). As is confirmed by the use of production functions and technical methods of production, in all these analyses production is considered as a process of physical transformation that can be represented by a set of functional relationships or as a sequence of fabrication stages. According to this broad approach, production is therefore a process of transformation carried out by a certain number of factors – usually registered under the headings of labour, capital, and 'land' – whose costs are covered by firms. But then no distinction is possible between the social (macroeconomic) and the microeconomic costs of production: both from the aggregate and from each single firm's point of view, production is a process of transformation whose costs derive from the different inputs entering the process. A truly macroeconomic analysis of production is possible only if human labour is recognized as a different conceptual status from the other factors, and money is no longer identified with a positive asset. According to a modern interpretation of Keynes's monetary analysis, production is thus an economic process resulting from labour alone and giving rise to an economic output defined in wage units. Since it is through the association of money with produced output that income is formed, and since income is the specific result of production, it follows that, from a purely economic viewpoint, production is the instantaneous event (the payment of wages) through which produced output is issued as a positive amount of money income. In its most rigorous definition, production is then an *absolute exchange* since it is the very transaction through which output is *changed* into a sum of money income, that is, through which output becomes the object of a bank deposit. The macroeconomic nature of production follows immediately from the fact that each single payment of wages increases the amount of national income currently formed. As far as consumption is concerned, its macroeconomic nature appears clearly as soon as it is related to the final expenditure of income, that is, to Keynes's identity between total supply and total demand. In contrast with the notions of consumption function and equilibrium advocated by mainstream economists, the macroeconomic analysis advocated here shows that, like production, consumption concerns the absolute exchange between money and output. Interpreted as the expenditure carried out for the final purchase of produced output, consumption is an instantaneous, macroeconomic event defining the destruction of a positive income.

The problem of the macroeconomic analysis of capital and interest is considered in Chapter 7. Leaving aside the neoclassical idea that capital is a factor of production on a par with labour and land, capital is analysed here according to the principles of the quantum monetary theory of production. In its first and most general form, capital bridges the gap between present and future, that is, between the moment income is created, t_1, and the moment it is finally spent (and destroyed), t_2. *At the very instant it is formed, current income is thus saved and transformed into capital-time.* From t_1 to t_2 income survives as the object of a financial claim that takes the form of the credit of income holders on banks and, simultaneously, of banks on firms. In its simplest form, capital is therefore related only to the flow of time and to reversible saving. Now, the formation of a truly macroeconomic capital requires capital-time to be transformed into fixed capital. This is indeed what happens when saved-up income is invested in the production of fixed capital goods. It is only when income is thus invested, in fact, that part of current income is changed into an equivalent sum of macroeconomic saving. Invested in the production of instrumental goods, the income initially transformed into capital-time is definitively subtracted from the commodity and financial markets and takes the form of macroeconomic capital, that is, of a capital that has become 'fixed' for society as a whole. Firmly built on Keynes's identity between macroeconomic saving and investment, the analysis of fixed capital is a necessary step towards the understanding of interest. Wrongly conceived of as the price of money or as the price equilibrating supply of and demand for liquidity, interest would still remain an arbitrary magnitude if it were not related to capital accumulation. In fact, even the existence of a positive interest on consumption loans would be difficult to justify if it were not backed by a positive interest derived from macroeconomic investment (saving). As claimed by Wicksell, 'interest on pure consumption loans [...] *parasitizes*, so to speak, on one of the large social income categories' (Wicksell 1997: 23–4). This means that, related to an exchange between a present and a future income, consumption loans refer to microeconomic saving and give rise to an interest that is also essentially microeconomic. Being simultaneously positive for an agent and negative for another, the payment of interest on consumption loans is a zero sum transaction, which leaves the amount of social income unaltered. In clear contrast with the microeconomic nature of interest on consumption loans, interest on fixed capital is a macroeconomic income. Through the investment of profits (that is, the 'capitalist' form of social saving), part of current income escapes consumption and is transformed into fixed capital. Hence, the accumulation of fixed capital implies a sacrifice by society taken as a whole (macroeconomic saving), and interest is nothing more than the compensation for this sacrifice. The investment of saving (profits) and its transformation into macroeconomic capital defines a final loss of income – which will no longer be available on the financial and commodity markets – and interest becomes the compensation for this loss, an income that, period after period, replaces the saving initially absorbed in the production of fixed capital goods.

In Chapter 8 the pathological working of the present system of national payments is opposed to the logical rules of positive analysis elaborated in Chapter 7. Also in Chapter 8 we show how inflation and involuntary unemployment are the twin results of an anomalous process of capital accumulation. The first part of the chapter is devoted to a critical appraisal of the orthodox approach to inflation. According to the majority of economists, inflation is due to an unexpected rise in money supply. Prices are both real and monetary. Inflation is identified with a process of continuously rising monetary prices caused by an increase in the quantity of money affecting aggregate demand. Now, a rapid growth in the money supply increases aggregate demand only if money has a positive value, that is, if it is issued as a positive asset. But the value of money is identified to the inverse of the price level. The vicious circularity of the traditional approach is thus patent: it is simultaneously maintained that money is issued already endorsed with a positive value and that this value depends on a price level that is itself dependent on the aggregate demand exerted by money. Another common feature of orthodox analyses is the widespread use of the price index as a standard of inflation. Yet, there are increases in market prices that simply lead to a new distribution of income without modifying money's purchasing power, which clearly shows how unreliable it is to measure inflation by a persistent rise in *microeconomic* prices.

The quantum theoretical approach to inflation implies a radical change with respect to traditional analysis. Starting from Keynes's identity between global supply (S) and global demand (D), it is shown that a numerical difference between these two terms arises when capital accumulation and amortization are carried out within a system of payments in which no distinction is made between money, income, and fixed capital. Today's pathological process of capital accumulation and amortization is also the cause of a worrying growth in involuntary unemployment, that is, of a situation in which unemployment rises 'whatever the behaviour *of all* economic agents' (Bradley 2003: 399). As suggested by Wicksell, pathological capital accumulation and over-accumulation leads to a fall in the natural rate of interest. When the natural rate is very close or equal to the market rate of interest, deflation sets in, and the economy starts suffering both from an inflationary increase in prices and from a deflationary rise in unemployment. The coexistence of inflation ($D > S$) and deflation ($D < S$) is a mark of today's monetary disorder. Traditional analysis cannot account for it, nor can it reconcile these two disequilibria with Keynes's logical identity ($D \equiv S$). Yet this is precisely what has to be done. Schmitt's quantum theoretical approach leads to this dialectical reconciliation within a truly macroeconomic analysis of inflation and unemployment.

Part III is concerned with the macroeconomic analysis of international economics. After a few general considerations about the specific nature of international transactions, Chapter 9 analyses the problem of eurocurrencies. Usually defined as bank deposits denominated in a currency of a given country but held abroad, eurocurrencies are deemed to be the consequence of tax and bank regulations. Thus, we are told that, because of official restrictions introduced by the US government, US banks were selling the dollar deposits of their clients and purchasing, on behalf of these same clients, deposits in dollars formed in their European branches. However, bank deposits are not multiplied by the transfer of claims between US banks and their European branches. The formation of eurodollars requires dollar-denominated credits to be created outside the United States, and this can result neither from an exchange of claims, nor from the lending of claims on dollar-denominated deposits. As macroeconomic analysis shows, eurocurrencies are not a financial innovation suiting economic agents' desire to diversify their portfolios, but rather the result of a macroeconomic pathology affecting today's system of international payments. The French economist Rueff (1963) was the first to observe that it is through the payment of US net trade deficit that eurodollars are formed. The dollars transferred by the United States in exchange for their net commercial imports are in fact immediately invested in US bank deposits or Treasury bonds, which means that, even though they are entered on the assets side of the creditor country's banking system, the dollars flow immediately back to the American banking system. Simultaneously deposited with US banks and with the creditor country's banks, the dollars spent for the payment of US net imports are thus duplicated and enter the international financial market as eurodollars. 'Entering the credit system of the creditor country, but remaining in the debtor country, the claims representing the deficit are thus doubled' (Rueff 1963: 324). Duplication is essentially due to the fact that key currencies are conceived of as the final term of a real exchange between money and imported goods. Hence, the duplication of dollars does not originate in the circular flow of dollars, but rather in the lack of understanding of the fact that dollars are always necessarily used as circular flows. Since any given country's domestic output cannot simultaneously define the real 'content' of the national currency deposited in the domestic banking system and of its duplicate, it follows that eurocurrencies are nothing more than 'empty' or valueless duplicates. As is shown in the last part of the chapter, the phenomenon of eurocurrencies can also be analysed by referring to the distinction between a country and its residents. In particular, it appears that, in today's system of international payments, the payment of net imports is twofold, and that, when it is carried out by a reserve currency country, it leads to the formation of eurocurrencies.

Chapter 10 is devoted to the macroeconomic analysis of exchange rate fluctuations. The first section of this chapter challenges the traditional conception of exchange rates, according to which these rates would merely be the (relative) prices of national currencies as determined on the foreign exchange market. The different theories proposed to explain exchange rate fluctuations are all grounded in the assumption that currencies are positive assets traded on the foreign exchange market and subject to the law of supply and demand. Current-account and asset-equilibrium models of exchange rate fluctuations as well as 'Keynesian' models focused on both current and capital account transactions are clear examples of the endless proliferation of models attempting to explain exchange rate fluctuations according to a microeconomic point of view. Indeed, if models are to mimic economic agents' behaviour, experts will always be confronted with a constantly changing parade of exchange rate models and the search for exchange rate stability will prove a hopeless exercise. Now, as shown in the second section of the chapter, the traditional approach to exchange rate fluctuations suffers from an even greater shortcoming since, contrary to what is often believed, current and capital account transactions do not affect exchange rates, so that neither monetary disorders such as inflation and deflation, nor interest rates can be a cause of exchange rate erratic fluctuations. The settlement of commercial transactions between countries implies, in fact, the perfectly circular use of the money chosen as a means of payment. This is certainly true when commercial imports are covered by equivalent commercial exports, but applies also when a country balances its net commercial imports through a net export of financial claims. The determinant criterion here is that of 'reciprocity'. If a transaction between two countries defines a reciprocal real exchange (goods and services against other goods and services or against financial assets), the money involved is used in a circular flow and no exchange rate fluctuation can derive from it. This is indeed what happens independently of whether we deal with key currency or non-key currency countries. Furthermore, monetary macroeconomic analysis also shows that the same result applies to capital account transactions. Exports and imports of financial assets give rise to reciprocal exchanges that leave exchange rates unaltered. By the same token, it is therefore also easily established that exchange rate fluctuations cannot derive from inflation, deflation, and interest rate variations, since each of these factors could influence exchange rates only through its effect on trade or capital movements. It thus appears that exchange rates fluctuate only insofar as currencies are not used in a circular flow, as simple *means* of payment. It is only when currencies are considered as if they were (positive) assets, *objects* of trade on the foreign exchange market, that their 'prices' fluctuate through their net sales and purchases. The transformation of currencies from simple means of payment into objects of trade takes place through the process of duplication described by Rueff (1963). Thus, in the present system of international payments euro or xeno-currencies generated by duplication feed a speculative capital market, and the transactions taking place on this market inevitably lead to exchange rate fluctuations. Finally, since duplication arises independently of economic agents' behaviour, speculation and exchange rate fluctuations are themselves the consequence of a macroeconomic disorder engendering pathological capital rather than the result of microeconomic agents' decision to invest on the foreign exchange market.

Chapter 11 is concerned with one of the clearest examples of a macroeconomic discrepancy whose origin cannot be attributed to microeconomic behaviour. Well known by experts of international economics, the problem relates to the necessary equilibrium of the balance of payments and, more precisely, to the necessary equality between world current account surpluses and world current account deficits. As unanimously recognized, a country's current account surplus/deficit is another country's (or group of countries') current account deficit/surplus, so that, on the whole, the global current account should always equal zero. However, this is not what happens in the real world. Statistical data in fact show that the global current account has constantly been negative, the amount spent by *LDCs* being currently greater than the amount entered as receipt in the rest of the world's (*R*'s) current account. Since *R*'s net commercial exports as well as the net interest on debt owed to it have regularly been paid by *LDCs*, the world current account discrepancy stands for an excess of payments carried out by *LDCs* and unrecorded in *R*'s current account. Dubbed by Krugman and Obstfeld (2003) as 'the mystery of the missing surplus', this discrepancy cannot be explained by referring to the microeconomic payments of commercial transactions, nor can it be maintained that *LDCs*' indebted residents pay their interest on debt more than once. Likewise, one cannot claim either that the missing surplus is nothing more than the effect of capital flight. In its current meaning, capital flight is the result of illegal transactions through which the residents of a given country are able to avoid taxation. By definition, any illegal transaction of this kind goes unrecorded, both in the country from which residents surreptitiously transfer their capital and in the country where the capital is transferred. We shall look in vain for a cause in the world current account discrepancy at the level of microeconomic payments. As confirmed by the two working parties appointed by the International Monetary Fund (1987, 1992) to examine current account discrepancies and world capital flows, the amounts corresponding to the 'missing surplus' are far too high to be explained by unreliable data collection. Furthermore, statistical observation shows that their rate of increase has not weakened despite consistent technical improvements. If we consider, moreover, that the longer the period of reference, the lesser the impact of misreporting – since errors tend to compensate – it appears that the increasing amount of world discrepancies is the mark of a macroeconomic disorder whose nature is indeed still mysterious. This first impression is then confirmed by the further observation that world capital and financial accounts do not match either. Does the world capital and financial account discrepancy have the same origin as the world current account discrepancy? Do the two discrepancies result from the same macroeconomic disorder? The aim of the chapter is to suggest a way of answering these questions by means of a flow analysis of the balance of payments.

Chapter 12 shows that a final solution to 'the mystery of the missing surplus' can be derived from the investigation of one of the most difficult problems of monetary macroeconomics: external debt servicing. Initially analysed by Keynes (1929), this problem has long been underestimated by mainstream economists, who seem to have entirely missed the originality of a transaction – the payment of interest – that substantially differs from any other international transaction. It is to a French economist – Bernard Schmitt – that we owe the complete and rigorous analysis of net interest payment. His undisputable premise is the fact that net interests on debt are paid out of the indebted country's current account. Of course, interests are paid by the country's indebted residents. Yet, the country itself is involved by the payment of its residents, which is entered in the current account balance. The payment of interest by the current account has a precise meaning: it clearly shows that the indebted country (A) pays its interests by transferring to the creditor countries part of its domestic resources. Thus, the payment in real terms of A's net interests on debt is a net transfer of A's domestic output. Now, this real transfer is conveyed by a monetary flow of A's current account. If the payment of net interests were of the same nature as any other payment, the monetary payment would be identical with the real payment, and the cost total for A would simply equal the amount of interest due. Yet, as shown by Schmitt, the payment of interest is of a different nature: it is an 'unrequited' transfer that does not allow for the circular flow of money, proper to any other payment. This means that country A does not benefit from the automatic reflux of the money conveying its real payment of interest. It thus follows that the monetary payment of interest has a positive cost added on to that of the real transfer of A's domestic resources. The total cost of A's net interest is therefore *twice* the amount due to its creditors. Half of the cost is paid by the indebted residents – and leads to an increase in A's external debt when A's commercial trade is balanced – the other half is paid by their country – and ends up with an equivalent reduction of A's official reserves. World Bank's statistical data confirm the double charge of interest payment. Over a period of 22 years indebted countries have paid 1,851,327 million dollars in net interests and, despite benefiting from a net total receipt of 2,428,975 million dollars (foreign direct investments, portfolio investments, and grants), their official reserves have been subjected to a decrease of 1,960,913 million dollars. By showing that the double charge is of a macroeconomic nature, Schmitt's analysis provides at the same time a consistent explanation of the missing surplus. In fact, while the first payment is microeconomic and leads to a debit of *A*'s current account – defining the payment of *A*'s residents – and to a credit of the creditor countries' current account, the second charge is macroeconomic and, though affecting *A*'s current account, has no effect on the current account of the creditor countries. *A*'s decrease in official reserves has no counterpart in the balance of payments of the rest of the world, which explains why global balance of payments' discrepancies have remained a mystery for such a long time.

Part IV of the book is entirely devoted to the macroeconomic approach to macroeconomics, to its laws, and to the way they can be implemented in the real world.

In Chapter 13 we stress once more that macroeconomic laws are not empirical laws derived from constant sequences of events and influenced by economic agents' behaviour. Independent of individual or collective behaviour, these laws derive from the flow nature of money and are concerned with the logical structure of payments relating to production and exchange. The first and fundamental law of macroeconomics establishes the necessary equality – or the *identity* – between macroeconomic supply and demand. Since it is through the payment of the macroeconomic costs of production that physical output is transformed into economic output, the measure of macroeconomic supply coincides with the numerical expression of these costs. Once it is established that labour is the sole macroeconomic factor of production, it necessarily follows that macroeconomic supply is expressed by the total amount of direct and indirect wages paid to workers: money wages are the standard through which physical output acquires its (economic) numerical form. As for macroeconomic demand, it can easily be shown that it is determined by the amount of income available in a given economy. Now, since it is through production that macroeconomic income is formed, it immediately appears that wages define both global supply and global demand: macroeconomic supply and macroeconomic demand are the two terms of an identity, the two aspects of one and the same reality. The second macroeconomic law is as strict as the first, for it establishes the *identity* between each single agent's sales and purchases. Once again it is because money is a simple flow that it cannot finance any net purchase. The instantaneous and circular flow of money necessarily implies, in fact, that both buyer and seller are simultaneously credited and debited for the same amount of money, which means that they are both and to the same extent sellers and buyers. Whether we consider the transactions carried out between residents of the same country or between countries, the law applies, since money does not change its nature when moving from the national to the international level. No single agent, resident or country, can therefore be a purchaser without simultaneously being a seller on the labour, commodity, or financial markets. The third macroeconomic law establishes the *identity* between saving and investment. As already shown in Chapters 2, 3 and 4, macroeconomic saving and macroeconomic investment form a unity. In fact, macroeconomic saving is precisely that part of macroeconomic income that is invested in the production of fixed capital goods. If an economy is to produce capital goods, it has to save part of its current income and invest it in this new production. Defined as the production of fixed capital goods, macroeconomic investment is therefore necessarily equal to macroeconomic saving. It is thanks to its macroeconomic saving that an economy can build up its fixed capital, and it is through macroeconomic investment that it transforms part of its income into fixed capital. Finally, in the last part of this chapter we show that the three macroeconomic laws mentioned here can be derived from the unique principle of *absolute exchange* established by Schmitt's quantum theoretical approach.

Chapter 14 deals with the role of positive analysis in setting the principles of the reform needed to fulfil the goal set by normative analysis, that is, the creation of an economic system free of any monetary pathology. In particular, we look at the measures suggested so far by mainstream economists in order to achieve monetary stability at the national level, and at the changes advocated by macroeconomic quantum analysis, in order to adapt the accounting structure of the banking system to the very nature of money, income, and capital. The first section of the chapter is devoted to a brief summary of the main steps that have marked the building-up of the present system of national payments. The development of double-entry book-keeping – made possible by the discovery of negative numbers – is at the origin of bank money, and represents the cornerstone of today's system of payments. Ricardo and Keynes are among the economists who have mostly contributed to the understanding of bank money. It is to Ricardo, for example, that we owe the distinction between money creation and financial intermediation. Taking over Smith's concepts of nominal and real money, Ricardo was able to show that, whereas nominal money is literally created, real money (income) derives from production, which is why credit must be backed by a financial intermediation instead of being wrongly identified with money creation. Keynes's monetary theory of production further contributed to improve monetary analysis, while bankers should be acknowledged the merit of radically ameliorating the workings of the monetary system by implementing an inter-bank clearing structure to settle inter-bank payments. In the second section of Chapter 14 it is shown that the monetarist approach to monetary policy is inadequate to deal with monetary disorders. A rigorous analysis of the way money is issued by banks and associated to physical output through production shows, in fact, that Friedman's microeconomic conception of money and of the way it interacts with the real world is highly unrealistic and misleading. By defining money as a positive asset, Friedman misses the distinction between money and income and fails to grasp the monetary nature of economic production. It thus follows that the price stability advocated by Friedman is neither a necessary nor a desirable requirement of economic growth. What really matters is not to grant only 'a limited amount of flexibility in prices and wages' (Friedman 1968: 174) by controlling the money supply, but to provide a sound monetary structure in which money plays its role in conformity with its own (banking) nature. The last part of the chapter deals with this specific point and shows that, at a national level, monetary disorders can be properly eradicated only through a reform of the banking system based on the structural distinction between monetary, financial, and fixed capital departments.

The need for a reform of the international system of payments is analysed in Chapter 15. The debate over the exchange rate regime best suited for a given country to achieve exchange rate stability has swung from fixed parity – currency boards and dollarization included – to free floating. European currency union excluded, none of these attempts at solution has proven satisfactory, the main reason for their shortcomings being the fact that today's exchange rate regimes belong to the category of relative exchanges, since currencies are considered as if they were real goods, and exchange rates are defined as their relative prices. Exchange rate instability is the unavoidable consequence of a world in which some national currencies are denatured through duplication and traded on the foreign exchange market. Every attempt at taming erratic exchange rate fluctuations without modifying today's system of international payments has therefore a cost. Alternatives range from foreign exchange market interventions and interest rate policies to the loss of monetary sovereignty. A price has to be paid even when full exchange rate stability is obtained by the most radical solution: monetary unification. In the case of the European Union, for example, since national currencies no longer exist, no interventions are needed any longer within the euro area. Yet, the loss of monetary sovereignty has a series of negative side-effects that seriously hamper the success of European unification. Free capital flows are the most worrying consequence of monetary unification and, together with the existing economic disparities between EU member countries, are likely to drastically increase unemployment in the regions suffering from capital outflows. Monetary macroeconomics helps us to envisage a new solution that, while preserving monetary sovereignty, prevents national currencies from being denatured into tradable goods whose price is subject to the law of supply and demand. The key novelty here is the shift from today's regime of relative exchange rates to a regime of *absolute* exchange rates, that is, to a system in which each transaction is carried out through the circular flow of money so that the currency used as a means of payment is never the object of a net sale or purchase. The reform advocated in this chapter is the reform proposed by Schmitt (1973) and already partially envisaged by Keynes in his plan for the establishment of an international clearing union presented at Bretton Woods in 1944. One of its key features is the intervention of the European Central Bank (ECB) both as a monetary and a financial intermediary. This means that the ECB will have to issue and allow for the circular flow of the euro, and manage a system of inter-European clearing guaranteeing the real content of inter-European transactions. Following this model, a system of fixed and stable exchange rates between three or more major currency areas can easily be worked out. The pyramidal structure depicted in Chapter 15 gives an idea of what the future for the world monetary system may be. But what about *LDCs*? Do they have to wait for a world monetary reform in order to avoid the double charge of net interest payments? Fortunately not: as shown at the end of Chapter 15, each single *LDC* can implement its own reform, thus protecting itself from the iniquity of the present system. Avoiding the second, macroeconomic, payment of interest, such reform will allow *LDCs* to benefit from a net inflow of foreign exchange and enter a new process of economic and social development.

Part I

Macroeconomics versus microeconomics

1 Neoclassical, new classical, and new business cycle economics

Walras and general equilibrium analysis: the triumph of microeconomics

Let us be clear. Walras was one of the greatest economists of all times and his attempt to make a rigorous science of economics deserves our unreserved admiration. Like Jevons and Menger, the French economist believed that pure economics is a branch of mathematics and that it is thanks to algebra that the rational method may be introduced into economics. '[G]iven the *pure theory of economics*, it must precede *applied economics*; and this pure theory of economics is a science which resembles the physico-mathematical science in every respect' (Walras 1984: 71). According to Walras, the pure theory of economics is the theory of value, and 'the theory of exchange and value in exchange, that is, the theory of social wealth considered in itself, is a physico-mathematical science like mechanics or hydrodynamics' (ibid.: 71). The founding father of general equilibrium analysis goes as far as to claim that the value in exchange 'partakes of the character of a natural phenomenon, natural in its origins, natural in its manifestations and natural in essence' (ibid.: 69).

Walras's desire to build economics on scientific and mathematical foundations was so strong that he did not hesitate to claim that the price of any given commodity (wheat in his example) is determined 'objectively', by scarcity or usefulness – 'both of these conditions being natural' (ibid.: 69). Hence, if wheat is worth 24 francs a hectolitre, '[t]his particular value of wheat in terms of money, that is to say, this price of wheat, does not result either from the will of the buyer or from the will of the seller or from any agreement between the two' (ibid.: 69). Unfortunately, Walras never really attempted to explain value in exchange independently of the will of the buyer or the seller or of any agreement between the two. He endeavoured instead to show that relative prices are determined through exchange in a competitive market where supply and demand are subject to individuals' preferences. 'Value in exchange, when left to itself, arises spontaneously in the market as the result of competition. As buyers, traders make their *demands* by *outbidding* each other. As sellers, traders make their *offers* by *underbidding* each other' (ibid.: 83).

Walras's revolution with respect to the theory supported by some great classical authors such as Smith, Ricardo, and Marx consisted mainly in switching from the analysis of production and absolute values to that of exchange and relative prices. The necessary rejection of the metaphysical concept of embodied labour led Walras to investigate the exchange between commodities, in search for a principle defining value as a mere relationship. Concentrating his attention on relative exchange, the author of *Elements of Pure Economics* reduced production to a subsidiary role, classifying it under the heading of applied economics. 'Thus the theory of economic production of social wealth, that is, of the organization of industry under a system of the division of labour, is an applied science. For this reason we shall call it *applied economics*' (ibid.: 76). The consequence of this choice is that pure economics is limited to the mathematical attempt to explain how supply and demand may determine relative prices and at the same time reconcile the maximization of individuals' well-being with that of the society as a whole. A difficult task indeed, which led Walras to transform the market into a *deus ex machina*, and which set the stage for any future microeconomic analysis based on the principles of general equilibrium.

The widespread acceptance of Walras's GEA marked the triumph of microeconomics over the classical authors' attempt to provide economists with a macroeconomic theoretical framework. Individual agents' behaviour became the key factor in an essentially subjective interpretation of the 'natural elements' of economics. Supply and demand were (and still are) considered the social forces through which individuals' preferences exert their action on the market in a continuous search for an equilibrium that, because of its very nature, can never be stable. Far from determining a set of logical rules economic agents have to conform to, neoclassical economists expect economic agents to find the best possible equilibrium allowing for the optimization of their individual utilities. Concerning the system taken as a whole, the state of the economy is thus seen as the result of a constant adjustment involving each individual agent in his relation with the others. No true macroeconomic criteria are envisaged and economics itself is conceived of as nothing more than a secondary branch of mathematics.

If economics were indeeed of a mathematical–physical nature and if relative prices could actually be determined by the simultaneous solution of a system of independent equations of supply and demand, Walras would be right in claiming that 'the theory of value in exchange is really a branch of mathematics which mathematicians have hitherto neglected and left undeveloped' (ibid.: 70). The triumph of microeconomic analysis is therefore closely related to the possibility of interpreting economics mathematically and, in particular, to the logical possibility of explaining economic events using mathematical formalism. Since Walras's publication of his *Elements*, the host of economists approaching economics from a mathematical viewpoint has never stopped swelling. Today the great majority of economists believe mathematics to be an indispensable analytical tool and make regular use of it. This simple observation is enough to give a clear idea of how far Walras's influence reaches and how deep-rooted microeconomic foundations are. Despite important differences, the main schools of economic thought share Walras's belief in mathematics as well as his microeconomic approach. Apart from a handful of heterodox thinkers, in fact, economists still reason in terms of adjustment, looking for a more or less perfect equilibrium in more or less flexible markets.

It is a fact that Walras's general equilibrium analysis led to a radical change in economic thinking, and that even Keynes's revolution did not succeed in overthrowing it. Indeed, Keynes's original contribution was submitted to a neoclassical interpretation that was implicitly, if not explicitly, accepted even by a vast number of Keynes's followers. As we shall argue at length in the following two chapters, both Keynesian and new Keynesian economists share the neoclassical point of view with respect to the need of explaining reality through mathematical modelling. Now, the use of mathematics rests on the possibility to determine a positive number of functional relationships between economic 'variables' (where the choice of the term 'variable' is itself evidence of the fact that economic magnitudes are axiomatically considered to be functionally related). Except for the particular case of identities, equations are conditional equalities, that is, equalities that are verified only for a given numerical value of the variables they relate to. Within GEA economic reality is represented by a series of models based on conditional equalities (the most famous being, of course, the equations relating supply and demand). Despite their notorious differences with the neoclassical models, Keynesian and new Keynesian models are also constructed on the same logical grounds. This explains why the search for microeconomic foundations has attracted so much interest. At the same time this clearly shows how deeply Walras's conception of economic analysis has influenced the history of our science in the last hundred and thirty years.

New classical economics: the microfoundations of econometric modelling

New classical economics: a short introduction

The first new classical models were elaborated in order to propose a valid alternative to Keynesian econometric models and in order to explain how monetary factors could generate business cycles, without abandoning the main features of GEA. As a first approximation, it may be said that new classical models reproduce the Walrasian general equilibrium system except for the introduction of imperfect information regarding prices. For example, Lucas (1972, 1973) showed that by dropping the assumption of perfect information the Phillips curve is compatible with the general equilibrium framework, so that monetary shocks can indeed have an influence (albeit only a temporary one) on real variables.

As claimed by Laidler, although the monetarists' criticism of the Keynesian analysis of inflation and unemployment jeopardized the reliability of particular functional relationships in the economy, monetarism 'constituted no radical theoretical challenge' (Laidler 1997: 335) to Keynesian orthodoxy. In fact, Keynesian econometric models did already incorporate a demand for money function and 'could easily enough be accommodated' (ibid.: 335) in order to account for a more stable relationship. Likewise, 'large-scale Keynesian econometric systems proved easily able to absorb monetarist ideas' (ibid.: 335), so that monetarism did not really provide a theoretical alternative to Keynesianism. What monetarism failed to do was successfully carried out – so we are taught – by new classical economics, which provided an analytical setting clearly distinct from the Keynesian framework. The central feature of the approach proposed by Lucas and his followers is the reintroduction of the main principles of general equilibrium analysis, in particular those of price flexibility and competitive market clearing. The originality of new classical models with respect to traditional general equilibrium models lies in the assumption that economic agents 'do not have full information about the structure of relative prices when they engage in trade' (ibid.: 338). The rational expectations hypothesis introduced by new classical economists has thus the advantage of accounting for equilibrium while leaving room for temporary disequilibrium. Uncorrelated random errors are in fact possible when agents form their expectations, but must necessarily reduce to zero if expectations are rational. Hence, output and employment fluctuations are perceived as 'voluntary responses to misperceived price signals' (ibid.: 336) occurring when the economy is subjected to random exogenous shocks. Agents may mistake changes in money prices for changes in relative prices and consequently modify their supply of goods. Yet, this change in real supply is not supposed to last. Economic agents will soon be aware of their mistake and modify their behaviour in accordance with the actual evolution of relative prices, thus re-establishing equilibrium at its proper level.

Reliance of new classical economics on price flexibility and market clearing is a sign of how closely related it is to microeconomic principles. It is not a mystery, of course, that new classical economists claim to derive macroeconomic models of reality from individual maximizing behaviour. What is particularly relevant here is the claim that new classical economics allows 'clearly defined links to be established between individual and market experiments without recourse to empirical laws' (ibid.: 340). It thus seems possible to avoid the traditional obstacle of aggregation facing

Keynesian macroeconomic theories. Derived from a Walrasian theoretical framework, new classical economics builds its macroeconomic system directly on it. The postulates of perfect competition and rational behaviour facilitate the transition from micro to macroeconomics, the distinction between the two being a matter of size and not of substance. It is clear that, in these conditions, macroeconomics is reduced to microeconomics, the state of the economy taken as a whole being the direct result of the decisions taken by individual agents. The claimed superiority of new classical economics over its rivals rests precisely on the principles of GEA, the logical coherence and rigour of which it shares. In particular, new classical economists are well aware of the fact that mathematical modelling has its natural origin in the neoclassical system of general equilibrium, which is still the most rigorous setting to date, at least as far as mathematical economics is concerned.

The new classical approach has been widely criticized, both outside and within mainstream economics. Akerlof, for example, in his inaugural lecture at the London School of Economics maintained that the continuous market clearing hypothesis is generally incompatible with the principle of profit maximization. Having claimed that profit-maximizing firms tend to follow standard business practice, which 'normally prohibit[s] firms and industries from paying the market-clearing wage at all times and in all places' (Akerlof 1979: 231–2), Akerlof goes on to prove that 'the firm which tries, contrary to the standard practice, to behave in the manner suggested by the market-clearing model will not in general maximise its profits' (ibid.: 232). Violation of widely accepted norms and of standard business practices will in fact prove costly, often too costly when compared to the advantages deriving from the adoption of market-clearing wages. Now, Akerlof's criticism is much less harmful than it might appear. Norms and business practices are historically determined and tend to evolve. Practices that are costly today may well become the norm tomorrow. We can openly disagree with the political and ethical implications of the new classical theory, of course. But this is not the point. What really matters here is whether or not the new classical macroeconomics depicts the logical workings of an ideal economic system.

New classical economists claim that their models are the only models that are logically self-consistent, and that the introduction of the continuous market clearing and rational expectations hypotheses is a logical requirement for a rigorous theory to be worked out at all. The free competition framework resulting from it would therefore be the unavoidable and 'objective' consequence of choosing the only empirical setting truly compatible with the sole theoretical model of the economy. If today's institutions do not entirely conform to the ideal model, this is no proof that the model itself is wrong. If we are to reject it, it must be on logical grounds, and not simply because its consequences do not fit our ethical or political choices.

A good economic theory must be able to explain the real world. The new classical theory is no exception to this rule. The fact that markets do not clear 'at all times and in all circumstances' (ibid.: 233) is apt to undermine the new classical approach, as is the fact that economic agents are far from acting rationally 'at all times and in all circumstances'. Yet, this discrepancy between theory and empirical evidence might be simply a matter of gradual adjustment. If no logical inconsistency were to be found in the new classical approach and if it were possible to show that its foundations rely on empirical axioms derived from the workings of the economic system, then new classical economists could indeed maintain that their theory has the twofold capacity to explain the present malfunctioning of the economy and to provide a model of how the economy should work in order to be consistent with its own logical laws (as determined precisely by the theory).

As we have already seen, the assumption of continuous market clearing and the postulate of price flexibility are a central tenet of new classical economics. While Keynesian macroeconomics rests on the assumption of price rigidity, new classical analysis states that a shift in demand is always matched by a change in prices allowing for the clearing of markets. If fluctuations in output and employment nevertheless occur in the real world, this is said to be due to misperceived price signals. Because of a lack of information about the meaning of money price variations, economic agents may mistake changes in money prices for changes in relative prices and react by modifying their real supply of goods and services. If this happens, output and employment fluctuate in the short run, giving rise to a real business cycle. Now, as observed by Laidler, the continuous market clearing hypothesis is apparently in contrast with individual agents getting their expectations wrong. Errors are costly, so that agents 'have every incentive to make their expectations as accurate as possible, and to use all available information in order to do so' (Laidler 1997: 31). This led new classical economists to resort to the rational expectations hypothesis. It is to this assumption that we shall now turn our attention.

The rational expectations hypothesis

Expectations were already taken into account by Friedman (1968), whose expectations-augmented Phillips curve suggested the existence of a relationship between the expected rate of change in real wages and unemployment. Yet, new classical theorists were not happy with Friedman's assumption since it privileged adaptive rather than rational expectations. In 1961, Muth put forward the idea that forward-looking agents form their expectations on a rational basis, which can be mathematically formalized. As noted by Gerrard, one great advantage of the rational expectations hypothesis is that it 'offers a more acceptable assumption in choice-theoretic terms since rational expectations display the twin properties of unbiasedness and orthogonality, thereby ruling out systematic expectational errors' (Gerrard 1996: 58).

According to the rational expectations hypothesis 'agents form expectations "as if" they were fully informed about the structure of the economy in which they operate, and make mistakes only to the extent that the economy is subjected to random exogenous shocks' (Laidler 1997: 34). Thus, models proposed by new classical theorists are greatly dependent on the way agents are expected to react to economic changes given their rationally determined behaviour. If they have insufficient information to distinguish relative from absolute changes in prices, monetary shocks may cause short-run fluctuations. However, if they behave rationally, pre-announced monetary policies will be ineffective, tax-financed and debt-financed fiscal expansions will be equivalent, and time-inconsistent policies will be less effective because they are less credible.

The rational expectations hypothesis was introduced as the principle required 'to reconcile the price distributions implied by the market equilibrium with the distributions used by agents to form their own views of the future' (Lucas 1980: 707). This reconciliation is a necessary requirement for the contingent-claim interpretations of a competitive equilibrium model suggested by Arrow and Debreu, and considered by Lucas as 'a powerful model-building apparatus specifically designed to help us deal with problems involving choice under uncertainty' (ibid.: 708). Yet, as observed by Buiter, the rational expectations hypothesis 'appears to be in danger of being consistent with any conceivable body of empirical evidence' (Buiter 1980: 38), and thus of 'becoming irrefutable' (ibid.: 38). In other words, what is apparently introduced as a verifiable (or falsifiable) hypothesis is in fact considered as an axiom, a principle stipulated to be true for the purpose of a chain of reasoning that would otherwise be impossible to establish logically. Hence, the assumption of rational expectations becomes the necessary foundation of a formal deductive system in which real economic variables are equally affected by alternative, anticipated fiscal and monetary policies. 'The issue of how economic agents acquire their knowledge of the true structure of the economy, which they use in making their rational forecasts is not addressed by the theory' (ibid.: 38). Indeed, the rational expectations hypothesis is not introduced in order to explain how forecasts are actually formed, but as a necessary element for the very existence of new classical models.

The main shortcomings of the rational expectations hypothesis

Both in its weak form (which Lucas calls 'vacuous') and in its strong form (defined as 'silly' by Lucas), the rational expectations hypothesis is hardly acceptable. If it is simply maintained that economic agents try to get the most out of the information they can get hold of, nothing will allow us to conclude that '[e]xpectations [. . .] tend to be distributed, for the same information set, about the prediction of the theory' (Muth 1981: 4–5). On the other hand, to claim that economic agents know the structure of the model that is supposed to describe the working of the economy and act accordingly seems too strong an assumption. Indeed, even in the softer version in which it is usually introduced by new classical economists, the rational expectations hypothesis is highly controversial. The claim that '[r]ational expectations imply that what they [economic agents] *do* expect is (within a serially uncorrelated error) what the true model says they *should* expect' (Hoover 1988: 16) amounts in fact to saying (1) that economists know perfectly well what the true model is, and (2) that economic agents *must* work out their expectations according to this model. The first assumption is anything but a faithful representation of the present degree of agreement among economists. Even though not every economist is prepared to admit it, nobody really knows what the true model really is. As for the second assumption, if it were true it would imply that expectations as well as decisions in general are necessarily formed according to the theoretical principles underlying the 'true' model, leaving no room for any form of uncertainty and free behaviour. It is not necessary to stress how far these assumptions are from reality and how little (if at all) they may help us to understand the world of economics.

Criticized by Keynesian economists and praised by new classical economists, the rational expectations hypothesis is one of the most awkward subjects of recent economic debate. Even an economist as sensible to Keynes's arguments as Vercelli is straight faced when claiming for its theoretical centrality. 'Although the prevailing interpretation and use of rational expectations is very questionable, this hypothesis has shown a remarkable heuristic value and remains the first systematic attempt at studying endogenous formation of expectations without violating economic rationality' (Vercelli 1991: 240). Now, what should be made clear first is what is meant by economic rationality. If it is supposed to mean that economic activity is rational when decisions are taken according to the theoretical principles of maximization under constraint, then rational expectations simply becomes a corollary of economic rationality. Moreover, if this is the case, economic rationality itself is then seen as an ideal state of affairs to which economic activity must tend. Hence, rational behaviour must tow in line with the principles of economic rationality, that is, with the principles that, according to a given economic theory, will make the economic system work at its best. Rational expectations are just part of this optimizing behaviour, and it is not at all surprising that new classical economists have unhesitatingly taken over this assumption. The whole of GEA is based on the axiom that, through supply and demand, economic agents are able to find the best possible equilibrium maximizing their utility.

The critical point of view adopted by non-neoclassical economists consists mainly in stressing the unrealistic character of the new-classical axiom. Because of market imperfections, rigidities, discontinuities, and so on, general equilibrium analysis appears rather artificial and various attempts have been made to transform it into a disequilibrium (non-Walrasian equilibrium) theory or to replace it altogether with Keynes's theoretical framework. However, if theoreticians were forced to choose between an analysis based on rigorous but totally unrealistic principles, and another that, in the attempt to be realist, is bound to be fundamentally useless, there would be little hope for economics to ever be an objective science explaining economic events. From a purely theoretical viewpoint, neoclassical theory seems better equipped than other theories to provide a rigorous framework of analysis. Its use of a sophisticated apparatus of mathematical formalization and its constant reference to rationality seem determinant in this respect. In fact, if another theory is to replace GEA, it must possess the same degree of scientific rigour and a higher heuristic value. This would prove rather difficult if economics were merely a social science. But, in this case it would be vain to look for a theory explaining economic reality, for its object of inquiry would unavoidably be beyond its reach. Human behaviour is highly unpredictable and no mathematical model would ever be apt to represent it. Indeed, as shown by one of the 2002 Nobel Prize winners for economics, Daniel Kahneman, far from being rational, people's decisions are often idiosyncratic. Behaviour is influenced by a host of psychological factors such as individual perceptions, emotions, judgements, and beliefs, which account for systematic deviations from economic rationality. In this situation the rational expectations hypothesis seems rather a heroic assumption, whose *raison d'être* is to make it possible to use new classical econometric models to represent a reality that is too complex and rich to be reconstructed mathematically.

As we will see in Part II, the microeconomic approach based on the analysis of economic agents' behaviour and focused on their capacity to maximize utility through exchange can be advantageously replaced by a macroeconomic approach emphasizing the role of a monetary structure whose 'logical' laws apply independently of economic agents' behaviour. In fact it is the explicit goal of this book to show that our perception of economics changes radically once we start thinking of it from the outset in monetary terms. This had already been done by the greatest economists of the past. Indeed, from Smith to Keynes, a common thread links together all the economists who have consistently tried to prove that economics is concerned with the structural laws governing the economic system as such. However, their message failed to convince the majority of economists, most likely because it did not demarcate clearly enough the domains of micro and macroeconomics respectively. In particular, macroeconomists of the past have not always been able to show that the social character of economic activity goes beyond the mere aggregation of individual forms of behaviour. A reason for their lack of success is to be found in their inability to convey the apparently odd idea that, although created by man, the economic system has a structure that is independent of human behaviour. Now, it is this structure that is the proper object of the economic science in its purest form. It then follows that it is the search for logical laws, as opposed to social or behavioural laws, which makes up the specificity of macroeconomics. The final rejection of the rational expectations hypothesis is therefore strictly related to the logical impossibility to derive macroeconomics from microeconomics. If economic laws are indeed of a macroeconomic nature, behaviour can no longer be a key factor and the rational expectations hypothesis immediately loses its centrality. The fundamental criticism of this assumption, therefore, does not merely lie in its unrealistic character, but in its total irrelevance for the building of a true macroeconomic theory. Hence, our critical analysis must move back from the level of the new classical assumptions to that of the neoclassical theory itself, and raise the question of whether a general equilibrium approach can ever form the conceptual cornerstone of (macro)economic theory.

New classical economics: a critique

Lucas's and Sargent's criticism of Keynesian macroeconomics is essentially based on econometric considerations and on the forecasting failure of Keynesian macromodels in the 1970s. On the one hand, both authors reproach Keynesian economists with attempting to derive their structural models by imposing a series of a priori restrictions on a number of variables as well as on the coefficients governing the behaviour of the 'error terms' (Lucas and Sargent 1997: 274). On the other hand, they claim that a structural model must be derived from a collection of economic time series. 'The problems of identifying a structural model from a collection of economic time series is one that must be solved by anyone who claims the ability to give quantitative economic advice' (ibid.: 273). According to Lucas and Sargent, Keynesians' failure to do so must be imputed to their models lacking foundations in microeconomic and general equilibrium theory. They reach this conclusion by observing that '[m]odern probabilistic microeconomic theory almost never implies either the exclusion restrictions that were suggested by Keynes or those that are imposed by macroeconometric models' (ibid.: 275). We thus get the flavour of Lucas and Sargent's analysis, which mainly consists in backing a microeconomic approach on the grounds that it allows working out more articulated econometric models than Keynes's macroeconomic approach.

As we have already seen, market clearing and agents' maximizing behaviour are the two main assumptions on which new classical economics rests. Now, Lucas, Sargent, and their fellow economists too, consider these assumptions as two postulates allowing the elaboration of econometric models based on decision functions. The close connection with Debreu's claim for the axiomatic nature of economic theory is evident. Yet, economics cannot be reduced to a series of axiomatic models structured according to mathematical principles. Debreu's attempt to establish definitively the priority of a mathematical approach to economics fails because he erroneously assumes, following Walras, that the object of economics is essentially mathematical. If, as he claimed right at the outset of his 1959 book, goods were numbers, his analysis would be unquestionable and would prove once and for all the validity of Walras's general equilibrium theory. As a consequence, Lucas and Sargent's contribution would also share the same scientific status. The two authors could then legitimately claim to have shown that 'Keynes and his followers were wrong to give up on the possibility that an equilibrium theory could account for the business cycle' (ibid.: 280). In reality, however, it is logically impossible to take goods to be numbers. It is true, of course, that physical goods and services have to be associated with numbers in order to become commensurable; and it is equally true that if they were not transformed into numbers, economics would not even exist for lack of a measurable object. Yet, this does not at all mean that goods themselves are numbers. To claim otherwise is to assume, rather arbitrarily, that axioms can be chosen at will, according to the theoretical structure one wishes to apply to one's object of enquiry. The absurdity of claiming that an apple is a number or that a chair, an aircraft, a juridical advice, a nuclear bomb – or whatever other real good or service – is a number should be obvious. No further proof should then be required to establish the logical inconsistency of GEA in its traditional Walrasian version as well as in its more recent versions. Nevertheless, given how deeply rooted in our minds neoclassical thought is, it is not superfluous to add a few more arguments to our critical analysis of new classical macroeconomics.

By all accounts, one of the most controversial assumptions of Lucas's analysis is that of rational expectations, that is, the belief that economic agents' expectations 'accord with those that would be generated with knowledge of the "true" model of the economy' (Snowdon and Vane 1997a: 267). Enough has been said about this unrealistic hypothesis. We shall therefore limit our analysis to the new classical economists' claim that '[t]he postulate that agents optimize means that their supply and demand decisions must be functions of real variables, including perceived relative prices' (Lucas and Sargent 1997: 280). This claim is perfectly in line with the choice of a neoclassical framework of analysis, the rational expectations hypothesis being 'imposed by way of adhering to the tenets of equilibrium theory' (ibid.: 281). Hence, its validity is subordinated to that of the principles of GEA, in particular to that stating that prices are *relative. If it were true that prices can be determined through the direct exchange of goods*, then it would be legitimate to claim that GEA is the best model of economic reality, and that economic agents form their expectations in accordance with it. Unfortunately for the supporters of neoclassical economics, relative prices cannot logically be determined within a system of relative exchange. Relative prices can only be derived from absolute or money prices, since it is impossible to introduce real goods and services to the realm of numbers through their direct exchange on the commodity market. The proof of the logical indeterminacy of relative prices has already been proposed elsewhere (see Schmitt 1984a, 1996a, Schmitt and De Gottardi 2003, and Cencini 1982, 2001). Let us here simply remind the reader that the over-determined character of the neoclassical system of general equilibrium is due to the fact that Walras's law is tautologically true once equilibrium is reached. However, in the whole adjustment process preceding exchange, the sum of demands does not equal the sum of supplies, since the number of independent equations is always greater than the number of unknowns (relative prices). If Walras's law were valid before an actual exchange, every (relative) price proposed on the market (by the auctioneer or by any other intermediary) would be automatically an equilibrium price. In either case relative prices remain undetermined and the system of general equilibrium is logically inconsistent. This being the case, it is clear that the new classical economists' assumption of rational expectations can no longer be upheld, since, as we observed earlier, it rests on the postulate that agents' supply and demand decisions are solely functions of relative prices.

The microeconomic nature of new classical economics is self-evident. Fluctuations in business cycles are attributed to economic agents' behaviour and the whole analysis is carried out in terms of equilibrium. 'The central idea of the equilibrium explanations of business cycles as sketched above is that economic fluctuations arise as agents react to *unanticipated* changes in variables which impinge on their decisions' (Lucas and Sargent 1997: 283). Now, as already noted, one of the new classical economics' postulates is that all markets clear, which is also one essential feature of equilibrium models. It is odd therefore that, in discussing criticisms raised against their new classical economics, Lucas and Sargent admit that '[c]leared markets is simply a principle, not verifiable by direct observation, which may or may not be useful in constructing successful hypotheses about the behaviour of these series [time series on employment and wage rates]' (ibid.: 284). If, as recognized by our two authors, market clearing is essential to equilibrium analysis, and if this assumption is unrealistic (ibid.: 284) and not necessarily useful, how is it still possible (1) to consider the market clearing hypothesis as a postulate, and (2) to keep relying on GEA as the basis for a new approach to macroeconomics?

The fact remains that new classical economics has been developed with the intent to provide a theoretical setting in which the business cycle could be analysed using a general equilibrium approach and in which Keynesian macroeconometric models can be advantageously replaced by equilibrium econometric models. This explains why several choices have been made mainly for technical reasons, the final aim being that of working out models amenable to the latest mathematical techniques.

Their choice of linearity and the neglect of learning are the effect of such strictures. 'There is no *theoretical* reason that most applied work has used linear models, only compelling technical reasons given today's computer technology' (ibid.: 288). Once again it appears quite clearly that micro-economic foundations are closely related to a conception of economics as an exercise in mathematical modelling. Equilibrium econometric models are the most sophisticated form of this attempt at transforming economics into a branch of mathematics – an attempt that could be successful only if the object of economics (produced output) could also be conceived of as an object of mathematics. In other words, economics could justify using the mathematical formalism of econometrics only if, as claimed by Debreu, real goods were numbers. This not being the case, it is in vain that economists keep on producing sophisticated pieces of mathematical virtuosity. As mathematically elegant and consistent as they may possibly be, models, of whatever breed, have nothing to do with the real world of economics. Mathematics can be introduced into economics once goods are given their numerical form. Yet, the process leading to this integration between goods and numbers is not of a mathematical nature. As we shall see, economics is a science in its own right that owes nothing to physics or mathematics and its laws are not derived from agents' behaviour. It will thus become clear that GEA is a blind alley, macroeconomics being logically founded on macroeconomic principles that have nothing to do with the search for equilibrium.

New business cycle economics: back to the homogeneity postulate

In the 1980s, new classical economics was put in jeopardy both theoretically and empirically, mainly because of its incapacity to give a satisfactory explanation of business cycles. 'With sticky prices ruled out on methodological grounds new classical models were left without an acceptable explanation of the business cycle involving money to output causality' (Snowdon and Vane 1997a: 14). As a result of this crisis, a new version of new classical analysis was built based on the assumptions of perfect information relating to monetary variables, predominance of real over monetary shocks, rational expectations, and continuous market clearing. Known as the 'real business cycle' approach, this new version of neoclassical economics reinstates the dichotomy between real and monetary variables. Hence, the economy is assumed to be subjected to random real shocks affecting the production function and resulting in relative price fluctuations. 'According to this approach observed fluctuations in output and employment are equilibrium phenomena and are the outcome of rational economic agents responding optimally to unavoidable changes in the economic environment' (ibid.: 16).

The transition from what has been dubbed the *mark I* (traditional new

classical theory) to the *mark II* (new business cycle analysis) versions of
new classical macroeconomics is characterized by the reversion to a full
information assumption and by the adoption of the real business cycle
point of view according to which economic fluctuations originate in persistent real shocks. Lucas's attempt 'to improve the microfoundations of
aggregate supply within a market clearing Walrasian general equilibrium
framework' (Snowdon and Vane 1996: 387) was thus replaced by the real
business cycle theorists' attempt to 'provide an explanation of aggregate
fluctuations which have their origins predominantly in shocks to the
supply side of the macro equation' (ibid.: 387). While in the *mark I* version
it is maintained that changes in output are only short-term effects caused
by unanticipated monetary fluctuations (so that systematic monetary
policy will be useless even in the short run), in the *mark II* version it is
claimed that 'fluctuations in output and employment are [...] Pareto
optimal responses to shocks to the production function, largely resulting
from fluctuations in the rate of technological progress' (ibid.: 389). This is
not surprising, of course, since new classical economics is derived from
Walrasian GEA, that is, from a theoretical framework where money plays
no essential role, and new business cycle economics goes back to the most
rigid form of the neutrality of money.

According to real business cycle theory, fluctuations in output and
employment are due to real changes, caused mainly by large random variations in the rate of technological change. In fact, so the story goes,
technological changes lead to fluctuations in relative prices. Since the
response of individual agents to these fluctuations in prices is rationally
determined, it necessarily brings about a change in the individual agents'
labour supply as well as in their consumption. The existence of a strict correlation between real business cycles and technological changes is thus
easily established on the basis of a very simple model derived directly from
the principles of GEA (in particular from those applied in standard intertemporal general equilibrium models).

As observed by Mankiw in his clear assessment of mainstream economics, real business cycle theory is highly controversial even from a
'conservative' viewpoint since it rests on three unrealistic assumptions.

> First, real business cycle theory assumes that the economy experiences
> large and sudden changes in the available production technol-
> ogy [...]. Second, real business cycle theory assumes that fluctuations
> in employment reflect changes in the amount people want to
> work [...]. Third, real business cycle theory assumes [...] that mon-
> etary policy is irrelevant for economic fluctuations.
>
> (Mankiw 1990: 1653)

Another criticism to real business cycle theory relates to the central
role played in this theory by the homogeneity postulate. As is well known,

the postulate of homogeneity states that a change in the quantity of money leaves relative prices unaltered. In the case of a monetary policy limited to a change in the number of monetary units, this assumption seems hardly controversial. Yet, as claimed by Fitoussi, if monetary policy is given a broader meaning it is possible to show that a change on the monetary side has 'an effect on the equilibrium level of production and employment because it influences the terms of trade between present and future' (Fitoussi 1983: 23). The French economist observes that the weakness of the homogeneity postulate results from the fact that it rests on 'the assumption of the uniqueness of the equilibrium. [While], in general, the equilibrium of an Arrow–Debreu model is not unique' (ibid.: 23). This implies that an increase in the quantity of money only exceptionally leads to a variation in nominal prices that is 'neutral' from the viewpoint of real magnitudes. Hence, in general, 'the real coordinates of the economy would not be invariant with respect to monetary policy' (ibid.: 23).

Referring to the widely shared assumption that macroeconomics must have microeconomic foundations, Fitoussi rightly observes that when macroeconomics is derived from microeconomics 'the qualitative properties of macroeconomic relations remain indeterminate' (ibid.: 2). He then concludes that '[t]he practical significance of this result is that macroeconomic theory should set itself up as an autonomous discipline and seek also other foundations' (ibid.: 2). Unfortunately, Fitoussi's own attempt is that of developing a non-Walrasian general equilibrium theory implying 'the existence of a multiplicity of equilibria whose real coordinates are different' (ibid.: 7). His rejection of Walrasian general equilibrium analysis as a meta-theory defining the framework within which macroeconomic models may be grounded on microeconomic relations is based on the belief that it is possible 'that price adjustment ceases before fully accomplishing its function of eliminating disequilibria' (ibid.: 6). Fitoussi pleads for the adoption of a theoretical approach allowing for equilibrium to be determined through the variation of both prices and quantities. The reasons for doing that span from the need for the economic system considered as a whole to ensure its existence, to the unwillingness that individual agents may display, in the absence of an auctioneer, to go on adjusting until a Walrasian equilibrium is reached. Hence, Fitoussi still looks for the foundations of macroeconomics within the framework of equilibrium analysis, even though he widens it to include 'quasi' or 'non-Walrasian' concepts of equilibrium. Nor can it be denied that the validity of Fitoussi's point of view is closely related to the validity of GEA. Fixed price models, temporary competitive equilibrium models, imperfect competition models are all derived from the Walrasian model of GEA. If it were proved that relative prices are logically undetermined, all these models would have to be rejected as lacking both logical foundation and justification.

2   Keynesian, new Keynesian, and post-Keynesian economics

Keynesian economics: a neoclassical interpretation of Keynes's theory

The expression Keynesian economics will here be used to cover the work of all those economists who, although more or less inspired by Keynes's macroeconomic theory, have not entirely rejected the market-equilibrium (or disequilibrium) approach. Apart from a small number of Keynes's followers who have consistently refused to read Keynes through neoclassical spectacles, a substantial majority of 'Keynesian' economists have *de facto* attempted to reconcile the *General Theory* with at least some principles of GEA. Among them we find most of the North-American Keynesians as well as all those who have accepted Hicks's *IS–LM* interpretation of Keynes's *General Theory*. We, following Coddington, and applying his analysis to our definition of Keynesian economics (and not only to what he calls 'hydraulic Keynesianism'), go further than him to actually show that, so defined, Keynesian economics and GEA 'are alternative programs for theorizing, rather than alternative theories' (Coddington 1976: 1265). Along similar lines, Blinder (1988) claims that Keynesians and monetarists share the same view of positive economics even though they part company where normative issues are at stake. He reaches this conclusion by showing that Keynesians and monetarists agree on what he considers to be the three principal theoretical tenets of positive Keynesianism, namely 'that both monetary and fiscal policy can change aggregate demand, that fluctuations in aggregate demand have real effects, and that prices and wages do not move rapidly to clear markets' (Blinder 1988: 280). Blinder's statement is exemplary of what the majority of economists thought of Keynesianism in the 1980s. Theoretical differences between monetarism and Keynesianism were mainly deemed to be a matter of emphasis rather than substance. Even those economists who disagreed with Friedman's claim to synthesis did not reject the neoclassical distinction between monetary and real variables, and struggled to show that Keynesian analysis had as sound a microeconomic foundation as the monetarist or new classical analysis.

As argued by a vast majority of Keynesian and new Keynesian economists, what distinguishes Keynesian economics from the rest of mainstream economics is the role played by market imperfections. Unlike
orthodox GEA, Keynesian theories do not rely on the principle of continuous market clearing since they assume the existence of a short-run slug-
gishness of wages and prices. 'The market imperfection that recurs most
frequently in Keynesian theories is the failure of wages and prices to adjust
instantly to equilibrate supply and demand' (Mankiw 1990: 1654). Now,
the assumption of wage stickiness was criticized on the grounds that it was
inconsistent with the maximizing behaviour of workers and firms, and
with 'models incorporating a predetermined nominal wage and movements along a standard, downward-sloping labor demand schedule' (ibid.:
1656). This clearly shows once again that Keynesian economists have
mostly been trying to introduce different hypotheses in a general theoretical framework that remains essentially neoclassical. Both the idea that
macroeconomic fluctuations are caused by individual agents' behaviour
(the very source of microeconomic foundations) and that the demand for
labour is a function of nominal wages are derived from GEA. If indeed
Keynesian analysis were of a radically different brand than GEA, there
would be no reason to worry about the inconsistency between wage stickiness and agents maximizing behaviour or movement along a labour
demand schedule. The fact that, '[m]ore generally, the classicals continue
to believe that the business cycle can be understood within a model of fric-
tionless markets, while the Keynesians believe that market failures of
various sorts are necessary to explain fluctuations in the economy' (ibid.:
1659) only goes to show that no fundamental difference exists between
Keynesian and general equilibrium analyses.

Of course, it could be objected that some of the assumptions adopted
by Keynesian economics as derived from GEA are generally agreed upon
by every economist and do not undermine in the least the originality of
the analysis proposed by the followers of Keynes. The assumption that
firms and consumers are maximizing agents is no more the hallmark of a
Walrasian than of a monetarist, new classical or Keynesian analytical
setting. Likewise, the law of supply and demand is the most universal law
of economics, and the assumption that markets are subject to it is
theoretically neutral. On second thought, however, it appears that the law
of supply and demand does not play the same, central role in every theoretical setting and that the assumption that individuals and firms are maximizing agents is not necessarily a determinant factor in the building of an
economic theory. Indeed, it is GEA that has made the law of supply and
demand into a key element of economic theorizing. And it is within the
neoclassical theory that maximizing behaviour acquires great significance.
As we shall see in the next chapter, the passage from Keynes's *identities* to
the *equations* used by Keynesian economists in their macroeconomic
models is thus not a harmless operation consisting in emphasizing the

role played by the law of supply and demand. By replacing the identities with conditional equalities, Keynesians have in fact transformed Keynes's theory into a particular case of the more general framework of neoclassical analysis. The clearest confirmation of this is given by the overwhelming acceptance by Keynesian economists of Hicks's *IS–LM* interpretation of Keynes's *General Theory*, an endorsement that led Patinkin to claim that Keynesian contributions to macroeconomics are essentially 'simultaneous-equation interpretations of the *General Theory* [that] can essentially be regarded as variations of *IS–LM*' (Patinkin 1990b: 213).

Let us then investigate further Hicks's conceptual interpretation of Keynes's theory.

Briefly, what Hicks attempted to do was to show that Keynes's '*special theory*' differs from the classical theory only insofar as the demand for money is made to depend on the rate of interest – $M = L(i)$ – while saving is not made to be determined by the rate of interest – $I = S(Y)$. His aim was therefore to reduce Keynes's analysis to a special case yielding 'the startling conclusion that an increase in the inducement to invest, or in the propensity to consume, will not tend to raise the rate of interest, but only to increase employment' (Hicks 1982: 107). Having done this, Hicks was then able to show that Keynes's special theory may be transformed into a '*general theory*' on condition that the demand for money be made to depend both on the rate of interest and on income. The introduction of the 'transaction motive' into the demand for money function transforms Keynes's special theory into a much more orthodox model, which allows Hicks to represent it with the aid of a diagram of a neoclassical nature (Figure 2.1).

The *LL* curve – known today as *LM* – relates the liquidity preference to the money supply and shows the combinations of income – *I* in Hicks's notation – and interest rate (*i*) that lead to equilibrium in the money

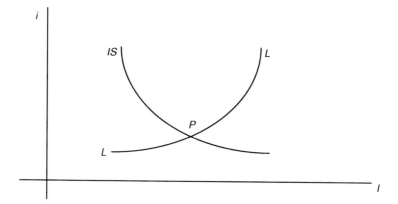

Figure 2.1 Hicks's diagram.

market. Since it is assumed that the demand for money increases when the rate of interest falls and varies positively with income, the *LM* curve is upward sloping and gets steeper 'the higher the income elasticity and the smaller the interest elasticity of the demand for money' (Vane and Thompson 1992: 7). The *IS* curve is the locus of combinations between interest rate and income allowing for the equality of saving and investment. It has a negative slope and implies that the equilibrium level of real income is a function of the rate of interest. Since national income depends on aggregate demand and aggregate demand is closely related to the multiplier, '[t]he slope of the *IS* curve depends on the responsiveness of investment to changes in the rate of interest and the value of the multiplier' (ibid.: 4).

The point of intersection between the *IS* and *LM* curves defines the simultaneous achievement of equilibrium on the goods and money markets. Hicks's *IS–LM* diagram is therefore the clearest attempt to show that Keynes's contribution can be reassessed in terms of general equilibrium analysis and thus emptied of its intended revolutionary content.

Being an earnest neoclassical economist, Hicks interpreted Keynes's theory according to the principles of neoclassical economics and it is not surprising to read in his 1937 article that in his *IS–LM* diagrammatic representation of Keynes's *General Theory* income and the rate of interest 'are determined together; just as price and output are determined together in the modern theory of demand and supply' (Hicks 1982: 109). Later on, in a paper published in the *Journal of Post Keynesian Economics*, and significantly entitled '*IS–LM*: an explanation', Hicks was to be extremely clear about the neoclassical origin of his diagram: 'It will readily be understood, in the light of what I have been saying, that the idea of the *IS–LM* diagram came to me as a result of the work I had been doing on three-way exchange, conceived in a Walrasian manner' (Hicks 1980–81: 320).

The neoclassical interpretation of Keynes's *General Theory* initiated by Hicks, Harrod and Meade, further developed by Lange and Modigliani, and taken over and re-elaborated by Clower, Leijonhufvud, Tobin, and Samuelson was to give rise to the neo-Keynesian approach to macroeconomics. Despite notable differences between their analyses, all these authors aim at formalizing Keynes's theory in order to make it workable in mathematical terms. Thus, while it is true that Hicks's attempt to interpret Keynes's theory along the path of general equilibrium analysis was worked out explicitly to reduce Keynes's contribution to a particular case of Walras's approach, it is also true that the success of *IS–LM* may be explained by the attraction it exerted on the majority of economists because of its simplicity.

Keynes's thought was too complex and in part counter-intuitive to be easily grasped. It was presented with the aid of very few and allegedly self-evident (if not tautological) equations and based on a macroeconomic approach that did not seem to be always consistent with the microeconomic perception of the real world that was supposed to be at the core of economics. Hicks's interpretation, on the contrary, had the great advantage of relying on a set of equations, of being easily represented by a simple geometrical diagram, and of incorporating Keynes into the microeconomic approach that was gaining acceptance among economists. It is not surprising, therefore, to find in *The New Palgrave Dictionary of Money & Finance* the following interpretation of Keynes's contribution to economic analysis: 'The main analytical innovation of Keynes's *General Theory* was to develop an alternative concept of equilibrium that allowed modified versions of supply and demand analysis to be applied to macroeconomic questions without assuming a state of ideal co-ordination' (Howitt 1992: 633). As Howitt's quotation clearly shows, the core of Keynes's message is reduced to a simple application of the law of supply and demand to the general concept of aggregate output. If this were the case, Keynes's revolution could be significantly played down, since it would amount to just another version of neoclassical analysis.

Though some of them do not go as far as Howitt, North-American Keynesians still believe Hicks's interpretation to be respectful of Keynes's thought and a very useful instrument both for teaching and for research. In a 1994 interview, Tobin, for example, does not hesitate to claim that 'the *IS–LM* model is the tool of first resort [. . .] it's a start and lots of times it's exactly right' (Tobin, in Snowdon *et al.* 1994: 129).

As shown by Keynes's correspondence with Reddaway, Harrod, Hicks, and Meade, the author of the *General Theory* never rejected either the neoclassical interpretation of his analysis or the *IS–LM* representation proposed by Hicks. The responsibility for the various attempts carried out by generations of economists to reconcile Keynesian and Walrasian economics within a neoclassical synthesis may thus be ascribed to Keynes himself. It may be deemed rather unfortunate that 'Keynes made no public protest when they [*IS–LM* and related diagrams and algebra] began to appear' (Kahn 1984: 160), yet this would not have been enough to make the *IS–LM* successful had Keynes's followers managed to prove that Hicks's model is logically inconsistent. The wide acceptance of *IS–LM* is due both to its clear and simple mathematical formulation and to the failure of its critics to show that it has to be rejected on logical–conceptual (and not ideological) grounds.

The *IS–LM* representation has often been criticized, mainly on the grounds that it is an oversimplification of Keynes's theory. Vercelli, for example, points out that 'the *IS–LM* model offers a profoundly distorted representation of Keynes's *General Theory*' (Vercelli 1991: 200) even though it may be taken to offer 'a fairly faithful analytic representation of some aspects of the *fixprice* heuristic model'. The Italian economist's conclusion about the *IS–LM* model is even stranger. He admits that 'it may well be useful for teaching or as a preliminary step in analysis' (ibid.: 200), but immediately adds that 'one should always be aware of its considerable distance, not only from reality, but also from Keynes's general heuristic model itself' (ibid.: 200). Vercelli's position is emblematic: it clearly shows the dilemma many economists face concerning Hicks's *IS–LM* analytical construct. Lacking a valid alternative to neoclassical analysis, they still do not know how to avoid the use of Hicks's model, which, despite its 'considerable distance' both from reality and from Keynes, seems to retain 'its continued analytical usefulness as it enters its second half-century' (Patinkin 1990a: 132).

New and post-Keynesian economics: the search for new microfoundations

New Keynesian economics

Dissatisfied with the tenets of new classical economics, a number of economists still influenced by the Keynesian approach to macroeconomics have worked out a new synthesis between Keynesian and neoclassical theories known as new Keynesian economics. After the monetarist synthesis, by which Friedman attempted to incorporate Keynes's contribution into what he believed to be a more general framework of analysis, the new Keynesian synthesis is the latest endeavour to provide Keynes's analysis with solid microeconomic foundations. To a certain extent, in the same way as it might be claimed that orthodox Keynesian economists tried to reconcile the need for government monetary and fiscal policies with the main principles of the neoclassical paradigm, the new Keynesian contribution might be seen as a further attempt to found Keynesian macroeconomics on the neoclassical axioms of individuals' utility and profit maximization, and rational expectations. As stated by Gordon, new Keynesian economics is essentially concerned with 'the search for rigorous and convincing models of wage and/or price stickiness based on maximizing behaviour and rational expectations' (Gordon 1990: 1137).

In the words of Gerrard, 'new Keynesian economics represents the attempt to examine, by a rigorous choice-theoretical method, the macroeconomic consequences of market failures at the micro level because of a variety of structural, informational and other imperfections' (Gerrard 1996: 60). Broadly speaking, new Keynesian models are supposed to determine the economic situation resulting from four categories of disequilibrium factors: imperfect competition; endogenous price and wage rigidity; multiple equilibria and coordination failures; and credit rationing (ibid.: 60).

Unhappy with orthodox Keynesian models based on nominal wage rigidity, some new Keynesian economists – such as Ball, Mankiw, Romer, Akerlof and Yellen – turned their attention to the commodity market and to the nominal rigidity of goods prices, trying to show how business cycles may result from a market in which monopolistically competitive firms operate in a context characterized by imperfect competition, transaction and menu costs, and asymmetric information. Endeavouring to provide adequate microfoundations for wage and price rigidities, these authors have worked out a theory of aggregate supply accounting for the non-neutrality of money.

One idea of their analysis is that of monopolistic competition, that is, the idea of building 'a macro structure on the foundations of monopolistic, rather than perfect, competition' (Blinder 1988: 289). The aim of this attempt is to show that imperfect equilibrium may be a correct frame of reference for economic theorizing, and that nominal variables can play a role even in a theoretical setting that is said to pertain to the determination of relative prices. As Blinder reminds us, Mankiw, Akerlof and Yellen introduced the fixed costs of changing nominal prices in order to show that nominal changes (or the lack thereof) may influence real balances, aggregate demand and social welfare. The logical sequence is the following. Suppose the money supply rises slightly. Because of the cost of changing nominal prices, most firms will not raise their prices, thus provoking an increase in real balances. As a consequence, aggregate demand will also rise; so will firms' profits and social welfare.

It should not be too difficult to realize that this logical chain of events rests on a series of highly questionable assumptions. The first is that money is being supplied as if it were a real asset 'produced' by the monetary authorities. Modern monetary analysis has got rid of this 'materialistic' conception of money and shown that there is no such thing as money supply proper. Banks issue money each time a transaction is carried out, it is true, but this does not define the creation of any positive amount of money income, and can therefore not lead to the formation of a stock or a 'quantity' of money being supplied by banks.

The second assumption is that aggregate demand is determined by real balances. If prices remain stable and the supply of money increases, so we are told, real balances rise, since consumers see their purchasing power go up. *What is totally missing here is the fact that a variation in microeconomic prices can never modify the amount of income available within the economic system.* Inflation notwithstanding, increases in the amount of income define equivalent increases in production, so that a variation or a lack of variation in prices can only modify the *distribution* of income, and not its total amount. On the whole, if we consider the totality of income holders, no real balance effect can thus occur.

In much the same vein, the third assumption is that aggregate demand is determined by the amount of income consumers and investors are prepared to spend given their propensity to save and the variation in the quantity of money and/or in nominal prices. Yet, here again the problem is ill-conceived, for global demand is determined by the amount of available income, and not only by that part of it their final holders are willing to spend. Behaviour has no influence on the determination of macroeconomic concepts such as that of global demand. If the amount of income deposited with banks is 100, global demand is perfectly known and numerically equal to 100 irrespective of the identity of those who are exerting it. It is obvious, for example, that if I am saving ten units of income somebody else will exert a demand in my stead. What really matters from a macroeconomic point of view is that my savings are immediately lent by the bank they are deposited with and are therefore not prevented from exerting an equivalent demand.

A fourth and last assumption is that social welfare may rise because of a nominal increase in the money supply (or because of a fall in microeconomic prices). This sounds rather odd, since it should be obvious that, economically speaking, an improvement in social welfare requires an increased production. The increase cannot be simply nominal, but it must be defined in both monetary *and* real terms. Moreover, it is only if the decrease in microeconomic prices is due to a rise in produced output that it determines a rise in social welfare.

Contrary to what is claimed by Ball, Romer and Mankiw, other new Keynesian economists (for example Greenwald and Stiglitz) argue that wage and price rigidities might have the opposite effect and dampen instead of amplifying a decline in economic activity. '[N]ational economic forces can magnify economic shocks that may seem small, and [...] existing price rigidities may *reduce* the magnitude of the fluctuations, as Keynes argued' (Greenwald and Stiglitz 1993: 26). According to Greenwald and Stiglitz, new Keynesian economics encompasses two broadly different approaches. The first, developed mainly by European economists, attempts to elaborate general disequilibrium models or general equilibrium models with price rigidities. The second assumes that, because of market failures to clear (mainly due to imperfect information and incomplete contracts), 'increased flexibility of wages and prices might exacerbate the economy's downturn' (ibid.: 25).

Greenwald and Stiglitz privilege the second approach and provide a detailed analysis of the reasons why price and wage flexibility may contribute to macroeconomic fluctuations. For example, they rigorously endeavour to show that changes in output may be caused by risk averse firms amplifying the effects of small shocks to the economy. Since '[t]he actions of firms are affected by their perceptions of risks', '[c]hanges in the economic environment will in general necessitate changes in some actions of the firm' (ibid.: 28), notably in its decision to produce and invest. Our authors individuate three key factors influencing the behaviour of risk-averse firms: the overall state of the economy, changes in the firm's cash position, and changes in the price level. In fact, these three factors may be reduced to one, since the firm's cash position is affected by its sales at a given price level, and the price level itself depends, together with the firm's possibilities of sale, on the overall state of the economy. In short, if the economy is in a state of recession, the theory of the risk-averse firm should explain why firms are willing to produce less, thus reducing the amount of produced output.

Now, the real problem here is not to find enough good reasons for firms to reduce their output in presence of an economic recession, but to explain why a recession exists in the first place. Could the theory of credit rationing and of risk-averse banks provide a satisfactory answer? Since banks are risk averse, their decision to lend is influenced by all the changes that are likely to modify their risk. Credit rationing is thus the result of the decisions taken by risk-averse banks in response to negative economic shocks. Once again, it is the initial state of the economy that is the triggering factor. 'This risk averse behaviour of banks will magnify an initial negative economic shock, and make recession deeper and larger' (ibid.: 31). Hence, our query remains: where does the initial recession come from? Broadly speaking, the new Keynesians' answer has been that, the economy being 'a complex organization, requiring coordination of decisions of the millions of households and firms [, u]nemployment and other macroeconomic problems can be viewed as a failure of society to solve the necessary coordination problem efficiently' (ibid.: 42). If the decisions of millions of households, firms and banks were optimally coordinated, no disturbances would occur. Hence, since in a social environment coordination is necessarily influenced by constantly changing behaviour, economic disorder will be the rule and the fight against it is bound to be an endless and hopeless attempt to square the circle. In this framework, the role left to economists' intervention would be to minimize economic fluctuations and their negative effects, by providing agents with better information. In contrast, our claim, and what we will argue throughout this book, is that economic disorder is not caused by any agents' behaviour, but by our systemic ignorance of the macroeconomic laws governing the framework within which economic agents act. But for the time being, let us make some additional critical observations on the new Keynesian approach to macroeconomics.

As clearly explained by Gordon in his 1990 critical survey of new Keynesian economics, the assumption of price stickiness derives from the absence of nominal GNP indexation and, therefore, from the fact that 'changes in individual prices will respond to changes in individual marginal costs, not changes in nominal GNP' (Gordon 1990: 1117). If individual prices are sticky, that is, if they do not mimic changes in nominal GNP, the aggregate price level will also be sticky, which means that the aggregate price level does not reflect the level of GNP expressed in prices. This sounds rather odd. Since nominal GNP is determined in terms of prices, how is it possible, for example, that individual firms' decision to keep their prices constant is not reflected in the level of nominal GNP? Reciprocally, how can a variation in the level of nominal GNP – real output remaining constant – not simply reflect a concomitant change in individual prices? If aggregate demand is derived from the aggregation of individual demands, can it vary independently of their variation? Keynesian and new Keynesian economists answer in the affirmative. They explain the possible inconsistency between individual and aggregate demands by the fact that aggregate variables are not simply derived from the sum of their individual components. Thus, a change in nominal aggregate demand can occur irrespective of changes in individual demands, which would explain why firms 'have no reason to accept the risk involved in indexing their price to nominal aggregate demand' (ibid.: 1117). Alas, the trouble is that Keynesian economists offer no adequate explanation of how aggregate demand can differ from the sum of individual demands. Under these circumstances, there seems to be little justification for maintaining that a rise in aggregate demand is not related to individual demands. Indeed, if demands vary jointly at the aggregate and individual levels, and if their variation has an effect on prices, it is no longer possible to maintain that changes in the aggregate price level 'do not mimic changes in nominal GNP' (ibid.: 1116).

Let us suppose that an increase in aggregate demand is caused by an equivalent inflationary rise in the supply of bank deposits. New Keynesians would maintain that while the increase in aggregate demand leads to a nominal rise of GNP, it may well have no effect on the aggregate price level since firms could decide not to modify their prices because of 'idiosyncratic elements of cost and demand' (ibid.: 1117). But, if the totality of the new bank deposits is lent and spent (as it necessarily is because of the very strictures of double-entry book-keeping), the demand of which firms benefit increases by the same amount as aggregate demand. Hence, if we assume – as Keynesian theorists do – that *caeteris paribus* a variation in demand gives rise to a variation in prices, we are forced to conclude that the aggregate price level is bound to increase to the same extent as nominal GNP. Of course, this is not to say that every increase in demand is necessarily matched by a rise in prices. What we are claiming is not that Keynesian and new Keynesian economists are bound to accept Walras's assumption that markets clear continuously through variations in prices. Market rigidities are not under dispute here. Nor are we denying that changes in demand may be matched by variations other that those in prices. Our contention is merely that the definition of nominal GNP accepted by the Keynesian school is in contrast with the claim that a variation in nominal GNP may not be mimicked by an equivalent change in the aggregate price level. In fact, nominal GNP is the expression of national output in terms of prices. If, for whatever reason, nominal national output increases while real GNP remains constant, this variation in prices is necessarily reflected at the microeconomic *and* at the aggregate levels. Macroeconomic prices being determined through the aggregation of microeconomic prices, any variation in microeconomic prices is necessarily mimicked by an equivalent variation in macroeconomic prices.

As a consequence, the close relationship assumed to exist between micro and macroeconomics is such that no true distinction is possible between macroeconomic and microeconomic prices. It thus follows that if the variation in aggregate demand influences nominal GNP it modifies microeconomic prices and, therefore, also the aggregate price level.

In order for the new Keynesian analysis to be a valid alternative to the neoclassical assumption that firms are price-takers, the theory must account for a degree of freedom between micro and macroeconomic prices. The Keynesian claim that economics is best described by non-market clearing models 'with demand-taking firms making voluntary choices of the price level' (ibid.: 1136) is sound. Yet, it requires macroeconomic prices to be distinguished from microeconomic prices, a distinction that Keynesian economists of every school (orthodox, new and post-Keynesian) fail to provide since they derive macroeconomic prices from the simple aggregation of microeconomic prices. Now, this problem cannot be separated from the question of global or macroeconomic demand. Here again Keynesian models have been unable to go beyond aggregation. But, if global demand is identified with aggregate demand it becomes impossible to explain both inflation and deflation. From the standard macroeconomic viewpoint, any level of aggregate demand is entirely justifiable on microeconomic grounds, which leaves no room for a macroeconomic theory of inflation and deflation. As a consequence, there seems to follow that variations in microeconomic prices have to mimic, at a disaggregate level, variations in aggregate demand.

It may be of interest to observe here that the elaboration of general equilibrium non-market clearing models – mostly by European economists – has rarely been taken into consideration by American new Keynesians. As noticed by Gordon, '[a]n interesting aspect of US new-Keynesian research is the near-total lack of interest in the general equilibrium properties of non-market-clearing models' (Gordon 1990: 1137). According to Gordon, this 'is understandable in light of the primacy of micro foundations as the prerequisite for macro discourse' (ibid.: 1137–8). If one observes that fixed price general equilibrium models rely heavily on the principles of neoclassical analysis and nevertheless are still regarded as too macro oriented by US new Keynesians, one can see that today's analyses are far removed from Keynes's original concerns and problems.

Gordon maintains that a genuinely Keynesian model must account for macroeconomic constraints and spillovers of the kind introduced in general disequilibrium models. But is this enough to consider new Keynesian models as truly macroeconomic? Has the claim that macroeconomic quantities belong to microeconomic choice functions anything to do with Keynes's project to build a (monetary) macroeconomic theory of production? Admittedly, a case can be made that Keynesian and new Keynesian economists are more concerned with microeconomic foundations than neo- and new classical economists. As claimed by Gordon, Keynesian economics rests on the factual observation that '[r]ational microeconomic agents care about the relation of their own price to their own costs, not to aggregate nominal demand' (ibid.: 1139). It thus appears that, while in neoclassical economics assumptions regarding individual microeconomic behaviour are introduced (along with the continuous market clearing hypothesis) as logical requirements of general equilibrium theories, *in Keynesian economics microeconomic behaviour is the stumbling block of the whole analysis*, microeconomic theories being worked out in order to conform with the initial macroeconomic assumptions and not the other way round. In the words of Greenwald and Stiglitz, Keynesian (particularly new Keynesian) economics 'seeks to adapt micro-theory to macro-theory. [...] The phenomena of unemployment, credit rationing and business cycles are inconsistent with standard microeconomic theory. New Keynesian economics aims to develop a micro-theory that can account for them' (Greenwald and Stiglitz 1987: 120).

Let us conclude this short overview of new Keynesian economics with a few critical remarks. In his paper on new Keynesian economics published in 1992 by the *European Economic Review*, Mankiw claims that 'the new classical challenge has been met: Keynesian economics has been reincarnated into a body with firm microeconomic muscle' (Mankiw 1992: 560). Confronted with such a claim, one cannot but feel sorry to see the father of modern macroeconomics 'reincarnated' in a microeconomic body. This is not surprising, though odd as Mankiw goes on to claim that reading Keynes is in no way an important part of Keynesian theorizing, and that 'the *General Theory* is an outdated book' (ibid.: 561). In a sense such claims should make one feel better for Keynes himself as his theory remains distinct from what the Keynesians have made of it. Be that as it may, it is disappointing to see to what extent Keynes's revolutionary message has been lost to the new Keynesians. It should also be admitted that the *General Theory* is not an easy book, and Keynes was not always crystal clear or consistent when developing on his main insights. It is all the same an unfair and contradictory assessment to conclude that '[d]espite its remarkable contribution the *General Theory* is an obscure book' (ibid.: 561). If Mankiw really finds it so obscure, how can he also claim that it is a seminal contribution to economics?

Of course, not all new Keynesian economists share Mankiw's point of view, either on Keynes or concerning wages and prices rigidity or stabilizing centralized policies. Stiglitz, for example, supports Tobin's belief that increasing flexibility in prices and wages may induce greater economic fluctuations than rigidity, and may then require some sort of stabilizing intervention by the government. By and large, however, the consensus is that macroeconomics must be founded on microeconomics and that it must do away with the neoclassical and new classical principle of continuous market clearing. Despite such denial of a key principle of Walrasian analysis, the neoclassical influence on new Keynesian economics remains so strong that a 'surprising number of new-Keynesian models share in common the neglect of aggregation; the aggregate economy is simply the representative agent multiplied by *n*' (Gordon 1990: 1136).

It seems therefore legitimate to conclude that the new Keynesian attempt to contrast GEA has in fact further reduced the differences between neoclassical and Keynesian economics. However, it has done so by gradually transforming a potentially novel and fruitful macroeconomic approach into an entirely microeconomic one, turning Keynesian economics into a branch of neoclassical economics. Disagreement as to whether nominal wages and prices should be considered rigid or flexible, or market failures should or should not enter the models, does not cancel the impact of the widely shared belief among new Keynesian economists, namely, that 'understanding macroeconomic behavior requires the construction of a (simple) general equilibrium model' (Greenwald and Stiglitz 1993: 24). The originality of Keynes's message is entirely lost due to the microeconomic usurpation of macroeconomics. Greenwald and Stiglitz's emphasis on price flexibility is another key instance where the convergence between new Keynesian and neoclassical economics is made manifest. At any rate, new Keynesian economics of whatever flavour has little to do with Keynes's own revolutionary insights on macroeconomics, or with his efforts to build a 'general' theory grounded on macrofoundations.

Post-Keynesian economics

Overtly opposed to neoclassical, new classical, Keynesian and new Keynesian economics, post-Keynesian economics encompasses the contributions of a number of authors who, inspired by Keynes, Kalecki and Sraffa, and dissatisfied with the strict dependence of macro on microeconomics asserted by mainstream economic analysis, attempt instead to argue for the primacy of a macroeconomic approach. By and large, post-Keynesians reject the Walrasian market-clearing definition of equilibrium as well as the new classical version of rational expectations and the assumption of individual profit-maximizing firms. They emphasize the key role played by money and by Keynes's effective demand, the notion of persistent involuntary unemployment, and the importance of oligopolistic and monopolistic markets. As far as choice-theoretical analysis is concerned, '[t]he Post-Keynesian position is that individual choice is limited. It is determined much more by income and class and the technical conditions of production than by relative prices' (Dow 1996: 78). As clearly stated by Dow, in post-Keynesian economics

> [i]nstitutional structure and industrial organization are [...] of considerable importance, since they determine the distribution of income, the level and composition of output, the capacity for

generating surplus, and the degree to which that surplus is expanded in such a way as to increase output and employment.

(ibid.: 78–9)

The position endorsed by post-Keynesian economists differs from that supported by mainstream economics to the extent that their 'analysis is in part based on postulates as to group behaviour' (ibid.: 99) rather than on axioms of individual behaviour. Believing that 'there are sufficient regularities between the chosen aggregates to allow useful analysis of policy questions, without grounding the analysis explicitly in individual behaviour' (ibid.: 98–9), post-Keynesians consider macroeconomics as being the science investigating group or aggregate behaviour and how this influences individual behaviour. Yet, this does not imply either a rejection of microfoundations or a new definition of macroeconomics. In fact, the macro level is still concerned with aggregates, and individual behaviour remains the cornerstone of the whole analysis. 'The first principle of micro-foundations within this [post-Keynesian] paradigm is that macroeconomics refers to the aggregation of the outcomes of individual action, and thus should not be logically inconsistent with the analysis of individual behaviour' (ibid.: 98).

One of the greatest difficulties with accepting this paradigm stems from the fact of taking macroeconomic magnitudes to be the outcome of aggregation of microeconomic data. Even as thoughtful a writer as Hoover, who openly maintains that the nature of macroeconomic relationships is such that it 'precludes direct reduction of the macroeconomic to the microeconomic' (Hoover 2001: 124), has no hesitation in claiming that '[o]n any interpretation, macroeconomics takes a larger view of the economy and deals with aggregates, which are, in turn, constructed from characteristic of individual economic actors' (ibid.: 113). It seems beyond dispute, in fact, that macroeconomics deals with aggregates, that is, with wholes formed by combining elements derived from the behaviour of single economic agents. Like the great majority of economists, post-Keynesians fully accept this broad definition. It is important then to investigate it further. We shall start by referring to two emblematic examples.

An exemplary case of a macroeconomic aggregate is national income. 'Considered as national income, nominal GNP adds up the incomes of each individual in the economy and is an obvious extension of the accounting framework for business or personal income' (ibid.: 117). According to this widely accepted definition, national income is thus simply the sum of all the individual incomes generated in a country during a given period of time. Yet, this definition does not give us any precise information as to whether, before aggregation, individual incomes are themselves an autonomous component part of national income. In other words, are we to hold national income to be the macroeconomic result of aggregating microeconomic or macroeconomic magnitudes?

Apparently, this question is almost absurd. If it is agreed that macro-economics deals with aggregates, then national income can only be a macroeconomic magnitude. However, it is precisely this account of macro-economics that we are calling into question here. We want to show that conceiving of macroeconomics as an economics of aggregates is arbitrary and seriously misguided. Is it not rather the case that national income sig-nifies the societal income, that is, the income of the society taken as a whole? And is it not also true that the income of each atomic individual is social precisely because it partakes of the income of the society he/she belongs? The income earned by a single producer defines his personal income, of course, but it also increases the income formed in the whole system. To the extent that the income of a single individual defines a con-comitant income for society (which does not mean that a single produc-tion will give rise to *two* incomes, but that the income so specified is simultaneously an income for the individual producer and for the society he/she is part of), it is a macroeconomic income. To claim otherwise means to stick dogmatically to a distinction between micro and macro-economics that rests on a superficial and confused 'quantitative' criterion. Instead of adopting a 'quantitative' criterion (as the number of individual agents concerned with a given economic event), we consider the eco-nomic system taken as a whole and observe how the occurrence at stake affects the situation for the entire society, now understood as consisting of the set of individual agents and not as their mere aggregate.

The second example of a macroeconomic aggregate usually referred to by economists pertains to consumption. As noticed by Hoover, in fact, '[c]onsumption as reported in the national income accounts [...] is just the summation of the purchases of a nation's citizens' (ibid.: 129). Here again the pertinent question to ask is whether individual consumption is a micro or a macroeconomic event. Now, the answer can be as straight-forward as it was with the case of national income: namely agreeing to identify consumption with the expenditure of a given income for the final purchase of produced output. In the same way that even a single produc-tion increases national income and has thereby to be viewed as a macro-economic event, so the single final purchase by an individual defines a final consumption from the standpoint of national output and hence counts automatically as a macroeconomic event.

A related difficulty that arises from the problematic mixing of micro with macro analysis is known as the fallacy of composition. The aggrega-tion of individual decisions may lead, in fact, to a result at odds with the aim pursued by each single agent. The most quoted examples are those of profit maximization in a general equilibrium framework, and of an increase in the propensity to save in a Keynesian setting. In a competitive market, if each single firm tries to maximize its extra profits, the result will be the overall disappearance of extra profits. In a Keynesian model, the decision of each single household to increase its savings will lead to a decrease of global saving through a fall in national income. Now, as a clear symptom of the logical error of any attempt to derive macro from microeconomics, the fallacy of composition problem cannot be really explained by post-Keynesian economics. Indeed, how is it possible to maintain that aggregate saving falls even as each individual saving increases? Once global magnitudes are considered the result of a process of aggregation, how can it be claimed that aggregates are now arrived at independently of the terms entering in their aggregation? In short, the fallacy of composition is at odds with the aforementioned post-Keynesian maxim that 'macroeconomics refers to the aggregation of the outcomes of individual action, and thus should not be logically inconsistent with the analysis of individual behaviour' (Dow 1996: 98).

To claim that, 'although macroeconomic reality is tied closely to micro-economic reality, macroeconomics is not reducible to microeconomics' (Hoover 2001: 131) is not enough to establish the autonomy of macro-economics. Indeed, Hoover readily admits that '[m]acroeconomic aggre-gates are what they are and behave as they do because of the underlying behaviour of individual people' (ibid.: 131), which amounts to admitting that macroeconomics is essentially based on microeconomics. Whether one can or cannot (as maintained by Hoover) 'give a complete accounting of macroeconomics from microeconomics alone' (ibid.: 131) is besides the point here. Heterogeneity of economic aggregates and informational complexity are undoubtedly serious obstacles in the way of the microfoun-dational programme. Nobody would deny that 'people who constitute eco-nomic aggregates are not alike and do not remain constant in their tastes and circumstances over time' (ibid.: 130). If we also add that '[f]ar from having complete, transitive, and reflexive preferences, people – subject to biding constraints to be sure and not completely inconsistent – choose in whimsical, partially informed, and arbitrary ways' (ibid.: 131), it becomes clearer how hopeless the attempt to derive macro from microeconomics is. Yet, the crucial autonomy of macro *vis-à-vis* microeconomics cannot be deduced from admitting the impossibility to account for the complexity of the real world. As long as macroeconomics is made synonymous with eco-nomic aggregates, there will be no opening for a genuine macroeconomic approach. As the examples of national income and consumption have brought out, aggregation is not the cornerstone for the construction of macroeconomics. What is needed is a more analytically rigorous distinc-tion between macro and micro allowing for the macroeconomic institut-ing of macroeconomics. As post-Keynesian economics does not succeed in that, it falls short of providing a viable alternative to mainstream economics.

3 Identity versus equilibrium

Equilibrium analysis: a critical appraisal

As is unanimously acknowledged, general equilibrium is the basis of neo-classical economics in all its different versions. Even advocates of disequilibrium analysis agree, in fact, on the essential role played by the equilibrium concept and by GEA generally. Whether it is seen as the ideal model economic reality should try to conform to, or as an unrealistic model that has to be modified in order to accord with the real world, general equilibrium is still the fundamental reference point for mainstream economic theories. Starting from a set of axioms relating to individual behaviour and from a number of assumptions of a formalist nature required for the system to yield a solution, economic models are worked out in terms of mathematical functional relationships. Economic entities are considered either as constants or as variables in a system of equations. By allowing for the solution of a system of independent equations, the value of the variables so determined is said to represent their equilibrium value.

Now, mainstream equilibrium analysis has also been criticized on different grounds. One of the most widespread criticisms is that equilibrium is made to depend on the value of exogenous variables whose definition is arbitrary. This does not mean, however, that the choice of exogenous variables is random. On the contrary, it strictly depends on the theoretical framework taken as analytical reference. In a real business cycle setting, for example, the choice of technological change as an exogenous variable is a logical consequence of the fact that Walras's GEA is based on relative prices determination and that money is essentially irrelevant. Be that as it may, it has also to be admitted that, being functional for the model one promotes, the choice of variables does not have to be consistent with the concerns of a realistic explanation of the world. Actually, some variables must just be presumed to be exogenous, irrespective of what the actual working of the economy indicates. Indeed, it may be argued that each of the chosen exogenous variables is completely independent with respect to the other variables that enter the model. Along this line of reasoning, for example, Fitoussi acknowledges that one major shortcoming of macroeconomic models – whether they are general equilibrium, Keynesian, non-Walrasian or rational expectations models – consists in the 'identification' problem: '[t]he reality approximated by our estimation method is always of a greater dimension than that of the models that we use' (Fitoussi 1983: 26). Thus, the structural form of economic models is bound to remain hypothetical (being determined on the basis of the set of assumptions chosen within the given framework) and hence too simplistic when compared to the complexity of the real world. 'This is particularly true of a macroeconomic model that restricts the space of phenomena to a very reduced dimension [...] but is also true of any economic model' (ibid.: 26).

Yet, reasonable as these critical observations may appear to be, they are far from being enough to force us to abandon equilibrium analysis in any of its versions. Conformity with the real world is a very important principle, of course, but of very little use, for reality is not simply here to be observed and described. If this were the case, we would need no theory to understand the world of economics. From the moment it is agreed that appearances are deceptive and that economic reality has to be read through theoretical spectacles, the direct comparison with the real world is no longer a discerning principle. In this respect Lucas's analysis is inconsistent. He starts, in fact, by claiming that '[a]ny model that is well enough articulated to give clear answers to the questions we put to it will necessarily be artificial, abstract, patently "unreal"' (Lucas 1980: 696). But then he adds that this state of affairs does not mean that closeness to reality cannot be a guideline for the choice between equally well-articulated models. On the contrary, the founding father of new classical economics maintains that models must be tested 'as useful imitations of reality' (ibid.: 696–7) and chosen according to the obvious principle that 'more "realism" in a model is clearly preferred to less' (ibid.: 697). Hence, model *A* would have to be preferred to model *B* if *A* provides a better simulation of reality than *B*. An economist's ability would therefore consist in increasing his technical ability to construct ever better imitations, simulated economies artificially reproducing the complexity of the real world. What Lucas seems to miss here is the fact that in order to establish whether a model is a better imitation of reality than another model we must know what the real world actually is, and not merely what it looks like. If the real world can be apprehended only by going beyond appearances, then how can we determine if our model is indeed a good replica of reality or a simple imitation of a deceptive representation of a reality that remains out of our reach? Plainly stated, this means that we need a more rigorous test than 'naïve realism' to evaluate economic theories. In the case of equilibrium analysis this implies that its rejection passes through a theoretical proof of its logical inconsistency as well as through the working out of an alternative analytical framework.

Now, insofar as an equation reflects a functional relationship and its solution defines the value of the variables allowing for the equality of its two sides, it may be claimed that its very presence is the mark of equilibrium analysis. In this respect equilibrium analysis is not only a characteristic of neoclassical theories, but spreads out to incorporate Keynesian and new Keynesian theories. The importance of equilibrium analysis is such that, despite the post-Keynesian rejection of the axiomatic approach endorsed by mainstream economists, post-Keynesian economics is essentially based on it. 'The common position which differentiates Post-Keynesian equilibrium analysis from that of general equilibrium theory is the rejection of mechanical time and the narrow conception of logical time equilibrium required by an axiomatic framework' (Dow 1996: 121–2). Post-Keynesian criticism of mainstream equilibrium analysis refers essentially to GEA and to the fact that 'it [GEA] encapsulates all endogenous variables by deterministic relationships within one system, producing a timeless solution which carries no explanation except with respect to any variables held back as exogenous' (ibid.: 124). In contrast with GEA, post-Keynesians support a more differentiated approach, alternating partial equilibrium analysis where the concept of equilibrium is related to historical time with an equilibrium analysis 'based on the logical notion of time, but with a less strict dichotomy between exogenous and endogenous variables; the alternative categorization of independent, given and dependent variables [allowing] for a richer causal explanation' (ibid.: 121). Yet, however strong the post-Keynesian rejection of GEA may be, it never goes as far as to imply the dismissal of the concept of equilibrium and its replacement with an alternative conception of the way economic magnitudes are determined.

Whether in its neoclassical or in its Keynesian version, equilibrium analysis is the hard core of today's economic theory. Both micro and macroeconomics rest on the idea that causality (logical, chronological or 'expectational') may be translated into a series of functional relationships and that the economic system may be represented by a set of models based on these fundamental relationships. Of course, as noted by Vercelli, '[c]oncepts of equilibrium and disequilibrium have long been involved in controversies over alternative macroeconomic theories' (Vercelli 1991: 11). However, the main differences between these alternative theories relate to the way the concepts of equilibrium and disequilibrium have been interpreted and applied rather than to the rejection or the acceptance of equilibrium analysis. As a matter of fact, equilibrium analysis has never been fundamentally questioned, either by neoclassical or by Keynesian economics. Indeed, having refused the idea that Keynes's identities might be much more than simple tautologies, Keynesians did not hesitate to transform them into conditions of equilibrium, apparently unaware that by doing so they were also transforming Keynes's theory into another version of GEA.

Vercelli is right in observing that the concept of equilibrium is functional to 'traditional' economic analysis since it 'permits considerable simplifications in the functional structure of a system. In particular: (i) a feedback is represented in equilibrium by a single relation [. . .]; (ii) certain variables become equal in equilibrium [. . .]; (iii) certain terms become zero' (ibid.: 16–17). This does not prove, of course, that the concept of equilibrium is a must within economic analysis, but rather that its importance is closely related to the logical possibility to model economics in functional (mathematical) terms. As we have already noticed, the need for equilibrium analysis derives directly from the transformation of economics into a branch of mathematics. *The generalized use of equations is indeed meaningful only insofar as economic magnitudes must be treated as variables and if some functional relationship can be established between them.* Up to now this has actually been the most widely accepted dogma in economics. Since Walras economists have been almost unanimous in believing that mathematics is what allows to make economics into a rigorous science, and that the only correct methodology in economics necessarily implies 'modelling' the real world. This is so much so that even post-Keynesians agree that '[f]ormal models are a requirement of all schools of economics, as they bring a form of rigour and may illuminate comprehension' (Lavoie 1992: 19). If one were to show that economics is of a conceptual and not of a mathematical nature, the usefulness of equilibrium analysis would be seriously challenged.

But what about Vercelli's claim as to the centrality of equilibrium for dynamic analysis? 'All the properties mentioned above, which give the equilibrium concept much of its methodological appeal, are indissolubly linked with the dynamic concept' (Vercelli 1991: 17). The distinction between endogenous and exogenous dynamic processes seems to require the concept of equilibrium as reference and seems to greatly simplify 'the "dynamic" configuration that permits the analysis of both equilibrium and disequilibrium' (ibid.: 17). Yet, it is wrong to identify dynamics with equilibrium and disequilibrium. In economics the word 'dynamics' refers to the study of the forces that produce change. Now, change itself may refer to two different states of equilibrium, or to the transition from equilibrium to disequilibrium (or vice versa), but it may also simply concern two states none of which can be defined in terms of equilibrium or disequilibrium. In a theoretical setting in which it is postulated that supply and demand are different interacting forces, equilibrium is obviously a key concept; and dynamics is quite naturally conceived of as the study of how exogenous factors may modify the initial relationship between the two forces. In such a framework it is not surprising to find a close similarity in the way dynamics is defined in physics as well as in economics, since the very postulate that supply and demand are distinct interacting forces is the unmistakable sign of the influence exerted by classical mechanics over economics. But what if supply and demand were shown to be the two aspects of one and the same economic entity, two sides of one and the same coin? If no adjustment between supply and demand were possible, dynamics would no longer be concerned with equilibrium or disequilibrium. The transition from one pair of supply and demand to another would still be possible, but it would not occur as the result of an interaction among functionally related variables. Dynamics would then be akin to a quantum-like transition rather than to a continuous or discontinuous type of change. The choice between these two approaches to economics is not arbitrary. The question then of whether supply and demand are two balancing forces or the terms of an identity is crucial, and may be settled only through a rigorous analysis. Let us therefore investigate further the concept of equilibrium.

In the words of Weintraub, '[e]quilibrium is a set of plans such that (1) for each agent, its plan seems best to it, (2) all plans are consistent among agents, and (3) actions based on those plans induce a well-defined outcome' (Weintraub 1979: 9). In a Walrasian theoretical setting, equilibrium on the commodity market obtains when the set of (relative) prices and quantities is such that economic agents' interaction leads to the maximization of their utilities and to the clearing of the market. The forces at work are those of supply and demand. If the economy is in a state of equilibrium, supply and demand balance, then their equality is assimilated to a condition of equilibrium. It is through the interaction of supply and demand, via their reciprocal adjustment, that equilibrium may be reached. This process of adjustment may take different paths and vary considerably according to the assumptions introduced in the model. However, independently of the specific model adopted, supply and demand are supposed to be functions of one or more variables classified as endogenous or exogenous according to the chosen theoretical frame of reference. The determination of the equilibrium set of prices is therefore that of the prices which, given the functional relationship represented mathematically by the equations of supply and demand, guarantee the perfect balancing of supply and demand as well as the best possible outcome for the economic agents involved in this market process.

The example we have just considered relates to the determination of relative prices, but it may easily be extended to other areas of micro or macroeconomics. The general features of equilibrium analysis remain in fact unaltered whether we refer them to individual or to aggregate variables, to individual or to aggregate behaviour, to a neoclassical or to a Keynesian framework. Let us verify this claim by looking at the way Keynesian economists deal with the problem of national income. What has to be determined is a variable whose value is to be discovered by solving a system of independent equations. National income is thus said to be functionally related to a number of endogenous and exogenous variables, whose specification depends on the model chosen as reference. For example, in the simplest Keynesian model usually proposed in textbooks, national income is related to consumption (the endogenous variable) and investment (the exogenous variable). The system is made up of two unknowns, income and consumption, and two independent equations. The unknowns are determined through the simultaneous solution of the two equations, $Y = C + \bar{I}$ and $C = a + cY$ (where Y stands for national income, $\bar{I}$ for investment, C for consumption, a for vital consumption and c for the marginal propensity to consume; and where $\bar{I}$, a and c are assumed to be given). Once again two forces are at work, aggregate supply (national income) and aggregate demand (the sum of consumption and investment), and once again it is through the balancing of these forces that a solution is to be found. The resulting value of national income is thus the equilibrium value, the only one for which aggregate supply and aggregate demand are at equality.

As in the case of relative prices, national income is subjected to a theory centred on equilibrium analysis. The possibility of entering national income into a functional relationship with consumption and investment is crucial. If this could indeed be achieved, the analysis would naturally unfold along the same line as neoclassical analysis. Despite their acknowledged differences, neoclassical and Keynesian analyses share in fact the belief that economic reality may be represented by one or more sets of equations derived from the relationships existing between economic magnitudes. While the various theories differ as to the choice of variables and the specific relationships that are supposed to exist between them, they agree as to the use of what is generally accepted as equilibrium analysis. Starting from its own specific set of assumptions, each theory offers a particular view of the economy, yet they all presuppose the concept of equilibrium and the uncritical use of mathematics in order to determine the state of the economy that induces individual agents or aggregates to behave in a coherent manner and allows them to reach a well-defined outcome.

As we have previously noted, equilibrium analysis relies heavily on the possibility of establishing reciprocal functional relationships between economic magnitudes. Relative prices are a function of supply and demand, but supply and demand are themselves dependent on prices; consumption and investment are functions of national income, but national income depends itself on consumption and investment. Yet, presuming such *reciprocity* is dangerous, particularly when we want to determine a causal relationship between dependent variables. If a depends on b and, simultaneously, b depends on a, how is it possible to establish a causal relationship between a and b (or b and a)? The simultaneous solution of the set of equations representing the reciprocal dependence of prices on supply and demand and vice versa gives no answer to the question whether supply and demand determine prices or the other way around. Similarly, how can we establish whether national income is determined by consumption and investment or whether it is Y that determines $C + I$?

This problem of causality has given rise to a vast debate among econo-mists. Since its richness and complexity cannot be summarized in a few pages, we shall confine ourselves to a very limited number of observations that may be relevant for the topic at hand. The first observation is that, despite some important exceptions, causality in economics has mostly been identified with 'exogeneity'. According to Koopmans, for example, we should regard 'as exogenous those variables which influence the remaining (endogenous) variables but are not influenced thereby' (Koop-mans 1953: 394). Exogenous variables are thus perceived as the cause and endogenous variables as the effect of an asymmetric relationship deter-mined on theoretical grounds. In this framework, causality is determined by the choice of exogenous variables, which is itself influenced by the theory adopted. In a model, therefore, a variable is exogenous because a theory defines it as a cause. '[T]he exogenous–endogenous relationship *reflects* the cause–effect relationship; the definition of exogeneity is instru-mental to the definition of causality' (Corti 1989: 147, our translation). Different theories imply the choice of different variables and of different causal relationships. '[T]he classification of components into exogenous and endogenous relates to their role in a model or theory: whether they are assumed to hold *a priori* or are to be determined within the model. A particular economic magnitude may be an exogenous component in one model and an endogenous one in another' (Howard 1979: 13). In neoclassical equilibrium models, for example, endogeneity and exogene-ity are determined by the microeconomic theory of individual choice. 'While, by definition, every endogenous variable can be seen to be the direct or indirect consequence of individuals making choices, exogenous variables are not chosen by anyone. They are the ultimate givens of the model' (Boland 1986: 9). Now, this is true only with respect to partial equilibrium models. When we refer to general equilibrium models things change, since in this theoretical setting all the economic variables are 'endogenized'.

Causality may therefore be attributed only to extra economic factors. 'A search for causes will take us inescapably to the primitive specifications of the atemporal model' (Bliss 1975: 35). As noted by Corti, this amounts to a 'methodological prescription: the ultimate task of the economist becomes that of expunging "causes" from his subject domain. By this logic no economic magnitude can ever be deemed to be a "cause"' (Corti 1989: 157, our translation).

To deal with this problem some economists prefer to replace the concept of causality with that of functional relationship. 'Functions, along-side other mathematical entities, help us to express some of the features of laws of whatever type, whether causal or not' (Bunge 1963: 94). Thus, for example, Weintraub asserts the priority of the mathematical solution of a model made up of functional relationships over the determination of causal relationships. However, as Koopmans appropriately points out, the mathematical form of a model has to be interpreted if the model is meant to explain anything. 'Without the interpretations, the postulates are bare statements establishing logical relations between unspecified entities represented by the symbols we have called terms' (Koopmans 1957: 133). This means that the functional relationship of a model cannot reflect symmetrical and reversible correlations, for symmetry and reversibility would necessarily lead to a circular explanation. But then it seems possible to maintain that in economics 'any "explanation" based on functional relationships counts as such only if it is *interpreted* causally' since 'irreversibility and asymmetry are obtained precisely by classifying the magnitudes entering the model as exogenous and endogenous variables' (Corti 1989: 181, our translation). We are thus back to the exogenous–endogenous distinction and to its circular link to causality.

Having established that the explanatory use of models requires their causal interpretation *via* the distinction between exogenous and endogenous variables, we are now confronted with a new difficulty arising from the necessary simultaneity of cause and effect. In fact, if exogenous and endogenous variables were to be simultaneously determined, the system would lack the asymmetry necessary for its mathematical solution to be economically meaningful. As Fisher observes, '[i]f one takes the model literally, the causal statement which it permits is that the endogenous variables are jointly determined by the remaining "predetermined" variables' (Fisher 1969: 493). Yet, how is it possible for exogenous variables to be *predetermined* with respect to endogenous variables given that the exogenous–endogenous relationship is a causal relationship, that is, as maintained by every expert in the field, a relationship implying the simultaneous occurrence of cause (exogenous variables) and effect (endogenous variables)? Predetermination guarantees the asymmetry, but it also introduces a temporal distinction between exogenous and endogenous variables that is 'sufficient in itself to raise a serious doubt about the validity of the exogeneity–causality association characteristic of economic modelling' (Corti 1989: 213, our translation).

Because of the impossibility of identifying the exogenous–endogenous correlation with a causal relationship, the choice of variables does not ensue from a logical necessity, but is specified on theoretical grounds. Once again we reach the conclusion that *it is the theory that establishes which variables have to be taken as being exogenous and how they are predetermined.* The axiomatic nature of economic models is derived, therefore, not only from the assumptions required to deal with them from a mathematical viewpoint, but also from the imposition of a relationship between exogenous and endogenous variables necessary for the models to explain the phenomena they are supposed to describe. Corti is right in observing that 'if the categories of exogeneity and endogeneity are deemed to be fundamental to any economic explanation this is exclusively due to the fact that modelling is supposed to be the only way to elaborate a theory in economics' (ibid.: 141, our translation). Indeed, modelling is the general method followed by every economist dealing with equilibrium analysis. Corti's criticism applies therefore equally well to GEA and to Keynesian-ism. However, the logical impossibility of taking the relation between exogenous and endogenous variables to be a causal relationship is not enough to justify the rejection of mainstream economics. It could still be claimed, in fact, that economic reality can be explained only by artificially reproducing it through a process of trials and errors in which theories, based on more or less realistic assumptions, get tested on empirical grounds. As we have already pointed out, this is not a very sound argu-ment, since there are no direct ways to submit an economic theory to empirical testing. The claim that, despite the lack of any causal relation-ship between exogenous and endogenous variables, economic phenom-ena can be approximated by using mathematical models can be definitively dismissed only if it is possible to work out an economic theory based on strict causality. The shift from an equilibrium analysis to analysing Keynes's logical identities is the first step in this direction.

Keynes's logical identities

It has often been observed that Keynes disregarded the classical concept of equilibrium, for he considered unemployment as a persistent phenom-enon rather than a temporary disequilibrium. His own concept of under-employment equilibrium must be correctly interpreted if one is to remain logically consistent. According to a classical interpretation, in fact, under-employment is a disequilibrium and, as such, it may only define an un-stable situation, a transitory state of affairs that is bound to be reabsorbed through an adjustment process leading to equilibrium. In Keynes's view, on the contrary, underemployment may well define a persistent character-istic of the capitalist system, a stable situation of 'equilibrium'. If one is prepared to think non-dogmatically, one can go as far as to maintain that Keynes's refusal of disequilibrium analysis led him to replace the notion of conditional equilibrium itself with that of logical identity. The correct understanding of a phenomenon such as underemployment requires economists switching from the theoretical setting of equilibrium model-ling analysis to one in which logical identities are addressed head on.

This is not the course taken by the majority of economists, of course. Puzzled by Keynes's use of identities, they have interpreted them as mere tautologies and have unhesitatingly transformed them into conditions of equilibrium. Even if it is true, so the story goes, that income is necessarily equal to consumption plus investment, and that saving is identical to investment, this is only a matter of nominal definitions. It is because saving and investment are both defined as that part of income which is not consumed that they are necessarily at equality. Likewise, it is because income is defined as the sum of its expenditures that Y is always equal to

$C + I$. Useless as identities, these same relationships become very relevant as soon as they are taken to be conditional equalities. Henceforth, saving is no longer identical to investment nor is income necessarily equal to consumption and investment. Their equality becomes the matter of an adjustment process and Keynes's original analysis is reduced to a particular case of equilibrium analysis.

In fact only two logical possibilities remain open to us. Either we think of Keynes's identities as 'simplifying assumptions of doubtful validity' (Vercelli 1991: 225), in which case Keynes's contribution becomes part of equilibrium analysis, or we try to understand the true meaning of Keynes's original message. In this second case, we must not be afraid of opposing a host of apparently well-established interpretations of Keynes's theory. Let us proceed slowly and gradually.

First of all, a clear distinction must be drawn between nominal and logical identities. The category of nominal identities is made up of tautological relationships, in which one term merely repeats the meaning conveyed by the other term. For example, the identity $I \equiv S$ is purely nominal if it is meant to describe the simple fact that I and S are given the same meaning. If we define S in the same way as I, the identity $I \equiv S$ becomes a truism, a relationship that adds nothing to our previous knowledge. A logical identity, on the contrary, is the result of a process increasing our knowledge.

Conceptual definitions, for example, are logical identities. As formal and concise statements of the meaning of a concept, they cannot be given a priori and are not the simple repetition of what was already known. In the case of the identity between I and S, we must conceive of it as a logical identity if I and S are proved to be the two complementary aspects of a unified structural whole, and not merely two interchangeable symbols referring to the same thing (like Frege's 'Morning star' and 'Evening star', which are synonymous expressions for the identical referent, namely the planet Venus).

Having distinguished logical from nominal identities, we now have to answer the rather absurd question of whether or not identities may be transformed into conditions of equilibrium. The absurdity is obvious: being the strongest possible structural condition between the two terms of an equivalence, an identity is a logical equality that always holds true and can therefore never specify a condition of equilibrium. No adjustment is ever possible between the two terms of an identity. This conclusion is straightforward and does not admit of any exception. It applies equally well to logical and nominal identities and leaves no room for a possible substitution of identities by conditional equalities.

The logical impossibility of transforming identities into conditions of equilibrium has direct consequences for the way Keynesian economics relates to the work of Keynes. In particular, the Keynesian interpretation of Keynes does not simply relegate Keynes's identities to the role of mere tautological definitions, but it also implies their necessary rejection. Let us address the identity between income (Y) and aggregate demand ($C+I$). The Keynesians' decision to consider $Y = C+I$ as a condition of equilibrium leaves no room for the simultaneous acceptance of Keynes's identity. In no way can the two interpretations of $Y = C+I$ – as an identity and as a condition of equilibrium – stand side by side. If we accept the first, the second is bound to fall and vice versa. By interpreting $Y = C+I$ as a condition of equilibrium, Keynesian economists support *de facto* a neoclassical rendition of Keynes's work and reduce his theory of income determination to an analysis of the adjustment between total demand and total supply. Y and $C+I$ are seen as two interacting forces whose matching point defines the only level of national income compatible with the equality of total demand and total supply. Mathematically, the equilibrium level of national income is determined by the solution of a system of independent equations whose form varies according to the assumptions introduced into the initial model. For example, in the simplest fixed-price Keynesian model of short-term income determination we have previously referred to, the system is made up of two equations: $Y = C + \bar{I}$ and $C = a + cY$, and can also be represented by the famous Keynesian cross diagram. Now, the impasse to which this neoclassical interpretation of Keynes's theory leads is particularly clear here. In fact, it may easily be observed that in the Keynesian model of income determination both consumption and investment are ill conceived. A quick glance at the consumption function and at the 45° line diagram highlights the fact that it is illogical to assume consumption and investment to be positive when national income is zero. Once it is admitted that both (economic) consumption and investment can be positive only if 'fed' by a positive income, the Keynesian 45° line diagram becomes totally irrelevant just like the system of equations from which it is derived.

The difficulties encountered by the Keynesian interpretation of Keynes's theory of national income raise the need for a reappraisal of the differences between identity and equilibrium. In this respect it may be of interest to show how Keynes's logical identity between Y and $C+I$ may be deduced from his fundamental equations. A first indication is given by Keynes at the beginning of Chapter 10 of his *Treatise on Money*. Here he states that the flow of the community's earnings or money income has to be divided '(1) into the parts which have been *earned* by the production of consumption goods and of investment goods respectively, and (2) into the parts which are *expended* on consumption goods and on savings respectively' (Keynes 1930/1971: 121). Thus, if we take C' and I' to represent the costs of production of consumption and investment goods respectively, and C and I to represent the final expenditure for the purchase of consumption and investment goods, we have the following relationship:

$$C' + I' = C + I$$

The reader well acquainted with Keynes's 1930 book will easily verify that this equality matches Keynes's second fundamental equation since 'the total value of the investment goods (new and old) coming on to the market for purchase out of current savings is *always* exactly equal to the amount of such savings' (ibid.: 131). In this case, in fact, output valued at its price level (OII) is necessarily equal to the total money income or earnings of the community (E).

$$OII = E$$

This result is reiterated by Keynes in the *General Theory*, where, in the chapter devoted to the definition of income, saving and investment, he states the following relationship:

'Income = value of output = consumption + investment'

(Keynes 1936/1973a: 63)

One of the implications of Keynes's 'fundamental equation' is that national income is defined in two equivalent ways: as the sum earned in the production of consumption and investment goods, and as the sum spent in the final purchase of consumption and investment goods. If this equality is taken to be a condition of equilibrium verified only for a given level of national income, Keynes's theory is but a particular case of equilibrium analysis. On the contrary, if it is conceived of as an identity, the logical equality between the formation and the expenditure of national income becomes the foundation of an entirely new, macroeconomic approach. In order for a true macroeconomics to exist, it is necessary to found it on conceptual invariants, that is, on laws that apply to the economic system taken as a whole, irrespective of the behaviour of its individual agents. Now, such laws take necessarily the form of identities. Without them, no macroeconomic structure could exist, and the search for equilibrium would be the only way to fight against economic disorder. Keynes's great merit has been that of opening the way to the discovery of true macroeconomic laws. Unfortunately, the novelty of his message was not always appreciated even by Keynes himself, who was the first victim of the difficulty 'in escaping from the old [ideas], which ramify, for those brought up as most of us have been, into every corner of our minds' (ibid.: xxiii). Thus, one of the main reasons that led to the neoclassical interpretation of Keynes's theory was Keynes's failure to convince his fellow economists of the significance of his logical identities. The controversy still raging on the necessary equality between saving and investment is evidence for this unresolved state of affairs.

Keynes's claim that S and I are always necessarily equal was indeed the object of an intense dispute during which the author of the *General Theory* endeavoured in vain to convince his adversaries that his identity was much more than a simple tautology. Robertson and Ohlin were the opponents with whom Keynes discussed in the most rigorous and passionate way the interrelations between S, I and the rate of interest. By his analysis, Keynes mainly purported to prove that it is the level of income and *not the rate of interest* that ensures the equality between S and I. 'The novelty in my treatment of saving and investment consists, not in my maintaining their necessary aggregate equality, but in the proposition that it is, not the rate of interest, but the level of incomes which [...] ensures this equality' (Keynes 1973c: 211). Robertson and Ohlin, on the contrary, defended the view that the equality between I and S is a condition of equilibrium, which may be satisfied only through a variation in the interest rate. Now, even though it is indisputable that most of the controversy was about the theory of interest, it is possible to interpret it differently by emphasizing the opposition between identities and conditional equalities.

In his article on 'Alternative theories of the rate of interest' published in the *Economic Journal* (June 1937), Keynes reaffirms the necessary equality of S and I – '[a]ggregate saving and aggregate investment, in the senses in which I have defined them, are necessarily equal' (ibid.: 211) – but makes it clear that the stated identity is not of a 'nominal' kind: saving and investment are not merely two different names for the same thing (ibid.: 211). At the same time, Keynes also claims that the necessary equality of the two terms is compatible with any realized level of income. Taken together, these two claims suggest an entirely new, 'macroeconomic' conception of production, saving and investment. Literally, they mean that for any given level of income, that is, of production, the amount globally saved can never be other than equal to global investment.

Aiming to fend off the difficult and revolutionary concept of the logical identity between S and I (and between total demand and total supply), Ohlin had recourse to Myrdal's distinction between *ex ante* and *ex post* magnitudes, maintaining that S and I are necessarily equal only once equilibrium is achieved, whereas they may, and usually do, differ during the search for equilibrium. Ohlin's attempt was to show that Keynes's identity is not opposed to the existence of a process of adjustment through time. Objectively, Ohlin's interpretation aims at replacing Keynes's identity with a conditional equality, that is, to transform Keynes's macroeconomic analysis into a neoclassical general equilibrium analysis based on the microeconomic adjustment between S and I. Now, the phase of adjustment that, *ex ante*, should allow for saving and investment to find their equilibrium is merely a fiction if production has not yet taken place. In fact, if no income is actually available, 'virtual' or 'desired' saving and investment have no real meaning. *Ex ante*, these magnitudes do not really exist since no income is available to make them positive. It is thus pointless to study their mutual interaction.

Whatever the impact of interest rates on the behaviour of consumers and firms, it remains true – as maintained by Keynes – that once macroeconomic saving is actually determined it can no longer differ from investment. Even if the identity between S and I allows for a degree of freedom between firms' envisaged decision to invest and consumers' decision to save, and an adjustment may occur between these two sets of planned decisions, once saving has found its final macroeconomic value investment can only match it, whether or not the process of adjustment has been successful in satisfying the desires of firms and consumers. Indeed, S and I are the dual aspects of a unified reality. Once one aspect is determined, the other is 'automatically' as well. To be precise, S and I are simultaneously determined, investment being financed by that part of income that is not definitively consumed, and macroeconomic saving being formed through the investment of the same part of current income. Hence, the adjustment between firms' and consumers' decisions cannot have any bearing on the logical identities of S and I and of total supply and total demand. In no way can Keynes's fundamental identities be transformed into conditions of equilibrium.

In order to avoid a possible misunderstanding, let us add that our analysis is only partially backed by Keynes's own statements. Thus, we would be wrong in claiming that Keynes always and consistently considered his identities as the necessary result of his conceptual analysis rather than as mere tautologies implicit in his nominal (i.e. purely conventional, terminological) definitions. There is also no getting around to the fact that Keynes defended his identities as following naturally from his nominal definitions of income, consumption, saving and investment: 'these two amounts [S and I] are necessarily equal, since each of them is equal to the excess of income over consumption' (Keynes 1936/1973a: 63). Keynes's himself was always acutely aware of the difficulties related to his novel conception of the relationship between S and I, and of his own inability to honour consistently this insight. The following quotation from a letter to Hawtrey, dated 24 September 1935 is symptomatic of Keynes's uneasiness: '[i]n any passages in which I seem to regard the adjustment of investment and saving as a process occupying time, I agree with you that I am expressing myself incorrectly and am departing from my own ideas' (Keynes 1973b: 581). Our aim is to show that, interpreted along the lines of a consistently coherent macroeconomic approach, Keynes's analysis reveals its true originality and its deep-seated opposition to the neoclassical approach and to any attempt to assimilate it into the neoclassical paradigm. As we will see in Part II, the identities between global demand and global supply, and between saving and investment acquire their full meaning only once it has been proven that production is a creation whose result is simultaneously monetary and real, and which defines the same time dimension as that associated with the final expenditure of the money income it generates. It is only after having developed a consistent macroeconomic analysis of production, consumption and investment that the significance of Keynes's identities will appear with the greatest clarity. For the time being, let us push our reappraisal of Keynes's theory a step further.

4 Keynes revisited

According to a widely shared interpretation, Keynes's theory may be represented by two kinds of models, one in which money wages are assumed to be constant and one which deals with flexible wages. In both kinds of models, markets are analysed by referring to supply and demand, equilibrium (of full, under, or over-employment) being conceived of as a state in which each of these two forces (supply and demand) is matched by the other. Yet, this interpretation of Keynes's work is both misleading and inappropriate. It is misleading since it gives the impression that the theory of the great British economist may easily be integrated in the wider framework of neoclassical analysis, at least to the extent that it could be worked out (1) in terms of equilibrium between supply and demand, and (2) by reverting to a mathematical formalization. It is inappropriate since it assumes the level of employment to be determined through the adjustment of virtual magnitudes, and because it introduces a deep disparity between demand oriented and supply oriented economics.

As shown by the key role played by demand disturbances in explaining economic fluctuations, Keynesian economists have always stressed the demand-side component of their theory. In every textbook, Keynes's analysis is defined as demand-side economics and opposed to the supply-side economics proposed by neoclassical economists. Now, this distinction has no great utility apart from providing another example of how the main schools of thought differentiate themselves on the basis of the variables they consider as central to their models. If one privileges the supply side, one will emphasize the centrality of 'shifts in the production function, variations in the stock of capital, effects of the tax system on the willingness to work, and so on' (Barro 1984: 502). On the contrary, if one believes economic activity to be mostly influenced by demand, one will investigate the impact of fluctuations in income distribution, the marginal propensity to consume (save) and all the conceivable factors that may affect expected demand.

In this chapter we will tackle Keynes's principle of effective demand in order to show that, once related to his macroeconomic identities, it implies a perfect symmetry between supply and demand and therefore does not support either a demand or a supply oriented economic theory.

The principle of effective demand

Every Keynesian economist will most probably share Tobin's view that '[t]he central Keynesian proposition is not nominal price rigidity but the principle of effective demand (Tobin 1993: 46). Tobin does not aprioristically reject the assumption of individuals' rational behaviour, yet he stresses the fact that institutions are not necessarily apt to guarantee perfect competition. Hence, he claims, 'if markets and price-setting institutions do not produce perfectly flexible competitive prices' (ibid.: 46), instantaneous and complete market clearing can no longer be taken for granted. In these conditions, aggregate demand may play a determinant role on output and employment. Let us try to understand to what extent the principle of effective demand is indeed related to the level of employment and to the relationship between global demand and global supply.

As every author interested in the principle of effective demand recalls, Keynes worked it out in order to dismiss the idea that full employment may always be reached simply through the implementation of Say's Law. According to the analysis developed in Chapter 3 of the *General Theory*, Say's principle that supply creates its own demand implies that competition between entrepreneurs inevitably leads to full employment. This is so because the aggregate supply and demand functions, which depend on the level of employment, coincide. 'That is to say, effective demand, instead of having a unique equilibrium value, is an infinite range of values all equally admissible' (Keynes 1936/1973a: 26). As suggested by Kregel, the same result may be reached through a neoclassical interpretation of Say's Law. Instead of deriving full employment from the identity between global supply and global demand, we would attain it through an adjustment in relative prices eliminating excess supply. It may therefore be claimed that it was '[t]he self-adjusting nature of the neoclassical version of Say's Law that Keynes chose to criticize' (Kregel 1992: 100). Kregel's claim is of a particular significance, for it shows that Keynes did not reject Say's Law out of hand. Actually, it would have been difficult for him to dismiss Say's Law entirely, while advocating the necessary equality between Y (global supply) and $C + I$ (global demand). What Keynes could not accept was the conclusion reached by classical and neoclassical authors as to the consequence on employment of the implementation of Say's Law.

> Thus Say's Law, that the aggregate demand price of output as a whole is equal to its aggregate supply price for all volumes of output, is equivalent to the proposition that there is no obstacle to full employment. If, however, this is not the true law relating the aggregate demand and supply functions, there is a vitally important chapter of economic theory which remains to be written and without which all discussions concerning the volume of aggregate employment are futile.
>
> (Keynes 1936/1973a: 26)

The principle of effective demand introduced by Keynes in order to replace Say's Law consisted in keeping the aggregate demand function distinct from the aggregate supply function and in showing that their equilibrium point does not necessarily coincide with the level of full employment.

> Thus the volume of employment is given by the point of intersection between the aggregate demand function and the aggregate supply function [...]. The value of D [the expected proceeds of entrepreneurs] at the point of the aggregate demand function, where it is intersected by the aggregate supply function, will be called *the effective demand*.
>
> (ibid.: 25)

Now, the principle of effective demand may be interpreted in two different ways, each corresponding to a distinct analytical setting. The first and most widespread interpretation relates the entrepreneurs' decision to produce to their selling expectations. As Keynes repeatedly maintained, entrepreneurs' decisions are influenced by the expected sale proceeds, so that expected demand is 'effective' not because it is 'actual' or 'realized' – which is obviously not – but because it is likely to push entrepreneurs to actually produce the output they expect to be able to sell. In the draft of Chapter 6 ('Effective demand and income') of the 1934 version of the *General Theory*, Keynes calls 'the actual sale proceeds *income* and the present value of the expected sale proceeds *effective demand*' (Keynes 1973b: 425) and adds that 'it is the present value of the expectation of income which constitutes the effective demand; and it is the effective demand which is the incentive to the employment of equipment and labour' (ibid.: 425).

Using Myrdal's distinction between *ex ante* and *ex post*, we would say that in its first interpretation the principle of effective demand applies to the *ex ante* relationship between planned production and expected sale proceeds. Since *ex ante* production has not yet taken place, supply and demand are purely virtual magnitudes and their relationship is in no way of a functional nature. Hence, being only a virtual magnitude, expected demand cannot really determine production. What it may do is to induce entrepreneurs to employ their available resources in order to satisfy at best the economic agents' prospective purchase of consumption and investment goods. 'Effective demand is made up of the sum of two factors based respectively on the expectation of what is going to be consumed and on the expectation of what is going to be invested' (ibid.: 439).

The second interpretation of the principle of effective demand refers to actual or realized magnitudes. Once production has indeed taken place, effective demand defines the actual amount of global demand for each level of produced output. Now, since a positive demand can only be exerted starting from an equivalent amount of income and since income is generated by production, the principle that supply creates its own demand is again brought to the fore. Rejected by Keynes as a mechanism leading to full employment *ex ante*, Say's Law may be interpreted as defining the *ex post* necessary equivalence between global supply and global demand. In other words, it may be shown that, *ex post*, Say's Law takes the form of Keynes's logical identity between Y and $C + I$. At the outset of the *General Theory* Keynes states in fact that 'the income derived in the aggregate by all the elements in the community concerned in a productive activity necessarily has a value exactly equal to the *value* of the output' (Keynes 1936/1973a: 20). This clearly means that, according to Keynes, output (global supply) has *necessarily* a value *exactly equal* to the value of produced income (global demand).

As we have observed in the previous chapter, the identity between $C' + I'$ and $C + I$ states precisely the necessary equality between the income formed in the production of consumption and investment goods and the income spent in their final purchase. Keynes's message is clear: every realized production gives rise simultaneously to a supply (output) and to an equivalent demand (income). Analogous to Say's Law, this proposition does not imply that production will always and necessarily reach the level of full employment. The decisions to produce are taken *ex ante* on the basis of expectations and there are no reasons to believe that expectations will adjust to allow for full employment. 'The volume of employment which will maximise his [the entrepreneur's] quasi-rent depends on the schedule of effective demand – which, again, depends on the entrepreneur's expectations of the sum of the sale proceeds resulting from consumption and investment respectively on various hypotheses' (Keynes 1973b: 436).

With a single exception – related to the pathological process of capital over-accumulation that eventually leads to unemployment – there are no macroeconomic laws forcing entrepreneurs' decisions. As a matter of fact, entrepreneurs enjoy a degree of freedom with respect to both macro and microeconomic laws. There are no behavioural laws forcing individuals to consume whatever amount of income results from production or pushing entrepreneurs to increase production beyond their expected sale proceeds. The identity $Y \equiv C + I$ expresses the fact that current production generates the amount of income necessary and sufficient for the final purchase of current output. This does not mean, however, that the entire amount of produced consumption goods will always necessarily be purchased by consumers independently of the actual level of output. Not only consumption does not automatically adjust to any amount of income generated by production, but entrepreneurs' forecast may prove wrong even when production is decided on the strict basis of expectations. What is important to understand is that Keynes's identity holds good even in these cases, since it is not influenced by economic agents' behaviour. Like

Say's Law, Keynes's identity is a macroeconomic law, which applies to the economic system as a whole, independently of the behaviour of its individual agents. The fact is that production determines simultaneously the output and the amount of income required for its purchase.

The necessary equality between global demand and global supply results immediately from the simple acknowledgement that current output is global supply and that global demand is defined by the amount of current income. There should be no need, in fact, to tell the reader that realized (*ex post*) effective demand is given by the amount of income available in the system and is not influenced by consumers and investors' behaviour. This is to say that, although it may modify the initial division of output into consumption and investment goods, economic agents' behaviour has no impact on the amount of global demand. *The distinction between the effective demand considered as a virtual or expected demand and the effective demand conceived of as an actual or realized demand is not easy to grasp, and Keynes himself did not introduce it explicitly in his writings.* Before getting deeper into the investigation of the relationship between the principle of *ex post* effective demand and Keynes's logical identities, let us therefore supplement the analysis we have developed so far by considering the contribution of two Keynesian authors who have dedicated much attention to the concept of effective demand.

The principle of effective demand: a Keynesian interpretation

As pointed out by Clower, the concept of effective demand as the expected sale proceeds to which entrepreneurs tend to adjust their aggregate supply was already put forward by Smith in Chapter VII, Book I of *The Wealth of Nations*.

> The quantity of every commodity brought to market naturally suits itself to the effectual demand. It is the interest of all those who employ their land, labour, or stock, in bringing any commodity to market, that the quantity should never exceed the effectual demand; and it is the interest of all other people that it never should fall short of that demand.
>
> (Smith 1776/1991: 50)

According to Clower's partial summary of Keynes's analysis, effective demand results from the adjustment between the aggregate supply and the aggregate demand functions, and thus defines the equilibrium level of output allowing for the equality between the expected sale proceeds of entrepreneurs and the aggregate supply curve. Now, the problem that has to be settled here is whether or not an adjustment may take place between aggregate supply and aggregate demand before production has actually occurred. Is it possible for what is but a planned or virtual output to adjust to a demand schedule that is itself purely virtual? What is the meaning of an *ex ante* interaction of two virtual forces? Entrepreneurs may well work out a series of possible scenarios, trying to figure out as accurately as they can how the public is likely to react to their decision to offer different quantities of output of different quality at different prices. On the basis of these expectations, entrepreneurs will then decide the combination of quantity, quality and prices that they think will maximize their expected yields. Yet, there is not a single instant at which, *ex ante*, a real (as opposed to virtual) force is confronted to another real force. Expected output is a mere 'potentiality', and so is expected demand. But how can two forces that do not even exist adjust one another in order to determine a magnitude that might or might not, depending on the decisions actually taken by entrepreneurs, become a realized magnitude?

The definition of effective demand as '[t]he value of D [the proceeds that entrepreneurs can expect to receive] at the point of the aggregate demand function where it is intersected by the aggregate supply function' (Keynes 1936/1973a: 25), may take us astray and justify a neoclassical interpretation of Keynes's contribution. In particular, if taken literally, it may suggest a way to reconcile Keynes's logical identity between global supply and global demand with the equilibrium approach so successfully generalized by Walras. It is only fair to recognize, of course, that Keynes himself is at the origin of this confusion. In order to clarify the terms of the problem it is necessary to recall that before production actually takes place, *ex ante*, effective demand merely defines 'the amount of the proceeds which the entrepreneur expect to receive from the corresponding output' (ibid.: 24). It is at this level that Clower's analysis sets in. 'Writing as J.M. Keynes', the American economist refers the principle of effective demand to the theory of employment and maintains that production is determined – through a process of adjustment between aggregate supply and aggregate demand – at the level at which the income generated by production will be entirely consumed and invested. In other words, Clower considers Keynes's necessary equality between Y and $C + I$ as a condition of equilibrium claiming that, given the marginal propensity to consume and the inducement to invest, there is only one level of income that satisfies it. The analysis is well known and supported by the great majority of Keynesian economists of any school. What we want to stress here, is that the adjustment of Y and $C + I$ is supposed to take place before production is actually realized. It is *ex ante*, therefore, that behavioural considerations are taken in and are assumed to be the factors influencing the determination of income. An increase in expected demand, so Clower tells us, may lead to an increase in income that, because of the marginal propensity to consume and the inducement to invest, does not allow for the equilibrium between Y and $C + I$. In particular, if the increase in income is not accompanied by an increase in investment, accounting for the fact that the marginal propensity to consume is smaller than one, $C + I$

will be less than *Y* and the system will fail to find its equilibrium. The loss that entrepreneurs would suffer in this case, if they were to increase production up to the level of effective demand, will induce them to modify their decisions until planned production will be matched by expected aggregate demand.

Now, this *ex ante* process of adjustment sounds strange for more than one reason. As we have already pointed out, one of these reasons is that no real adjustment can take place between virtual magnitudes (and there may be no doubt that *ex ante* global demand and global supply are purely virtual). But the feeling of uneasiness about the adjustment between planned supply and expected demand is also grounded on the fact that we are asked to believe that an increase in effective demand may lead entrepreneurs to plan a production whose expected demand cannot match it. In other words, we are told that, except when planned production coincides with the equilibrium level of income, entrepreneurs take their decisions on the basis of an expected global demand that is bound to be different from the expected demand resulting from the value of the marginal propensity to consume and the inducement to invest. A numerical example will help us to clarify the issue. Let us suppose entrepreneurs to expect a global demand (made up of the expected demand for consumption and investment goods) of 100 money units. Let us also assume that this demand defines an increase in expectations of ten money units with respect to the previous, equilibrium level of 90 money units (made up by 63 units of consumption and 27 units of investment). If the marginal propensity to consume remains equal to 70 per cent and if the inducement to invest can account for an increase in investment of two money units, effective demand will be equal to 99 money units (70 per cent of $100 + 27 + 2$), and entrepreneurs will have to modify their plans accordingly. The effective demand determined on the basis of entrepreneurs' expectations (100 money units) is thus different from the effective demand determined by the theory (99 money units). Does this mean that entrepreneurs are usually wrong and that they should take their decisions only after their expectations have been adjusted by the theory? Or does it mean that entrepreneurs should become theoretical economists in order to correctly determine the only level of production compatible with the equilibrium between aggregate demand and aggregate supply? Is it not true, on the contrary, that entrepreneurs' expectations take implicitly into account economic agents' behaviour so that they should not differ from the expectations of the theory? Is it not simply true that, consistently with what was claimed by Keynes, entrepreneurs plan their production referring to their expected sale proceeds? '[T]he *effective demand* is simply the aggregate income (or proceeds) which the entrepreneurs expect to receive [. . .] from the amount of current employment which they decide to give' (Keynes 1936/1973a: 55).

Clower, 'writing as himself', analyses the problem of effective demand

and of its relationship with unemployment attempting to reconcile Keynes's approach with that of Walras and Marshall. He claims, in fact, that the clearing of the commodity market does not necessarily imply the clearing of the labour market and therefore does not automatically lead to full employment. 'On this showing, Keynes's theory of effective demand is a straightforward reconcoction of Marshallian short-period demand and supply analysis. [...] Unemployment equilibrium in Keynes's partial equilibrium macromodel is a consequence of non-clearance of "the labour market", *not* non-clearance of "the market for output" ' (Clower 1997: 42). According to Clower, it would thus be possible to interpret Keynes's adjustment between the aggregate demand function and the aggregate supply function along the lines followed by neoclassical economics. As even a cursory look at the Keynesian literature reveals, Keynes's analysis may indeed be interpreted in this way. Effective demand would thus result from the simultaneous solution of a set of equations derived from the aggregate demand and supply functions. Yet, our criticism based on the logical impossibility for any adjustment to take place between virtual magnitudes holds good even in this case. Clower's functions are only virtual themselves and can exert no real pressure on the commodity and investment markets.

The *ex ante* adjustment hypothesized by Clower's analysis is thus nothing more than the principle according to which entrepreneurs' decisions are influenced by their expectations. To postulate the existence of a mechanism allowing for the reciprocal interaction of supply and demand before production occurs, amounts to assuming arbitrarily, and quite absurdly, that a planned output defines a real supply (and not, as is obviously the case, a purely virtual supply) and that an expected demand is a real force (and not an imaginary demand). On one hand, Clower seems to miss entirely the nature of the 'adjustment' occurring *ex ante*. On the other hand, he does not seem to understand the true meaning of Keynes's *ex post* logical identity between Y and $C+I$. Clower's use of the 45° line as the identity relation between aggregate demand and aggregate supply shows that he entirely misses the point that no reconciliation is logically possible between identities and conditional equalities. If we accept Keynes's identity between global supply and global demand we cannot simultaneously maintain that, except for their equilibrium value, these two magnitudes are unequal. An identity is the strongest possible relationship between the two terms of an equation. This means that if it is certainly true that the 45° line is the locus of points whose coordinates satisfy the necessary equality between Y and $C+I$, it is also certain that it is the point corresponding to the production that actually takes place which determines current demand. Expected demand may indeed influence the decisions of entrepreneurs. Yet, once decisions are taken, whether they adjust or not to expectations, demand will always match its corresponding supply. Even if the deep meaning of this identity may appear somewhat mysterious, it should be clear that it is realized production that generates the income necessary to exert a positive demand. Thus, the identity $Y \equiv C + I$ is verified for whatever level of current production and therefore cannot be 'determined' by a process of adjustment.

In no case do the identity and its value result from the solution of an equilibrium equation. The identity $Y \equiv C + I$ is the logical starting point of Keynes's theory of national income and cannot be subordinated to any conditional equation whatsoever. Now, the mistake made by Clower in his analysis of effective demand is precisely that of privileging conditional equilibrium over logical identities. Referring to Samuelson's presentation of the problem of income determination, Clower states in fact that 'Paul Samuelson appears to confound the *conditional* equilibrium condition $E = F$ (Z) [...] with the national income accounting *identity* $Y \equiv C + I$, thereby converting a conditional equation in one unknown into an identity that holds for every value of Y' (ibid.: 45). Clower deems effective demand to be the pivotal conditional equation of the system of income determination, and does not perceive the importance of accounting identities such as $Y \equiv C + I$. This is closely connected to his assumption that output is offered 'in exchange for units of a *commodity* called "money"' (ibid.: 37, our emphasis), and clearly shows how difficult it is, even for a clever and sophisticated Keynesian as Clower, to grasp the nature of macroeconomic laws. In order to perceive that Keynes's accounting identities are not mere terminological tautologies but true macroeconomic laws it is necessary to understand that money is neither a commodity nor a net asset, and that macroeconomics is not simply a matter of aggregation. What has to be clearly realized is that Keynes's theory refers to the macroeconomics of monetary production, and not to the microeconomics of relative exchanges.

Before coming back to the meaning of the identity between Y and $C + I$, let us briefly analyse the contribution of another famous Keynesian economist, Pasinetti, whose approach differs substantially from that of Clower, yet falls under the same criticism. Pasinetti seems to hesitate between two different conceptions of effective demand. In his 1974 paper on the economics of effective demand the Italian economist starts by reproducing Hansen's famous diagram in which production is always matched by an equivalent demand and states that 'whatever total demand may be [...], net production will turn out to be precisely the same' (Pasinetti 1974: 32). Pasinetti's use of the terms total demand and total net production and his claim that there is always a perfect correspondence between the two magnitudes that they represent may lead us to think that he is referring here to actual or realized production and to actual demand. The first impression is therefore that Pasinetti uses Hansen's diagram to represent the *ex post* relationship between income and $C + I$, that is, Keynes's identity $Y \equiv C + I$. Yet, if this were indeed the case, how is it that Pasinetti claims that 'demand generates income' (ibid.:

32)? The simplest answer would be that Pasinetti merely follows Hansen and takes over his claim that '[s]o long as there are unused resources, every increase in demand is matched by an increase in supply' (Hansen 1938: 321). If this were the answer, then Pasinetti would not avoid the ironical remark addressed by Clower to Hansen. 'If we are to call the proposition "supply creates its own demand" Say's Law, we should with comparable abandon restate Hansen's assertion as "demand creates its own supply", and call it Hansen's Law' (Clower 1997: 42). Now, everybody will agree that, since actual demand must be 'fed' by an equivalent income, in the domain of realized magnitudes it is production that determines demand and not vice versa. Pasinetti's next sentence seems to dispel every doubt about his position. 'If producers were to expect a fall in demand, they would reduce production accordingly, *quite irrespective* of the level of their productive capacity. And they would do the opposite if they were to expect an increase of demand' (Pasinetti 1974: 32). It is planned or virtual production that Pasinetti has in mind, and it is *ex ante* effective demand that, by influencing entrepreneurs' decisions, indirectly 'generates' income.

If, as suggested by Pasinetti, 'Keynes's Aggregate Demand Function and Aggregate Supply Function are [taken to be] behavioural relations' (Pasinetti 1997: 95), then they must be assigned to the domain of planned or virtual magnitudes. In this theoretical setting 'they are supposed to incorporate all information concerning the decisions of consumers and entrepreneurs acting in a given framework of a specific market structure' (ibid.: 95). According to the Italian economist, this is the way Keynes conceived of the aggregate demand and supply functions when determining effective demand. 'When the analytical purpose is that of determining effective demand, the appropriate procedure is that adopted by Keynes in Chapter 3 of *The General Theory*, namely the setting up of functions expressing the behaviour of an economy within a specific institutional set-up' (ibid.: 98). Using the analytical distinction between virtual and realized magnitudes we may say that Pasinetti's interpretation of Keynes's effective demand establishes a close correspondence between virtual demand and virtual supply on one side, and the behaviour of consumers and investors and the behaviour of entrepreneurs on the other side. Yet, Pasinetti's analysis of Keynes's principle does not stop at this first, behavioural level. Indeed, Pasinetti emphasizes the importance of a more fundamental level going beyond behavioural aggregate demand and supply functions. 'But when the analytical purpose is to single out the basic characteristics of a "monetary production economy" – as Keynes called it – one must make an effort to descend to a deeper level of investigation' (ibid.: 98).

For Pasinetti the move towards fundamentals passes through the replacement of the behavioural aggregate supply and demand functions by a 'basic, non-institutional, or if we like pre-institutional, characteristic' (ibid.: 100) 'of the way in which industrial economies come to be set up' (ibid.: 100). According to the Italian economist, this characteristic, which represents the principle of effective demand, consists in the fact that, up to the level of full capacity utilization, production is determined by expected demand. 'Actual production will thus turn out to be whatever effective demand is expected to be' (ibid.: 99). What Pasinetti considers as a fundamental characteristic of individual economies is thus simply the principle according to which entrepreneurs take their decisions on the basis of the expected sales of their planned output. 'Any producer must try to estimate the demand that is likely to be effective *before* starting any production at all and quite irrespective of existing productive capacity' (ibid.: 101). This sounds far too simplistic a consideration and it is hard to believe that a serious criticism of Keynes's analysis of effective demand may be based on it. Yet, this seems to be the very object of Pasinetti's critical analysis. 'He [Keynes] had (correctly) developed, at the behavioural level, the consequences of the principle of effective demand, but had not yet been able to penetrate to the deeper level of the foundations' (ibid.: 102).

Pasinetti's conclusion is relevant for promoting his own positive analysis, which consists in the search for 'a macroeconomic equilibrium *condition*, in which the relevant components are productivity coefficients and demand coefficients, at a stage of analysis which is independent of institutions and thus precedes any analysis of behavioural relations' (ibid.: 102). If the attempt to avoid behavioural relations is one of Pasinetti's great merits, his preference for conditional equilibrium takes him far away from Keynes's logical identities and from the possibility to ground the fundamental principle of effective demand in the domain of actual or realized magnitudes. His definition of Keynes's principle, on the contrary, confines it to the domain of virtual or planned magnitudes, that is, to a level of generality that, precisely because it lies 'behind any institutional mechanism that may be invented for an individual economy' (ibid.: 103), denies it any explanatory power. Finally, let us observe that Pasinetti's 1997 conclusion that 'effective demand generates income' (ibid.: 100) is exactly the same as the one he had reached in his 1974 analysis and shares with it the same shortcomings. In particular, as we have already noted, it is highly questionable to infer that virtual demand generates income from the fact that entrepreneurs take their decisions on the basis (among other factors) of the expected demand for their planned output. Indeed, a virtual magnitude cannot determine or generate anything at all. No income would be formed if production did not actually take place, which clearly means that production 'feeds' demand and not that demand creates its own income.

Pasinetti's interpretation of Keynes's concept seems sometimes too simple to be entirely satisfactory. If it is planned production that is influenced by the expected sales of consumption and investment goods, there is no compulsory reason for planned production to be precisely the same as expected demand. *Ex ante*, effective demand is undoubtedly a major factor influencing entrepreneurs' decision to set production at a certain level, but it is by no means the only factor, and entrepreneurs may well decide not to conform strictly to the principle of effective demand. It thus appears that Pasinetti himself is the victim of the apparent simplicity of Keynes's principle. The idea that expected demand may not be enough to induce entrepreneurs to produce at full capacity is very simple indeed. Likewise, it is not difficult to imagine 'the possibility and disastrous consequences of a gap between potential production and effective demand' (Pasinetti 1974: 34). In particular, it is easy to understand that if expectations are not high enough, available resources may not be fully employed. Things get more complicated, however, when we pass from the *ex ante* conception of effective demand to its *ex post* conception. Once production is actually realized, global demand can but be equal to global supply. Whatever the level of production, demand is necessarily equal to it, that is the meaning of Keynes's logical identity between Y and $C + I$.

Two difficulties arise at this stage. The first is concerned with the impossibility to transform an identity into a condition of equilibrium, the second with the necessity to reconcile the identity $Y \equiv C + I$ with the possible numerical divergence between global demand and global supply. Pasinetti does not seem to be at ease with either of these two difficulties. Immediately after having claimed that Y is identical to $C + I$ since '[t]otal effective demand is the sum of demand for consumption goods (C) and demand for investment goods (I) [and since] effective demand generates income' (ibid.: 36), he introduces the functions of consumption and investment and transforms the initial identity into a condition of equilibrium. Since Pasinetti's explicit aim is 'to distinguish, in Keynes' analysis the principle of effective demand from the analytical tools he used in order to put it across' (ibid.: 41), and since the Italian economist shares with most Keynesian authors the belief that these tools are derived from the adjustment of aggregate supply and aggregate demand and depend on the marginal propensity to consume and on a new theory of interest, it is not surprising that he underestimates the importance as well as misses the significance of Keynes's identity. As for the second difficulty mentioned before, Pasinetti cannot be held responsible for not having faced it, since it unveils once the two conceptions of effective demand, the virtual and the realized, have been properly understood, and only after the identity $Y \equiv C + I$ has been fully recognized as a true macroeconomic law.

Effective demand and Keynes's identities

$Y \equiv C + I$

The identity between Y and $C + I$ establishes that, whatever the level of output actually produced, global demand is necessarily equal to it. In this respect, Keynes's identity is analogous to Say's Law since output generates *de facto* its own demand. This does not mean, however, that some sort of *deus ex machina* forces consumers and investors to spend the totality of their income. In reality consumers are free to decide the amount they spend for the purchase of consumption goods. As a consequence, the identity $Y \equiv C + I$ does not in the least guarantee the direct sale of the totality of the consumption goods actually produced. Entrepreneurs may well get their expectations wrong and be unable to sell part of their production. The point is that the income required to finance the output's final purchase does not disappear if its initial holders decide not to spend it. In other words, saving does not destroy income, and, since income 'feeds' demand, saving does also not decrease total demand. What is saved by consumers is lent by banks to other agents who will exert a demand in their place. What really matters here is the fact that the amount of income created by production defines global demand, independently of whether it is entirely spent by consumers or partly spent and partly saved. The amount saved is invested. If the entire production of consumption goods is purchased by consumers, the entrepreneurs' expectations are fulfilled and the distribution of total output between consumption and investment goods coincides with the planned production of these two categories of goods. If consumers act differently from what expected by entrepreneurs, demand is still enough to match global output, but the ratio between consumption and investment goods no longer coincides with what was initially planned.

Let us assume, for example, the final purchase of a given output of consumption goods (equal to 100 units of value) to be equal to 90 units only. The remaining, unsold goods will have to be purchased by firms, which are bound to cover their cost of production. In order to do so, firms spend an equivalent part of the income currently saved. In sum, the entire production of consumption goods (100) will be demanded, in part by consumers (90) and in part by firms themselves (ten). No shortage of global demand may therefore be caused by consumers' behaviour, the effect of their reduced final purchase being the partial transformation of consumption goods into investment goods. It should be superfluous to note that this transformation is obviously not physical. Goods are physically unchanged, yet their economic classification into the category of consumption or investment goods may vary, the determinant factor being the kind of income that is spent for their final purchase. Moreover, it is clear that if consumers were never to purchase part of the consumption goods currently produced, firms' forced purchase would decrease their profits and, consequently, their investment. Unsaleable consumption goods would thus be better defined as a negative amount of investment goods. Their presence would be the mark of entrepreneurs' mistaken planning of production and may even have some serious, albeit temporary consequences on employment. The fact that global demand does not fall short of global supply, however, is enough to exclude the possibility of pathological (Keynes's involuntary) unemployment.

The case of truly unsaleable goods is almost exclusively related to deflation, a situation in which the amount of available income is insufficient to finance the final purchase of produced output. Since savings are necessarily deposited with the banking system, consumers' behaviour cannot be the source of deflation. It thus follows that entrepreneurs' unfulfilled expectations are much more likely to cause a delay in the selling of output than a final loss for their firms. Be that as it may, Keynes's logical identity between Y and $C+I$ provides the macroeconomic theoretical framework within which we have to analyse the effect of microeconomic behaviour. $Y \equiv C+I$ is a true macroeconomic law resulting from a positive analysis of production started by Keynes in his *Treatise on Money*. In that book, Keynes asserted, against the opinion of orthodox economists, not only that global demand is always necessarily equal to global supply, but also that total saving is always necessarily on a par with current investment. In the previous chapter we have already introduced a few considerations about the identity $I \equiv S$ and Ohlin's attempt to transform it into a condition of equilibrium taking advantage of the distinction between *ex ante* and *ex post* magnitudes. Let us complete them here by attending to Keynes's own critical analysis.

$S \equiv I$

Our point is that even if we were to accept the existence of *ex ante* S and I in the form of planned saving and investment, this would not imply that their actual or realized values are the result of their mutual adjustment. Let us follow Keynes's argument. Having admitted that '[p]lanned investment – i.e. investment *ex ante* – may have to secure its "financial provision" *before* the investment takes place; that is to say, before the corresponding saving has taken place' (Keynes 1973c: 207), he adds that '[i]t is, so to speak, as though a particular piece of saving had to be earmarked against a particular piece of investment before either has occurred' (ibid.: 207–8). This is a very clear and deep argument indeed. Planned investment may be decided before production actually takes place, which is obvious. But it must also secure its financial provision before then. Keynes observes, however, that in this case an equivalent amount of future saving is earmarked against the planned investment. As he immediately explains, this means that '[t]here has, therefore, to be a technique to bridge this gap between the time when the *decision* to invest is taken and the time when the correlative investment and saving actually occur' (ibid.: 208). Hence, planned investment can find a financial backing before saving takes place provided that banks are willing to bridge the gap between the present and the future through their financial activity. If this happens, investment is financed 'in advance' with respect to the *ex ante* equality between saving and investment.

To make things clearer, Keynes argues that ' "finance" has nothing to do with saving. At the "financial" stage of the proceedings no net saving has taken place on anyone's part, just as there has been no net investment. "Finance" and "commitments to finance" are mere credit and debit book entries, which allow entrepreneurs to go ahead with assurance' (ibid.: 209). What Keynes is telling us is, therefore, that *ex ante* investment may be financed by banks and that, even though saving has not yet been determined, this does not introduce any discrepancy between saving and investment. This argument is not easy to grasp. The only true financing of investment is saving and this can occur only *ex post*, once investment and saving have actually taken place. Nevertheless, planned or *ex ante* investment and its financing by banks is a possibility that cannot be discarded. Now, Keynes maintains that the two expenditures, 'finance' and investment, must not be taken to have the same meaning. *Ex ante* banks advance an income not yet formed, *ex post* investment is backed by an equivalent sum of income actually formed and saved. But, if this was intended to mean that *ex post* saving and investment are necessarily equal, what about their *ex ante* relationship?

Keynes claims both that planned investment is financed by banks and that 'finance has nothing to do with saving'. Since he distinguishes investment from the decision to invest, we may infer that in his mind the *ex ante* relationship between saving and investment is replaced by the relationship between planned investment and its financial provision. We could thus be led to conclude that there are two distinct relationships, each of which implies the necessary equality of its terms. Yet, this could be interpreted as implying that investment financed by banks is entirely different from investment financed by saving, which is certainly not what Keynes would have been prepared to admit. While it is true that Keynes distinguished planned from actual investment and 'finance' from saving, it would be ingenuous to claim that he considered the two investments and the two expenditures as distinct and unrelated. Indeed, when he speaks of the financial intervention of banks, he explicitly affirms that this technique is necessary to bridge the gap between the time when the decision to invest is taken and 'the time when the *correlative* investment and saving actually occur' (ibid.: 208; our emphasis). The existence of this correlation has far-reaching consequences, one of which is the fact that actual saving can 'retroactively' modify the size of *ex ante* investment.

Let us take a very simple numerical example, where the unit is understood to be a monetary unit. Suppose planned investment is equal to 100 units in period p_0. This means that in p_0 firms plan to invest 100 units and that, if banks agree to do so, they provide a financial backing of the same amount. Suppose now that at the end of the given period global saving is actually equal to 80 units. Global investment is thus also set at the level of 80 units. Does this imply that the economy ends up with two distinct investments of a different nature? Certainly not, since the only investment that actually takes place is equal to 80, which therefore cannot exceed 80 units even though the amount of investment is initially set at 100 units. The exact amount of income actually saved in p_0 is crucial here. Since only 80 units are globally saved, macroeconomic investment must be equal to 80. This means that only 80 units out of the 100 advanced by banks in p_0 are in fact financing planned investment. The other 20 units are absorbed by consumption, which reduces the production of investment goods to 80 units (the remaining 20 units of investment goods being indirectly purchased by wage-earners, an indirect purchase that transforms them into consumption goods 'by destination'). What was planned as a production of investment goods is in part transformed into a production of (future) consumption goods. In the following period, the investment goods unsold in p_0 will in fact be replaced by an equivalent production of consumption goods. If, instead of the planned figure of 100 units, macroeconomic saving does not exceed 80 units, this means that 20 units of money income are spent by wage-earners in the purchase of future consumption goods. This forward purchase takes the form of a loan extended by wage-earners to firms. The investment goods that wage-earners purchase today indirectly (through their loans to firms) will then be replaced by an equivalent amount of consumption goods produced in a subsequent period.

Finally, it is important to notice that S and I are always equal, not only *ex post*, but also *ex ante*. True, in the interval between the instant wages are paid (t_0) and the instant income is spent (t_1) an adjustment may occur between what firms plan to invest and what income holders are prepared to save. But, whatever the decisions taken by these agents, at each point of the interval t_0–t_1 the amount of macroeconomic saving (determined by the amount of invested profit incurred so far) sets the limit to investment, so that no difference can ever be found between the two. Macroeconomic saving and macroeconomic investment are thus jointly determined. It is only at t_1 that the amount of macroeconomic saving is definitively established and that S and I find their final numerical expression. Before t_1, that is, *ex ante*, S and I may differ from their *ex post* level; yet, they define a series of possible 'equilibrium' values. To any of the points in the interval t_0–t_1 corresponds a given amount of macroeconomic saving (invested profits) that, if realized, would define an equal amount of investment. No adjustment ever takes place between S and I, which are always equal *ex ante, ex post*, and '*ex* anything else' (ibid.: 222).

Keynes's rejection of *ex ante/ex post* analysis as an attempt to transform the identity between S and I into a condition of equilibrium is uncompromising and shows clearly the substantial difference between his own analysis and that put forward by Ohlin, Robertson, Hicks and all those authors who read the *General Theory* with neoclassical spectacles. It also provides the proof that Keynes's analysis cannot be represented by Hicks's *IS–LM* diagram. *If I and S are always equal, whatever the level of income actually produced, it is no longer possible to consider saving and investment as functions of income.* For a given level of income and interest rate, for example, we do not necessarily find only one possible value of the identity between S and *I.* There is only one actual value, of course, but it cannot be determined before S and *I* actually take place. Even if decisions are influenced by the level of income and of the rate of interest, no function can be established between S and *I* since every assumption we may make as to their possible correlation can always be overruled by the actual decision of consumers and firms. We are thus led to the conclusion that *ex post IS* can only be represented by a series of unrelated points (Figure 4.1). Each point defines the level of *IS* in any given period when saving and investment actually occur, and is independent of any other point.

Ex ante no *IS* curve can be drawn as a function of Y and r. Income of p_0 is determined by the production taking place at t_0 and does not vary between t_0 and t_1. In this interval of time an infinity of combinations between S and *I* are possible, which most of the time do not satisfy both desires: the firm's to invest and the income holders' to save. Each combination defines an *ex ante* equality between S and *I* and, were it possible to know the amount of planned saving at each point of time, it would also be possible to draw a curve representing the various levels of S = *I* corresponding to different levels of the interest rate (Figure 4.2).

The implications for the *IS–LM* diagram can easily be imagined. If we take the *ex post* representation, *IS* is a series of unrelated points and no adjustment is possible between it and the *LM* curve. If it is the *ex ante* representation that is considered, no unique *IS–LM* diagram can be drawn since the coordinates of the *IS* curve (r and time) are not the same as the coordinates of the *LM* curve (r and Y). To conclude, let us observe that if it is a fact that even today economists are not unanimous as to the analysis of S and *I,* it is also undeniable that not everybody is prepared to address Keynes's identities in order to prove that, far from being nominal tautol-

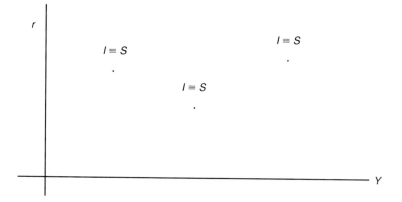

Figure 4.1 The *ex post* representation of *IS.*

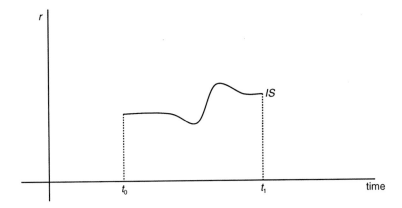

Figure 4.2 The *ex ante* representation of *IS.*

ogies, they are the building blocks of modern macroeconomics. Even the most faithful followers of Keynes accept the idea that *I* and *S* are equal only at equilibrium, unaware that, in so doing, they are advocating a neoclassical interpretation of Keynes's theory. The analysis of the debate between Keynes, Robertson, Ohlin and Hicks shows how difficult it was for Keynes to get his message across. Things are not radically different today, even though developments in banking since provide the basis for a new understanding of Keynes's monetary theory of production. It is precisely through a rigorous analysis of bank money and production that it is possible to derive a monetary macroeconomic theory encompassing that of Keynes.

Before starting such an analysis, let us conclude this chapter by observing that despite the necessary equality of *Y* and *C + I* and of *S* and *I*, Keynes's interpretation of Say's Law is not opposed to the numerical difference between global demand and global supply. Even though *Y* is always equal to *C + I*, *C + I* may in fact be *numerically* different from *Y*. Indeed, it is precisely because *Y* and *C + I* are the two terms of an identity that their numerical difference defines a pathological disequilibrium. Keynes's identities do not amount to a superficial version of Say's Law according to which supply generates its own demand in such a way that no difference whatsoever will ever be possible between supply and demand. In a pathological state of the economy, supply and demand may actually diverge, yet their difference will not be inconsistent with their deeply-rooted identity. Hence, Keynes's identities become the necessary condition for the very definition of inflation and deflation. This is the third possible interpretation of Keynes's principle of effective demand. *In the case of inflation, for example, effective demand will be numerically greater than global supply yet substantially identical to it.* This means that the value of global demand will still be the same, but would now be carried by an increased number of monetary units, which is precisely what inflation leads to: a decrease in the purchasing power (value) of each single monetary unit. Since this subject matter pertains to the analysis of the pathological workings of our monetary economies, let us postpone its investigation to the second part of the book and terminate this first part by noting how much we still need to understand Keynes's principle of effective demand as well as his fundamental identities in order to spell out the logical–conceptual foundations of macroeconomics.

Part II

The macroeconomic analysis of national economics

5 Money and income as macroeconomic magnitudes

Money and income: a few introductory remarks

As economists know well, within orthodox neoclassical economics money is irrelevant, since (relative) prices are deemed to be determined through direct exchange, independently of the money stock and the absolute price level. The homogeneity postulate, the Walrasian assumption of continuous market clearing, and the absence of market frictions are the mark of general equilibrium analysis. Money has no proper role to play in this theoretical setting, where even Walras's *numéraire* is assumed to be a commodity.

For new classical economists, expectations are supposed to adapt to changes in the money supply even in the short run, so that monetary policy is likely to have an effect on real variables only if changes were to be totally random. If expectations are perfectly rational, individuals will know the set of equilibrium prices obtaining on any possible assumption regarding the monetary policies adopted by the government and will be able to neutralize any unexpected effect of changes in the money stock on real variables.

In real business cycle economics, the basic model is a 'stochastic dynamic equilibrium growth model without money and nominal prices, and without market imperfections and coordination problems' (van Els 1995: 240). In its basic version, the real business cycle model is therefore very closely related to the models of traditional Walrasian general equilibrium analysis. Money is superfluous, and unexpected changes in the money supply are replaced with changes in other exogenous variables – in particular technological capacity – as determinant factors of economic fluctuations.

In contrast to orthodox economics, the neutrality of money over relative prices was to be limited to the long term by economists such as Patinkin, who showed that Walras's Law and the homogeneity postulate do not hold good when equilibrium is subjected to an unexpected change in the money stock. In order then to account for market imperfections some mainstream theorists attempted to introduce non-Walrasian elements in their models, while others investigated the possible influence of money on business cycle models. For example, King and Plosser developed a model with 'two productive sectors with one intermediate and one final good' (King and Plosser 1984: 364), the intermediate good being the output of the financial industry and an input 'into production and purchase of final goods' (ibid.: 364). King and Plosser's attempt to integrate money and banking into real business cycle theory is based on the clear perception that money is endogenous and that private banks play an essential role in our monetary systems. They even claim that 'empirical analysis [...] provides general support for our focus on the banking system since the correlation between monetary measures and real activity is primarily with inside money' (ibid.: 363). Yet, we would look in vain for a true process of integration between money and output in the works of monetary economists of a neoclassical breed. In King and Plosser's analysis what we find instead is the description of production in the final goods industry as a function of labour, capital and financial trans-action services. Nothing is said about the logical (im)possibility to insert in the same equation such heterogeneous quantities as commodity units, hours worked and book-keeping entries. Money is not truly integrated into the real world, but is simply considered as a device facilitating exchanges that could almost equally well be carried out without its inter-mediation. Thus, King and Plosser's theory remains akin to GEA, the accounting services provided by the financial industry being introduced in their model only to 'facilitate the exchange of goods by reducing the amount of time and other resources that otherwise would be devoted to market transactions' (ibid.: 365).

The way of looking at money adopted by the great majority of (Amer-ican) Keynesian economists was influenced by equilibrium analysis and is exemplified by the general acceptance of Hicks's *LM* curve. Attempting to show that if the demand for money was made to depend on income and on the rate of interest Keynes's theory was only a special case of a more general theory, Hicks introduced the 'transaction motive' as well as the 'speculative motive' into the demand for money function. The resulting *LM* curve shows the combination of income and interest rate at which the demand for money will just equal the money supply, that is, which will maintain equilibrium in the money market. Now, in Hicks's interpreta-tion, the *LM* curve is supposed to be 'a stock relation' (Hicks 1982: 329) and is meant to define the equilibrium points between the supply of and demand for money income and not simply of nominal money. But this makes it impossible to consider *LM* as a function of income, the rate of interest and time, for – as claimed by Keynes – current national income defines current total supply and is always necessarily equal to total demand, whatever the level of income itself and the rate of interest. By taking over Hicks's neoclassical interpretation of Keynes's theory, Keynes-ian theorists are therefore missing the originality of Keynes's monetary analysis. In particular they entirely miss the distinction between money and money income, do not fully understand the monetary nature of production and circulation, and fail to see the need to replace conventional functional relationships with conceptual identities.

As for new Keynesian economists, they emphasize the role played by credit creation in a world where access to capital markets is differentiated and firms may be forced to rely entirely on bank credit in order to finance their activity. In this framework, credit rationing becomes a key factor in the search for equilibrium. By and large, new Keynesian economists seem more concerned with monetary consistency than their Keynesian colleagues. 'The mechanism by which the monetary authorities affected the level of economic activity in Keynesian analysis is implausible' (Greenwald and Stiglitz 1987: 129). Yet, their own monetary analysis is too superficial and confused to represent a valid alternative. The new-Keynesian definition of money, for example, is so wide and *ad hoc* that one cannot avoid feeling lost when presented with theories filled with concepts such as money, quasi money, high powered money, inside money, outside money, money supply, demand function for money, opportunity cost of holding money, cash balance, cash management accounts, money substitutes, cash-in-advance, credit money, bank money, state money, private money, and so on. Things become even worse when one is simultaneously told that 'money is not required for most transactions, only credit' (ibid.: 129), and that 'the relationship between transactions and income is tenuous' (ibid.: 129), or that 'transactions are exchanges of assets' (ibid.: 129) and that '[t]o the extent that money demand is based on asset considerations, what is relevant, of course, is not income, but wealth' (ibid.: 130). As these few quotations clearly show, we are asked to believe that in a monetary economy money is not required for most transactions, and at the same time that, even though the relationship between transactions and income is tenuous, most transactions require only credit. But in a monetary economy economic transactions are monetary. How is it thus possible for (monetary) transactions not to require money? This is not to say, of course, that credit is not also involved. But if credit is involved in most transactions as suggested by Greenwald and Stiglitz, how can the relationship between transactions and income be tenuous?

Like their Keynesian and new Keynesian colleagues, most post-Keynesian economists base their monetary theory on the money supply endogeneity, where '[e]ndogeneity refers to the capacity for institutions to create money instruments, or a few financial institutions to emerge, to satisfy excess demand for money' (Dow 1996: 174). The idea that money is endogenously determined seems thus to result from the belief that money is an asset and that there are different kinds of monetary assets that may be issued by monetary and financial institutions in order to satisfy the demand for money. 'The path of endogeneity mirrors, and is interdependent with, that of liquidity preference, accommodating demand for credit in the upturn, but frustrating it in the downturn' (ibid.: 185). Central or high powered money is the most liquid monetary asset, and its demand increases when 'confidence in the prospect of capital gains collapses' (ibid.: 185). In a business cycle upturn, on the contrary, capital gains are sought after, demand for credit rises, and less liquid monetary asset are increasingly preferred to central money. This clearly shows how the concept of money is still a blurred one even in the works of a great number of economists who consider themselves to be the most faithful followers of Keynes's monetary theory. In particular, it is immediately obvious that no clear distinction is made between money and credit, as well as between money and income, and that too much emphasis is laid on the behavioural aspect of the demand for money.

Let us conclude this very short and incomplete overview by observing that, according to the majority of economists, the study of money pertains both to the micro and macroeconomic fields. Supply of and demand for money are supposed to be functions relating the behaviour of private and central banks on one side, and of consumers, savers, speculators and firms on the other side, in response to changes in interest rates, income distribution, marginal efficiency of investment and other such factors. Given the importance attributed to supply and demand by equilibrium analysis, it is therefore not surprising to find that monetary economics is essentially based on microeconomics, macroeconomics entering the picture only insofar as the supply of and demand for money 'are pervasive in their influence on virtually all the major macroeconomic variables in the short run' (Handa 2000: 3). Opinions differ as to the stability of the demand function for money. For example, while monetarists believe the demand for money to be a stable function of a few measurable arguments, most Keynesian theorists emphasize the destabilizing role played by institutional changes on the demand for money function. On the other hand, it seems correct to state that the majority of mainstream economists would agree as to the importance of the supply of money function, and, as a consequence, of the central role played by the behavioural or microeconomic approach related to monetary institutions.

> The microeconomics part of monetary economics focuses on the study of the demand and supply of money and their equilibrium. No study of monetary economics can be even minimally adequate without a study of the behaviour of those financial institutions whose behaviour determines the money stock and its close substitutes.
>
> (ibid.: 3)

On the whole it appears that the state of the art in monetary economics is rather messy and still very much influenced by the tenets of equilibrium analysis. The distinction between supply of and demand for money, their adjustment, and their limited effect on real variables are a clear sign of the dependence of monetary theory on the neoclassical analysis of relative exchanges. Likewise, the definition of money as a positive asset is reminiscent of the neoclassical concept of commodity money.

Despite the efforts of post-Keynesian economists, money is still mainly conceived of as a stock made up of different kinds of monetary assets, more or less liquid and more or less apt to circulate among economic agents. In an attempt to clarify the modern macroeconomic concept of money, we shall therefore devote this chapter essentially to showing that money is not an asset and that, as such, it must be carefully distinguished both from credit and from income.

Is money an asset?

In his famous 1967 article entitled 'A reconsideration of the microfoundations of monetary theory', and republished two years later as 'Foundation of monetary theory', Clower uncompromisingly argues that neoclassical theory is inappropriate to describe a monetary economy since what 'passes for a theory of a money economy is in truth descriptive of a barter economy' (Clower 1969: 205). In a few words, his main argument against GEA is that within this conceptual paradigm money is considered as an element of the commodity set, indistinguishable from any other element of the set. 'The fact that fiat money is included among the set of tradable commodities is utterly irrelevant; the role of money in economic activity is analytically indistinguishable from that of any other commodity' (ibid.: 204–5). Unfortunately, even an author as convinced as Clower that 'money matters' and that 'money buys goods but goods do not buy goods' is not immune from the temptation to identify money with a commodity, albeit of a particular nature. 'The natural point of departure for a theory of monetary phenomena is a precise distinction between money and non-money commodities' (ibid.: 205). Hence, Clower maintains that '[a] commodity is regarded as money for our purposes if and only if it can be traded directly for all other commodities in the economy' (ibid.: 207).

Now, Clower claims also that the distinction between money and the other commodities is a matter of kind and not of degree. It is not at all obvious, however, to what kind of real goods money pertains. Moreover, if money is a real good (however peculiar it may be) it seems curious to maintain that 'goods do not buy goods'. This claim would be clearly false, in fact, if the money used to buy goods is itself a good. Although it is true that money is not 'just one of many commodities that may be bartered directly for other commodities' (ibid.: 209), Clower fails to notice that barter can be avoided only if money is not a commodity at all. If the analysis does not go as far as to recognize the immaterial nature of money, it is bound to fall back into the neoclassical theoretical framework. There is no essential difference, in fact, between direct and indirect barter. Even if sales and purchases are mediated by a commodity money, it should be clear that goods are still exchanged against goods. The fact that one of them is made to play the role of money or of a medium of exchange does not substantially modify the situation. This is so much so that neoclassical economists have no difficulty in agreeing to define money as a veil, while still conceiving of it as an asset. Indeed it is precisely because money is conceived of as an asset that it is said to split barter into a succession of sales and purchases and thus conceal the reality of the direct exchange between commodities. Direct barter is concealed by two transactions, which, as they define two separate exchanges between real goods and a commodity money, are also of a barter kind.

Monetarism is the clearest example of the way money has so often been misconceived. The whole theoretical framework of monetarism is based on the assumption that money is a *stock*. The money supply is said to determine the quantity of money, changes in nominal income are made to depend on changes in the money stock, balance effects are related to the public willingness to hold money, and so on. Yet, monetarists are not alone in conceiving of money as a stock. In its function as a store of value, for example, money is related to a demand for money to hold, both by monetarists and Keynesians alike. This conception derives directly from the belief that money is essentially an asset, either a commodity chosen as general equivalent or a monetary asset issued by banks as counterpart of the real assets deposited by the public. Let us leave aside the question of whether or not money has historically been generated out of gold or other precious metals. It is a fact that today national currencies have no link whatsoever with gold and that money is issued by banks through their use of double-entry book-keeping. What has to be clarified, therefore, is whether banks issue a positive stock of money in exchange for a stock of real goods, or if their intervention is of a very particular nature that does not pertain to the world of relative exchanges.

If, as still maintained by the great majority of economists, money is a positive asset in itself, then it is perfectly legitimate to consider it as a stock and its flow as the circulation of a stock. Yet, for this to be the case, banks should have the power to create a positive asset equivalent to the real goods (financially) deposited by their clients or, as suggested by supporters of the state conception of money, governments should be endorsed with the privilege to finance their purchases using their own IOUs. Let us postpone the analysis of state money and concentrate on the study of bank money. Two main difficulties have to be dealt with here. The first concerns the actual possibility for banks to act as 'creators', the second pertains to the numerical measure of the goods deposited by the public. Even if it were possible to overcome the second kind of difficulty, the first would, alone, be sufficient to challenge the traditional analysis of money. It should be obvious, in fact, that if banks cannot create any positive asset simply by acknowledging their indebtedness to the public, money cannot be conceived of as a stock.

When they issue money, *banks act as monetary intermediaries, and not as purchasers* (which they would do if the money they create were given to the public as counterpart of the public's real deposit). This means that money creation has nothing to do with relative exchanges, which require the presence of at least two distinct and positive assets. But if money is issued in an act of pure intermediation, banks are necessarily confronted with two clients and not only just the one who deposits the real assets entered on the banks' balance sheets. A typical intermediation is one as represented in Table 5.1, where the bank pays a client C on behalf of its other client A.

Let us call money B (MB) the monetary units issued by the bank (B), and let us suppose to start from *tabula rasa*. The only presupposition we make at the beginning of our thought experiment is that *the bank can use its double-entry book-keeping in order to issue its own acknowledgement of debt*. Since nobody can pay by getting indebted, and since no positive purchasing power can be created (that is, obtained out of nothing), we know for certain that the bank is not a net purchaser. The asset deposited by agent A as guarantee of the payment carried out by the bank on his behalf is therefore not purchased by B. What we want to know is the exact definition of the money units issued by the bank.

As a simple bank IOU, money cannot be issued as a net asset. This is a first result easily derived from the book-keeping nature of bank money. No relative exchange takes place between the asset entered on the liabilities side of B's double-entry book-keeping and MB, precisely because money is not a new asset equivalent to the asset deposited by A. The bank has not the power to create a positive monetary asset and give it to the public in exchange for an equivalent real asset. Benefiting from a positive creation of money, A is a creditor to the bank. It is certain, in fact, that banks' debits to the public have a real object: money is a real credit owned by the public towards the issuing banks. But what is the 'object' of A's credit? Certainly not gold, or any other real asset of the sort. Indeed, the object of the banks' debit to the public is not a stock, but a flow. This means that, as a beneficiary of a money creation, A acquires the right to ask the issuing bank to carry out a payment on his behalf. Since the object of A's credit is a payment, it follows that the object of money itself is a flow. This means that money comes into existence at the very moment a payment is carried out. In other words, money is the means by which a payment is conveyed from the payer to the payee through the

Table 5.1 A monetary intermediation

	Bank		
Liabilities		*Assets*	
C	x MB	A	x MB

intermediation of a bank. Now, since payments are instantaneous events, money's existence is itself instantaneous: each time a bank pays C on behalf of A a sum of money is created on A and destroyed on C.

With respect to money creation two moments can be distinguished. First, a bank merely credits and debits the same client, A, with a given sum of money. Corresponding to the opening of a line of credit, this double entry defines a creation of money in favour of A and a simultaneous destruction of money for A: the same amount of money is entered as a debit and a credit for A, and, conversely, for the bank. Since no payment has yet occurred, no money has actually been created so far. Subsequently, when the bank pays C on behalf of A, the same amount of money is entered both on the assets side and on the liabilities side of the bank balance sheet as a debit of A and as a credit of C respectively. More precisely, a sum of money is simultaneously created and destroyed both for A and for C. This is so because neither A nor C can be credited by the bank without being immediately debited and vice versa. The flow nature of money does not allow money to be positively created without being destroyed at the same time. Thus, A is credited with a sum of money obtained by getting indebted to the bank, and is debited with the sum spent by the bank in order to pay C on his behalf. Reciprocally, C is credited with the sum of money paid by the bank, and is debited for his purchase of a bank deposit. The result of the payment is a net debit of A to the bank and a net credit of C whose object is not money but a bank deposit. Money does not survive the payment carried out by the bank, which is a necessary consequence of the fact that the object of money is the payment itself. What remains is a bank deposit, a stock, owed by A and owned by C.

As shown by Schmitt's definition of money as an asset–liability, money proper can never be stocked. First introduced by Schmitt (1966), this definition accounts for the peculiar nature of bank money as well as for the intermediary role played by banks. It thus follows that, being an asset–liability, money proper can never finance a net purchase, and is bound to define an instantaneous and circular flow. It is both its nature of asset–liability and its circular use that makes money a flow. Once the originality of bank money has been fully perceived, it becomes clear that it is not possible to consider money as a stock that may be put in motion and thus made to flow. The nature of bank money is such that money is always a flow. Stocks exist too, of course, but they are not made up of money proper, and they have to be explained in accordance with the asset–liability definition of money. Before investigating further the relationship between flows (money) and stocks (bank deposits), let us spend a few words on the chartalist definition of money adopted by a number of post-Keynesian economists.

State money: a wrong conception

Lerner, Minsky, Tobin, Wray and some young post-Keynesian economists support Knapp's idea that money is essentially state money, since state money is what is accepted at public pay offices to settle taxes or other liabilities to the state. According to the chartalist definition, 'money is a creature of the state' (Lerner 1947: 313), for the state is the ultimate institution that can enforce the acceptance of its IOU both as a unit of account and as a means of payment. Now, *the important point is not the choice of the denomination or of the unit of account in which taxes are expressed, but the way in which the chosen unit is introduced in the economy.* According to Minsky, this is done simply through the government's decision to force people to pay taxes using the acknowledgement of debt issued by the central bank. '[T]he fact that taxes need to be paid gives value to the money of the economy' (Minsky 1986: 231). This is enough, according to Wray and those who accept the chartalist point of view, to convince the public to accept government money and to claim that 'government spending is always financed through creation of fiat money – rather than through tax revenues or bond sales. Indeed, taxes are required not to finance spending, but rather to maintain demand for government fiat money' (Wray 1998: 75). What our authors do not see is that money's validity cannot derive from an act of faith, whether voluntary or induced.

Instead of claiming that, like any other economic agent, the state cannot finance its purchases (public spending) simply by issuing its own acknowledgement of debt, Wray maintains that '[g]overnment spending is constrained only by private sector willingness to provide goods, services or assets to government in exchange for government money' (ibid.: 87). Thus, according to Wray, public spending could at most provoke an excessive increase in bank reserves. The sale of government bonds would then be the means by which the Treasury undertakes to drain excess reserves.

But, if this happens, does it not mean that public spending has in fact been financed by the money income transferred from the private sector? Instead of advocating a complex mechanism of government intervention whose *raison d'être* is merely that of justifying the state money axiom, would it not be better to recognize that the government itself has to comply with the logical rules of bank money? Nobody *pays* by getting indebted, not even the state. Hence, public spending is indeed constrained by the amount of money income the government can obtain through taxation and the sale of public sector output and bonds. Actually, even if government spending chronologically precedes the payment of taxes, it is the money income transferred by tax payers that eventually finances public expenditures and not the other way around. The principle is simple: purchases can be financed only out of corresponding sales and not out of the mere acknowledgement of debt issued by the purchaser. Let us repeat that the state's activities are subject to the same logical requirements as those of other economic agents. In particular the state can finance its purchases only through simultaneous and equivalent sales on the commodity and financial markets. Let us represent in Table 5.2 a state's expenditure carried out through the intermediation of the central bank.

If the transaction occurs prior to the payment of taxes, the state's purchase of *C*'s real assets or services is balanced by an equivalent sale of financial claims to the central bank, entry (1). Now, the money issued by the central bank and used – through the intermediation of a private bank – to finance the state's purchase of *C*'s output – entries (2) – is an advance of money income that the central bank will recover as soon as it sells the state's financial assets to the public, represented here by agent *D* – entries (3). Finally, it is not central money but the income lent by *D* that finances public spending. Like in the case of private bank money, central or state money is a mere asset–liability that cannot finance any net purchase. What is true for every private bank is also true for the central bank. Whether created by a private or a central bank, money as such is a flow. The state cannot modify this state of affairs and must find in its sales the financing of government spending. Wray is not far from hitting the target when he writes that 'if the tax system were removed, the government would eventually find that its fiat money would lose its ability to purchase goods and services on the market' (ibid.: 81). In fact, 'the ability to purchase goods and services' does not derive from the supernatural power of the state to issue its own IOUs in the form of net assets, but from the ability to *'sell' taxes and Treasury bonds*.

In conclusion, let us observe that a monetary system would work perfectly well even in the absence of the state and its tax system (whose role is useful and necessary from a social rather than a monetary viewpoint). Conceived of as the money of the government, state money is therefore irrelevant systemically speaking. In fact, what is indispensable is a central money conceived of as the common standard issued by the central bank in its role of settlement institution for inter-bank payments (bank of banks).

Table 5.2 The financing of public spending through private loans

Central bank			
Liabilities		*Assets*	
1. State	x	State's financial assets	x
2. Private bank	x	State	x
3. State's financial assets	x	Private bank	x

Private bank			
Liabilities		*Assets*	
2. C	x	Central bank	x
3. Central bank	x	State's financial assets	x
State's financial assets	x	D	x

Acting as a clearing house, the central bank is indeed behaving as an intermediary between private banks, in much the same way as private banks act as intermediary between their clients. Central bank money, which plays the role of the common denominator between bank monies issued within a country, is therefore also a flow. When, as in Table 5.3, the central bank pays bank B_2 on behalf of another bank, B_1, it uses its own acknowledgement of debt as a *means* of payment.

In this transaction, both the private banks involved and the central bank itself are simultaneously sellers and purchasers. Bank B_2 sells a real asset (on behalf of its client C) and purchases a financial claim – entry (2) – its partner B_1 sells a financial claim and purchases a real asset (on behalf of its client A) – entry (1) – and the central bank sells to B_1 the real asset purchased from B_2 and sells to B_2 the financial claim purchased from B_1 – entry (3).

Whether we refer to private or to central bank money it is thus confirmed that money is an asset *and simultaneously* a liability, an asset–liability of no intrinsic value whose sole role is that of *conveying* reciprocal payments *via* its instantaneous flow.

First introduced by Adam Smith, the concept of vehicular or nominal money has been given a fuller explanation by Bernard Schmitt, who, in referring to double-entry book-keeping, has shown that, as an asset–liability spontaneously issued by banks, money is a purely numerical form required to monetize produced output. As such, money can be issued at zero cost and without there being any logical limits to its emission (except, of course, those set by production). Applied to this framework, money supply simply defines the capacity that banks have to provide the economy with a numerical form. Whatever the number of money units needed, banks can issue it through a book-keeping double-entry that is costless and instantaneous. Thus, with respect to nominal money, money supply does not define – as wrongly assumed by the monetarist school – a given stock

Table 5.3 The central bank's intermediation

	B_1		
Liabilities		*Assets*	
1. Central bank	x	Client A	x

	B_2		
Liabilities		*Assets*	
2. Client C	x	Central bank	x

	Central Bank		
Liabilities		*Assets*	
3. B_2	x	B_1	x

or a quantity of money. Actually, money is immaterial and the very idea of it being a quantity is wrong and misleading.

As Trautwein recalls, Wicksell in his book on interest and prices coined the expression 'pure credit economy' meaning 'a state of affairs in which all money is held in interest-bearing bank deposits and in which all payments are effected by means of book-keeping transfers in the banking system' (Trautwein 1997: 3). What was for Wicksell a 'purely imaginary case' (Wicksell 1965: 70) was later considered to be 'the essence of reality rather than pure science fiction' (Trautwein 1997: 5) by the German economist Albert Hahn. Now, with Trautwein, it is interesting to observe that Hahn considered obsolete the belief 'in the primacy of a well-defined *stock* of money' (ibid.: 5) and maintained that 'bank lending does not depend on prior saving' (ibid.: 5). This leads us straight to the question of the logical relationship connecting money to credit.

Money and credit

According to Wicksell's definition, pure credit economics is not about a monetary economy in which money does not exist. Unless we insist identifying money with cash, it is obvious that money is implied in all payments even if none of them is actually carried out with banknotes or coins. Does the fact that payments are carried out by means of book-keeping transfers in the banking system imply that in a pure credit economy money needs to be identified with credit? Certainly not, since while money is a *flow*, credit requires the presence of bank deposits, and bank deposits are *stocks*. There is therefore a categorial difference between money and credit. Those economists who identify money and credit have an asset definition of money in the back of their minds. They more or less explicitly hold that a monetary economy requires the presence of a monetary (standard) asset, which is usually supposed to be the liability of the central bank. But, even if it is obviously true that the debt of the banking system is the credit of the public, this does not mean that, when issuing money, banks (or the central bank) can incur a net debt and thus issue money as a positive asset. Banks can grant a positive credit to the public only on the basis of a pre-existing bank deposit. Every bank loan is necessarily backed by an equivalent borrowing, so that credit is the outcome of a financial intermediation, and not of a monetary creation.

Yet, the confusion between money and credit is widespread and the source of endless misconceptions. Let us just consider, as an example, Trautwein's claim that '[t]he conflict [between the requirement of a stable standard of value and the flexibility of credit money] is in the nature of a standard of value and a definite means of payment that in itself is nothing but a form of credit' (ibid.: 15). It immediately appears that money is supposed to act as a reliable standard of value only insofar as it is identified with a stable, positive asset, and yet, being nothing but a form of credit, money may be issued with a degree of flexibility that is in contrast with the requirement of stability. Trautwein's statement is thus a curious mixing of old-fashioned and modern concepts. The idea that value is a kind of substance that has to be expressed by a standard whose value is constant goes back to the Classics and has since been definitively superseded by Walras and Keynes's thesis that value is a numerical relationship and not a materialization of an economic 'quality' of produced output. By contrast, the idea that money is created by banks through their use of double-entry book-keeping is modern and perfectly in line with the activity of intermediation carried out by private and central banks. The conflict put forward by Trautwein should not therefore be taken at face value, as it were. The flexibility required for banks to be able to meet the needs of their clients should be reconciled with the reliability of money's purchasing power and not with some mysterious economic value of which money would be the standard. Thus, the problem faced by Trautwein would become one of determining whether or not the emission of bank money adjusts to the demand for money in such a way as to allow for the stability of prices and, subsequently, of money's purchasing power. Now, this very problem may be addressed in two different ways: whether the creation of bank money is identified with that of credit or with that of a pure numerical form or 'vehicle'. By stating that, as a means of payment, money 'in itself is nothing but a form of credit' (ibid.: 15), Trautwein is explicitly choosing the first alternative and that explains why he is worried about the possibility that the banks' creation of money may be dangerously excessive. This shows also that what should merely be the creation of a simple *means* of payment is perceived by Trautwein as the creation of an *object* of payment – in conformity with the neoclassical axiom of relative exchange according to which every payment implies the exchange of two equivalent assets.

The shortcomings of the monetary circuit approach

The confusion between money and credit is widely spread also among post-Keynesian economists as well as among the so-called circuit theorists. For example, in a book on the theory of the monetary circuit published in 2003, Graziani reiterates the idea that money is issued by banks as a credit to firms, used by economic agents on the commodity and financial markets, and finally given back to banks where it is destroyed. 'The very term "monetary circuit" draws its origin from the fact that the theory examines the complete life cycle of money, from its creation by the banking system, through its circulation in the market, to its being repaid to the banks and consequent destruction' (Graziani 2003: 19). The logical consequence of this analysis is that '[e]ntrepreneurs, being admitted to bank credit, can rely on a potentially unlimited purchasing power' (ibid.: 19). The emission of money is thus conceived of as a creation of purchasing power carried out by banks and required in order to finance the production of firms.

Parguez and Seccareccia push this analysis to its extreme consequences and claim that 'money is, and has always been, a debt created *ex nihilo* by bank credit advances that are granted either to permit the generation of real wealth or to acquire existing physical assets' (Parguez and Seccareccia 2000: 102). It is obvious that this is possible only if banks can create a positive purchasing power. But, are banks actually up to this task, which obviously amounts to a process of 'spontaneous generation'? Parguez and Seccareccia's answer in the affirmative maintains that '[m]oney is at all times the liabilities issued by banking institutions which have been endorsed by the state primarily for the purpose of financing the formation of future real wealth. This money has a real extrinsic value because every holder of these liabilities has acquired a claim on the future physical wealth that results from the initial bank credit advances' (ibid.: 107). Besides the ingenuous idea that endorsing banks' activity the state has the power to invest their IOUs with a positive value, it is striking to read that the formation of real wealth has to be financed by a monetary wealth created *ex nihilo*. The idea that banks can create wealth, not through their activity as consultants and intermediaries, but merely by issuing their IOUs is very strange indeed. Yet, it is even weirder to claim that the wealth thus created has an extrinsic value (where does it come from?) that *finances* the formation of real wealth. Parguez and Seccareccia's model seems to work as follows:

1   Banks issue credit money by spontaneously acknowledging a debt to the public.
2   The money thus created has a positive value guaranteed by the endorsement of banks' activity by the state.
3   Production is financed by this newly created credit money.
4   The purchase of physical output takes place through the expenditure of credit money and leads to its destruction.

Two main shortcomings affect this analysis. First, it is metaphysical to believe that a positive value can be created *ex nihilo*. Second, if money had a positive value before production actually takes place, once output has indeed been produced total wealth would amount to twice the value of total output. As Adam Smith has already shown more than 200 years ago, money and output are the two faces of one and the same reality and not two distinct realities of equal value.

The mistake of the circuit theorists derives from a still microeconomic conception of production. They miss the particular nature of labour and end up sharing the neoclassical view that labour is nothing but a factor of production among others. If it is maintained that firms need to 'spend money to acquire the labour services required for the production of the planned output of consumption and capital goods out of their existing capital stock' (ibid.: 107), it becomes obvious that labour is to be conceived of like any other factor that the firm has to purchase in order to carry out its production. Circuitists also share, at least implicitly, the weird idea of the earning-through-spending theory of income, since they maintain that firms spend a given sum of credit money in order to purchase labour services and that this expenditure determines the formation of an equivalent sum of income. Their analysis is confused. They claim both that the expenditure of bank liabilities on the commodity market implies their destruction, and that the purchase of labour services engenders a new income. Given that there is no purchase of labour *per se* but only of labour services and since the purchase of labour services is nothing else than the purchase of labour's output, circuitists ask us to accept that:

1 when it is carried out by firms, the purchase of current output requires the expenditure of a positive purchasing power that is transformed into an equivalent sum of labour income, and that
2 the same purchase leads to a destruction of purchasing power when it is carried out by consumers.

Graziani correctly points out that a monetary economy must be based on a 'system of payments [...] in which payments go through a third party acting as an intermediary' (Graziani 2003: 60). It is the bank that plays this role. Money may thus be used as a means of payment because, being issued by an element outside the set of purchasers (and sellers), it never defines the acknowledgement of debt of one of them. Nobody pays by getting indebted, of course, and this is why bank money is rightly foregrounded by Graziani as the sole necessary element of a true monetary economy. Now, the fact that money is issued by a third 'agent' functionally distinct from the set of purchasers is not enough to give money the power to settle debts. Money must acquire a positive purchasing power that cannot simply be created. Yet, the theorists of the monetary circuit persevere in their error and attempt to show that the emission of money is the creation of a positive asset to the benefit of firms. '[M]oney *always* emerges as a debt (or liability) issued by this third agent on itself, which has as counterpart a credit simultaneously granted by buyers of goods and services within an economy' (Parguez and Seccareccia 2000: 101). But how can the buyers of goods and services grant a credit to the bank? Who are the buyers liable to grant a credit to the bank before a positive income has actually been formed? Most likely, Parguez and Seccareccia are thinking of firms. In this case, the credit matching the bank's debt is defined as the debt incurred by the firms benefiting from the money creation process. It should therefore immediately follow that money is issued as an asset–liability of the bank (and, simultaneously, of firms). If the advocates of the theory of the monetary circuit were prepared to follow the analysis of bank money till the end, they would have to conclude that, in conformity with the principles of double-entry book-keeping, the creation of money amounts to no positive asset.

Let us attend to Graziani's claim that money '*only comes into existence the moment a payment is made*' (Graziani 1990: 11) and to Goodhart's observation that '[w]hen the current accounts of the payer and payee have been respectively debited and credited by their banks, the payment is completed; nothing further needs to be done' (Goodhart 1977: 218). From these quotations it follows that every payment is logically instantaneous and that money actually exists only instantaneously. No need to talk of money stock or asset creation here. Existing only while a payment is carried out, money is a flow. To understand this 'vehicular' nature of money it is necessary to enter the world of purely numerical magnitudes and of double-entry book-keeping. The theorists of the circuit have clearly seen that money is *bank* money. What they have failed to notice so far is that banks create a magnitude that is simultaneously positive and negative. By supporting an analysis in which money and credit are mixed up, these authors miss the opportunity to grasp the immaterial (numerical) nature of money and go on considering money as an asset – which is indisputably the major shortcoming of neoclassical theories. A truly novel theory capable of overcoming the dichotomous vision of neoclassical economics must give up any dimensional conception of money. Failing to apprehend money as a purely numerical form, the theorists of the monetary circuit envisage the emission of money as a credit creation and inadvertently end up proposing a 'mechanistic' analysis of the economic system. An example of this can be found in the stock–flow relationship. As we have already observed, according to the theory of the monetary circuit, money flows back to banks when firms reimburse their debts. The time and size of the inflow are uncertain, and there is no guarantee that the amount that flows back will always be equal to the outflow. If this were the case, firms would remain partially indebted to banks and the system would be crisis prone. As may easily be seen, such an analysis follows the mechanics of flows, since money is supposed to flow (more or less rapidly and not necessarily for the entire amount issued by banks) within a pre-existent circuit. It is also worth noting here that economic agents' behaviour plays a relatively important role in the analysis developed by the circuitists, which is a clear sign that their analysis is still strongly influenced by *microeconomic* considerations.

The difference between the theorists of the monetary circuit and those who follow Schmitt's quantum theoretical analysis is analytically speaking quite clear cut. Whereas according to the former money is created by banks as an asset whose circulation has a positive duration in continuous time, the latter conceive of money as an asset–liability that is instantaneously created and destroyed each time banks carry out a payment. The definition of money as well as the temporal dimension of its 'circulation' are thus entirely different in the two analyses. But what about the relationship between money and money income? Let us conclude the chapter by briefly analysing this problem.

Money and money income

The distinction between money as a numerical form and money income – very familiar to classical economists – may sound strange to modern economists, who do not even seem aware of its existence in the first place. Is it not true, in fact, that every time a payment is carried out by banks it amounts to the simple transfer of a sum of money income? If we leave aside transaction costs, it seems obvious that a payment of 100 money units involves a total expenditure of 100 units of money income. For what reason should there be another intermediation (purely monetary) mixed up with the transfer of 100 units of money income from the payer to the payee? Following double-entry book-keeping, banks transfer the sums deposited with them from one client account to another. Is that not enough to allow us to conclude that money income is the only reality here and that, insofar as it is the object of a deposit, it is a stock? Actually, while no one disputes the fact that money income is a stock, it can be argued that the distinction between the deposit and its object is not that between the banks's accounting books and the money income that gets recorded in these banks. *Money income is itself the deposit, not the object of the deposit.* Indeed, the object of the bank deposit (that is, of the money income that makes it up) is that part of current output that it 'contains', as it were. Since money income is a stock whose value is positive and since banks cannot create it *ex nihilo*, it is not surprising to find that money income owes its positive value to its real content: the output it is made to 'contain' through the payment of production. Hence, it would be a mistake to claim that income is a stock of money issued by banks (or the monetary authorities), and which defines the money supply.

As we have already seen, money as such is an acknowledgement of debt issued by banks and whose object is a payment that banks agree to make on behalf of their clients. No pre-existing bank deposit is required for the emission of money to occur. Yet, it is obvious that if no bank deposits were involved the payment would have no real content, and would therefore be entirely meaningless. The apparent contradiction between these two statements can be avoided by showing that it is the payment initially carried out by banks that generates the positive bank deposit required for the transaction to be effective. This is indeed what happens when, through the payment of wages, output is associated to money. A bank can pay an agent, C, on behalf of another agent, A, only if the object of the payment is deposited with it. Now, when wages are paid out to income earners (IE) on behalf of firms (F), output is deposited on the assets side of the bank – it is the object of F's debt to the bank – and defines simultaneously the object of *IE*'s credit on the bank. Through the payment of wages output is transformed into a positive amount of money income, of which it is the real object or 'content'. Money income is therefore the result of an *absolute exchange* through which physical output is converted or changed into a sum of money deposited with the banks. Since money proper is a simple means of payment with no positive value whatsoever, it can never be the object of an exchange. This means that money can never enter a relative exchange with output. Money cannot be exchanged for goods, nor goods for money, since in no circumstances can money be considered as the *counterpart* of output. It is thus confirmed that the only conceivable exchange between money and output is an absolute exchange, money income being nothing other than the output itself (in the form of money), and not its counterpart.

Going back to the distinction between money as such and money income, we can say that nominal or vehicular money is a 'form' whose creation is necessary if we are to give physical output a numerical expression. It is because banks are made to issue this numerical form that they perform a monetary intermediation. Without it, physical output would simply be a heap of heterogeneous objects. Thanks to banks' monetary intermediation, physical output is made homogeneous and becomes the object of a deposit. The reason why this all-important intermediation goes unnoticed is because it is always associated with a financial intermediation. Since every payment relates to an income – which is either created, destroyed, or transferred in the operation – we are easily led to forget that it is monetary intermediation itself that allows the transaction to occur in the first place. Our microeconomic perception of economic reality encourages us to think that it is enough to own a positive income to finance a payment. Yet, we should always keep in mind that no money income could ever exist if banks did not give a numerical form to physical output, and that every payment requires both a financial *and* a monetary intermediation.

As far as the supply of and demand for money is concerned, we have to analyse whether or not a functional relationship between them may exist. Let us start with nominal or vehicular money. Any claim that the higher the income actually produced, the higher the amount of nominal (arithmo-morphic) money required to express it, would be merely tautological. Moreover, being created and destroyed at the very moment a payment is carried out, money proper is never submitted to an interactive adjustment between demand and supply. In fact, since vehicular or nominal money is not a stock, there is no point in talking about its supply and its demand (unless the demand for money is conceived of as a request for payments to be carried out and the money 'supplied' as the capacity of banks to satisfy this request). But what about money income?

This time we are confronted with a stock, a bank deposit of a given positive amount that cannot be modified at will and at zero cost. Yet, it must also be remembered that the available money income is not the making of banks, not even of central banks. A mere double-entry in the central bank's book-keeping is obviously not enough to create a positive amount of riches in the form of national money income. Production is what is needed to give a real content to money creation. This means that the supply of money income is determined by production or, more precisely, by the monetization of production. Money income is thus the result of a payment by which current output is given its numerical form. But if the supply of 'real' money is defined by the amount of income generated by production, would there be any sense in considering the money supply as a function of national income? Income is the 'real' money supply and its level is a function of production only in the very strict sense that output is precisely defined by the amount of income of which it is the real 'content'. Hence, the supply of money income is determined by the amount of bank deposits formed at the very instant when production is given its numerical form, that is, through the payment of its costs. For every given period the amount of the 'real' money supply is thus perfectly determined by the amount of bank deposits. Can there be an excess demand, positive or negative, for money income? Apparently yes, if one were to consider only the demand explicitly exerted by consumers. On further reflection, however, things do not work out this way. Saved income, in fact, is also subject to a necessary demand since, according to double-entry book-keeping, the entire amount deposited with banks (that is, entered on the liabilities side of their balance sheets) is lent out by them (that is, it is balanced by an equivalent entry on their assets side). What is not demanded by consumers is lent to firms, which need it to finance their debt to banks. On the whole, the amount of money income is demanded in its totality and no adjustment occurs or is needed between the supply of and demand for money income.

The lack of any *functional* relationship between the supply of and demand for money income has a devastating consequence on Hicks's interpretation of Keynes's *General Theory*. From what we have just seen it becomes immediately obvious that no *LM* curve can logically be drawn with respect to bank money. Hicks's mistake was to believe that money could be created by banks already endowed with a positive value. It must be admitted, however, that Keynes himself was not entirely aware of all the consequences of his monetary theory of production. In particular, his analysis of what he called the liquidity preference confuses more than enlightens, and resembles more of a baffling attempt to show that the rate of interest is not determined by the supply of and demand for loanable funds than to a coherent insight on monetary theory. Were banknotes and coins to be entirely done away with, the liquidity preference would no longer play any role, yet the system would remain substantially unchanged and work just as well as before. Keynes's own fundamental contribution is to be found elsewhere. His basic identity between total income (Y) and total demand $(C + I)$, for example, is clear evidence for the necessary equality between the supply of and demand for money income. As soon as it is realized that money as such is issued by banks as a valueless numerical form and that it is through its association with current output that it is transformed into income, Keynes's analysis acquires its real significance. Production, which from a physical point of view is a time-consuming process of transformation, becomes a proper subject of economic inquiry only once it is expressed in money terms. Income is thus formed at the very moment the macroeconomic costs of production are paid for through an absolute exchange. While the payment of the microeconomic costs of production requires the expenditure of a positive income, wages (the only macroeconomic costs of production) are paid out of a purely nominal sum of money. This is so because of the very nature of economic production. Being an instantaneous event through which physical output is given a monetary form, production is the source of the macroeconomic income resulting from the absolute exchange between money and output. Far from requiring the expenditure of a positive income, the payment of the macroeconomic costs of production allows its very formation. In fact, the macroeconomic costs of production concern the economy as a whole, so that their payment cannot imply a transfer of income between economic agents, but requires a particular kind of transaction. Through the payment of the macroeconomic costs of production the economy pays itself, which explains why the payment of wages is an absolute exchange giving rise to a positive, macroeconomic income. Human labour alone is the source of value, that is, of a new utility, neoclassically put, resulting from the creative power of the human mind and from the capacity of (human) labour to give a new form to matter and energy. By giving a monetary form to output, production allows the physical outcome of human labour to acquire a numerical expression, transforming it into an object of economic inquiry.

Confirmed by the way banks actually enter the payment of wages in their books, this analysis may be traced back to Keynes's concept of wage units as well as to some of the intuitions to be found in Smith, Ricardo, and Marx. Taken to its extreme consequences it shows that from a monetary viewpoint economics is a true, autonomous science. This is not to deny, of course, that economics is also a social science. Yet, it is only when money enters the picture that economics acquires its proper status. *What makes economics such a difficult science to master is precisely the fact that it is simultaneously concerned with an immaterial form and its physical counterpart. In order to understand the specifically economic aspect of production, it is necessary to go beyond its physical characteristics.* Only then is it possible to accept the idea that, economically speaking, production is an *instantaneous* process by which current output is expressed in numerical form and becomes thus the object of the bank deposits formed through the payment of wages. As noticed by Keynes, national income is the definition of national output and, therefore, of total supply. For any given period, production is determined at the very moment wages are paid. At the same instant the money income thus formed is available as a bank deposit. Then, banks being led by double-entry book-keeping to lend their deposits, money income is also necessarily subject to an equivalent demand as soon as it is formed. It thus follows that, instead of being represented by a curve, *LM* is reduced to a *massless point* for any level of produced income.

Thanks to what we have found about the nature of *IS* (see Chapter 4) and *LM*, it is now easy to see that Hicks's diagram has nothing to do with the actual working of a monetary economy. Once *IS* and *LM* are properly understood, it becomes evident that they cannot be represented by two intersecting curves. Neither *IS* nor *LM* is a function of the sort claimed by Hicks. Once the production of a given period has actually taken place, *LM* may be represented by a single point, while *IS* is still numerically undetermined. At the moment income is finally spent, *LM* is again nothing more than a single point, and so is *IS*, the amount of macroeconomic saving being fully determined and necessarily equal to investment. In no circumstances is it possible, therefore, to support the neoclassical and Keynesian claim that the equilibrium level of income is specified, together with the equilibrium level of interest rates, by the *intersection* of *IS* with *LM*.

6 Production and consumption as macroeconomic events

The analysis of production: some conceptual considerations

As clearly summarized by Scazzieri, 'the extension of the analytical core of Walrasian general equilibrium from exchange to production, already attempted by Walras himself, led a number of economists to outline a complete reduction of production theory to exchange theory' (Scazzieri 1993: 7). Thus, production was conceived of as a time-consuming process of transformation subjected to the same mechanism governing relative exchange, 'no feature of production activity [being] associated with conceptual issues different from those dealt with in exchange theory' (ibid.: 7). As noted by Scazzieri, production has mostly been described 'as a combination of transformation stages that follow one another in time' (ibid.: 27), or 'as the combination of the productive factors in use at any given time' (ibid.: 27). The first representation was that proposed by Austrian and neo-Austrian theorists, while the latter was at the origin of a mathematical formalization that led to the neoclassical version of the production functions. In modern economics, these two approaches have been combined with Leontief's input–output analysis in an attempt to overcome the shortcomings related to the linear conception of production developed by Austrian economists and the general equilibrium approach adopted by neoclassical theorists.

As was repeatedly pointed out during the Cambridge controversy on capital, neoclassical and Austrian theories of production have a problem in explaining how capital may simultaneously be a final output and a factor of production, or how capital may be determined independently of income distribution and the rate of interest. In fact, the sequential Austrian models and the neoclassical general equilibrium models differ on some important points. In particular, while neoclassical models rely on production functions that are meant to establish a functional relationship between factors of production (traditionally land, labour and capital) and final output, Austrian models emphasize the role of time (production period) and draw a clear-cut distinction between factors and means of production (that is, between non-produced and produced factors of production). Thus, whereas in general equilibrium analysis final goods and productive services enter on a par the same system of simultaneous equations, in the Austrian version of neoclassical economics a distinction is made between means of production of different order. (Böhm-Bawerk goes as far as to claim that the means of production of the highest order are produced by labour alone.)

Even though the linearity implicit in the Austrian theory of production partially contrasts with the simultaneity of the Walrasian models of GEA, these two approaches have traditionally been classified as belonging in the same broad family since they are opposed to the circular vision of production shared by Quesnay, Sraffa, Pasinetti and a number of economists emphasizing the technical aspect of production. It is within this latter theoretical framework that Leontief's input–output analysis found another field of application.

Sraffa's endeavour to determine prices through a system of simultaneous equations relating physical outputs to physical inputs is arguably the most elaborated and influential example of the circular analysis of production. Unfortunately the solution proposed by Sraffa is logically flawed. The equations representing what he calls a 'self-replacing state' that is made up of heterogeneous physical goods are logically meaningless unless it is assumed that wheat, iron and pigs (Sraffa's inputs and outputs) are always exchanged according to their technical coefficients of production. 'There is a unique set of exchange-values which if adopted by the market restores the original distribution of the products and makes it possible for the process to be repeated; such values spring directly from the methods of production' (Sraffa 1960: 3). This may either mean that exchange values are directly determined by the methods of production or that they are the specifications of the self-replacing state. In both cases, Sraffa's 'exchange values' are determined independently of exchange. If we exclude – as done by Sraffa – the metaphysical hypothesis that inputs and outputs are one and the same object under different guises, we may reach the conclusion that in Sraffa's model prices are predetermined. Instead of being determined through exchange, prices are imposed to it by the technical relationships implicit in the definition of the self-replacing state.

The previous result should not come as a surprise to those economists well acquainted with Walras's general equilibrium analysis. Sraffa's theory is in fact closely related to Walras's. Both authors attempted to derive prices from exchange, they both formalized their models by using a system of independent equations that should admit of a simultaneous solution, and they both were confronted with the heterogeneity problem. Even their solution is similar. Walras, for example, in the case of a two-agents, two-goods model assumed that the equivalence between supply of *a* and demand for *b* holds good before exchange actually takes place. Sraffa assumed the technical relationships between wheat, iron and pigs to be known before these goods are exchanged by their producers. Finally, the reason for their failure to provide a logical theory of (relative) price determination is also the same. Both Walras and Sraffa were in fact the victims of a *petitio principii*, since they assumed as given a relationship that, on the contrary, should have been derived from their system of independent equations. Thus, Walras's Law plays the same role in GEA as does Sraffa's self-replacing state in *Production of Commodities by Means of Commodities*.

That Walras and Sraffa's conceptions of production were different is a fact. Yet, both their analyses aim at determining market prices rather than physical coefficients. Walras considered the economic system as a set of markets on which prices of goods and productive services are simultaneously determined through exchange. Sraffa started his analysis from production and looked for the prices at which goods (entering the system as inputs and as outputs) would have to be exchanged to allow for the system to be in a self-replacing state or to admit of a surplus compatible with a uniform rate of profit. Even if it is true that Sraffa eventually identified prices with the physical coefficients determined by the methods of production, it can hardly be denied that he worked out his theory in order to provide a valid alternative to Walras's GEA. Like Walras, Sraffa was looking for a theory of price determination, perfectly aware that, without such a theory, real goods would remain incommensurable. Like his predecessor, Sraffa was also convinced that prices may be determined simultaneously with their unit of account. Thus, neither Walras nor Sraffa realized that (relative) exchange cannot determine a unique standard of value, and cannot therefore solve the heterogeneity problem. All this leads us to the conclusion that both Walras and Sraffa mark the (neoclassical) endeavour to explain production *via* the determination of prices through the simultaneous solution of a system of equations derived from exchange (between firms and consumers or between firms).

Emphasizing the role played by the technical methods of production and by the social division of labour, some economists influenced by the work of Leontief, Sraffa and Pasinetti, have developed a structural approach to production. For example, Scazzieri privileges an analysis of production conceived of as a 'network of tasks' or as a 'sequence of fabrication stages'. 'The distinction between technical subdivision of a job and social division of labour suggests the possibility of considering the production process as a network of operations performed in a sequence to be determined (tasks), quite independently of the agents (workers or machines) who are performing such operations, and also independently of the flows of materials in process and finished products' (Scazzieri 1993: 13). In short, Scazzieri advocates a task-process approach to production analysis in which production is 'characterized by a dual sequential structure: the *subjective* structure connected with the role of initial and intermediate decisions in arranging tasks over time, and the *objective* structure reflecting the physical linkages between fabrication stages' (ibid.: 16). It is easy to see that Scazzieri's analysis of production is essentially centred on the physical process of transformation and on the relationship between a set of abstract task-processes and the factors and productive structures that are meant to execute these tasks.

Now, Scazzieri's attempt suffers from the logical impossibility of establishing an equivalence between goods entering a physical (technological) relationship. In fact, two physically heterogeneous goods do not become homogeneous only because they are exchanged for one another. 'Homogeneity is a common measure. To say that two commodities are homogeneous means therefore that they belong to the same "space of measure"'(Cencini and Schmitt 1976: 116, our translation). The exchange of iron and wheat, for example, does not make iron equivalent to wheat. After having being exchanged, the two goods remain as distinct as they were before exchange. The reason for the persistence of the heterogeneity of wheat and iron is that their (relative) exchange cannot determine a unique standard. If it is true that, being exchanged one against the other, iron is the standard of wheat, it is also obviously true that this same exchange defines wheat as the standard of iron. Exchange being a reciprocal transaction, '*the transformation of iron into the standard of wheat defines identically the transformation of wheat into the standard of iron. It is therefore formally impossible to end up with a unique standard*' (ibid.: 119, our translation). Whether exchange is said to take place on the market for real goods and services (Walras) or between firms (Sraffa, Scazzieri), it never establishes the equivalence of its two terms, which therefore remain heterogeneous.

The shortcomings of a purely physical conception of production are well known and range from the heterogeneity of inputs and outputs to the impossibility of determining any net product (see Cencini 2001: 95–9). A way out of this impasse was already sketched by the Classics and then carried forward by Keynes in his effort to build a monetary theory of production. Two factors are of a particular significance here: human labour and money. According to neoclassical economics as well as in conventional input–output analysis, labour is essentially on a par with the other factors of production. Nobody denies the centrality of human labour, of course, yet mainstream economists never go as far as to recognize that labour has a different conceptual status with respect to other factors. This explains why they were led to conceive of production as a functional relationship of which labour is nothing more than one element among others. Moreover, this explains also why production has mainly been the object of microeconomic analysis. If labour is only one among other factors of production, an input not fundamentally different from the rest, production itself is perceived as a mere process of transformation. Labour participates in this process together with capital goods (produced means of production) and what is still called 'land' (raw materials, energy, natural resources). Firms cover the cost of these factors. Wages are therefore only one of the firms' costs of production and there seems to be no reason to consider this cost having essentially a different status from the others. But then no differentiation is possible between the social (macroeconomic) and the microeconomic costs of production. Both from an aggregate and from each single firm's point of view, production remains a microeconomic process of transformation whose costs derive from the different inputs entering the process. Keynes, taking over from the Classics the idea that human labour is the sole factor of production, shifted the emphasis from a micro to a macroeconomic analysis of production. In his attempt to analyse production as an economic process, Keynes was obviously not denying that firms have to cover a great variety of costs. His claim that labour alone is at the origin of production is not at odds with the fact that, from a physical viewpoint, production remains a process of transformation involving a great number of inputs and requiring labour to be backed by capital equipment and natural resources. 'It is preferable to regard labour, including, of course, the personal services of the entrepreneur and his assistants, as the sole factor of production, operating in a given environment of technique, natural resources, capital equipment and effective demand' (Keynes 1973c: 454).

The choice of labour as the sole factor of production cannot be grounded on technical factors. The original contribution of labour is not physical. This is why the Classics did not succeed in working out an entirely satisfactory macroeconomic analysis. In Smith's, Ricardo's, and Marx's theories labour is indeed the unique source of value, yet value is still thought of as a 'substance' and, as such, it cannot account for the peculiar, economic nature of produced output. Given that, it is to Walras that we owe the discovery of the dimensionless conception of value. '[A]ll valuable and exchangeable things, to the exclusion of everything else, are useful and at the same time limited in quantity' (Walras 1984: 83). According to Walras, produced goods and services are valuable because they are apt to satisfy needs and wants of the population and not because of some 'substantial' quality incorporated into them. With Walras, value becomes a simple relationship between (exchanged) real goods expressing the utility of currently produced output. What is still lacking in Walras's analysis, however, is (1) the awareness that it is thanks to human labour alone that matter and energy are given a new utility form, and (2) the capacity to express value numerically. This is clearly shown by Walras's essentially microeconomic approach to production and by his attempt to determine real (as opposed to monetary) prices. Keynes's great merit is to have provided a theory in which the dimensionless nature of value is perfectly consistent with the particular status of labour and with the numerical specification of economic output.

The second, decisive element of Keynes's contribution is precisely his choice to measure output in wage units and to use bank money as a unit of account. Henceforth, production is seen as an economic process resulting from labour alone and giving rise to an economic output defined in wage units. From an economic point of view, output is a new utility form, which the human mind conceives of and that is imposed on matter and energy through a process of physical transformation implemented by human labour aided by capital equipment and resources. Keynes's macroeconomic conception of production is thus based on his insight that labour is the only source of value and that money wages are the only possible standard for a value that is necessarily dimensionless.

From the moment economic production is conceived of as the proceedings through which current output becomes identified with a sum of money wages, the problem of whether or not production can generate a surplus finally finds a solution. Logically impossible if production is considered solely from a purely physical viewpoint – once matter and energy are fully taken into account, Lavoisier and Einstein's principles do not allow for physical output to be greater than physical inputs – the surplus covers the totality of current output if production is analysed as a monetized economic event. The sum of wages that defines current output is in fact a new, net income literally created by production. A monetary theory of production is a theory in which production is uniquely specified in money terms. *In Keynes's analysis, this means that output is indistinguishable from the sum of money paid out to wage-earners and is thus a net surplus in its entirety.* The contrast between Keynes's and the neoclassical analysis of production could not be greater. What is conceived of as a microeconomic process of transformation by mainstream economists is seen by Keynes as a macroeconomic event, as an act of creation whose result concerns the economy taken as a whole.

The quantum theoretical approach to monetary economics confirms Keynes's analysis. Let us investigate it in some detail.

The macroeconomic analysis of production

Let us start from the distinction between money and income. As we already know, money, an asset–liability of the bank, is a flow, while income is a bank deposit, a stock. Thus, whereas money is issued (at near to zero costs) as a numerical form of no intrinsic value, income defines a positive value and therefore cannot result from a creation *ex nihilo*. Money corresponds to the capacity of banks to carry out payments on behalf of their clients. Hence, banks create money each time their clients ask them to act as monetary intermediaries on the labour, commodity, or financial markets. What banks obviously cannot do is to create both the means (money) and the object (income) of payment. It is true, of course, that banks act also as financial intermediaries for their clients. But it should also be patent that the object of these financial intermediations cannot be the result of an act of faith or of a miraculous, spontaneous generation. In fact, banks lend to some of their clients what has been deposited by other clients. What has to be determined, therefore, is where the deposits come from. The answer that immediately suggests itself is production. But what does it mean to claim that production generates income?

A first, obvious remark is that income is not an outcome of the process of physical transformation through which matter and energy are given a new form. Furthermore, income is also not the expression of a metaphysical economic 'essence' of real goods. Thus, since production is the source of both current output and of current income, and since income is not added on to produced output (an outcome already arrived at by Adam Smith), income and output must necessarily be the two sides of one and the same event. In other words, current production engenders simultaneously current output and its monetary alter ego: income. To claim that current income corresponds to or is made equivalent to current output is not correct, since, literally interpreted, this would mean that production gives rise to two different and separate entities: current output and a monetary counterpart that are joined to form a total product whose real and monetary sides should add up doubling the value of current output. What is happening instead is entirely different: output and income are the result of one and the same process, the dual sides of the same coin.

Let us be as clear as possible. To state that income is identical to real output amounts to recognizing that income *is* real output. This would obviously not be the case if money was not already associated with production. Income originates therefore from this association of money with produced output. Hence, income defines the unification of money (as a numerical form) with its real content, and, alternatively, of produced output with its monetary form. Issued by banks as an asset–liability, money transforms into income as soon as the output of a given production becomes its intentional object.

What is the intentional object of nominal (numerical) money? The answer is straightforward, given that money is simply a spontaneous acknowledgement of debt of the bank that issues it. The object of nominal money is money itself. This is why there is no logical limitation to money creation. Banks can easily supply any amount of nominal money because (1) the cost of issuing the money is almost zero, and (2) whatever the amount created, the principles of double-entry book-keeping are such that money's reflexivity entails its instantaneous return back to its source. As already observed, banks cannot create a positive amount of income. The object of income is output, not nominal money, and output cannot be created by banks (except when banks are themselves the producers of services, in which case they must be considered as firms). Yet, as output is transformed into a positive amount of income when it is given its monetary form, banks are the intermediaries through which output and money enter what Schmitt calls an absolute exchange. Indeed, economic production is a case of absolute exchange because it does not account for an exchange between two distinct objects (one taking the place of the other and vice versa), but is rather synonymous with a transaction through which output is *changed* into a sum of money income. The problem is then one of explaining via what operation output is made into the intentional object of a bank deposit.

Once again the answer is well known by monetary economists favouring double-entry book-keeping. When a bank carries out a payment in favour of a firm, the firm's output becomes the object of its debt to the bank. The operation we are looking for is thus the payment of the costs of production carried out by banks on behalf of firms. Yet, this does not entirely address our problem. It remains to determine, in fact, whether the payment concerns the micro or the macroeconomic costs of production. Firms are confronted with a whole series of costs. Does the payment of any of these costs transform firms' physical output into the object of a bank deposit? If we assumed as an axiom that labour is the sole macroeconomic factor of production, we could immediately infer that the payment of wages is the only payment achieving this result. Yet, this result would amount to a *petitio principii*, since it was assumed to hold good from the outset. Instead, the fact that labour alone is a macroeconomic factor of production must be explained, not axiomatically posited. This can be done by showing that the payment of wages differs substantially from the payment of any other cost of production. The crucial point here is that output becomes the intentional object of a bank deposit only in a monetary economy of production. As we know, money is the means by which payments are carried out. Thus, banks pay the costs of production through an instantaneous flow. This means that money itself is never the object of the payment. Double-entry book-keeping implies, in fact, the simultaneous credit and debit of each agent entering a monetary payment.

Let us represent in Table 6.1 the payment of a cost of production.

In the same instant, firm *F* and its economic correspondent, *C*, are credited and debited by the bank, *B*, with a sum *x* of money, which flows back to its source of emission. As a result of this monetary flow, *F* is indebted to the bank, and *C* is the owner of a positive bank deposit. Given the nature of bank money, it should be clear that *B*'s payment on behalf of *F* cannot be made on the profit of capital or land, for neither of these microeconomic factors of production can be debited and credited. The transaction through which a positive income is formed can only be referred to human labour since this is the only 'factor' that may be

Table 6.1 The payment of a cost of production

	Bank		
Liabilities		*Assets*	
Agent *C*	*x*	Firm *F*	*x*

credited and debited in terms of a purely nominal money. Through the payment of wages, production is therefore identified with a creation of income, owned by workers, deposited with the banking system, and defining the physical output, object of the firms' debt to the banks.

Another argument in favour of the particular status of human labour is derived from the simple observation that the payment of produced means of production or of any other real good (raw materials, energy, natural resources) entering the production process requires the expenditure of a positive income. Capital goods must be purchased, and their purchase implies the expenditure (advanced or not) of an income whose origin would remain mysterious if human labour were not clearly distinguished from the other 'factors of production'. Capital and land must be purchased by using an income that can obviously not be derived from their purchase. The payment of wages, on the contrary, gives rise to an income allowing for the transformation of physical output into the real object of an actual bank deposit. As we have already seen in Chapter 5, this is so because the macroeconomic costs of production are not paid by some economic agent to the advantage of others. Wages are the costs of production of the economy taken as a whole, and their payment is an absolute exchange transforming physical output into a sum of money income. In other words, it is workers who pay themselves through the intermediation of banks and firms, and thus convert or 'change' the physical outcome of labour into a sum of money wages.

The idea behind the macroeconomic analysis of production is therefore phenomenological: wages are the monetary definition or description of output. The transformation of physical output into a sum of money income is thus nothing but the transformation of real production into a monetary production. Banks and firms are the intermediaries through which workers change their product into a sum of money income. This is what the absolute exchange between money and output is all about. Through the payment of wages, (a flow), production – which is also a flow – is transformed into a creation of money income. The association between output and money (conceived of as a purely numerical form) takes place through this transformation of the real flow of production into a monetary creation, that is, through the monetization of production.

In its emission, money is instantaneously created and destroyed for each of the three poles implied by the payment of wages: bank, firm, and workers. Now, an instant is just what is required for money to flow to and fro and transform current output into the object of a bank deposit. The instantaneity of production derives therefore from its monetary nature. Following Schmitt's quantum theoretical analysis, we can further observe that production *quantizes* time. The obvious fact that a physical process of production is time-consuming while from an economic point of view production is an instantaneous event is enough to posit that the payment of wages be referred to a finite period of time. Now, if production is a flow it must necessarily be a quantum flow, since if a finite period of time is covered instantaneously this can only mean that it is emitted as an indivisible span of time: a quantum of time. 'This means that production is not a flow following the direction of time but, on the contrary, a flow *defined in a circle*, from t to t_n and simultaneously from t_n to t. This is the exact definition of production as a quantum; it quantizes the period of time $(t_n–t)$ since, instead of being a unidirectional flow it is a "flux–reflux"' (Schmitt 1984a: 443–4, our translation).

The macroeconomic definition of production as a sum of money wages as well as the identification of production with an instantaneous flow quantizing time may come as a surprise to the reader accustomed to general equilibrium analysis. Actually, what is really surprising is that, after Keynes, economists can still endeavour to explain production in real terms. The fact that production is a monetary phenomenon is beyond dispute. The meaning of Keynes's message is therefore not subject to controversy: it relies on the nature of bank money and of its association with real output. Keynes's concept of wage units finds its full expression when production is analysed as an absolute exchange between money and physical output. From the moment the result of production is no longer seen as a physical object but as the unity of physical output with its (numerical) monetary form (as 'output-in-the-money'), it becomes clear that *the whole output is a net product.* Current income is indeed an entirely novel economic product resulting from the integration of physical output into its monetary form. This also shows that, *in economics, production is an instantaneous event concerning the system taken as a whole, independently of the number of economic agents involved.* The production by every single agent is therefore a macroeconomic event in that it increases not only the income of each such single producer, but also the income of the entire system. At the moment wages are paid to any individual economic agent, a new income is created that defines his economic output as well as a component part of society's total product. Each singular 'monetized' output is therefore a *net* product, since the positive formation of the new income – resulting precisely from the association between money and output – is not counterbalanced by any negative formation of income. The (instantaneous) result of economic production is entirely new and takes the form of a macroeconomic income. Thus, the macroeconomic nature of every single instance of production follows immediately from the fact that each single payment of wages increases the amount of national income currently formed. It is thus clear that both the concept of 'net output' and of 'macroeconomic event' would not be possible if production were considered only as a physical process and if bank money were not identified with a dimensionless entity (a purely numerical form). The nature of modern bank money leads us forcefully to the conclusion that, economically speaking, production is an instantaneous event through which output is given a monetary form and is thus 'emitted' as an indivisible whole.

The modern conception of bank money makes it possible to vindicate the Classics' intuition about production being the creation of a value originated by human labour. We abandon any substantial conception of value and identify production with an intentional act connecting numerical money and physical output. The new analysis of production is further elaborated in Schmitt's description of the complementary nature, namely both wave-like and particle-like, of production. As rigorously explained by the French economist in his 1984 book on money and capital accumulation, the 'output-in-the-money' captures the corpuscular aspect of production, while the wave-like aspect pertains to the spread of a finite period of time happening the moment productive services are paid for. This leads Schmitt to the new definition of economic output as a quantum of time, and of production as an emission, understood as an instantaneous event quantizing time.

Given the novelty and the importance of the argument, let us represent the production period corresponding to the physical process of transformation by the interval t_0–t_1 along the abscissa of time, and economic production by a single point corresponding to the instant, t^*, when output is issued in its monetary form (Figure 6.1). t^* can be any instant, within or outside the interval t_0–t_1. Independently of whether they are paid in advance, during or after the period of physical transformation, wages refer to the interval t_0–t_1, which is thus covered by a 'wave' that quantizes it. At t^* the whole period of time, t_0–t_1, during which matter and energy are physically transformed is covered in both directions, from t_1 to t_0 and from t_0 to t_1: 'at instant [t^*] production is a "wave", a movement in time, going from t_n [t_1] to t_0 and identically from t_0 to t_n [t_1]' (Schmitt 1984a: 58, our translation). At the very moment a money income takes the place of physical output (with which it enters an absolute exchange), a period of

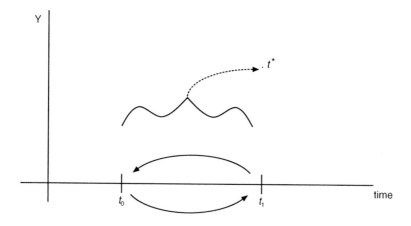

Figure 6.1 The quantization of time.

time (the finite and indivisible interval $t_0–t_1$) is thus issued as a quantum. Production is therefore an instantaneous (and therefore time-dimension-less) event whose result is a sum of money income referring to the finite period of time during which workers transform matter and energy in order to give it a new utility form. Instantaneous event that has no proper time dimension, production is nevertheless referred to a quantum of time. It is this finite and indivisible period of time that defines the peculiar 'dimension' of wages and produced output. Production is claimed to 'quantize time; that is, *to capture instantaneously a slice of continuous time*: the first result of production is therefore the definition of a quantum of time. Output is not deposited in time; it *is* time' (ibid.: 54, our translation).

Highly abstract and original, Schmitt's quantum analysis is nonetheless the logical consequence of a monetary macroeconomic conception of production originating in the work of Keynes. A truly macroeconomic analysis of production is thus in sharp contrast with the mainstream, microeconomic approach in which production is conceived of as a process of physical transformation. As clearly perceived by Keynes, these two approaches may co-exist only if one is logically subordinated to the other. Now, the priority of macro over microeconomics derives directly from the nature of money and from the need to integrate money with the real world. The logical indeterminacy of relative prices (Schmitt 1966, 1996a; Cencini 1982; Schmitt and De Gottardi 2003) is the best proof that the neoclassical microeconomic approach fails to give physical output a numerical form and therefore leaves production totally unexplained as an economic phenomenon. If goods cannot be expressed numerically (that is, monetarily), they remain heterogeneous, and value (or prices) can no longer be accounted for: production can only be described from a physical point of view and its economic analysis is beyond reach of scientific speculation. The need for a monetary, macroeconomic approach is directly motivated by the failure of the neoclassical attempt to determine relative prices. If economics is to become a true and original science, it has to put money at its centre. Once this is done, and once the nature of money is properly understood, production can finally be apprehended as an economic event. The novel conception of quantum time follows then as a cogent and relevant theoretical explanation.

The macro versus the microeconomic analysis of consumption

Economists' analyses of production and consumption span from the uni-directional conception of the neoclassical school to the circular vision of Sraffa and his followers. Whether the economic process is viewed as a one-way avenue leading from factors of production to produced output, or treated as a circular process in which commodities are produced by means of commodities, a correlation is supposed to exist between inputs and outputs as well as between present and future outputs. Since today's outputs will become the inputs of tomorrow, the idea of productive consumption derives quite naturally from observing this physical process of production and consumption. If the two processes are analysed from a physical–physiological perspective, consumption appears not only as the other face of production, but also as the necessary step leading to new production. In this perspective, consumption of foodstuff by workers is seen as the reproduction of workers' labour potentiality: capital goods too are consumed in the production of new final goods, and so are raw materials and natural resources. Consumption, in short, is seen as the goal of production and vice versa.

A decisive progress towards an economic analysis of consumption was made by Keynes, who related consumption to the final expenditure of income. Given this theoretical setting, we must now choose between two different and mutually exclusive interpretations of Keynes's analysis. According to the interpretation shared by Keynesian, new Keynesian and most post-Keynesian economists, consumption is a function of income and the interest rate, and the complement of investment in the definition of aggregate demand. Thus defined, consumption becomes the object of investigation of a series of models trying to pattern the behaviour of consumers with respect to changes in their disposable income affecting different periods of their life-cycle. The way is thus opened to the microeconomic analysis of consumption and to the building of the microeconomic foundations of macroeconomics. On the contrary, according to the alternative interpretation of Keynes's theory we are advocating in this book, consumption relates to the final purchase of consumption goods and is therefore an exemplification of Keynes's logical identity between total supply and total demand. In this theoretical framework, consumption is identified with the final *destruction* of the income created by the production of consumption goods. Now the analysis is macroeconomic right from the outset, consumption being determined independently of economic agents' behaviour.

Let us spend a few more words about these two interpretations.

The Keynesian idea that consumption is a function of income goes back to Keynes's own notion of the marginal propensity to consume. In this sense, it has to be admitted that Keynes himself contributed to the microeconomic interpretations of his theory. It is clear, in fact, that as soon as it is accepted that the part of income which is spent for the purchase of consumption goods is determined by the propensity to consume and that the part which is spent for the purchase of investment goods is determined by firms' inducement to invest, the presumed equality between Y and $C + I$ is perceived as a condition of equilibrium rather than as a logical identity. Economic agents' behaviour thus remains a central element of the theory whose objective now becomes to determine the level of income allowing for total demand to equate total supply. What has not yet been completely understood by Keynesian theorists is that by accepting the notion of consumption function and of equilibrium they are endorsing the point of view of equilibrium analysis. Keynesian income analysis and neoclassical GEA become therefore two alternatives within the same broad theoretical framework. Now, the price Keynesian economists have to pay for their taking up the neoclassical challenge is to slide down the slippery slopes of equilibrium analysis. By foregoing Keynes's identities, they lose, in fact, the opportunity to develop a macroeconomic analysis of production and consumption. Instead they proceed to advocate one of the most misguided albeit ingenuous theories in the history of economic thought: the theory of the multiplier.

Since this deceiving theory has already been rigorously criticized (Schmitt 1972; Cencini 1984), let us limit our analysis to a few observations. First of all it has to be noted that the idea of the multiplier rests on the assumptions that (1) consumption is an expenditure through which income is *reproduced*, and that (2) the income saved is no longer available in the system and cannot therefore finance any expenditure. The first assumption is clearly at odds with Keynes's claim that income is the result of production and not of consumption. The second assumption openly contrasts with the fact that income is a bank deposit, that is, with the fact that – it is the very logic of double-entry book-keeping which requires it – that part of income which is saved remains entirely available within the banking system and is thus necessarily lent to the economy. This leads straight to our first inference: if it were true that income is reproduced through its expenditure, the multiplier would be an asymptotic process since, through lending, banks would allow for the totality of income to be spent. Instead of decreasing through time, the series of incomes generated from the expenditure of the initial (separately given) income will go on for ever. The choices facing the theoretician are the following: either (1) he sticks to the initial assumption that expenditures reproduce income and accepts the idea of an infinite multiplier, or (2) he abandons the 'earning-through-spending' theory of income and maintains that the final expenditure of income leads to its destruction, which obviously amounts to saying that there is no multiplier effect. Keynesian economists, alas, are not aware of the correct terms of the problem, of course. In fact, they still believe the multiplier process to be a decreasing process over time. What they do not understand is that the double-entry book-keeping nature of bank money does not allow to identify saving with hoarding. Were they able to see that the entire amount of income saved takes necessarily the form of a bank deposit, they would immediately realize that saving does not decrease expenditures in the least. Indeed, since they are involved as monetary and financial intermediaries in every transaction, banks cannot avoid lending the totality of the sum deposited with them. If the whole banking system is taken into account (central bank included), it can be easily verified, in fact, that this logical implication of double-entry book-keeping applies irrespective of the rules imposed to the banks' activity. Thus, if Keynesian economists were not lacking a clear understanding of the logical laws governing a monetary economy, they could surmise that the theory of the multiplier is based on a totally absurd assumption. How can it be possibly maintained that the expenditure of a positive income gives rise to another, equivalent income? Is it not rather the case that consumption and investment define the destruction of the income spent for the final purchase of consumption and investment goods? Is it not evident that any new income requires a new production? If no production takes place, no new income is formed and it would be very curious indeed to claim that in order to get a new income it is enough to spend the one we already have.

The theory of the multiplier is a clear example of the absurdity to which a superficial and microeconomic 'reading' of economic activities may lead. If agent *A* spends his income to purchase the goods and services sold by another agent, *B*, it seems legitimate to claim that what is spent by *A* is earned by *B*. Yet, if one pushes his reasoning a bit further one immediately realizes that the income earned by *B* originates from the productive activity of *B* rather than from the expenditure of *A*. The 'miraculous' concatenation of incomes generated from the expenditure of previous 'autonomous' incomes (whose origin remains mysterious within the 'earning-through-spending' theory of income) is totally alien to a monetary theory of production.

Let us now turn to the second interpretation of Keynes's theory of consumption, which we advocate.

Interpreted as an expenditure carried out for the sake of a final purchase of produced goods, consumption is an instantaneous event that has nothing to do with the process of wear and tear to which physical output is submitted. Economically speaking, consumption is a transaction earmarked by the opposite sign with respect to production. Thus, while production defines the creation of a positive income, consumption defines its destruction. The physical output that was momentarily transformed into the object of a bank deposit loses its monetary form at the very moment it is purchased. Consumption coincides therefore with the transformation of produced output from an economic product into a physical object or service. Literally this means that economic consumption is the transaction through which produced output ceases to exist as an economic entity. *While physical consumption entails the 'disappearance' of physical output, economic consumption is thus identified with the 'disappearance' of economic output.*

If one identifies consumption with the expenditure of income for the final purchase of produced output, one may extend it to include both the final purchase of consumption and investment goods. This allows us to rewrite Keynes's identity between total supply, *Y*, and total demand, *C + I*, as $Y \equiv C$. Considered as the expenditure defining the final purchase of produced output (independently of its subdivision into consumption and investment goods), consumption appears thus to be the complementary part of production. What is created by production is destroyed by consumption *in its entirety*. This is the message conveyed by Keynes's identity, which leaves therefore no room for any positive hoarding and is the clearest example of the incompatibility of Keynes's analysis with the theory of the multiplier. Now, the identity $Y \equiv C$ establishes not only that the income created by production is entirely destroyed by consumption, but also that production and consumption are the two aspects of one and the same occurrence. Literally speaking, this means that production and consumption coincide; a result that even Keynes would have probably recoiled from and that seems incompatible with our common-sense perception of the economic reality. Is it not logically inevitable that, if consumption coincides with production, income is destroyed the very moment it is formed? And if so, does it not necessarily follow that economic output is also concurrently destroyed so that its very existence is put in jeopardy? Keynes's logical identity appears thereby as a useless conceptual device, since it reduces the economic world to a series of instantaneous events that leave no mark in the real world.

One of the great merits of Schmitt's quantum theoretical approach is precisely that of reconciling Keynes's identities with the need to explain how income can have a positive existence in time. As the reader will remember, production is an instantaneous event that quantizes time. At the very instant wages are paid, physical output enters its monetary form and a positive income is thereby formed. At the same instant, t^*, the interval $t_0 - t_1$ corresponding to the period of time during which the physical process of production has taken place is covered by a wave-like movement that defines the interval $t_0 - t_1$ as a quantum of time. Let us suppose consumption to occur at another, later instant of time, t_2. What has to be shown is that Schmitt's notion of quantum time allows for consumption to coincide with production even though t_1 and t_2 are different points on the arrow of time. This is done by observing that production and consumption are instantaneous, chronologically distinct events that quantize the same period of time. Consumption defines in fact, negatively, the same income specified, positively, by production. Like production, consumption defines thus a wave-like movement referring to the interval $t_0 - t_1$ and entailing its emission as a quantum. The new conception of time involved by the macroeconomic analysis of production advocated here enables production and consumption to coincide in quantum time while differing in chronological time. This would obviously not be the case if production and consumption were considered on purely physical grounds. Yet, what makes economics a science *sui generis*, distinct from physics, is the dimensionless character of money and of every monetary transaction. To enter the realm of economics proper is to enter that of numbers and of instantaneous, dimensionless events relating numbers (money) to produced output. Production and consumption pertain to this category of events. This is why their relationship with time is of a very particular kind.

Indeed, since production and consumption circumscribe the same quantum of time, they can be made to coincide despite their chronological distinction. The simultaneity of consumption and production in quantum time obviously does not imply their simultaneity in chronological time. Wages are paid at t_1 and income is finally spent at a different instant, t_2. Nevertheless, the fact that they refer to the same output, which is positively emitted at t_1 and negatively emitted at t_2, transforms production and consumption into the two sides of a unique emission. Production and consumption 'are given as of a piece: each *positive* production immediately defines an equal, *positive* consumption. The object of economic analysis is not production followed by consumption, but a unique, double-faced reality, the *production–consumption*' (Schmitt 1984a: 447, our translation). The fact that production and consumption coincide in quantum time has a precise meaning, which is independent of whether t_2 is retroactively superposed on t_1 – as in the case when t_2 follows t_1 chronologically (as it happens in our representation) – or t_1 is retroactively superposed on t_2 – which is what happens when banks allow for income to be spent in advance. The quantum co-occurrence of the two events happening at t_1 and t_2 actually means that production and consumption take part in the joint determination of output. Thus, before income's final expenditure produced output is only partially determined as far as its economic nature is concerned. It is only after it has been purchased that it becomes possible, for example, to establish which part of produced output was made up of wage goods and which of investment goods. Before its final purchase, output pertains to the sole category of consumption or wage goods. It is only in the light of what happens at t_2 that it is possible to improve our knowledge of the exact economic nature of the goods produced at t_1. Thus, investment is an economic category that cannot be determined on the basis of the physical aspects of produced output. Economic consumption, that is, the expenditure of income for the final purchase of produced output, participates to its joint determination and provides the pieces of information required to distinguish wage or consumption goods from investment goods.

Since production and consumption are two instantaneous events coinciding in quantum time but occurring at different moments in chronological time, the income created at t_1 subsists – albeit in the form of capital-time (see Chapter 7) – during the whole interval t_1–t_2. At the same time the co-occurrence of the creation (production) and destruction (consumption) of income as conveyed by Keynes's logical identity between global supply and global demand is respected in quantum time, since t_2 retroactively coincides with t_1.

The macroeconomic nature of consumption comes straight out of the previous analysis. Being the reciprocal side of production, consumption implies the destruction of the income created by production. Thus, irrespective of whether it is carried out by a single agent or by the totality of agents, the final purchase of produced output modifies the amount of income available for the system as a whole. In the same way as production is a macroeconomic event increasing national income, consumption is therefore a macroeconomic event decreasing it. As opposed to macroeconomic consumption, microeconomic consumption does not alter the amount of income available, its effect being simply an alternative distribution of the very same income. The purchase of a second-hand car, for example, defines the transfer of a sum of income from the purchaser to the seller without increasing or decreasing the total amount of income already present in the system. In today's mainstream economic analysis there is no clear-cut distinction between micro and macroeconomic consumption. This conceptual confusion explains why economists have been so far incapable of providing a satisfactory theory of consumption.

In fact, in its economic sense, consumption is the final appropriation of output. This clearly means that if money did not exist, consumption would not be chronologically distinguished from production. In the absence of money, real goods would be consumed at the very instant of their formation, since they would immediately be appropriated by their producers. Thanks to money this is not the case. Produced output is no longer appropriated, either by firms or by householders, at the moment of its formation. Instead of physical output, wage earners obtain a sum of money income. Hence, while production is positive, consumption is chronologically postponed until money income is finally spent, thus allowing the final appropriation of produced output: consumption. What supporters of traditional economic analysis have failed to understand is (a) that production and consumption can be chronologically separate only through the intervention of money, and (b) that once money has fulfilled its task, production and consumption coincide, one complementing the other. Production and consumption are fundamental objects of inquiry of macroeconomics, and so is money. By conceiving of money as a commodity or as an asset, mainstream economists are trapped in the realm of relative exchanges. Their analysis of production is thus necessarily limited to microeconomic considerations whose validity is itself seriously hampered by the lack of a consistent theory of money. Macroeconomics is the domain of money, and no serious economic theory can do without it. As we will see in the following chapters, this explains the conceptual difficulties encountered by most current theories when dealing with the problems of interest, capital, inflation, and involuntary unemployment.

7 Capital and interest: their macroeconomic origin

From capital-time to fixed capital

As a first approximation capital may be identified with the produced means of production available in a given economic system at a given period of time. Yet this definition is far from being satisfactory and applies mainly to capital in its material form. From an economic point of view, capital could then be conceived of as 'a fund providing command over productive goods' (Nell 1988: 14). However, Nell goes on to point out that even this definition is inadequate. A clear understanding of what capital really is requires a thorough analysis of the way capital is formed and of its implications for a capitalist system. In this chapter we will be dealing only with the logic of capital accumulation, whereas the pathological process of capital accumulation characterizing the current working of the capitalist system is analysed in Chapter 8. Moreover, we will make very little explicit reference to the neoclassical and Keynesian analyses of capital. The reasons of this choice are perfectly in line with the results of our analysis of production as developed in Chapter 6. Both the neoclassical and the Keynesian approaches to capital are based on an unsatisfactory theory of production and growth. The idea that capital is a factor of production on a par with labour and land, and that accumulation is concerned with the adjustment of this particular factor to its equilibrium level is as unrealistic as the theories of the multiplier and the 'accelerator' on which the Keynesian growth models rest. Problems such as factors substitution and reallocation, steady growth and traverse (the transition from one growth path to another), reswitching of techniques (the impossibility of determining a unique method of production when a technique proves to be the most profitable at more than one level of the rate of profit), technical change as a technological progress function, and other related questions will therefore be left aside from the outset. Referring to the main tenets of the quantum theoretical analysis of production, we will instead investigate, first, the logical–conceptual relationship existing between capital, income, and time and, then, the peculiarities of fixed capital.

Capital, income, and time

Let us start from production. Even if money did not exist, human labour would still be at the origin of new utility forms. Yet these forms could not find their numerical expression and real goods would remain hetero-geneous. Relative prices being logically indeterminate, no logical *system* could arise and exchange would be limited to isolated barter. Money is therefore what allows for production being accounted for as an economic event. The unique nature of economic production and its peculiar rela-tionship with time are at the core of macroeconomics. It is because pro-duction is an instantaneous event that transforms physical output into a sum of money that current income defines the totality of current output as a net product. And it is because current income refers instantaneously to a finite interval of time that we can say that production quantizes time. As we have already seen, the fact that both the production and consump-tion of the same output are instantaneous events, the quantization of one and the same interval of continuous time reconciles our perception of these two events as both distinct (in chronological time) and concurrent (in quantized time).

The simultaneity of production and consumption is indeed a state of affairs that has often been advocated by economists. For example, in his criticism to Böhm-Bawerk's theory of capital, Clark argued that no pro-duction lag exists since production and consumption are necessarily syn-chronized; the former comes to an end only when the latter starts. According to Clark, capital 'is the means of avoiding all waiting. It is the remover of time intervals – the absolute synchronizer of labor and its fruit' (Clark 1899: 308). The same point of view was later taken over by Knight, who went as far as to claim that '[i]n the only sense of timing in terms of which economic analysis is possible, *production and consumption are simulta-neous*' (Knight 1934: 275). His statement is obviously perfectly consistent with the tenets of general equilibrium analysis and with the simultaneous solution of the system of independent equations that is said to describe the overall equilibrium of production and exchange. Yet its justification goes beyond the theoretical framework of GEA. If the period of produc-tion is stretched in order to account not only for the process of physical transformation but also for the time required to bring the product to market, production will indeed be accomplished the very moment output is purchased, which allows production to coincide with consumption. Moreover, given production is a positive creation, logic requires it to be immediately matched by a concurrent and equivalent, positive destruc-tion. This necessarily implies that the income formed at t_1 is also spent at this very instant, even though actual consumption might take place at a later instant, t_2, in continuous time. One of quantum theoretical analysis' great merits is to succeed in reconciling such apparently contradictory requirements, namely, that income cannot survive its creation at t_1 and that nevertheless it is in the end spent after a positive interval of time elapses.

It is capital that, in its first and most general form, allows for bridging the gap between present (t_1) and future (t_2). At the very moment it is formed, instant t_1, current income is saved and transformed into capital. More precisely, the entire amount of income initially saved is lent to firms, F, in order to finance their initial purchase of current output in the form of a stock. Yet consumption – the final purchase of current output – will only take place at a later instant of continuous time. Between its initial, temporary expenditure at t_1 and its final expenditure at t_2 income takes the form of capital and it is as such that it covers the interval t_1-t_2. The beneficiaries of the payment of wages occurring at t_1, are credited by their banks with a positive amount of bank deposits corresponding to their income. However, workers are immediately transformed from income holders into the holders of an equivalent amount of *capital: the financial claim over a future income.* Although their initial income is instantaneously lent by banks and 'spent' by firms, income earners, *IE*, are entitled to recover it at any time in the future. This would not be possible, of course, if firms' initial expenditure defined also their final purchase of current output. This is not what happens at t_1. The expenditure of firms is in fact only the implicit consequence of the automatic lending by banks of the deposits recorded with them. Because of the very principle of double-entry book-keeping, banks cannot avoid lending to firms, F, the entire amount of income saved by *IE* and entered on the liabilities side of their accounting books (Table 7.1).

As this perfect balancing of assets and liabilities clearly shows, *IE*'s deposits cover F's indebtedness. This means that *IE*'s savings are invested by firms in the initial purchase of current output. The income formed and saved at t_1 is therefore 'spent' by firms in the sense that it allows them to replace income earners as the initial owners of the newly produced output. *Because of production, firms are financially indebted to income earners, whose income finances F's initial investment and, thus, the transformation of current output into a stock held by firms.* Current income is thus the object owed by firms to banks and by banks to income earners. *B*'s financial intermediation at t_1 does not lead to the final destruction of income but rather to its transformation into capital. From t_1 to t_2 income survives, in the form of capital, as the object of a financial claim. If, at t_2, *IE* were to decide to give up their current savings in order to purchase current

Table 7.1 The automatic lending of deposits

	Banks		
Liabilities		*Assets*	
IE	x	F	x

output, they would instantaneously recover their initial income. What has initially been transformed into capital becomes income again and disappears with the final purchase of current output.

Let us summarize the crucial steps of our analysis so far.

1   The payment of wages by banks, on behalf of firms and to the benefit of income earners, is carried out through a monetary intermediation. Banks debit and credit firms with a given amount of money, and they simultaneously credit and debit income earners with the same amount.

2   The income generated by the association of physical output with money is immediately deposited with the banks and lent to firms, which borrow it to finance their initial investment in the stock of current output.

3   Banks' monetary intermediation is therefore coupled with their financial intermediation. Thus, the debit and credit of firms correspond to their purchase of the stock of produced goods and services, and to their sale of financial claims to the banks respectively, while the credit and debit of income earners correspond to their sale of current output and to their purchase of financial claims on bank deposits.

4   Firms are not the final owners of current output, for the simple reason that they are financially indebted to the banks. The stock formed at t_1 will in fact be sold by firms to income holders at a later moment in time, t_2.

5   From t_1 to t_2 income takes the form of a capital, and current output is stocked by firms. Capital is thus the form taken by income as soon as it is saved by its initial holders and lent to firms. As a result of the transformation of income into capital, firms owe a sum of bank deposits, while income earners own an amount of financial claims corresponding to the bank deposits lent to firms.

6   At t_2 capital recovers its initial form of income and is spent for the final purchase of current output. Through the intermediation of banks, firms are credited with a positive sum of money earned through the sale of their stock of physical output, and are debited with the same amount of money because of their purchase of the financial claims initially sold to banks (at t_1). Simultaneously, income earners are credited for their sale of claims on bank deposits, and debited for their purchase of the physical output stocked by firms.

In its first and simplest form, capital is therefore related only to the flow of time and defines a *reversible* transformation of income. Let us follow Schmitt (1984a) and call capital-time this first kind of capital. As we can already see, the 'survival' of income in the form of capital-time during the interval t_1–t_2 is compatible with the quantum concurrence of production and consumption. In quantum time t_1 and t_2 coincide retroactively, which allows for the positive existence of capital in chronological time. The income created at t_1 is thus retroactively destroyed at this same instant. At the same time, however, the income created at t_1 can be destroyed at a later instant, t_2, because capital *is* this very filling of the gap between t_1 and t_2. On no occasion has income as such a positive existence in time. The financial intermediation performed by banks transforms income into capital at the very instant it is formed. It is capital, therefore, and not income that can be found in the interval t_1–t_2. Given that the initial transformation is reversible, this is enough to allow for the final expenditure (and destruction) of current income at t_2.

Let us now consider a second form of capital, namely, the capital-time related to consumption loans. Let us suppose, therefore, that at time t_1' comprised in the interval t_1–t_2 the income formed and saved at t_1 is lent to agents C, who spend it for the final purchase of current output. This time *IE*'s income can no longer be recovered at t_2 since it is destroyed by C at t_1'. From t_1 to t_1' everything happens as in the previous case, except that the final expenditure of current income is now carried out by C rather than by its initial holders, *IE*. The capital-time formed at t_1 because of the financial intermediation of banks comes to an end at t_1'. Yet *IE*'s claim on banks does not also come to an end. Even though the income saved and deposited by *IE* is lent to C, banks remain indebted towards *IE* – a debt that is matched by the banks' credit on C. What changes at t_1' is not the claim of *IE* with respect to banks, but the object of income earners' financial claim, which is now no longer *IE*'s own income – which is spent by C – but an equivalent, future income of C. At t_2, when *IE* are supposed to recover their initial income, banks will give them the income transferred by C in order to settle their debt with the banking system. The capital-time formed at t_1 and cancelled at t_1' will thus be replaced by another capital-time formed the moment C earn their own income. Thanks to the financial intermediations of banks, *IE* can therefore substitute their present income with C's future income, and vice versa, and change the object of their initial claim on the bank. In our simplified example, at t_1' C borrow *IE*'s current income in order to purchase *IE*'s current output and, at t_2, *IE* get in exchange C's current income and the 'power' to purchase C's current output.

The two cases of capital-time we have analysed so far are very similar and illustrate well the relationship expressed between the flow of time and the role of financial intermediation played by banks. They both pertain to microeconomic saving, of course, and cannot therefore account for the accumulation of macroeconomic capital. Yet what they show is that, even in its simplest forms, capital is essentially related to time. As observed by Wicksell in his defence of Böhm-Bawerk's theory, 'the *time element* in consumption and production becomes the *exclusive* content in the concepts of both capital and interest' (Wicksell 1997: 37). One key element implicit in Böhm-Bawerk's theory of capital is the threefold distinction between money, income, and capital. Both production and consumption require the use of money as a means of payment and define the two complementary parts of the circuit of income. Through the assimilation of physical output within its monetary form, production leads to the formation of a positive income, which is destroyed through consumption, that is, through the final purchase of produced output. Capital arises to bridge the gap between production and consumption. What is difficult to understand is that, despite appearances to the contrary, income cannot logically survive its formation and cannot therefore be transferred over time as such. The dual aspect of production and consumption (two events specifying one and the same magnitude) can be properly explained only by Schmitt's quantum theoretical approach. It is *qua* quantized time that consumption can coincide retroactively with production. But if production and consumption are dual, it follows that income does not last over time. No income can ever be found in the interval shared by the instant income is formed and the instant it is finally spent. It is here that capital enters the picture: saved the very instant it is formed, income is immediately replaced with a financial claim and henceforth transformed into capital-time.

To properly understand the nature of capital it is necessary to examine it in close connection with money and income. This suggestion is not always heeded by economists. Thus, for example, Graziani rejects the idea that savings in the form of bank deposits are lent by banks to firms. 'It has to be excluded that banks [...] *transfer* to firms the liquidity collected from the owners of bank deposits' (Graziani 1988: xxiii, our translation). This is so, according to Graziani, 'because the bank cannot transform a deposit on call into a medium or long-term deposit, so that the owners of the deposit will remain entitled to the same "liquidity" whatever the amount of financing granted to firms' (ibid.: xxiii, our translation). Graziani's understanding of money income and of its circular flow remains too physicalist to allow him to describe it in its fullest extent. Of course, if bank deposits were like physical assets, their transfer would prevent their owners from spending them at will, at any moment of their choice. If transferred literally to firms, these deposits would no longer be available to their owners, a situation that banks obviously cannot allow to occur. However, bank deposits are not material and their transfer does not imply any spatial displacement. To be precise, the transfer concerns the sum of money income deposited with banks and is the necessary consequence of double-entry book-keeping. This has no effect whatsoever on the possibility owners of the deposits on call have to spend them as they like. Liquidity is not in the least affected by the loan granted to firms. Used to momentarily back the debt of firms, the sum saved by income earners can at any time be recovered in order to be spent on the product and financial markets. Like the circular flow defining nominal money, the circular flow of income can be correctly understood only if one analyses economic transactions from the immaterial bank money point of view and in line with the principles of double-entry book-keeping.

Another example of today's limited understanding of the 'circuit' of income is given by Davidson's recent re-introduction of the notion of liquidity preference. In fact, the Keynesian concept of liquidity preference is highly unsatisfactory since it rests on the erroneous assumption that money can be saved and made to play the role of a store of value. The idea that money is subject to liquidity preference since it may be demanded 'as a liquid store of value, that is, a vehicle for transferring savings (generalized purchasing power) over time' (Davidson 2002: 82) is actually at odds with any clearly maintained distinction between money, income, and capital. Of course, if money were a positive asset, it could function as a store of value. However, the fact remains that money's value derives from its association with produced output. It is nevertheless correct, as claimed by Davidson, that saving is not simply a sum of money but of purchasing power. But money's purchasing power can exist only with respect to produced output. The existence of positive saving implies therefore the non-expenditure of a positive money income and the formation of a stock of goods. Now, how can a generalized purchasing power be transferred over time? Is it by leaving the unspent part of money income deposited with the banking system, and its correspondent stock of unsold output deposited with firms? According to this simplistic view, income could be transferred over time simply by not spending it (and on condition that its real object or 'content' – output – maintained its use-value unaltered). This is to forget, however, the inexorable logic of double-entry book-keeping. What is deposited with banks enters on the liabilities side of their ledger and is immediately matched by an equivalent entry on the assets side.

Correctly interpreted, the relationship between bank assets and liabilities means that deposits are never idle. On the contrary, they are lent as soon as they are formed, so that each penny saved is immediately invested. *This is precisely the true meaning of Keynes's identity between saving and investment: what is not spent by households on consumption is necessarily spent by firms on investment.* In contrast with Keynes's identity, the concept of liquidity preference introduces the idea that an increase in saving is not matched by an equivalent increase in the demand for produced output. Defined as a demand for liquid financial assets, saving is thus said, *caeteris paribus*, to 'reduce today's effective demand for the products of industry and therefore depress real economic activity' (ibid.: 82). Quantum monetary analysis shows instead that saving always finances an equivalent demand and that it is through its transformation into capital that money (income) allows the bridging of the gap between present and future. Schmitt's analysis appears therefore as further vindication of Böhm-Bawerk's idea that capital is intrinsic to the process of production and consumption. As claimed by Wicksell in his reply to Brisman, in fact,

> Böhm-Bawerk's really epoch-making idea [...] was to recognize in the
> *capitalistic production process* itself [...] the simple primary concept, of
> which capital in all its guises is then only derived or secondary. If so, it
> soon becomes clear that there is nowhere to draw a boundary line suc-
> cessfully; rather everything produced but not yet consumed, and
> which has some exchange value, becomes capital.
>
> (Wicksell 1997: 18)

Saving can either result in the substitution of present for future consumption, or lead to the formation of fixed capital. In both cases the income
initially saved is spent, albeit in two quite different ways. When saving is
merely the exchange between one agent's future income and another
agent's present income, it is obvious that it does not imply any net transfer
over time. What is saved by one agent is spent by the other: this is the zero-
sum nature of microeconomic saving. Things however radically change
when one is confronted with a positive macroeconomic saving. In this
case, part of the available income is conserved over time through its transformation into fixed capital. It is this transformation that defines the
'expenditure' of macroeconomic saving for society as a whole. More precisely, that part of current income that is macroeconomically saved cannot
logically remain available as a deposit in the financial department of
banks. Its 'expenditure' is nothing else than its investment in the production of fixed capital goods.

Let us next analyse in some detail the shift from capital-time to fixed
capital.

The formation of macroeconomic capital

Classical economists considered capital accumulation as 'the productive
investment of part of society's net product – the surplus of output over
necessary consumption and the requirements for maintaining capital
intact – in order to expand productive capacity' (Nell 1988: 14). As we
have already seen, the classical notion of net product is highly controversial and does not account enough for the macroeconomic nature of production. Nevertheless, the classical analysis of capital accumulation
provides the right introduction to the problem by emphasizing the fact
that fixed capital results from the productive investment of part of
society's income.

The first step towards the formation of fixed capital is the formation of
what we may call *circulating capital*, that is, a sum of saved-up income at the
disposal of firms for the financing of a new production of investment
goods. This sum can be derived either from profits or from the selling of
financial claims. Yet, since the capital obtained through a financial loan
can be assimilated to an advance of profits (Schmitt 1984a), we will consider profit as the only source of circulating capital. This is not to say that

the whole amount of profits defines a circulating capital, that is, a sum of capital-time that will be transformed into fixed capital. Profits are in part distributed as dividends or interests to households that will spend them for the final purchase of current output and, to this extent, they will never give rise to a new fixed capital. What we are calling circulating capital corresponds therefore only to that part of profits (realized or advanced) that represents the part of current income that will be finally saved by society as a whole.

That macroeconomic saving is a necessary step towards capital accumulation does not come as a surprise. It is rather obvious, in fact, that a sacrifice in consumption will be required in order to produce instrumental goods. Workers producing tools have to be fed, and in a primitive society this can be done only if workers producing foodstuff agree to give up part of their current consumption. A stock of consumption goods is the prerequisite for the production of capital goods. The same requirement applies to our industrialized economies, the difference being that in a monetary economy the stock of consumption goods is the real object or 'content' of a monetary capital held by firms. Before fixed capital is formed, firms produce consumption goods only. Now, if firms are able to earn a profit through the sale of part of their produced output, a stock is formed that is made up of the consumption goods firms have yet to sell. It is this stock of real goods that will 'remunerate' the workers producing fixed capital goods.

For the sake of analytical clarity, let us distinguish the period in which profits are formed, p_0, from the period in which they are invested, p_1. At p_0 part of current output is sold at a profit and part is stocked. The profits formed at p_0 are therefore the monetary aspect of the circulating capital corresponding to this real stock of consumption goods. In the following period, p_1, part of the workers employed in p_0 to produce consumption goods are employed in order to produce instrumental goods. The wages earned by these workers can now be spent for the purchase of the consumption goods stocked in p_0. This leads to the disappearance of real circulating capital and to its replacement by an equivalent amount of real fixed capital. The new instrumental goods replace in fact the stock of consumption goods sold in p_1 and define the real content of the new capital resulting from the investment of profits.

As said before, this chapter is concerned solely with the logic of capital accumulation. This means that we are considering here only the way in which fixed capital would be formed in an orderly system, that is, one in which the differentiation between money, income, and capital is actually enacted by banks. In period p_0 profits are formed and saved. As in any other case when income is saved, profits are thus immediately transformed into an equivalent amount of capital-time. The difference here is that this time, because of the investment of profits occurring at p_1, saving will be of an irreversible kind. In other words, the transformation of the capital-time formed in p_0 into a fixed capital will never be followed by a reverse transformation (from fixed capital into capital-time) allowing for the expenditure of the income saved in p_0. Thus, it is through the formation of fixed capital that the amount of income saved in p_0 is transformed into a *macroeconomic saving.*

In the interval between the instant profits are formed (and saved) and the instant they are finally invested, capital exists only as capital-time and saving is not yet of a macroeconomic kind. However, the fact that profits will actually be invested in p_1 gives a particular significance to the sum saved and to the stock of current output defining its real 'content'. As it were, the stock of unsold consumption goods corresponding to the profits that will be invested in p_1 becomes a real wage fund, and this is why it may be useful to *call 'circulating capital' the capital-time that is going to be invested in the production of investment goods.* Now, in p_1 a new income is formed corresponding to the production of fixed capital goods. Workers producing investment goods are thus able to purchase the consumption goods stocked in p_0 and making up the real wage fund. As for profits, they become the monetary form of instrumental goods and are definitively saved up as a sum of fixed capital. In a way, the goods making up the real 'content' of the income (that is, profits) saved up in p_0 replace the goods making up the real content of the wages paid to workers producing fixed capital goods in p_1, and vice versa. The final result is that part of p_0's current income has been macroeconomically saved in the form of fixed capital and, thanks to this sacrifice, instrumental goods will increase future labour's physical productivity.

Quantum theoretical analysis confirms Böhm-Bawerk and Wicksell's intuition that *capital is essentially saved-up labour and time, and shows that fixed capital is the logical result of the investment of profits.* It shows also that through their transformation into fixed capital, profits define a *macroeconomic* saving and cannot be considered, therefore, merely as a part of current income. They are derived from current income, it is true, but they enter the category of macroeconomic entities as soon as they are invested and converted into fixed capital. If we now compare this approach to that advocated by general equilibrium analysis we immediately realize how far apart they are.

By accepting Walras's theoretical framework, neoclassical economists are forced to determine profit and capital simultaneously and, by identifying 'normal' profit with interest, they logically subordinate profit to capital. According to GEA, in fact, the rate of interest is the price level of capital goods, which is determined through the (relative) exchange between capital and non-capital goods. But if the rate of interest is the price of capital goods (c) in terms of non-capital goods (b), how can capital derive from profits? If $1c/2b$ is the relative price of c in terms of b, this simply means that the rate of interest is a price among others and that interest – obtained by multiplying the rate of interest times the initial endowments of capital goods – is part of produced output. It thus follows that profits correspond to the services yielded by capital goods. '[W]e have a third category of capital, namely *capital proper*, capable of yielding *capital-income* or *capital-services*, which we shall also call "*profits*" ' (Walras 1984: 215). According to Walras, profits are the services yielded by capital goods (capital proper) and their price corresponds to the amount of interest paid in order to benefit from these services. This means that *profits derive from capital proper and not the other way around.* In claiming that capital yields profits, Walras mistakenly confuses two magnitudes (profit and interest) that should logically be kept separate. Moreover, he misses the fact that *capital is the result of production and not a factor of production that may arbitrarily be considered as given.* What GEA fails to provide is an explanation of the logical origin of capital. Thus, despite the efforts of Wicksell, Hicks, Bliss and many other distinguished economists, GEA has never succeeded in proposing a satisfactory theory of capital accumulation.

As we have seen, capital accumulation is a process through which new fixed capital is added to the system. This process requires the renewed formation of profits and their investment and must not be confused with amortization, which refers to the replacement of fixed capital goods used up by wear and tear as well as by technological obsolescence, and which implies the constancy of fixed capital and not its growth. Thus, while production of new instrumental goods beyond amortization increases the amount of fixed capital by adding a new macroeconomic saving to it, amortization defines the production of replacement goods and maintains the amount of fixed capital at its previous level. As monetary macro-economics shows, the real and monetary aspects of capital form a unity, they define one and the same thing. This clearly means that if one is modified, the other immediately changes also. For example, in the case of capital-time the decision to spend at t_2 part of what had been saved at t_1 reduces both the amount of monetary capital and of its real 'content': the sum spent for the final purchase (at t_2) of part of the goods produced and stocked at t_1 disappears and the goods purchased give up their economic form. In the case of fixed capital, the income saved in period p_1 will never be spent on the commodity market for the purchase of the instrumental goods produced in period p_2 precisely because, through the investment of profits, income is transformed into a macroeconomic capital. If instrumental goods were purchased on the commodity market, they would in fact pertain to the category of consumption goods: consumption would extend to the entire production and capital would not even exist. However, instrumental goods are used as means of production and are subject to a physical and technological process of wear and tear. This decrease in the real aspect of fixed capital entails therefore also a decrease in the amount of financial capital. Amortization derives essentially from the need to restore fixed capital to its former level. Thus, as we have already observed, amortization consists in the investment required for the production of replacement goods and for the renewal of fixed capital.

Both capital accumulation and amortization are closely related to the increase in the physical productivity of human labour and to the problem of interest. Let us therefore try to sketch the principal lines of a macroeconomic theory of interest based on the concepts of fixed capital and amortization analysed so far.

Interest and capital

Interest is one of the most central and controversial concepts in economics. Indeed economists are still far from a general agreement as to the meaning of this concept. Our aim in what follows is therefore to attempt to explain the terms of the problem in light of quantum analysis.

Interest and profit

The first point that must be clarified is that interest is not related to money proper but to capital, which means that the interest rate is not the price of money. Not only '[i]t is no doubt somewhat easier to understand that wood and meat cost money, than that money costs *more* money' (Wicksell 1997: 21), but it is clearly meaningless to speak of the 'price' of money. As a unit of account as well as a means of payment, money is the unit in which prices are expressed but has obviously not itself a price. The confusion comes from the past use of a commodity money, of course. Even when a real good is used as money, however, its price is not the price of money but the price of the good used to physically represent money. If this were not the case, to wit, if money had itself a price, then a money's money would have to be found in order to express the price of money, and so on down a bottomless pit that is the mark of the absurdity of looking for the price of money in the first place.

As quantum analysis shows, money is a flow whose existence is limited to the instant in which payments are actually carried out. Thus, money as such cannot be deposited in 'real' time and therefore cannot be the source of interest. All those economists who are still talking about the quantity of money and the adjustment between its supply and its demand conceive of money as a stock. Today this old-fashioned conception of money is overtly in contrast with the reality of banking. To consider bank money as a 'mass' (a physical dimension) is greatly mistaken and an atavism. More careful consideration shows that money must be distinguished from income, and that it is income and not money that is deposited with the banking system.

Unfortunately this distinction has not been fully recognized yet. Even Keynes, the economist who pioneered the monetary analysis of production, did not always respect it. In particular, dealing with the problem of interest he was so much sidetracked by the desire to show that saving and investment are adjusted through a variation of income that he claimed that the interest rate is the price equilibrating supply of and demand for liquidity.

> Liquidity-preference is a potentiality or functional tendency, which fixes the quantity of money which the public will hold when the rate of interest is given; so that if r is the rate of interest, M the quantity of money and L the function of liquidity-preference, we have M = L (r). This is where, and how, the quantity of money enters into the economic scheme.
>
> (Keynes 1936/1973a: 168)

The idea that the quantity of money may be modified by economic agents' willingness to spend more or less of it is both ill-founded and logically inconsistent. In the first place, money is destroyed as soon as it is created in the flows of payments. On the other side, even if money were a stock, its quantity could not be determined by economic agents' behaviour. What is spent by some consumers, for example, is necessarily earned by other economic agents so that, on the whole, the quantity of money cannot be modified in the way suggested by Keynes. The theory of interest advocated by the great British economist is thus at odds with his own analysis of money, and particularly with Chapters 6 and 7 of the *General Theory*, in which he endeavoured to explain the transformation of money into income. Ironically, what Keynes claimed to be the most original contribution of his monetary analysis (namely, the theory of interest) appears to be a dead end, a hopeless attempt to avoid identifying the interest rate with the capital rate of return. By distinguishing the interest rate from the capital efficiency (that is, from the relation between the prospective yield of capital and its supply price), Keynes was *de facto* maintaining that real and financial capital are two separate objects determining two distinct magnitudes. 'The schedule of the marginal efficiency of capital may be said to govern the terms on which loanable funds are demanded for the purpose of new investment; whilst the rate of interest governs the terms in which funds are being currently supplied' (ibid.: 165). Yet, as observed by Schmitt, real and financial capitals are the two aspects of one and the same object. Since investment funds are both supplied and demanded, and real investment is also supplied and demanded, this shows that interest rate and capital efficiency are not two distinct concepts. Interest is an income derived from a capital that is both real and financial and not, as suggested by Keynes, a magnitude totally independent of real capital.

Another point in need of clarification is the nature of interest on consumption loans. In his comments on Brisman's articles published by the *Scandinavian Journal of Economics*, Wicksell observes that 'interest on pure consumption loans [...] is no part of the return on social capital; instead it only *parasitizes*, so to speak, on one of the large social income categories: wages, rents and (with respect to the whole economy, as derived from social production) interest' (Wicksell 1997: 23–4). Thus, as was already very clear in the mind of the brilliant Swedish economist, interest on consumption loans must be distinguished from the interest derived from social production. This does not mean that interest on consumption loans is not related to capital. In fact, interest of any kind is always related to saving and, therefore, to capital. For the same reason, capital resulting from income being deposited in time, both interest on consumption loans and interest on investment are related to time. The true distinction between these two kinds of interest is that the former is linked to a *reversible capital-time* (that is, a capital that will eventually be reconverted into income and spent on the commodity market) whereas the latter is derived from an *irreversible, fixed capital* (that is, a capital defining a macroeconomic saving). The income saved and lent to consumers defines an exchange between a present and a future capital. Some consumers spend today the income saved by other potential consumers and will in the future save part of their new income in order to pay back the initial loan. Consumption loans are therefore related to a microeconomic saving. What is saved by some agents is being spent by others; no net saving is formed for society as a whole. Moreover, precisely because the income lent to consumers is spent for the final purchase of produced output, no net income can be derived from consumption loans, which means that interest on consumption loans is not a macroeconomic income.

Wicksell's image of interest on consumption loans as parasitizing on social income is somewhat crude but conveys straightforwardly the idea that interest on consumption loans is derived from the macroeconomic income generated by production. The payment of interest from borrower to lender does not increase social income but merely transfers part of the new income of the former to the latter. Being simultaneously positive for an agent and negative for another agent, the payment of interest on consumption loans is a zero-sum transaction, which leaves the amount of total social income unaltered. Now, if saving were lent to consumers only, the very existence of interest would be put in jeopardy. Since interest on consumption loans is not a net or macroeconomic income, it would be difficult to justify the increased transfer of income from borrower to lender. It is true, of course, that lenders may run a risk by allowing borrowers to spend an income before having earned it. Yet it might also be claimed that risk is very much reduced when banks act as financial intermediaries and that borrowers allow lenders to preserve their income (or, more correctly, their claim to a new, equivalent income) until a later date, when, thanks to technological progress, they will be able to purchase more and better goods. In the absence of a macroeconomic interest, the interest on consumption loans would itself lose its *raison d'être* and correspond to Wicksell's image of parasitic income.

A third clarification concerns the origin of interest as a macroeconomic income. According to neoclassical analysis, interest is a social income simply because capital is a factor of production whose price, the rate of interest, is determined by the adjustment between supply of and demand for capital exerted on the financial market. Now, this is the result of a truncated view of reality, where production is conceived of as a mere process of physical transformation and where money plays no essential role. When production is considered as an economic event *sui generis*, money becomes an essential element of the theory. Incapable to account for the monetary nature of production, the neoclassical postulate of homogeneity based on the dichotomy between real and monetary factors has to be replaced by an integrated approach in which money and physical output define one single economic object. When this is done, it appears that economic production is an absolute exchange (between money and output) that occurs through the payment of a unique factor of production: labour. Since capital goods are produced means of production and not a macroeconomic factor of production, they absorb the very income formed by their production and therefore cannot be the source of the additional income identified as interest.

As clearly perceived by some prominent economists, interest derives from capital. Yet there is no obvious causal relationship between capital and interest. In particular it is not true that interest is a net, macroeconomic income because capital has a cost determined by its supply and demand. If capital has indeed a cost justifying the formation of interest, this cost cannot originate in the financial market. In other words, if interest is a macroeconomic income, it cannot have its source in the adjustment between supply and demand but must be derived from production.

The problem that has to be faced now is how to explain the formation of interest as a macroeconomic income within the monetary circular flow of wages. Referring to Marx's claim that the process of capital accumulation implies a growth in the flow of money, Wray observes that '[m]onetary accumulation occurs where the circuits are not closed and occurs as the "revolving fund" is continually renewed and as the volume of short-term credit grows over time' (Wray 1996: 451). He then adds that '[a]s the monetary IOUs issued to finance the wage bill must carry interest, it is apparent that closure of the circuit is not possible unless firms issue enough short-term debt to include interest commitments' (ibid.: 451). Even if Wray's analysis is still largely unsatisfactory (since the American economist does not distinguish money from income – which leads him to claim, erroneously, that monetary IOUs *finance* the wage bill – and since he believes that 'interest [. . .] ensures nominal economic growth' (ibid.: 447) – thus implying that interest is only a nominal magnitude) it raises nevertheless a central and difficult question that is not new among thoughtful economists. For example Graziani, a specialist of the monetary circuit, has observed that firms have to pay interest but that the necessary money income cannot come from the market as 'firms cannot derive from the market an amount of money greater than that they have themselves given to the market' (Graziani 1988: xxiv, our translation).

Assuming that the amount paid out in wages is equal to 100 units of money income, this is the sum that firms can obtain through the sale of produced output. Yet, in order to pay the interest due to banks, firms must derive more that 100 units of money income from their sales. According to Graziani this is possible only if banks increase the liquidity available on the market. But how is that done? By regularly spending 'the totality of interest perceived from firms' (ibid.: xxiv, our translation), claims Graziani. A perfect example of circular reasoning, this explanation can obviously not be accepted, since it amounts to explaining the formation of interest through its expenditure. According to Graziani, firms can pay a positive interest to banks because banks spend this very interest to purchase goods from firms. 'If banks spend their net revenues [...] in order to purchase goods, firms – for whom these expenditures are equivalent earnings – can in this way pay the interest due' (ibid.: xxiv, our translation). If this were actually the case, interest would be determined mechanically, through the expenditure decided by banks. Whatever the amount of interest required by banks, firms will always be able to pay for it since banks themselves would provide them with the necessary amount. Hence, banks would pay themselves (through the intermediation of firms) the very interest they spend in advance.

Even though Graziani's solution is not appropriate, his problem is a real issue and cannot be avoided if one is to work out an all-embracing theory of the monetary circular flow. Let us reformulate the terms of the problem: since wages are the only macroeconomic income generated by production, how is it possible for firms to realize a positive profit and pay a positive interest out of it? The answer given to this question by Schmitt has not been entirely understood yet, and there are still economists who believe that no positive profit can be obtained by firms as a whole if it is accepted that wages define the totality of income available in a given system. Let us show that this is not the case by following a very simple, arithmetic example.

Suppose firms, *F*, to pay 100 wage units to their workers and sell current output at a market price of 125 units. If income holders spend the totality of current income, they will get only 100/125 of current output, that is, an output worth 80 wage units (100/125 × 100). This means that of the 100 units spent by income holders only 80 units define a final purchase, the remaining 20 units being simply transferred to firms. It is true that firms still owe 20 to banks, but it is also clear that 20 units of current output have not been sold yet. It is therefore enough for *F* to sell these 20 units to be able to cancel their debt. This can easily be done, *since 20 units of income (in the form of capital-time) are still available in the system.* Firms can, for example, distribute their profits as dividends and interest, and then sell the remaining 20 units of output to shareholders and financial lenders.

The fact that profits are obtained through the sale of current output at a market price (125 units) higher than value (100 units) is also clearly dealt with by Schmitt, who shows that *once quantum time is taken into account prices and values no longer differ.* The difference between prices and values, which is necessary for the formation of profits on the commodity market, finally dissolves because, as is shown by the quantum theoretical approach to production and consumption, *the payment of wages includes the expenditure of profits.* Formed on the commodity market, profits are in fact spent on the labour market. As implicit in Smith's concept of 'labour commanded', profits allow firms to purchase the product of labour from the outset, that is, from the moment workers are paid their wages. The retroactive effect of consumption over production, made possible by the concurrence of these two events in quantum time, allows for the reinterpretation of the emission of wages and explains why any difference between price and value is bound to disappear at the macroeconomic level.

> Finally, and even though it is a necessary step both analytically and from the viewpoint of the chronological order of concrete events, the formation of any difference between prices and value disappears in the logical reinterpretation of the emission of wages: the positive difference between price and cost of wage goods defines the production of non-wage goods.
>
> (Schmitt 1984a: 136, our translation)

In a few words, '*[t]he price of wage goods is greater than their value only because it is inclusive of the price of non-wage goods*' (ibid.: 142, our translation). Once it is understood that the payment of wages is inclusive of the purchase of non-wage goods and that profits are formed through the expenditure of wages, it becomes clear (though there is still difficulty since the problem is a very hard issue indeed) that the macroeconomic price at which goods are sold is given by the price actually paid by the purchasers of wage goods minus the price of non-wage goods. In our numerical example, wage goods of a value of 80 units are sold at a price of 100 units, which are inclusive of the price of non-wage goods (20 units). It thus follows that the actual price of wage goods only (100 units − 20 units) is exactly equal to their value.

In order to avoid a possible misunderstanding it is important to observe here that *the market price at which the entire output is sold by firms* (125 units in our example) *must not be mixed up with the macroeconomic price at which wage goods are sold.* Before current output is subdivided into wage and non-wage goods, firms set the market price at the level of 125 units. But the actual price of wage goods will be settled by consumers. If wage earners were to decide to spend the totality of their income for the purchase of current output (as we have assumed in our example), firms would sell 80 units (in value) of wage goods at a price of 100 units. *The price of goods (of any kind) is therefore univocally determined by the amount of income spent for their purchase.* The initial market price (125 units) is only a 'coefficient of redistribution' proposed by firms. According to the way consumers react to this signal, output is subdivided into wage and non-wage goods, each of which has its own price (in our example wage goods have a price of 100 units, while profit goods are sold among firms at a price of 25 units). Now, what quantum analysis shows is not only that the 'redistribution' price must not be confused with the price proper of each kind of goods, but also that, finally, prices and values are always equal. In other words, the macroeconomic price of goods is given by the amount of income required for their *final* purchase, that is, for covering their macroeconomic cost of production.

We have maintained so far that profits are included in the circuit of wages, so that a positive payment of interest may be derived from the payment of wages. The problem of the origin of interest, of its *raison d'être*, however, has still to be addressed and with it the question of whether or not interest is a macroeconomic income on its own. To answer these questions we have to go back to the analysis of fixed capital accumulation.

Interest and fixed capital

That interest is related to fixed capital seems now beyond dispute. Yet economists are far from being unanimous about the origin and the nature of interest. In particular, disagreement is still high about whether or not capital is a factor of production and interest an income generated by this factor. What can immediately be observed in this respect is that if capital were a factor of production interest would define the output of capital and, given the enormous increase in physical productivity allowed by instrumental goods, its amount would be far greater than that of wages. As Böhm-Bawerk, one of the greatest experts in the theory of capital, has shown, interest is not derived directly from the increase in physical productivity (Böhm-Bawerk 1959). As a means of production, capital increases physical productivity but is not the source of a net return. Capital as a means of production must therefore be carefully distinguished from the yields of capital, and a way must be found in order to transform the increase in physical productivity into an increase in value *without* transforming capital into a macroeconomic factor of production.

The fact that fixed capital is not a factor of production and that the increase in physical productivity is not a measure of interest does not prove that interest is not a macroeconomic income derived from fixed capital. Recall that fixed capital is formed through the investment of profits and defines a macroeconomic saving. A part of current income escapes consumption and is transformed into a fixed capital whose real object is a given amount of produced means of production. The investment of profits implies therefore a sacrifice by the entire society. Interest can thus be seen as a kind of compensation for this initial sacrifice. As suggested by Schmitt, interest finds its analytical justification in the formation of macroeconomic saving and takes the form of an income whose origin lies in the accumulation of fixed capital. *This does not mean either that fixed capital loses part of its value in the form of interest or that capital is itself the source of income.* In fact, fixed capital cannot be at the origin of a net transfer of value to the benefit of produced output. Even if it were admitted that, through its use, fixed capital transfers part of its value to produced output, it would still be necessary to account for the replacement of what is lost by wear and tear. The value lost by fixed capital is restored through amortization. From a macroeconomic point of view, amortization is the production of replacement goods required to restore fixed capital at its previous value. It thus becomes clear that *capital transfers part of its value to labour (to its output) only to the extent that labour gives back to it an equal value: capital works for labour only insofar as labour works for capital, which amounts to saying that value comes from labour alone.* Whereas amortization is the simple replacement of an old value with a new one, interest is a net income whose origin is related to the fact that production of fixed capital goods absorbs a net amount of saving. It is precisely this increase in the demand for saving that is the cause of interest. The transformation of saving into a macroeconomic capital – its investment – defines the final loss of an equal amount of income, and interest is the compensation for this loss.

Even though capital is not directly the source of interest, it is nevertheless the cause of an increase in value measured in money terms by the interest distributed by firms out of their profits. Since it remains true that value is determined by labour alone and that wages are the sole source of income, interest can be a macroeconomic magnitude only if it is derived from wages. This may be shown to be the case in two different ways. The first is the one we have already dealt with in the previous section and amounts to showing that interest must not be added to wages when measuring national income. The second is based on the contrary possibility: adding interest to wages. To avoid contradiction it is necessary to state that in this second case interest is obtained through a *multiplication of wages.* The idea is that the use of fixed capital increases the value produced by labour, so that the total amount of income produced is obtained by multiplying the total wages paid out (directly and indirectly) to workers by a coefficient determined by the amount of capital and the rate of interest.

Let us suppose, following our previous numerical example, that fixed capital is equal to 20 units and that the rate of interest is equal to 3 per cent. Interest is then equal to 0.6 units and measures the amount of income added by the production of interest goods. If wages are initially measured by 100 units, the use of fixed capital will thus multiply them by a coefficient equal to 0.6 per cent, and the total amount of income produced by labour will amount to 100.6 units. 0.6 units define the amount of value added because of the use of fixed capital and correspond to the wages paid for the production of interest goods, that is, the goods purchased through the final expenditure of interest. In the absence of fixed capital and if we abstract from the formation of profits, production would have been made up of wage goods only and its value would have been equal to 100 units. The presence of fixed capital changes things. Even if the increase in the physical productivity of labour has no direct impact on the economic value of current output, interest derived from fixed capital entails a new production of interest goods whose value, measured in wage units, adds up to the value of total output. In our example, workers producing a physically increased amount of wage goods with the aid of instrumental goods earn an income of 99.4 units, while those producing interest goods are paid 0.6 units. Nevertheless the total income formed in the system is equal to 100.6 units, since interest is a new income generated by the multiplication of wages. Wages paid out to workers are equal to 100 units (99.4 + 0.6). Yet the value of total output is 100.6 units because the production of interest goods adds a new value to a production that would otherwise have consisted of wage goods only. Thanks to fixed capital, workers are able to produce wage *and* interest goods, and this new production is an added value justifying an increase in income of 0.6 units.

All in all, interest proves to be a macroeconomic income derived from fixed capital and determined in wage units (corresponding to the production of interest goods). As for the amount of interest formed in each period, it depends on that of fixed capital and on the level of the interest rate, that is, the rate at which the compensation of the macroeconomic saving defined by fixed capital takes place. According to Schmitt (1996b: 38), in an orderly system the natural interest rate would be equal to the number of Euler. Thus, the number discovered by the Swiss mathematician would also set the target for the market rate of interest. The interest rate on consumption loans finds therefore its justification in the existence of a positive interest on fixed capital. If consumers want to benefit from saving, they are forced to offer an interest rate at least as high as the natural interest rate savers would derive from the productive investment of their income. The fact that interest is paid both on consumption and on productive loans, however, should not lead us to the conclusion that time itself is the direct source of a new income. As claimed by Böhm-Bawerk and by Wicksell, capital is time, yet interest is an income derived from time only when it is related to fixed capital, that is, to an irreversible capital-time. Thus, only part of the interest paid to savers is a new macroeconomic income, namely that derived form the transformation of saving into fixed capital. Let us say it once again, interest is a macroeconomic income only to the extent that it is formed in order to replace, period after period, the initial investment of profit absorbed in the production of instrumental goods.

8   Inflation and unemployment as macroeconomic disorders

The microeconomic analysis of inflation

A critical appraisal of the orthodox approach to inflation

The traditional analysis of inflation is based on a dichotomous perception of reality. Real goods and money are conceived of as distinct objects related to one another through the price level. Theories differ as to the way they explain the determination of the original price level; yet it is widely agreed that its stability may be threatened by an unexpected rise in the money supply leading to a variation in aggregate demand. For example, both Keynesian and new classical economists consider a fluctuating growth rate in the money supply as the main variable generating variations in the level of output and prices. The mechanism through which the effects of a variation in the money supply are transmitted to the price level or affect other economic aggregates varies according to the approach endorsed by a specific theory. Keynesian economists will emphasize the role of the wealth effect as well as of investment, consumption, and interest, rates; new classical economists will stress the importance of individual's behaviour and rational expectations together with incomplete information; real business cycle theorists will maintain that a variation in the value of money and credit is induced by a (technological) shock affecting real output. The common element of these alternative approaches is that inflation is always defined as 'a process of continuously rising prices' (Laidler and Parkin 1975: 741) essentially due to an increase in the money supply.

The quantity theory of money is arguably at the origin of the monetary theory of inflation. As shown by Setterfield in his recent review of the alternative theories of inflation, '[t]he quantity theory remains the cornerstone of inflation theory in the classical macroeconomic tradition' (Setterfield 2002: 346). Despite their differences, monetarism, new classical macroeconomics, and new Keynesian economics 'maintain that an, increase in the money supply initiates an excess demand for goods that, in the long run, translates wholly into an increase in prices' (ibid.: 246). Other causes of inflation are given by the cost-push theories of inflation and by economists referring to the orthodox Keynesian model of aggregate demand fluctuations. As claimed by Romer, 'when it comes to understanding inflation over the longer term, economists typically emphasize just one factor: growth of the money supply' (Romer 2001: 470). Taking for granted the existence of a direct relationship between the level of prices and the quantity of money, the majority of economists maintains that, for a given level of (real) output, a variation in the quantity of money determines a nominal change in prices. It is also widely and wrongly believed that central banks can determine the quantity of money and, through it, the price level. In fact, the actual working of our banking systems shows that things do not happen in this way. Money is issued by commercial banks as their own acknowledgement of debt and central banks are called upon to provide the common form to these different acknowledgements of debt. Thus, through inter-bank clearing central banks transform commercial banks' monies into homogeneous components of the same national currency. It is also true that, besides operating as clearing houses, central banks are in charge of the emission of banknotes and coins. Yet, these are merely alternative ways by which the money issued by commercial banks can be represented. Banknotes and coins are not money proper, but a claim (the most liquid one) on bank deposits. Thus, even if central banks have indeed the monopoly on the emission of banknotes and coins, the simple fact that banknotes and coins have to replace commercial banks' IOUs in order to enter circulation shows that central banks do not actually control them. As empirical evidence confirms, even commercial banks are unable to determine the amount of banknotes and coins in circulation. In fact, it is the public who decides what the sum of cash is, which central banks have to supply. Depending on both social and psychological factors, the public demands a certain amount of cash from commercial banks, and commercial banks have no choice but to ask central banks to satisfy the public's desire.

The very idea that banks (either central or commercial) can control the money supply is closely related to a net-asset conception of money. Indeed, the very expression 'money supply' is already clear evidence of the wide acceptance of this axiom. Money is deemed to be supplied as if it were a positive asset 'produced' by the banking system. It is true that, at the same time, money is also defined as a 'veil', a nominal amount that leaves real magnitudes unaltered. But this is indicative of the conceptual ambiguity that leads economists sharing this theoretical framework to claim that money matters while endorsing the homogeneity postulate, or to assert that inflation is always and everywhere a monetary phenomenon, and that money is neutral. Be it as it were, it is obvious that had money no value whatsoever, its quantity would then be irrelevant for the determination of prices. If growth in the money supply is supposed to cause an increase in aggregate demand, it is because money is deemed to have a positive value. Yet at the same time we are told that the value of money is the inverse of the price level: the higher the level of prices the lesser the value of money and vice versa. Thus, we are asked to believe that money is issued already endorsed with a positive value, but that this value depends on a price level that is itself dependent on the aggregate demand exerted by money. Once again the vicious circularity of the traditional approach to monetary economics is a clear sign of its unsoundness.

As shown by the quantum theory of emissions and confirmed by the actual workings of the banking system, money as such is not an asset. This is easy to see, since if money were a positive asset issued by banks instantaneously and at a near to zero cost (the reader should remember that money is a banks' IOU spontaneously issued through double-entry book-keeping), money creation itself would pertain to the world of metaphysical production – the instantaneous production of a positive asset pertaining to the realm of 'spontaneous generation' rather than to the world of physics proper – and economics would have to be based on metaphysical rather than micro or macro-foundations. However, once money is correctly perceived as an instantaneous flow and rigorously distinguished from bank deposits (stocks), it becomes immediately clear that the quantity theory of money is highly misleading. The flow aspect of money is indeed in sharp contrast with such monetarist notions like 'quantity of money', 'velocity of circulation', or 'money supply'. As we have repeatedly attempted to show, there is no such thing as 'the quantity of money', and money does not circulate in any physical sense akin to a physical-process type of circulation. The monetary flow cannot be compared to the flow of water, electric charges, human blood, and so on. Money is immaterial and its flow is instantaneous. To be precise, we should not even speak of the flow of money. If such a thing as the flow of money existed, money would have to be conceived of as a material entity (matter or energy) flowing more or less rapidly within a circuit that would exist independently of money's circulation. In fact, money does not flow; it *is* a flow. It is money itself that defines its own flow in each payment it carries out. Thus, no distinction can be made between the circuit and the circulation of money. 'Circuit' means nothing else than the instantaneous flow of money itself.

Understanding the true nature of money involves grasping the importance of introducing negative numbers in economics. This is not to say, of course, that negative numbers are not already used by economists. Yet, they are merely used in order to describe the decrease of a quantity as arithmetically represented. Thus, a negative rate of growth means a decrease in wealth; a negative income is a decrease in somebody's financial assets; a negatively marked price stands for a price falling below the cost of production, and so on. What is still missing in this positivist economic account is any conception of the relevance of negative magnitudes. The primacy of real variables and the identification of money as a positive asset do not allow for the existence of negative magnitudes. The inability to envisage such a state for money is the main reason why no true macro-economic theory can be developed by mainstream economics. It is only once it is recognized that money exists as *simultaneously* positive and negative (an *asset–liability*) that economic output can be seen as a net, macro-economic product (see Schmitt 1984a and Cencini 2001). To enter the world of macroeconomics proper is to become aware of the special relationship existing between negative numbers and real goods. The shift from a physicalist conception of production as a process of transformation to an economic conception of production requires an understanding of the true nature of money and the way physical output is integrated into its monetary form. Now, as shown by quantum analysis, production is an *absolute exchange* taking place between money and physical output, which results in the transformation of physical output into a sum of money income. The monetary form and its real 'content' are thus perceived as the joint aspects of one and the same reality: economic production.

The traditional approach to inflation based on the growth of the money supply does not explain any such absolute exchange and advocates, instead, a mechanistic conception of production and the relationship between money and output. This leads mainstream economists to an impasse: either they claim that money is a simple veil and that only relative prices matter, or they identify money with a positive asset and replace relative with monetary prices. The first alternative is chosen by the followers of a pure general equilibrium approach and reflects the respect for the homogeneity postulate. Demand is defined in real terms and is totally independent of variations in the money supply. Needless to say, this theoretical vision of economics has no connections with the real world and owes its success essentially to the prestige it derives from its *ad hoc* use of mathematics. Apparently adequate, its purported scientific status is closely linked with the logical possibility for determining relative prices and therefore follows in the footsteps of Walras's axiom of relative exchange. The second alternative is closer to reality insofar as it recognizes the importance of money, but is incapable of providing the theoretical elements required to show how nominal demand can differ from effective demand. *If money is issued as a positive asset, the money supply specifies total demand.* In such a framework there is no place for the classical distinction – introduced by Smith and successively taken over by Ricardo and Marx – between nominal and real money, and it is therefore impossible to distinguish a nominal from a real growth in the money supply. Instead of exploiting and developing the classical notions of nominal and real money, the monetary analysis of inflation advocated by mainstream economics assumes prices to be directly related to the quantity of money. But if a growth in the money supply defines an increase in aggregate demand that leads to a rise in prices (and/or in produced output), how can inflation be identified with a monetary anomaly? Banks issue money on request and according to the principles of double-entry book-keeping.

How is it possible to establish to which extent and for what transactions their intermediation is justified and when it is pathological?

According to Laidler, '[i]n dealing with the interaction of the quantity of money, money income and prices, the essential monetarist contribution has been to postulate the existence of stable relationships among these variables as an *empirical* matter' (Laidler 1981: 6). The strength of monetarism seems to stem directly from the empirical nature of its main postulates. If, as claimed by Laidler, empirical evidence strongly supports the existence of a stable relationship between money supply, money income and prices, there seems to be little point in trying to counter this result on purely theoretical grounds. Economics must deal with an empirical activity of human beings and a theoretical explanation cannot be at odds with its empirical working. This concern is fundamentally sound, of course. Yet, it does not mean that empirical evidence is to be directly derived from observation. That is a positivistic stricture, not required by a scientific explanation. The phenomenon rarely coincides with its appearance. Phenomena must be interpreted and their results evaluated, which can be done only through a conceptual detour as it were. A theoretical framework is thus always required in order to determine the empirical givens. As a consequence it is disingenuous to claim that a theory is better suited than another on purely factual grounds. Theories must be compared both conceptually and empirically, then tested *vis-à-vis* the phenomenon in order to assess to what extent they are capable of doing it justice.

Inflation and the price index: a few critical considerations

Let us consider further Laidler's claim about the empirical superiority of monetarism. If we take prices as an example, how can we consider their increase as empirical evidence of positive inflation? Obviously, this can be done only if inflation is identified with a nominal rise in prices. This clearly means that we would determine our choice of empirical evidence on the basis of a given theory (in this case the monetarist theory of inflation). Had we started from another theory, our choice of factual evidence would have probably been different, yet equally justifiable from an empirical point of view. What really matters, then, is the logical consistency of the theory under scrutiny and its capacity to explain reality. In the case of inflation, the problem is to establish the true nature of this phenomenon. In particular, our concern here is to examine whether inflation is a micro- or a macro-phenomenon. If one considers the way inflation has historically been conceived of, it is noticeable that authors hesitate whether to view it from a micro or a macroeconomic point of view. The traditional analyses of demand-pull and cost-push inflation are essentially sectoral and rely heavily on microeconomic concepts such as the propensity to consume, the behaviour of firms, workers, States, banks, foreign exporters, and so on. On the other hand, the monetary theories of inflation promote a more global approach and reason in terms of global demand and global supply. On the whole, however, the difference between these two broad approaches is much less than it appears. This can easily be seen by referring to the way inflation is identified with a continuous rise in prices.

Economists are unanimous in measuring inflation through a variation in the price index, mostly the consumer price index. We are thus told that, all things being equal, a constant increase in the price of one or more elements of the consumer basket leads to a rise of the price index and, therefore, to inflation. Prices that are considered here are market prices of specific goods and services. It is therefore immediately evident that inflation is measured by (and therefore identified with) a persistent rise in microeconomic prices. Now, the lack of distinction between micro and macroeconomic prices has a disruptive consequence concerning the analysis of inflation: increases in prices that lead to a new distribution of income without modifying money's purchasing power are in fact liable to provoke a rise in the consumer price index and lead to an erroneous conclusion as far as the existence of positive inflation is concerned.

Let us consider the following example. Suppose global supply (current output) to be equal to 100 units of money income. In the absence of inflation, global demand is also equal to 100 units, corresponding to the amount of income available in the system. Using a mainstream terminology we might say that the money supply is just enough to finance an aggregate demand exactly equal to aggregate supply. Suppose now the government to permanently rise its taxes on cigarettes and/or fuel. As a consequence of the government's decision the market price of cigarettes and/or fuel will also rise, for example by 20 per cent. This will lead to a persistent increase in the price index, say of 0.5 per cent, but would not modify the amount of aggregate demand. It would therefore be mistaken to infer that the rise in taxes is the cause of an inflationary rise in prices. In fact, the only effect of the new taxes will be to modify the initial distribution of income. A greater part of households' income will be transferred to the state, which will thus be able to exert a demand for current output in their stead. On the whole aggregate demand will remain the same and no inflationary gap will appear between global demand and global supply.

In our example the rise by 0.5 per cent of the price index defines an increase in the cost of living but has nothing to do with inflation, since it leaves money's purchasing power unaltered. This conclusion, which can easily be understood when income is conceived of as the result of an absolute exchange between money and output, is concealed by the generalized use of the price index as a measure of inflation. Now, our example is just one among many that entail the same result and that corroborate the fact that numerous variations in *microeconomic* prices lead to a simple redistribution of income without altering the relationship between global demand and global supply. Moreover, the frailty of the traditional analysis of inflation should easily catch one's eye if one considers

1   that the consumer price index is calculated by including imported goods into the standard basket (which is openly in contrast with the obvious fact that money's purchasing power is defined by the relationship – established by production – between a currency and the *national,* current output);
2   that it does not account for the effect on prices of technological progress,
3   and that actual price-level measurements suffer from substitution, new-goods, quality-change and 'aging' biases (see Rossi 2001: 31–42).

Let us conclude this first part of our analysis of inflation with a quotation that clearly shows the great inadequacy, not to say confusion, characterizing the present state of mainstream economics with regard to inflation. '[T]hese are many potential sources of inflation. Negative technology shocks, downward shifts in labor supply, and other factors that shift the aggregate supply curve to the left cause inflation; the same is true of increases in the money stock, downward shifts in money demand, increases in government purchases, and other factors that shift the aggregate demand curve to the right' (Romer 2001: 470).

The quantum theoretical approach to inflation

Inflation and Keynes's logical identity between Y *and* C + I

> Keynes in Book I of the *General Theory* denied that real aggregate demand was related at all to the price and money wage level. In effect, he turned the classical neutrality proposition against the classicals. If all money wages and prices are lowered in the same proportion, how can real quantities demanded be any different? Thus, if a real shock makes real demand deficient, how can a purely nominal price adjustment undo the change?
>
> (Tobin 1993: 59)

Tobin's observation may be interpreted either to mean that real magnitudes are all that matters, nominal variables being incapable to counter any real shock, or that the neoclassical dichotomy between real and monetary variables has to be replaced by an integrated vision of the world in which money and (real) output form a unity. The first interpretation is nothing but another version of the homogeneity postulate of GEA and its acceptance would make of Keynes a neoclassical economist (an unavoidable consequence of accepting Samuelson's neoclassical synthesis). The second interpretation leads to a new macroeconomic analysis based on

Keynes's logical identities. It is with respect to such an alternative that inflation and deflation have to be investigated.

Let us start from the identity, resulting from production, between money (a numerical form) and physical output (its real 'content'). The payment of wages is an instantaneous transaction through which money and output enter an absolute exchange. As a result of this particular exchange, an income is formed as a bank deposit entered on the liabilities side of banks' balance sheet. The very object of the banks' debit to the public is the physical output entered on the assets side of their balance sheet and making up the banks' credit with respect to firms (Table 8.1).

Debit and credit are the negative and positive poles of a unique event and define a unique, two-sided state. Thus, consistently with Keynes's logical identity between Y and $C+I$, the quantum theoretical approach to production shows that supply (current output) and demand (current income) are always necessarily equal. In fact, supply and demand are the two sides of the same coin; one cannot exist without the other, so that either they can exist side by side or they disappear together. Through production, an income is formed whose object is current output: supply and demand coexist. Through consumption income is destroyed in the final purchase of current output: supply and demand disappear simultaneously.

Now, an identity being the strongest relationship of coincidence between the two terms of an equation, how is it possible for global demand to be greater than global supply? How can two magnitudes be simultaneously identical and numerically different? The presence of inflation urges us to answer these questions, while logical analysis sets the constraints and, inexorably, 'forces' on us the conclusion that inflation as a purely monetary anomaly is impossible. Prices are still allowed to rise, but they now do so for reasons that have nothing to do with inflation. Global supply and global demand remaining necessarily equal, the rise in the level of prices would result solely from microeconomic fluctuations causing a new distribution of income. What has been considered as the outcome of a monetary pathology now appears to be a simple increase in the cost of living. However, empirical evidence shows that this is not the case. Monetary units are subjected to diminution of their purchasing power that cannot be explained by referring to microeconomic rises in prices. Inflation is thus a real issue despite the fact that global supply is always identical to global demand.

Since, obviously, inflation cannot be written off solely on theoretical

Table 8.1 The book-keeping exchange between money and output

Bank			
Liabilities		*Assets*	
Public (income holders)	x	Firms (current output)	x

grounds, it is equally clear that its correct understanding cannot write off the logical strictures. If it is analytically argued that current output and current income are the two terms of an identity, inflation must then be accommodated within this theoretical framework. Instead of being an obstacle to the explanation of inflation, the identity between global demand and global supply helps address it head on. In other words, the identity between Y and $C + I$ makes it easier, not harder, to dispense with the familiar theories of inflation advocated by mainstream economics. Let us illustrate this with a few examples.

Let us suppose global demand to increase because of the state paying formerly unemployed people to dig holes and fill them up again. According to Keynesian economists, the rise in demand will increase production *via* the multiplier effect unless the productive sectors are already working at full capacity, in which case the rise in demand will lead to an inflationary rise in prices. In both cases, however, the intervention of the state is said to create at first an inflationary gap between aggregate demand and supply. The argument here is very simple. Since workers digging and filling up holes are remunerated for their job, they earn a positive income that increases aggregate demand, whereas aggregate supply remains fixed at its previous level. But on what grounds can it be claimed that filled up holes are not part of global supply? Certainly not because of their physical irrelevance, for services, though evanescent, nevertheless form an important part of national output. The quantum theory of production settles the issue easily. Filled-up holes are actually part of global supply because they are the very object of the debt incurred by the state to the (central) bank that carries out the payment of wages on its behalf. Thus, the production of filled-up holes specifies simultaneously a supply and an equivalent demand. This is so much so that the state will have to sell its output in order to pay its debt back to the central bank. Once the state has recovered the sum invested in the production of filled-up holes (through direct or indirect taxation or through the sale of Treasury bonds), supply and demand will recover their previous level, which is further confirmation that the state's intervention can neither cause inflation nor start off a process of multiplication.

The fact that in some countries budget deficits have been and in some cases still are financed through money creation can hardly be denied. It is also true that, in countries where central banks are controlled by the state, public firms' losses may be covered in the same way. If this happens, global demand is subjected to a nominal increase of an inflationary nature owing to the extra 'nominal' money created by central banks. Yet this will not work for industrialized countries or for any country in which central banks are independent and enacting the principles of modern banking. If a central bank acts in conformity with these principles, budget deficits can be financed only by transferring to the state part of the currently produced income. In some cases a central bank may also advance to its government an income not yet produced. But even in these cases the extra expenditure of the State is no cause of inflation, since part of the country's future income having been spent in advance, the central bank will destroy it as soon as it is formed. *To 'advance' an income is not equivalent to creating one* ex nihilo. What is spent today (in advance) will no longer finance an expenditure tomorrow (when it will be actually formed) so that, on the whole, global demand is not artificially risen by this particular banking practice. As far as firms are concerned, the analysis follows the same path. Compliance with the principles of banking does not allow a priori any public firms' losses to be financed by central banks' money creation. Similarly, and *a fortiori*, within a modern and politically independent banking system, private firms' deficit cannot be covered by money creation. Firms must find in the financial market the resources necessary to back their *losses*, which means that what they spent in excess necessarily decreases the demand for current output exerted by the suppliers of financial resources.

Keynes's logical identity between supply and demand can help us get rid of another traditional theory of inflation, the so called wage-push analysis. According to this interpretation, inflation would result from repeated rises in wages unmatched by corresponding increases in labour's physical productivity. For example, if in one or more sectors' workers were able to obtain a 5 per cent nominal increase in wages and their physical productivity remained unaltered, the cost of production of their output would rise by 5 per cent, which, in turn, would cause a concomitant inflationary rise in prices. Now, suppose that prices did indeed rise by 5 per cent. This does not mean that the nominal growth of wages is the cause of the discrepancy, numerically expressed, between global supply and global demand. In fact, global supply is no more than the measure of current output, and the economic measure of current output has been given by its macroeconomic cost of production. Measured in wage units, current output is therefore defined by the amount of (direct and indirect) wages allotted to workers. Thus, a rise in wages entails a rise in both global demand *and* global supply. Each single output is independent of any other and determines its own demand. If output of period p_0 is equal to 100 wage units, 100 is the numerical expression of the global supply at p_0 and of the income formed in this period, that is, of the concomitant global demand. If in the following period, p_1, wages rise from 100 to 105 units, global supply (output of period p_1) and global demand (income formed in p_1) also become subjected to the same numerical increase. No divergence can appear between supply and demand, either with respect to p_0, p_1 or $(p_0 + p_1)$'s output. This is tantamount to saying that wage-push theories provide no explanation of inflation.

The logical identity between global supply and global demand seems conceptually too tight to allow for inflation – typically defined as a situation in which global demand is greater than global supply – to even occur. Nevertheless, it is thanks to this inexorable identity that the true sense of inflation can be appreciated. A logical identity establishes the strongest possible relationship between its two terms. Applied to our case this means that global supply and global demand remain always dual, regardless of their numerical specification. It is thus not inconsistent to have a situation in which global supply (S) and global demand (D) are identical despite the fact that S is numerically equal to 100 while D is numerically equal to 105. The identity establishes that S (100) $\equiv D$ (105) – and not, of course, that from a purely numerical point of view 100 is equal to 105. Using the Classics' distinction between nominal and real money, we claim that global demand expressed in *nominal* money terms is greater than global supply expressed in real money terms. If we expressed both S and D in real terms, no such difference would arise. But if one of the two is measured in nominal money a numerical discrepancy can arise. This is what happens in the case of inflation, where the numerical expression of global demand is greater than that of global supply. Now, the logical identity between S and D tells us that, despite their numerical difference, S and D define the same economic value. In other words, the identity D (105) $\equiv S$ (100) signifies that a global demand measured by 105 units of nominal money is still worth 100 units of real money, that is, that an income equal to 100 units of real money is distributed over 105 units of nominal money. But if an income worth 100 units is distributed over 105 units of money this entails a loss of each single wage-unit's purchasing power. The nominal rise in global demand leaves its value unaltered, but decreases the value of each single unit charged to carry it over. Inflation is therefore a situation in which global demand rises with respect to global supply *in nominal money terms*. The identity between D (105) and S (100) shows this very clearly. Global demand is still worth 100 units, yet, instead of being distributed over 100 units of money, it is now 'vehiculated' by 105 units of money. Each monetary wage-unit loses part of its initial value or purchasing power, which indicates that inflation is the altering of the initial relationship between produced output and its monetary form.

The theoretical coexistence of a substantial identity and of a numerical divergence both pertaining to global supply and global demand is a result that can be appreciated only if money is clearly distinguished from income and if production is conceived of as an instantaneous, absolute exchange between money and output. What must still be explained, however, is how it is indeed possible for global demand to rise, in nominal terms, with respect to global supply. As shown by Schmitt (1984a), Cencini (1996), and Rossi (2001), the origin of inflation is to be found in the anomalous investment of profits characterizing what we might call today's pathological capitalism. If inflation is still a mysterious disorder, it is probably because its analysis is closely connected with that of capital accumulation, a process that, quoting Wicksell, is the '*testimonium paupertatis* of political economy' (Wicksell 1954: 106) and whose investigation is 'very complicated and very difficult' (Solow 1963: 11). Complexity and difficulty inherent in the analysis of capital are due to the need to clearly distinguish between money, income and capital, as well as to the confusion of these three concepts in practice. The theorist attempting to explain inflation is therefore confronted with a double task: how to understand the logical relationship existing between money, income and capital, and then to figure out what happens when the distinction between these concepts is not recognized in the accounting of an actually existing economic system. In Chapter 7 we investigated the logical link relating fixed capital to saved income (capital-time) through the investment of profits. What we have now to analyse is the way profits are invested in today's monetary economies.

Inflation, capital accumulation, and fixed capital amortization

Our starting point is a piece of fieldwork evidence: at the level of banking practice no book-keeping structure reflects today the logical and conceptual distinction between money, income, and fixed capital. Analytically, all the transactions entered into by and through banks are lumped together in the same T-account. The main reasons for this logical confusion are (1) the lack of a true analysis of monetary *flows*, and (2) the conflation of income with capital. Thus, on the one hand flows are not the object of any specific double-entry book-keeping and, on the other hand, capital is never entered into a specific capital account. As far as capital accumulation is concerned, the consequence of this confusion means that the investment of profits leading to the formation of fixed capital is unbalanced financially. Let us try to explain this.

When profits are invested in the production of fixed capital goods, the income transferred by households to firms is for ever transformed into a macroeconomic saving through its investment by firms. Having been thus transformed into fixed capital, profits should therefore no longer be available on the financial market. Yet this is not what happens in the present system. In the absence of a fixed capital department where they would be entered into by banks, invested profits are deposited in the overall T-account of banks. To be precise: once invested, profits disappear as such. Having spent it, firms are no longer the holders of a positive income. Yet, what is destroyed as profit reappears as a bank deposit and 'feeds' an equivalent demand on the market for produced goods and services. The anomaly of the present system lies in the fact that *invested profits are still available on the financial market even though they have been expended and transformed into fixed capital.* Despite having been spent by firms, they reappear in the form of wages.

A comparison between what should logically happen and what actually happens today may prove useful. Let us start with Schmitt's differentiation into monetary, saving (or financial), and fixed capital departments, by which banks should organize their books by if they are to comply with the requirements of a coherent monetary system.

> – The department of emissions [or monetary department] is concerned with the creation and destruction of money, whether it is created when output is formed, transferred or sold.
> – The saving (or capital-time) department is where ordinary bank deposits are entered into in order to 'recycle' them on the financial market, to the benefit of their owner or of those who borrow them.
> – The fixed capital department is in charge of all the saving initially formed in the second department that must be withdrawn from this department precisely because it has been invested in the production of instrumental capital.
>
> (Schmitt 1984a: 321–2, our translation)

Our main concern here is the investment of profits, so let us reproduce only the book-keeping relationships between the second and third departments by describing the way capitalization should be entered into an orderly system (Table 8.2).

Entry (1) defines the formation of a monetary profit of 20 units whose object is the stock of real goods carried over from period p_1. Entries (2) and (2') show how F's profit is transferred to the third department. The production of instrumental goods, entry (3), gives rise to a new income that workers spend (and destroy) in the final purchase of stocked output, entry (4). Finally, entries (5) and (2') describe the situation at the end of period p_2, real capital goods being the object of a capitalized saving deposited in department III.

In the present system no accounting classification is designated to dis-

Table 8.2 The book-keeping formation of fixed capital

Department II			
Liabilities		*Assets*	
1. F	20	Output	20
2. III	20	F	20
III	20	Output	20
3. W	20	F (fixed capital goods)	20
4. Output	20	W	20
5. III	20	F (fixed capital goods)	20
Department III			
Liabilities		*Assets*	
2'. F	20	II	20

tinguish between monetary, financial and fixed capital departments. As a consequence, the investment of profits is wrongly allotted to their expenditure. What has to be clarified then is the effect of an expenditure so instituted. If firms spent their profits toward the final purchase of investment goods on the commodity market, income would be destroyed. Yet, if this happened no fixed capital could be formed (fixed capital goods would in reality remain, economically speaking, indistinguishable from consumption goods) and no macroeconomic saving would appear. What actually happens is that profits are spent on the labour market. The purchase of fixed capital goods by firms does not entail the destruction of profits but leads to their re-emission in the form of wages (Table 8.3).

Entry (1) refers to the profits in p_1. The expenditure of profits within the payment of wages to workers producing fixed capital goods is represented by entry (2). Entry (3) describes the expenditure of the income obtained from the investment of profits for the purchase of the stock of real goods formed in p_1.

If we consider the flows inherent to the investment of profits and not merely their outcome, we observe that they amount to a total of 40 units, of which 20 units are the expenditure of profits for the purchase of fixed capital goods and 20 units the payment of wages financed through the expenditure of profits. Instead of being transferred to the fixed capital department, profits are spent on the labour market and are thus re-emitted as wages and spent again, in this new form, on the market for produced output. The same income (20 units of profit) is thus spent twice. If profits were saved-up in the third department, the purchase of output would be financed by a new amount of wage income that would not be derived from the expenditure of profits. In this case a single flow of 20 units would correspond to the production of fixed capital goods. Today it is not so. The production of instrumental goods is financed out of profits, which entails the coexistence of two flows of 20 units each. What Schmitt calls '*la dépense gigogne*' – the 'dyadic' expenditure – is precisely the expenditure of profits through the payment of wages.

Now, the anomaly in the second period does not lead to an inflationary rise in prices, since the wages generated by the investment of profits can be spent for the purchase of the goods stocked in the first period, while profits themselves are spent for the purchase of fixed capital goods. If one

Table 8.3 The re-emission of wages

Banks			
Liabilities		*Assets*	
1. F	20⎞	Output	20
2. W	20⎠	F (fixed capital goods)	20
3. Output	20	W	20

compares the situation in which capital is transferred to the third department with what happens today, one can observe that whereas in the first
case a new income is spent on the market for products while profits are
capitalized, in the second case the same income is spent twice, once on the
labour market and once on the commodity market. This double expenditure is anomalous and ends up transforming capitalization into a pathological process. What is wrong is not that firms decide to invest their profits
into the production of instrumental goods, but that this decision leads to
the expenditure of profits on the labour market instead of transforming
them into social capital. The substitution of stocked consumption goods
produced in the first period for investment goods produced in the second
period masks the fact that fixed capital goods are purchased by firms with
the payment of wages. By spending their profits on the labour market,
firms purchase the very goods that should mark the real object of social
capital, thus depriving the whole society of the economic ownership of
fixed capital. It is through the investment of profits that fixed capital is
formed, and it is through their investment that profits are transformed into
a macroeconomic saving. If fixed capital goods were to define the real
'content' of this macroeconomic saving, they would be owned, economically, by firms on behalf of society (represented here by the individual
owners of firms). Now, the fact that profits are spent with the payment of
wages, instead of being transferred to the third department, entails the
final purchase of fixed capital goods by what Schmitt calls 'depersonalized
firms'. The expenditure of profits does not allow for their transformation
into social (macroeconomic) saving, and thus gives to 'depersonalized
firms' the ownership of fixed capital goods. Firms themselves, and not their
individual owners, become the final holders of fixed capital goods, which
are thus hopelessly out of the reach of society (considered as the set of
individuals operating in our economic system). Instead of being owned by
society (through 'personalized' firms), fixed capital is appropriated by
'depersonalized' firms and thus pathologically transformed into a reified
capital, the objective antagonist of economic society.

Let us straightforwardly emphasize that the origin of pathological capital
is not to be found in the behaviour of firms. What goes awry today cannot
be attributed to the entrepreneurs' decisions but to the absence of a fixed
capital department that can prevent banks from paying wages out of the
income (profits) meant to correspond to macroeconomic saving. Given the
skewed bank accounting, the investment of profits generates a pathological
capital to which human labour is in turn pathologically attached. In today's
ill-functioning capitalism, economic agents are the victims of a system in
which fixed capital is appropriated by impersonal *Capital* itself.

On the whole, capitalization can take place in two different ways, a
coherent and a pathological one. In an orderly system, fixed capital would
be represented by an amount of monetary capital entered into the third
department and by its real 'content' (instrumental goods), physically

stocked with firms. In a pathological system, fixed capital is represented by an amount of capital goods purchased by firms on the labour market. Thus, a coherently logical capitalization does not entail the appropriation by impersonal *Capital* ('depersonalized' firms) of the produced means of production, while pathological capitalization does. Now, the purchase of fixed capital goods by firms defines a nominal increase in global demand. 'Every invested profit is an expenditure of F [firms] on F and every expenditure of F on F is an excess demand on the products market exerted through the mediation of an expenditure on the pro- ductive services market' (Schmitt 1984a: 214, our translation). This nominal increase in demand has no inflationary effect on prices only because it is entirely absorbed by the formation of pathological capital. Yet inflation is just around the corner as soon as amortization is taken into account. The effect of the particular relationship between impersonal *Capital* and income holders is such that the amortization of instrumental goods amounts to a profit's formation whose investment gives rise to an excess demand that can no longer be counter-absorbed by the purchase of the unsold stock of consumption goods produced in the first period.

Let us compare what happens in periods p_1 and p_2, when profits are first formed and invested, with what happens in period p_3, when the produc- tion of amortization or replacement goods is added to that of wage and investment goods (Figure 8.1).

As shown in Figure 8.1, the initial investment of profits has no inflation- ary consequences since the excess demand exerted by firms leads to the appropriation of fixed capital goods by *Capital* and since workers whose income is lacking its real 'content' – precisely because fixed capital goods have been appropriated by *Capital* – can nevertheless purchase the consumption goods stocked in p_1. Things are different in period p_3, when

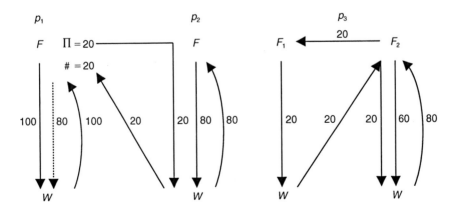

Figure 8.1 Inflation and fixed capital amortization.

part of firms F, F_1, are producing replacement goods. Since fixed capital goods are appropriated by impersonal *Capital* ('depersonalized' firms), production of amortization goods is carried out to the benefit of *Capital*, which means that the income earned in the production of replacement goods will necessarily be spent for the purchase of the goods produced by firms F_2. As a consequence, in period p_3 firms F_2 will derive a positive profit from the expenditure of the income earned by workers employed in the production of replacements goods. Now, besides leading to an increase in pathological capital (corresponding to a new production of fixed capital goods), the investment by F_2's of their new profit defines an inflationary gap between D and S. Since in period p_3 no stock of consumption goods is available to fill up the wages distributed to workers producing the new amount of fixed capital goods, the rise in demand caused by the new investment of profits can no longer be neutralized. If we sum up the demand exerted on the commodity market we reach the amount of 120 units (100 exerted by W and 20 by F). Global supply being equal to 100 units, a numerical divergence appears defining the new distribution of value owing to inflation.

Reminding the reader that a fully detailed analysis of the quantum theory of inflation can be found already in Schmitt (1984a), let us conclude this brief overview by emphasizing the fact that inflation is a macroeconomic disorder whose cause lies in the still imperfect accounting structure of monetary payments. Independently of economic agents' behaviour, inflation arises today because the investment of profits implies their expenditure on the labour market and the simultaneous formation of pathological capital.

Involuntary unemployment: its macroeconomic origin

A few remarks about mainstream analyses of unemployment

From the outset economic analysis of unemployment has been treated either as a microeconomic disequilibrium concerning the market for labour, or as the consequence of a macroeconomic imbalance between global demand and global supply. Accordingly, theories of unemployment have attempted to determine its causes either starting from economic agents' behaviour or from the macroeconomic laws governing production, circulation and capital accumulation. Since the widespread and long-lasting success of Walras's general equilibrium analysis the balance has radically shifted in favour of a labour market approach to unemployment. So, today, it has become extremely difficult to find an explanation of this phenomenon that is not based on microeconomic considerations.

In a pure Walrasian system, unemployment is a temporary disturbance due to a disequilibrium between supply of and demand for labour generated by a rise in real wages. In the simplest GEA model, equilibrium is restored through a fall in nominal wages, which brings down the level of real wages and encourages employers to increase their demand for labour. '*[E]quilibrium in the market for services, as in the market for products, is attained by raising the prices of those services the demand for which is greater than the offer and by lowering the prices of those services the offer of which is greater than the demand*' (Walras 1984: 477). In this theoretical setting, unemployment is therefore conceived of as a matter of equilibrium, a state of affairs where workers' and firms' desires are not perfectly matched given the level of real wages.

The analysis proposed by the monetarists is only slightly different from Walras's GEA. According to the followers of the quantity theory of money, the institutional setting of our real economies may not correspond to that of a perfectly competitive economy. Under these conditions, the labour market could still be assumed to clear, provided that one is allowed to modify the equations of GEA in order to account for market imperfections, which, in the case at hand, means to account for a 'natural rate of unemployment'. In his paper on the role of monetary policy, Friedman defines the 'natural' rate as

> the level that would be ground out by the Walrasian system of general equilibrium equations, provided there is imbedded in them the actual structural characteristics of the labor and commodity markets, including market imperfections, stochastic variability in demands and supplies, the cost of gathering information about job vacancies and labor availabilities, the cost of mobility, and so on.
>
> (Friedman 1968: 8)

Like in traditional neoclassical theories, unemployment for monetarists is thus made to depend on the supply of and demand for labour, and is said to be independent, in the long run, of nominal variations entailed by changes in monetary policies. The resulting analysis of unemployment is both microeconomic and 'real'. What Friedman reproaches Phillips for is precisely his failure to distinguish nominal from real wages, so that the impact of monetary policies is played down by anticipations and real wage effects. In short, according to Friedman, unemployment is a real quantity determined by a Walrasian system of general equilibrium and beyond the influence of monetary authorities (which merely control nominal quantities). Interventions on the rate of money growth would, therefore, have only a short term impact on real magnitudes so that Phillips' permanent trade-off between inflation and unemployment must be replaced by a temporary trade-off, which 'comes not from inflation per se, but from unanticipated inflation, which generally means, from a rising rate of inflation' (ibid.: 11).

New classical economists take over the monetarists' analysis as well as

Friedman's idea that real wage may fail to adjust to its equilibrium value because of workers' incorrect expectations with regard to inflation. Were inflation not accurately forecasted, workers would be led to settle for a real wage at a level that does not allow equilibrium to reach its full employment level.

According to the real business cycle approach, economic fluctuations are caused by persistent real shocks such as random changes in the rate of technological progress. Emphasis is thus moved from monetary to real shocks, that is, from demand-side to supply-side unanticipated variations. Evolved out of new classical economics, the real business cycle school adopts a rational expectations hypothesis and claims that shifts in the aggregate production functions lead economic agents 'to optimally respond to the resultant fluctuations in relative prices by altering their supply of labour and consumption' (Snowdon and Vane 1997a: 361).

As an attempt to explain variations in employment, real business cycle analysis proves extremely poor compared to the efforts made by other schools of thought. In particular, it seems highly restrictive to relate unemployment mainly to technological shocks. As clearly maintained by Keynes, technological unemployment pertains – together with that caused by frictional disturbances such as bad management, imperfect information, imperfect competition, and so on – to the category of voluntary unemployment. Implicated in the development of an economic system, however, technological progress may be viewed as a positive factor even from the employment point of view, since it allows machines to replace workers in dangerous and repetitive tasks that have nothing to do with the creative aspect of human labour. According to Keynes, the truly pathological category is that of involuntary unemployment, workers being led out of work by a permanent excess supply in the commodity market. Known as *deflation*, this situation is defined as one in which total demand fails to match total supply because money income is less than that required to meet the supply of real goods and services. This cannot result from an autonomous variation in the money supply, and has nothing to do with the inflation–unemployment trade-off suggested by Phillips. The question is much more difficult to deal with than it may at first appear, and requires a deep knowledge of the pathology of capital accumulation. Before addressing it, let us briefly observe that Keynes himself was unfortunately the source of another, more conventional theory of unemployment.

Davidson, for example, rejects the traditional, microeconomic analysis of unemployment in favour of Keynes's suggestion that unemployment is 'basically always a liquidity problem' (Davidson 2002: 25). According to the American economist, Keynes's crucial insight is that 'there is a fundamental psychological law where the marginal propensity to spend income on the products of industry is less than unity' (ibid.: 25). Hence, unemployment would essentially be due to the households' decision to save part of their income or, what amounts to the same thing, to hold it in its liquid form. We are thus encouraged to switch from a vision in which unemployment is mainly caused by the workers' refusal to accept lower wages to one in which workers are on the dole as consumers refuse to spend the totality of their income. Now, none of these interpretations is truly appealing. If it is naïve to impute involuntary unemployment to the unwillingness of workers to accept lower wages, it is likewise ingenuous to maintain that consumers' behaviour may be the cause of unemployment since saving reduces global demand. And Davidson is not the only post-Keynesian to argue for the negative impact of saving on employment.

Wray too claims, for example, that unemployment is caused by the desired level of net nominal saving being higher than the actual level, which is tantamount to saying that unemployment rises with the increase of households' propensity to save. Wray argues in fact that, 'if the desired net nominal position were lower, the population would be spending more and creating more jobs for the unemployed' (Wray 1998: 129–30). As shown by quantum monetary analysis, however, saving cannot be a cause of unemployment for it does not affect global demand. Saved money income exists in the form of bank deposits and, because of double-entry book-keeping, bank deposits are always necessarily lent and spent. Now, as we have seen in Chapter 6, the logical and empirical impossibility of identifying savings with a loss of money income (what the concept of hoarding was supposed to capture) has a disruptive consequence for the Keynesian multiplier. Hence, there seems to be no room for the claim that public spending can, through the multiplier effect, induce an increase in the production of the private sector (and therefore, as a direct consequence, a fall in unemployment). In fact, this conclusion is corroborated by another straightforward argument: the supposed rise in demand due to the government acting as employer of last resort is entirely absorbed to cover the costs of public production. In other words, if it is true that the money income generated by the new production increases global demand, it is also certain that the newly produced output increases global supply by an equivalent amount. Independently of their physical characteristics, public goods and services must be sold by the government. Whether this happens through a direct sale or through taxation, it does not matter. In every case, demand and supply are modified in tandem, so that the government's intervention does not raise global demand alone, nor does it induce a rise in private sector employment.

In conclusion, we see how Davidson and Wray's analyses are no less microeconomic than those of their neoclassical, monetarist, new classical, and new Keynesian competitors. Whether the blame is put on workers or on consumers, the fact remains that the cause of unemployment is identified with the microeconomic behaviour of one category or another of economic agents. Finally, Davidson's lack of a rigorous distinction between micro and macroeconomics is highlighted in such claims as: 'Keynes's aggregate supply and demand curves are behavioral functions' (Davidson 2002: 27), and 'Keynes's aggregate supply function is derived from ordinary Marshallian macro flow-supply functions' (ibid.: 31).

Capital over-accumulation as the cause of involuntary unemployment

Naïvely conceived, involuntary unemployment may be defined as a situation concerning all those people who are ready, willing, and able to work at the going wage rate and nevertheless unable to find a job. There is nothing obviously wrong in this definition, of course, yet it may induce the reader to believe that unemployment is a matter of personal will or its lack rather than the consequence of a structural pathology afflicting the entire economic system. In fact, as claimed by Bradley, '[i]nvoluntary unemployment will be a relevant concept only on condition that involuntariness is proven comprehensive; this implies that unemployment will arise whatever the behaviour of *all* economic agents' (Bradley 2003: 399). This is the right interpretation of Keynes's concept of involuntary unemployment, which clearly distinguishes a situation where unemployment arises because of the anomalous behaviour of one or more categories of economic agents or, alternatively, because of frictional or technological reasons from a situation in which it is the effect of deflation. Now, like inflation, deflation is a macroeconomic disorder deriving from the present pathological process of capital accumulation. Let us try to show it.

First of all, it is important to note that deflation can no more be identified with a persistent fall in prices than inflation can be assimilated to a persistent rise in prices. Indeed, prices may fall for a host of reasons that have no consequence whatsoever on the relationship between physical output and its monetary form. Second, deflation must not be considered as a negative inflation. Derived from the apparent inverse correlation existing between inflation and deflation, the belief that these disorders are mutually exclusive is in sharp contrast with the reality of facts. It can indeed be easily observed that while inflation does not cumulate over time, its effects do, which means that whereas today's inflation is entirely new with respect to past inflation, any positive rate of inflation adds up to the previous rates and denotes an overall growth of inflation itself. *What is wrongly taken to be the rate of inflation is thus the rate of increase in inflation.* Hence, for example, a rate of inflation equal to 2 per cent means that today's inflation has grown by 2 per cent with respect to yesterday's inflation. If we suppose inflation to have started in period p_1, where it reached 3 per cent, a new rate of inflation of 2 per cent in period p_2 will denote a total inflation of more than 5 per cent occurring in p_2. The reader can therefore easily imagine how important inflation at period p would have been had the disorder first appeared several periods before. This is to say that, contrary to what is commonly believed, inflation is an expanding disorder, increasingly affecting money's purchasing power. The fact that technological progress counterbalances the fall in the standard of living that would otherwise accompany inflation shall not lead us astray: inflation is a growing, constantly renewed disorder perverting the money–output relationship. It is now easy to understand how deflation is also becoming a cause for worry in capitalist economies. *The simultaneous presence of high levels of inflation and deflation is a good indicator that these two disorders are not inversely correlated.*

The coexistence of inflation and deflation is not easy to grasp. Empirical evidence notwithstanding, how is it possible for global supply to be simultaneously lesser (inflation) and greater (deflation) than global demand? This apparent contradiction can be successfully dealt with only by referring to Keynes's logical identity between global supply and global demand. If S and D were two distinct magnitudes, it would be logically impossible to write down the following relationship:

$$S \gtreqless D.$$

But since S and D are the two faces of one and the same coin, their identity is the common feature of their numerical divergences. It is precisely because S and D are identical that their numerical difference acquires an unambiguous meaning, and it is because the meanings of S (100) $\equiv D$ (120) and S (120) $\equiv D$ (100) are rigorously differentiated that inflation and deflation can coexist.

It should be obvious from the analysis above that inflation and deflation have a common cause: the pathological process of capital accumulation and over-accumulation. To show this, it is worth referring to Figure 8.1 and to Wicksell's distinction between natural and market rates of interest. As the reader will remember, inflation is the unavoidable consequence of (pathological) capital amortization and coincides with a new investment of profits defining a further increase in fixed capital. *Over-accumulation refers therefore to the duplication occurring when the object of amortization is a fixed capital of pathological origin (that is, a fixed capital formed by the expenditure of profits).* If the system did not set a limit to capital accumulation, fixed capital would rise *ad infinitum* and inflation would be the sole disorder caused by it. Now, the fact is that capital has a cost, determined by the market rate of interest, and that this cost (interest) has to be paid out of profits. With the persistent growth of fixed capital the amount of its remuneration rises too, and given that capital grows more than profits, Wicksell's natural rate of interest (the ratio between profits and capital) is doomed to fall. As the gap between natural and market rates of interest closes down, it becomes clear that the rate of growth of fixed capital must slow down, since future profits would not be enough to remunerate a capital growing at the same pace as before. As maintained by Schmitt, 'being unable to remunerate sufficiently the totality of new capital' (Schmitt 1984a: 237, our translation), firms can either reduce its formation or invest their profits in the production of wage goods instead of new capital goods. In the former case, national production would also be reduced, thus provoking a positive measure of involuntary unemployment. In the latter case, a pathological production of wage goods replaces the pathological production of fixed capital goods and leads to a deflationary gap between global supply and global demand. Let us explain this further.

As the reader knows, the pathology we are referring to consists in the fact that the production of new capital or wage goods is financed through the investment of profits. When new fixed capital goods are produced, their final purchase by firms on the labour market entails an excess demand leading to an inflationary rise in prices. When new wage goods are produced instead of instrumental goods another disorder appears, the supply on the commodity market being pathologically increased by the new wage goods already purchased on the labour market. 'To the extent that inflationary profits are spent in the production of wage goods, these goods are offered on the commodity market, where no income is available for their purchase' (ibid.: 238, our translation). Having already been purchased on the labour market, wage goods must therefore be sold a second time on the commodity market. But 'the national economy provides only *once* the necessary purchasing power' (ibid.: 238, our translation). As a result of this redundant offer of the same goods, global supply rises in nominal terms with respect to a demand that remains unaltered in real money terms.

Inflation and deflation are two different disorders arising from the same cause: the pathological investment of profits. While inflation is a disorder in which global demand is increased by a renewed expenditure of an income already spent on the labour market, deflation is defined by a pathological increase in global supply. Does this not then mean, contrary to what we have been claiming, that inflation and deflation eventually balance each other out? The answer is certainly no with respect to the possibility of inflation compensating deflation. In fact, the numerical gap between supply and demand means that global demand, expressed in real money terms, is insufficient to meet global supply. In other words, the income available in the system is insufficient for the purchase of the goods offered by firms. It should be clear, therefore, that this lack of income cannot be compensated through inflation because the pathological excess demand characterizing inflation is precisely not the effect of an increase in income.

Is the answer also in the negative when the question is raised as to the possibility of deflation 'correcting' for inflation? This time things are slightly different, since it is not impossible for the effects of a pathological excess demand to be balanced by the effects of a pathological excess supply. Specifically, the goods offered a second time may well be matched by an income spent a second time, which explains the compensation of the inflationary rise by the deflationary fall in prices. However, it has to be made very clear that this does not in the least mean that deflation can be a remedy against inflation, or even that a persistent deflation can constantly reduce inflation. It must be clearly understood, in fact, that inflation and deflation share a common cause and that:

1   the production of wage goods instead of fixed capital goods is the first step towards an overall fall in production, and that
2   a high level of inflation is necessary for deflation to settle in.

Point (1) is almost self-evident. Being unable to sell the entire output, firms have no other choice than to reduce production and thus put workers on the dole; which is a further confirmation that deflation is a major cause of involuntary unemployment. Thus, whether firms invest part of their profits in the financial markets or toward the production of wage goods, national employment is bound to be reduced, that part of profits which is not invested in the production of new capital goods being the measure of involuntary unemployment (see Schmitt 1984a: 239). Point (2) recalls the fact that deflation settles in when capital accumulation can no longer expand any further because of the increasing cost of its remuneration. Deflation is thus the last stage of a process that initially leads to growing levels of inflation. As long as the rate of profit (Wicksell's natural rate of interest) is much higher than the market rate of interest, capital accumulation grows and so does inflation. Before capital accumulation approaches the limit set by the necessity to remunerate capital out of profits, there is in fact no need for the system to switch from the production of fixed capital goods to that of wage goods. It is only once the gap between natural and market rates of interest closes up that the growth in capital accumulation must be reduced. Deflation thus takes the place of inflation only to the extent that it reduces the rate of growth of capital accumulation. Under no circumstances does deflation cause a decline in inflation, which at most, when the pathology reaches its peak, stabilizes itself at its highest level.

The coexistence of inflation and deflation is the mark of a system in which pathological capital accumulation and over-accumulation have gone on for so long that it becomes necessary to reduce the rate of growth of fixed capital. Inflation, deflation, households' growing indebtedness, and rising unemployment are the unavoidable consequences of this pathological development of modern capitalist economies. All these disorders have therefore a common cause that is independent of economic agents' behaviour. Determining the origin of inflation and involuntary unemployment is a process that requires a macroeconomic analysis of capital accumulation, which in turn is grounded on Keynes's crucial identities between global supply and global demand and between saving and investment. The time has come to finally abandon the fruitless, microeconomic approach to inflation and unemployment and switch to a macroeconomic quantum theoretical approach putting the analytical differentiation between money, income, and capital at centre stage.

Part III

The macroeconomic analysis of international economics

9 Eurocurrencies
A macroeconomic occurrence

Before dealing with the specific problem of eurocurrencies it is necessary to introduce a few general considerations about the particular nature of international transactions. We will therefore devote the first part of this chapter to a short introduction to the peculiarities of international macroeconomics, which should prove useful for a better understanding of what follows as well as of the arguments analysed in the other chapters of this Part.

From national to international macroeconomics

A first, almost self-evident difference between a national and an international economy is that the former is an economy of production and exchange while the latter is merely concerned with exchange. In fact, no truly international production exists, world output (multinational output included) being entirely the making of nations. It thus follows that a hypothetic international money could not derive its value from international production. At the international level the integration between money and output must first pass through the intermediation of national currencies. The shift from national to international exchanges highlights a second important difference between national and international economies.

Within any given country there is monetary homogeneity. The monetary units issued by banks pertaining to the same banking system are undifferentiated elements of the same set: national currency. Homogeneity, however, is not an intrinsic characteristic of banks' money but the result of a process leading to the creation of a proper banking system. It is through inter-bank clearing that the monetary units issued by each single bank are made homogeneous. Each commercial or private bank is a different institution whose spontaneous acknowledgement of debt would remain heterogeneous with respect to that issued by any other private bank was it not for the system of clearing operated by the central bank. Through what Schmitt likens to a catalytic process, the different bank monies are given a common form (central money) and become part of a unique national currency. Things are radically different at the international level. Each national currency is obviously distinct from any other, and their heterogeneity is not dealt with by any system of international clearing. Yet, the problem seems to be solved through the determination of exchange rates. If the exchange rate between money A (MA) and money B (MB) is, say, of one MA for every two MB, the shift from one currency to the other is a simple question of arithmetic calculation, MA and MB being *de facto* homogeneous and therefore interchangeable elements of the same set. Yet, as claimed by Schmitt, this is precisely the question that has to be settled. *Does the exchange rate between MA and MB establish their homogeneity or do they remain heterogeneous despite their exchange?* The answer depends on whether or not the exchange between MA and MB is an *absolute* exchange, that is, on whether or not it defines the identity of its two terms. '[M]onies A and B are homogeneous elements of the same set if the exchange of x MA for y MB defines the equivalence or the identity of its terms' (Schmitt 1984b: 89, our translation).

If the transaction taking place on the foreign exchange market specifies the identity between MA and MB, it then establishes their homogeneity. On the contrary, if the exchange is essentially a barter between MA and MB, it leaves them fundamentally as heterogeneous as they were before being exchanged. The distinction between *relative* and *absolute* exchange is crucial here. If the transaction between MA and MB is conceived of as a relative exchange, MA simply taking the place of MB and vice versa, the two currencies remain heterogeneous. The consequence of this state of affairs is that 'exchange rates are "barter prices" instead of equivalences [which means they] do not follow the relative value of currencies, determined by each national economy of production' (ibid.: 91, our translation). A different result can be reached only if MA and MB enter an absolute exchange, where, for example, money A is changed *into itself* through the intermediation of money B (Figure 9.1).

As claimed by Schmitt, in fact,

> [w]hen *the same* (instantaneous) *foreign exchange transaction* implies *twice* money A, through money B, *two relations of equivalence* are simultaneously determined, equivalence
>
> $$y \, MB = x \, MA$$
>
> being formed within the tautological equivalence
>
> $$x \, MA = x \, MA.$$
>
> (ibid.: 90, our translation)

MA ————————▶ MB ————————▶ MA

Figure 9.1 The absolute exchange of money A.

The transformation of foreign exchange transactions from relative into absolute exchanges requires the implementation of an international clearing system operated by a *central bank of central banks* along the same principles already at work within the majority of domestic banking systems. In the absence of such a monetary infrastructure, national currencies are bound to remain heterogeneous and the world will go on lacking of a true international monetary system.

The latest observation may be further buttressed by attending the concept of monetary 'space'. At the national level transactions between residents are carried out through the intermediation of money, which acts as a unit of account and as a means of payment. The 'space' of domestic transactions is thus covered by bank money – a vehicular flow. Moreover, the monetary intermediation of banks being combined with their financial intermediation, the domestic banking system provides the structural framework required for the existence of an efficient system of payments. A new problem arises, however, when transactions concern more than one country and payments have thus to be carried out between different nations (Figure 9.2).

The 'space' between country *A* and the rest of the world (*R*) has to be covered by a vehicular money capable of conveying to *R*'s residents the payment of *A*'s residents and vice versa. Banks in *A* and *R* can take charge of the payments made by their residents, but only within the national boundaries of *A* and *R*. In order for a payment to be carried over from a country to another, it is necessary to create a structure providing a monetary link between national currencies. Logically and factually, the validity of money A is limited to *A*'s banking system. *Once it abandons its country of origin, a currency's nature changes* and this is why it has to be replaced by an international money whose unique task is to cover the 'space' between nations. It is true, of course, that today international payments are carried out by private or public banks without recourse to the intermediation of an international central bank and of an international vehicular money. As we will repeatedly see, however, appearances mask a serious disorder

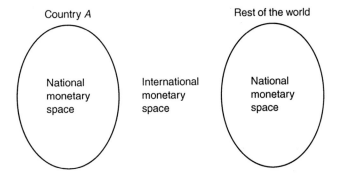

Figure 9.2 The national and international monetary 'spaces'.

that severely hampers especially the world's developing economies and that, if nothing is done to reform the present situation, will eventually lead to a systemic breakdown, which would be catastrophic.

The problem of international payments is to create a system of international monetary flows *connecting* national flows. If money were a commodity, payments could be easily traced down, and the flow of money would indicate nothing else than the physical transport of commodity money. Monetary economics would amount to the formal description of these real flows and the whole economic system would have to be worked out only in real terms, along the principles already proposed by neoclassical microeconomics. It is also beyond dispute, however, that modern bank money is no commodity. Being immaterial, money cannot circulate, like commodities, in the traditional sense. A mere acknowledgement of debt whose object is a payment (a flow), money cannot be conceived of as an object or an asset moving from one place to another. The 'flow of money' is therefore an instantaneous 'movement' to and from the issuing bank. What we have to investigate is what happens when international payments are carried out by means of the instantaneous (circular) flow of a national currency and compare the results with those that would have obtained if this flow were replaced by that of an international money covering the 'space' between countries.

The laws of money and their impact at the international level

Let us refer again to money conceived of as an immaterial 'means' of payment and to the implications of its being an instantaneous flow. At the national level, one of the consequences of such a flow is that money can never be hoarded. Being a flow, money can never be at rest or hidden somewhere. Issued by a bank at the very moment a payment is carried out, money flows instantaneously back to it. Indeed, it is because money defines at a stroke both a debit and a credit of the payer and of the payee that it can 'vehiculate' the bank's payment. Now, the law of the instantaneous reflux of money to its point of emission ought to apply also at the international level. When a bank in country A, BA, pays a bank in country B, BB, the money issued by BA flows immediately back to it. Double-entry book-keeping imposes a very rigorous discipline. The necessary balancing of assets and liabilities leaves no room to creative imagination in the interpretation of BA's payment (Table 9.1).

Table 9.1 The circular flow of money A

Bank of country A			
Liabilities		*Assets*	
Bank of country B	x MA	Client	x MA

The fact that money A is simultaneously entered on the assets and on the liabilities sides of B*A* shows that in the same movement it is issued to the benefit of B*A*'s client, transferred to B*B*, and deposited with B*A*. One clear and perhaps surprising implication of the flow nature of bank money is that a national currency can never leave its country of origin. Our claim can be contradicted of course by those who, due to their imperfect understanding of money, can counter that foreign currencies (like the US dollar) can be found in every other country of the world. Yet appearances deceive, while logic is compulsory. If it can be shown that, from a logically consistent viewpoint, the nature of money is such that it defines an instantaneous circular flow, the inference is unavoidable: a national money can only be deposited with its national banking system.

The opposition between appearances and logic can either mean that appearances deceive or that logic is faulty. If logic is systematically applied, it leads to correct results that might seem odd when compared with 'common sense' and empirical observation. In the case at hand, the fact that national currencies are held abroad has to be interpreted in the light of the conceptually backed impossibility of any national currency abandoning its banking system. If dollars are all necessarily deposited with US banks and if, nevertheless, dollars are entered into the balance account of foreign banks, the reconciliation of conceptual logic with factual evidence calls for a further investigation into the nature of the 'dollars' deposited with non-US banks.

Before analysing the problem of *eurocurrencies*, let us consider another implication of the immaterial and vehicular nature of money. As the distinction between money and income confirms, money is the 'vehicle' or 'means' by which payments are carried out, but it is not itself the 'object' of any payment. It is income that discharges debts and not money proper. Within countries, money acquires its purchasing power (that is, it becomes income) through its association with production. It is because produced output becomes the real 'content' of money that payments are effective. Two events come together to validate domestic payments: (1) the use of a money defining the IOU of banks, and (2) the integration of money with current output through the *absolute* exchange defined by production. What happens then when we move from domestic to international payments?

It is not difficult to see that presently at the international level neither of the following conditions is fulfilled, namely:

1   payments cannot be carried out using the debtor's own IOU, and
2   every payment must have a real 'content'.

The first condition is self-evident: nobody *pays* by getting indebted. In every country residents pay their debts by using banks' IOUs and not their own acknowledgements of debt. At the international level, reserve currency countries pay their net external purchases with their own national money. By so doing they 'pay' their creditors by acknowledging to be still indebted to them. A very curious payment indeed, which, as we will soon verify, is at the origin of the pathological formation of eurocurrencies. The second condition requires debtor countries to transfer to their creditors part of their (present or future) output as the real 'content' side of their payments. Once again reserve currency countries do not comply with the logical requirements of an orderly monetary system. As the US example clearly shows, there are countries whose trade balance deficits are 'paid' without this implying any net transfer of financial claims (that is, of claims on their future output). This leads us to one last observation concerning the peculiarities of the present system of international payments.

In a national setting, residents are all subject to the same logical rules as far as monetary payments are concerned. Internationally this is not the case. *A great disparity exists between reserve and non-reserve currency countries.* In particular, the asymmetry is such that while reserve currency countries can 'pay' for their net purchases simply by crediting the exporting countries with an amount of national money, *non-reserve currency countries are forced to purchase a foreign currency in order to pay for their trade deficit.*

Let *A* and *B* represent a reserve and a non-reserve currency country respectively. Since money A defines a circular flow from and to country *A*, the payment of *A*'s net imports 'vehiculates' to the creditor countries (the rest of the world, *R*) an equivalent amount of claims on *A*'s banking system (Figure 9.3).

Through the vehicular use of money A, country *A*'s net imports of real goods and services are thus matched by a transfer of claims whose object is a monetary deposit with *A*'s banks.

Things work out differently for *B*, the non-reserve currency country.

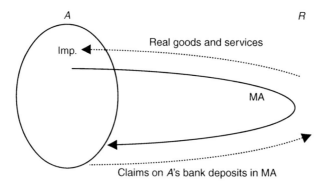

Figure 9.3 The payment of a reserve currency country's net commercial imports.

Since its national money is not accepted for the payment of its net commercial imports, B has to pay its creditors by means of a reserve currency. In order to do that, however, B must first get hold of the necessary amount of, say, money A. Two possibilities are offered to it: it may obtain a loan through the sale of financial securities or reduce its international reserves. In both cases the result would be the same: a rise in B's external net indebtedness (it is clear, in fact, that a reduction in official reserves defines a fall in B's external credits and therefore a rise in its net external debt). Since the use of official reserves implies the selling of financial claims (previously obtained through the investment of reserves on the foreign exchange market), let us represent B's payment in the case in which B obtains the necessary amount of MA (reserve currency) through the sale of financial securities (Figure 9.4).

As Figures 9.3 and 9.4 clearly show, the difference between A's and B's payment of a trade deficit is that B is forced to increase its financial debt in order to get hold of the reserve currency required for its payment, whereas A can use its own national currency to this effect.

At this point it is useful to note that all aspects of international economics highlighted so far pertain to the domain of macroeconomics. None of them is in fact directly influenced by economic agents' behaviour. In particular, the monetary laws we have been referring to are valid independently of whether or not they are complied with by individuals or institutions. This is not to say, however, that the choice of a specific structure or system of payments is irrelevant. On the contrary, if the logical principles of monetary macroeconomics are not complied with, the conflict between logical laws and the actual working of the economic system leads inevitably to a pathology, a disorder that can be addressed only through a (macroeconomic) institutional reform of the system itself, which will be analysed in Part IV.

Let us stop here our brief introduction to some of the problems related

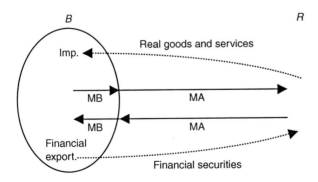

Figure 9.4 The payment of a non-reserve currency country's net commercial imports.

to the specificity of the system of international payments and turn our attention to the analysis of eurocurrencies.

The traditional analysis of eurocurrencies

Eurocurrencies are usually defined as bank deposits denominated in the currency of a given country but held abroad and their causes identified with 'the existence of incomplete financial markets; and inefficiencies in the process of financial intermediation and in the operation of securities markets' (McKenzie 1992: 781). A great number of factors are then assumed to have played an important role in determining an excess supply of or demand for funds inducing 'an innovative response mechanism on the part of the financial sector which led either to the expansion of the eurocurrency system or to a widening in the breadth of instruments which it offered' (ibid.: 781). Among the factors listed by McKenzie we find changes in banking regulations and in tax legislation, inflationary expectations, and technological advances in banking and in securities market trading. Davis emphasizes the influence of fiscal regulations claiming that 'the development of the euromarkets is largely explicable in terms of various fiscal and prudential regulations which have been applied to domestic financial markets' (Davis 1992: 783). On the whole, experts are unanimous in considering tax and bank regulations as the main reason for the formation of eurocurrencies.

Regulation Q introduced by the US government in the mid-1960s and limiting the interest rate US-based banks could pay on dollar deposits is the most quoted example of a restrictive measure leading to the development of offshore markets. Introduced in order to restrict aggregate demand, Regulation Q discouraged short-term money market investment in the United States. Thus, '[i]n an attempt to alleviate the loss of funds, the largest US banks expanded the deposit taking activities of their London branches which were subject to UK rather than US regulation' (McKenzie 1992: 781). Other official restrictions such as reserve requirements, the interest equalization tax, and the 'voluntary foreign credit restraint programme' are also mentioned as factors enhancing the formation of dollar deposits in Europe. Let us analyse in some more details the mechanism that is supposed to have led to the creation of eurodollars.

Because of the restrictions before mentioned, US banks were selling to their American clients dollar denominated deposits in their European branches. The transaction may be represented as in Figure 9.5.

Through the vehicular use of dollars, claims on US bank deposits denominated in dollars are transferred from the US banks to their European branches in exchange of the claims on their dollar denominated bank deposit. In fact, the US bank is selling the deposit in dollars of its client and purchasing, on behalf of this same client, a deposit in dollars

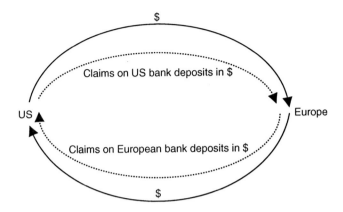

Figure 9.5 The reciprocal transfer of claims on dollar denominated deposits.

formed in its European branch. The book-keeping entries in the US and European banks are shown in Table 9.2.

Having converted his American deposit into a European deposit, the client of the US bank is debited by his bank and credited by the European bank, while the two banks concerned by this transaction are reciprocally indebted for the amount of x dollars. As may easily be inferred from Figure 9.5 as well as Table 9.2 the whole transaction amounts to a reciprocal transfer of claims on dollar denominated deposits. Although the exchange of claims on dollar deposits between the US and the European bank may be analysed as an international transaction, its effect is similar to what would have happened if it had taken place between two US banks operating in two American states. Now, a creation of eurocurrencies (eurodollars in our example) cannot result from a simple exchange of claims that leaves fundamentally unaltered the situation existing prior to the exchange. Bank deposits are not multiplied by the transfer of claims between the US bank and its European branch. Dollars are entirely deposited with the US banking system and no new deposit arises in the European branch, which is merely the owner of a claim on its American

Table 9.2 The reciprocal transfer of claims on dollar denominated deposits

B *(US)*		
Liabilities	*Assets*	
B (Europe) x \$	Client	x \$

B *(Europe)*		
Liabilities	*Assets*	
Client x \$	B (US)	x \$

head office. If x dollars were actually transferred from the United States to Europe it would indeed be possible to speak of a European deposit of dollars formed outside the United States. Yet, as we have already seen, dollars are defined in a circular flow, so that not a cent can abandon the US banking system. Moreover, if the formation of eurodollars were to define the deposit in a foreign bank of dollars previously deposited with a US bank, the United States would suffer from a deflation corresponding to the net outflow of their national currency, which obviously is not the case. The relentless rise of eurodollars has not been accompanied by a fall in the deposits of dollars held in the United States and has therefore not been the cause of a deflationary decrease in domestic demand.

Even if the exchange of claims on dollar deposits does not create eurodollars directly, is it not possible that the lending of dollars by a foreign branch of a US bank will have this effect? This is what is suggested by McKenzie, who claims that '[i]n order to maintain their customer relationships, UK banks began to lend their dollar balances instead of sterling to European traders. For the first time dollar-denominated credits were being created outside the US on a large scale' (ibid.: 781). In order to settle the question of whether or not the lending of claims on dollar denominated deposits is at the origin of eurodollars, we have to analyse what happens when the beneficiary of the loan spends the dollars to purchase goods and services from a third country *C*. It is rather obvious that if the dollars (obtained by giving back to the US bank the claims on its dollar deposits) were spent for the purchase of US goods and services, no eurocurrency would be formed. Likewise it is also clear that if the dollars were spent on the financial market they would merely give rise to a new loan of the same deposit, a result that does not explain the creation of eurodollars any more than the initial exchange between US and European banks.

The only interesting case here is therefore that in which the dollars are used to finance a commercial net import of Europe with respect to the rest of the world. Let us represent this possibility as in Figure 9.6.

If the beneficiary of the loan is a non-American resident, the lending of dollars by the European branch of the US bank defines a purchase of European financial claims or securities and ends up financing the European imports of goods and services from the rest of the world. If the beneficiary is a US resident, the transaction amounts to a net commercial purchase of the United States and can simply be represented as in Figure 9.7.

The mystery of eurocurrencies is hidden here. Yet, most authors leave the payment of commercial deficits by reserve currency countries aside, believing that the transfer of key currencies and their lending is enough to 'multiply' them and thus provide the euromarket with an inexhaustible source of eurocurrencies. It is currently maintained in fact that even if '[m]ost of the restrictions which acted as a catalyst for the growth of the

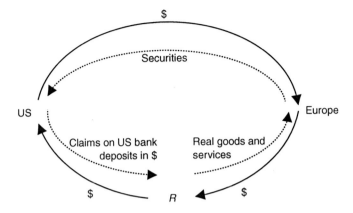

Figure 9.6 The payment in dollars of Europe's net commercial imports.

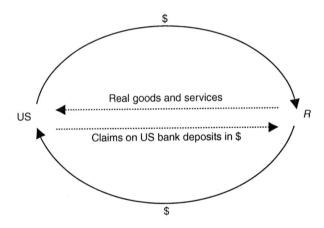

Figure 9.7 The payment of US net commercial imports.

eurocurrency system have been removed [...] the system continues to grow [because] it provides services that are highly competitive with those in national markets' (McKenzie 1992: 782). Although the higher competitiveness of euromarkets may account for a rise in the transactions taking place in this market and, eventually, for the rise in the exchange rate of eurocurrencies (we will address this problem in the next chapter), it cannot explain the continuous increase in the amount of eurocurrencies (Table 9.3).

As shown in Table 9.3, the total amount of eurocurrencies has never ceased to rise in the last ten years. This is clear evidence of the increasing importance of this phenomenon and of the existence of its causes, which cannot be identified with the provisory restrictions adopted in the

Table 9.3 The external positions of banks in individual reporting countries (in foreign currencies vis-à-vis all sectors)

Reporting countries	Amounts outstanding	
	1993 December	2003 December
	Assets (in billions of US dollars)	
All countries	**4,726.2**	**9,533.1**
Australia	–	56.9
Austria	46.7	45.5
Bahamas	167.0	226.1
Bahrain	56.4	86.4
Belgium	185.3	180.4
Brazil	–	21.1
Canada	39.1	114.0
Cayman Islands	394.0	1,038.7
Denmark	36.9	72.0
Finland	10.5	28.6
France	373.4	342.4
Germany	180.8	506.1
Greece	–	13.3
Guernsey	–	81.4
Hong Kong	503.6	394.9
Ireland	22.7	166.9
Isle of Man	–	13.7
Italy	87.5	50.8
Japan	432.1	1,001.6
Jersey	–	205.7
Luxembourg	311.6	252.3
Netherlands	143.5	241.1
Netherlands Antilles	–	33.6
Norway	6.2	18.0
Portugal	–	18.2
Singapore	341.7	442.6
Spain	71.7	60.5
Sweden	23.3	60.5
Switzerland	272.5	773.0
Taiwan, China	–	80.6
United Kingdom	951.6	2,767.0
United States	60.2	77.9
Other	7.9	61.3

Source: Data elaborated from *BIS Quarterly Review*, August 1996 and September 2004.

past. The fact that, once created, the euromarket attracts an increasing number of speculative transactions is an obvious sign of its growing import-ance, but it does not exonerate us from the task of explaining how eurocurrencies are formed in the first place. Now, while it is recognized that 'the US current account deficit played a role' (Davis 1992: 783) in the development of euromarkets, very few authors have investigated how the payment of this deficit led to the creation of eurodollars. Why has the majority of economists been fooled by the apparent 'naturalness' of the phenomenon?

The answer to this question is once again to be found in an insufficient understanding of the nature of money and its laws. Erroneously considered to be issued as positive assets, currencies are deemed to be part of a unique, homogeneous monetary 'space', so much so that eurocurrencies are supposed to add to the total stock of international liquidity. If this were actually the case, it would be impossible to distinguish the creation of eurocurrencies from the emission of any other currency, and the phenomenon could no longer be considered as pathological. Like in Dr Pangloss' world, everything would be at its best in the best possible world. This naïve view of the international monetary system is further confirmed by the use of an essentially microeconomic approach to the eurocurrency problem. As claimed by McKenzie, the expansion of eurocurrencies would be limited by economic agents' willingness to diversify their portfolios, matching their demand for liquidity with a mix of domestic money and eurocurrencies. '[T]he application of conventional portfolio theory suggests that economic agents will diversify their portfolios and hence any expansion of eurocurrency liabilities will be limited by the preferences of investors' (McKenzie 1987: 782). The eurocurrency system is simply viewed as a financial innovation potentially beneficial, since '[i]f the assets created are close substitutes in terms of liquidity for domestic money, then the demand for money schedule will shift to the left [...] the interest rate will decline [and] this will stimulate an increase in economic activity' (ibid.: 782). Unfortunately, as we will see in the following section, eurocurrencies are a form of pathological, international capital whose continuous growth limits actual economic development and increases the risk of a worldwide financial melt down.

The macroeconomic analysis of eurocurrencies

Eurocurrencies and the payment of net commercial imports

The terms of the problem are clear: how is it possible for a national money to become a reserve currency and still remain deposited with its national banking system? The author who more than anybody else contributed to explain this mystery was Rueff. Having observed that the dollars transferred by the United States in exchange for their net commercial imports were immediately invested in US bank deposits or Treasury bonds so that the United States recovered within the same day the liquidity they had lost (see Rueff 1980: 303), the French economist claimed that 'everything happens as if these currencies had never been exported in the first place. Entering the credit system of the creditor country, but remaining in the debtor country, the claims representing the deficit are thus doubled' (Rueff 1963: 324). Entered on the assets side of the creditor country's banking system while remaining deposited with US banks, the dollars are thus subjected to a *duplication*. Now, since the original dollars are bound to flow back to the US banking system, those that are invested on the euromarket are simply *duplicates* of the original US dollars.

An indirect result of the conference held in Genoa in 1922 and of the Bretton Woods agreements in 1944, the duplication of dollars is essentially maintained by the belief that the US currency is an asset both within and outside the national borders. The phenomenon of duplication would apply also, of course, to any other currency accepted internationally as 'object' of exchange. As in our previous examples, let us call A the net importing country and MA its national currency. The payment of A's net commercial imports from the rest of the world, R, is entered as follows into A and R's banking systems (Table 9.4).

Used to 'vehiculate' A's payment, money A is an instantaneous flow. The entry on the assets side of R's balance sheet defines therefore the claims on A's bank deposits earned by the rest of the world and not an amount of MA. As shown in Figure 9.3, in exchange for its net purchases of real goods and services country A gives to R an equivalent amount of financial claims on its bank deposits. No duplication has occurred so far and nothing can be reproached to A's payment. In order to spot the anomaly leading to the actual duplication of MA, let us compare the present state of affairs to what would happen if the structure of international payments conformed to the logical principles of monetary macroeconomics.

If countries were aware of the vehicular nature of money, the reflux of MA to A's banking system would be explicitly carried out by R's banks. In other words, banks in R would immediately invest in country A the money A entered on their balance sheet's assets side. R's export of real goods and services would thus be immediately matched by an equivalent import of A's financial assets (Figure 9.8).

In Figure 9.8 the real exchange between A and R is perfectly balanced, an amount of R's current output being exchanged against an equivalent amount of A's future output. Money A is used, consistently with its own

Table 9.4 The payment of A's net commercial imports from R

A's banking system			
Liabilities		*Assets*	
R's banks	*x* MA	Importer	*x* MA

R's banking system			
Liabilities		*Assets*	
Exporter	equivalent in MR of *x* MA	A's banks	*x* MA

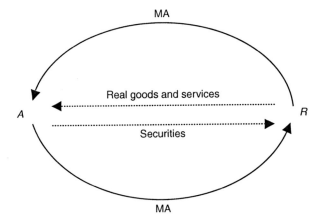

Figure 9.8 The 'orderly' payment of *A*'s net commercial imports.

nature, in its vehicular function and no amount of MA is given in exchange for *A*'s net commercial imports. However, this is not how things happen today. Money A is not perceived as a simple IOU, and the exchange between *A* and *R* is formed by a real (*R*'s output) and a monetary term (MA). Instead of considering Figure 9.8 as a representation of the correct way in which *A*'s net commercial purchases must be analysed, bankers and economists have been side-tracked by the erroneous belief that money itself can be the final term of a real exchange. The duplication of MA does not derive from the fact that MA defines a circular flow, but rather from the lack of recognition of this fact. Thus, claims on *A*'s bank deposits are simply entered as a sum of money A into *R*'s banking system. The same sum of money A is therefore entered, at the same time, into *A* (as bank deposit) and into *R*'s banking system.

The process of duplication incurred by money A is confirmed by the fact, shown in Table 9.5, that *R*'s exporters are finally paid in money R

Table 9.5 The increase in *R*'s international reserves

R's commercial banks			
Liabilities Exporter	equivalent in MR of *x* MA	*Assets* *R*'s central bank	equivalent in MR of *x* MA
R's central bank			
Liabilities *R*'s commercial banks	equivalent in MR of *x* MA	*Assets* *R*'s commercial banks	*x* MA

and that x MA are entered into R's central bank, where they define an increase in R's international reserves.

Instead of flowing into R's official reserves, MA could increase the reserves of R's private banks, it is true. Yet, even in this case the increase in reserves would define a net gain for the country as a whole (represented by R's global banking system – private banks plus the central bank). In order to simplify our exposition, we will henceforth subsume the latter case – an increase in R's private bank reserves – under the more specific case of an increase in R's official reserves. It thus appears that it is because countries R are willing to accept it as a reserve currency that money A is duplicated, and that it is because of its duplication that money A actually increases R's official reserves. It is the mistaken way in which the payment of a key-currency country's net commercial imports is entered into its creditor country's banking system that begets eurocurrencies as an effect. As mere duplicates of national monies, eurocurrencies form an international capital whose pathological nature should be easily grasped by the attentive reader. It is obvious, in fact, that the output available in any given country cannot be the intended real 'content' of both the national currency deposited in the domestic banking system and its duplicate. What is wrongly identified with an asset is therefore a duplicate of no real value. An 'empty' or 'hollow' money takes the place of a real payment and becomes the object of another country's official reserves.

The mechanism we have analysed so far refers to the payment of a key-currency country's net commercial imports. But what about countries that are net commercial exporters and whose money is nevertheless a eurocurrency? Does this mean that there are other transactions leading to the formation of eurocurrencies? In fact, it can be shown that the origin of eurocurrencies is unique. Let us take the example of Japan. It is well known that Japan's commercial balance has been and still is positive, its exports of real goods and services regularly exceeding its imports. At the same time it is also a well established fact that euroyen are a non-negligible part of today's eurocurrencies. How can these two facts be reconciled with the claim that eurocurrencies are formed through the payment of a commercial *deficit*?

Let us consider a possible exchange between the United States and Japan leading to the formation of both eurodollars and euroyen. Suppose the US imports of real goods and services from Japan to be equal to x million dollars and the Japanese commercial imports from the United States to reach a sum of y million dollars, where x is greater than y and z is the amount of dollars satisfying the equality $x = y + z$ (Figure 9.9).

Furthermore, suppose Japan to be a net importer of American securities up to an amount of z million dollars (Figure 9.10). To the extent that US commercial imports are balanced by an equivalent amount of Japanese commercial imports, no problem arises. The reciprocal payment of y million dollars may be carried out using the American currency, the

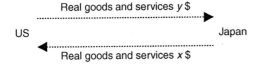

Figure 9.9 The US net imports of Japanese real goods and services.

Figure 9.10 Japan's net imports of US securities.

Japanese, or both: in no circumstances will it entail the formation of eurocurrencies, whether eurodollars or euroyen. If Japan paid its commercial imports in yen and the United States paid theirs in dollars, the two countries would end up being reciprocally indebted. The United States would hold an amount of claims on Japanese bank deposits equal to the amount of claims on US bank deposits held by Japan. It is thus clear that, after compensation, no claim on dollars or yen subsists in Japan and in the United States respectively. A positive formation of eurodollars occurs only with respect to the US payment of its net commercial imports. The payment of z million dollars has in fact the annoying consequence of duplicating the deposits of the American currency, which is entered both into the American and into the euromarket banking systems. The dollars earned by Japan through its net exports of real goods and services increase the official reserves of the Bank of Japan, and are immediately invested on the euromarket.

Let us now analyse what happens when Japan imports from the United States an amount of financial claims equivalent to z million dollars (Figure 9.10). Since Japan is a reserve currency country, its net imports of US financial assets can be paid in yen. If this is the case, through the vehicular use of its national currency Japan exchanges an amount of claims on its bank deposits against an equivalent amount of US financial assets (Figure 9.11).

In contrast with what happens when the payment refers to a net export of real goods and services, the yen entered on the assets side of the US banks do not define a gain for the US nation taken as a whole and do therefore not lead to a net increase in its official reserves. As a result of the exchange of financial claims represented in Figure 9.11, US banks are credited with an amount of yen defining their ownership of Japanese bank deposits, while US exporters of financial claims are credited by their banks in dollars. Now, if these US banks were to exchange their yen against dollars on the euromarket, the Japanese currency would take the place of

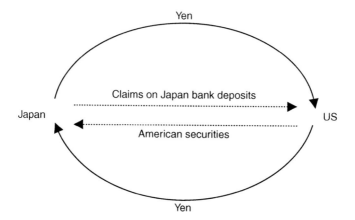

Figure 9.11 Japan's payment of its net imports of US securities.

the US dollars and become a eurocurrency. In this case, the formation of euroyen would not increase the total amount of eurocurrencies available offshore. Table 9.6 shows how the yen would replace the dollar in the set of eurocurrencies.

Eurobanks act as an intermediary between euromarket and domestic banking systems. Thus in entry (1) eurobanks owe the Bank of Japan the amount of eurodollars they lend to the euromarket on behalf of the Japanese central bank, while in entry (2) they owe the US banks (USB) the yen invested on the euromarket in exchange for dollars. Entry (1) represents in fact the initial investment of eurodollars made by the central bank of Japan, and entry (2) the investment of euroyen carried out by the US banks and the eurobanks (where z' is the equivalent in yen of z million dollars).

If the dollars earned by Japan through its net commercial exports were not entered into its central bank's official reserves, the purchase of US financial assets by Japanese residents would entail a compensation between the commercial banks of the two countries, so the formation of eurodollars would *de facto* be neutralized. However, this is not what happens in actual fact. Because of the existence of monetary sovereignty,

Table 9.6 The investment of yen on the euromarket

			Eurobank		
Liabilities			*Assets*		
1. Central bank of Japan	z \$		Euromarket	z \$	
Euromarket	z \$		USB	z \$	
2. USB	z' yen		Euromarket	z' yen	

the gain derived from a trade surplus benefits the country itself (its banking system), whose official (or private bank) reserves increase by the amount of foreign currency earned through the commercial surplus. Entered on the assets side of the Japanese central bank, the dollars obtained in exchange for the Japanese net commercial exports are invested on the euromarket and thus avoid being compensated by the yen entered on the assets side of US commercial banks.

It appears that the duplication of dollars and yen can be explained by referring to the fact that both currencies are taken to be positive net assets. It is the nation Japan that benefits from the net inflow of dollars (or, more precisely, from the net creation of eurodollars) corresponding to the Japanese commercial surplus, whereas the yen obtained through the American net export of US financial assets are earned and invested by US banks. And it is because of its status as reserve currency that the yen is accepted in exchange for US securities. Were it not considered to be a positive asset in itself, the Japanese currency would not be used either as a means or as an object of payment internationally. Japan would be forced to pay its net purchases in dollars and the yen would not be duplicated into a eurocurrency. Things being what they actually are, Japan's net purchases of US future output are paid in yen, and since the United States can pay for their external purchases in their own currency, the Japanese money entered as an asset into the US banks is invested on the euromarket.

The twofold payment of net imports

The macroeconomic nature of eurocurrencies appears with great force once this phenomenon is related to the distinction between a country taken as a whole and the sum of its residents, and is enhanced by Schmitt's analysis of the double payment of a country's net imports.

The fact that countries exist and cannot be assimilated to the sum of their residents has its source in the nature of money and is the clearest instance of the macroeconomic aspect of international transactions. As unanimously recognized by economists as well as bankers, money is an acknowledgement of debt spontaneously issued by a banking system. This means that, outside its national borders, a currency defines the acknowledgement of debt of the country whose banking system has issued it. Now, if a country were to be identified with the sum of its residents rather than with their *set*, it would never be possible to find a situation in which no residents are indebted to the external world but their country is, or, vice versa, no residents are creditors while their country is one. Yet this is precisely what happens today. Suppose A to be a reserve currency country whose residents have fully paid (in money A) for their external purchases of real goods and services. After the payment no resident of A is indebted towards the rest of the world but country A is, precisely because of the payment carried out by its residents. The money A held abroad or, more accurately, the claims on A's bank deposits held by R define the indebtedness of country A considered as a whole, whose status can therefore not be deduced from that of its residents. If we now suppose A's residents to be net exporters paid by R's importers in a reserve currency whatsoever, we have another example of how a country is not reducible to the sum of its residents. A's exporters are in fact paid through the intermediation of A's banking system. Independently of A's banking regulations, the final payment of A's exporters is made by a conversion of money R into an equivalent amount of money A. Once this final payment has been carried out, no resident of A remains a creditor with respect to R. Yet the amount of money R entered into A's banking system defines a net credit of country A. This is so much so that the reserve currency earned by A through its net commercial exports is transferred to A's central bank, where it increases that country's official reserves. The existence of A's international reserves denotes the external earnings of the undifferentiated set of its residents, which are not owned by any particular resident.

The distinction between countries and residents is the starting point of Schmitt's analysis of the double aspect of a country's payment of net imports. In fact, countries are necessarily involved in the transactions carried out by their residents and – as we have just seen – their involvement persists even when their residents have entirely fulfilled their obligations. In particular, in the case of a country's net imports, even if its residents have paid in full their external purchases the country itself remains indebted to the rest of the world and will therefore have to take over itself the payment of its residents.

Two broad cases must be distinguished, according to whether the indebted country is a reserve or a non-reserve currency nation. The 'dual' payment relates to the distinction between countries and residents, and applies to both cases. Yet, its consequences are not exactly the same. Indeed, if A is a reserve currency country the first payment is immediately compensated while the second can be postponed *ad infinitum*. Figure 9.3 represents the payment in money A carried out by A's residents and the subsequent indebtedness of A's banking system. As shown by the circular flow of money A, initially reduced by the payment of A's net imports, the income available in country A is immediately restored to its previous level. This means that R is lending to A the very income earned through its net exports. The claims on A's bank deposits earned by R have precisely this significance: all the incomes formed in country A remain deposited with its banks, part of these deposits being now owned by R. If R's claim on A's bank deposits were transformed into financial claims (through the purchase of financial assets), A's net commercial imports would be matched by its net financial exports. However the fact is that, because of the particular status attributed to money A, the rest of the world identifies its entry of MA with the entry of a positive asset entirely autonomous with respect to its original deposit into A's banking system. As a consequence of this duplication country A does not pay even once its net imports. The analysis runs as follows. The outflow of internal resources due to payment by A's residents is immediately balanced by an equivalent inflow corresponding to R's investment of MA into A's banking system. Now, since R's credit is replaced by a simple amount of (duplicated) money A, the reconstitution of A's internal income through R's lending is almost costless for country A, which will have to pay only the interests on the amount of MA lent by R. Since no financial claim on A's economy is transferred to R, the external indebtedness of country A – defined in money A entered into R's banking system – is purely nominal (it has no real object). Thus, MA being a reserve currency, A is entitled to honour its debt simply by renewing it (that is, by crediting R with another, equivalent amount of money A).

If A is a non-reserve currency country, the payment of its commercial deficit entails a twofold charge that is simply due to the fact that the country itself has to take over the payment carried out by its residents. Since MA is not a reserve currency, A's net commercial imports have to be paid in money R. This implies that A (its banking system) has to convert into MR the payment in MA of its residents. In order to do so country A has to get indebted by selling a net amount of domestic financial claims on the international market. A's net commercial imports are thus balanced by an equivalent export of financial claims (see Figure 9.4) and A's effective payment is postponed to the moment it will amortize its external debt.

It might be worth observing here that there is nothing wrong about A financing its net commercial purchases through equivalent net sales of financial assets. Actually this is one of the principles an orderly system of international payments would have to comply with. Now, the fact is that in today's system only Less Developed Countries (*LDCs*) are bound to match their net imports of real goods and services with a net export of national financial assets, while key currency countries are allowed to pay for their trade deficit by crediting the rest of the world with a simple duplicate of their own money. Thus, it is the way the present system of international payments is structured that leads to the pathological payment of net imports. The existence of nations and their necessary involvement in the transactions carried out by their residents is not *per se* a cause of monetary disorder. As we will see in Part IV, a system can be envisaged in which payments are the making of residents as well as their nations, yet their overall charge is 'single'.

For the time being let us summarize our argument by saying that *today's asymmetry between reserve and non-reserve currency countries has an impact on the formation of eurocurrencies*. While reserve currency countries can avoid paying their net purchases of foreign output, non-reserve currency countries must get indebted in order to 'backup' the payment carried out by their residents. The non-payment of reserve currency countries' net imports defines the formation of an equivalent amount of eurocurrencies, whereas the payment of non-reserve currency countries' trade deficit entails their external indebtedness. This chapter having being devoted to the analysis of eurocurrencies, will conclude with a few observations concerning the nature of the euromarket and of its transactions.

The euromarket

By definition, the euromarket is the market on which reserve currencies are traded together with financial items such as eurobonds, euronotes, foreign currency options, and futures. Transactions on primary and derivative securities have greatly increased the size of the euromarket as well as its potential destabilizing impact. To avoid any possible confusion, let us reaffirm that the formation of eurocurrencies is a phenomenon related to the payment of international trade deficits by key currency countries. Transactions having eurocurrencies as their object do not increase their formation, but may have an impact on their composition and/or on their relative value. Thus, for example, the purchase of eurodollars by, say, EU residents will not add a sum of euro-euros to that of the eurodollars but will simply substitute the EU residents to the initial investors of eurodollars (Table 9.7).

The first transaction entered into Table 9.7 refers to the investment of eurodollars by the central bank of a country whatsoever (CBC_w). Entries (2) and (3) describe the substitution of European Union banks (EUB) to CBC_w as lenders of eurodollars. Through the intermediation of the eurobank, CBC_w sells its eurodollar deposits and purchases an equivalent amount of claims on European banks' deposits. Acting on behalf of EU residents, EU banks replace CBC_w but neither the amount nor the composition of eurocurrencies is modified.

A change in the composition of eurocurrencies would occur if the loan in eurodollars was replaced by a loan in euros, which would indeed be the case if EU residents were to use the eurodollars they purchase on the euromarket to finance their own international transactions. As shown in Table 9.8, after the replacement caused by the purchase of eurodollars carried out by the EU banks on behalf of EU residents, the euromarket benefits

Table 9.7 The change of investor in the euromarket

	Eurobank		
Liabilities		*Assets*	
1. CBC_w	$x\,\$$	Euromarket	$x\,\$$
2. EUB	$x\,\$$	CBC_w	$x\,\$$
3. CBC_w	y euros	EUB	y euros

from an investment in euro-euros. The central bank of the country whose
eurodeposit provided the initial endowment of the euromarket is now the
owner of a new deposit in euro-euros, a result that does not come as a surprise since a change in the composition of eurocurrencies is necessarily the
mirror image of the change in the composition of the official reserves of
countries lending to the euromarket. The same would happen if the client
asked his eurobank to change his initial investment in eurodollars into
euro-euros. To satisfy its client, the eurobank would change dollars into
euros on the foreign exchange market, a transaction that would lead to the
replacement of dollars with euros in the eurocurrencies basket. Now, while
the change in eurocurrencies composition does not increase their number,
it may alter their value. For example, the net purchase of eurodollars on
the foreign exchange market is bound to raise their exchange rate and
thus increase the total value of eurocurrencies (Table 9.8).

As already observed, the euromarket has been growing steadily and so
have transactions on eurobonds, syndicated euro-credits, euronotes,
options, futures, and so on. As noted by Davis, all these sectors 'have
grown rapidly since their inception to a size comparable with or in excess
of many corresponding domestic markets' (Davis 1992: 783). Changes in
eurocurrencies composition and in their exchange rates have contributed
to this expansion and so have conjunctural factors such as the series of oil
price increases in the 1970s, when 'OPEC countries had deposited a large
proportion of their surpluses in relatively short-term deposits in the
eurocurrency system' (McKenzie 1992: 782). *To be precise, the growth of
eurocurrencies that occurred then was not caused by the rise in oil prices but by the
duplication of the currencies (mainly the US dollar) spent by the industrialized
countries purchasing oil from OPEC countries.* It is also interesting to note that
a consistent part of eurocurrencies are lent to *LDCs*, which have to meet
an ever increasing charge of their external debt servicing.

Economists certainly are not unanimous about the impact of the euromarket on monetary order or disorder. Some maintain that it can affect
the foreign exchange market inducing changes in interest rates, others
argue 'that euromarket flows have tended to make balance of payments
deficits more sustainable and hence aggravated the eventual adjustment

Table 9.8 A change in eurocurrencies composition

		Eurobank	
Liabilities		*Assets*	
EUB	*x* $	Euromarket	*x* $
CBC_w	*y* euros	EUB	*y* euros
Euromarket	*x* $	EUB	*x* $
EUB	*y* euros	Euromarket	*y* euros
CBC_w	*y* euros	Euromarket	*y* euros

which is required' (Davis 1987: 784). The lack of clarity as to the effects of eurocurrencies as well as the controversies over whether the euromarket creates credit, or over whether there are limits to its expansion are essentially due to a misperception of the nature of eurocurrencies. Once it is understood that eurocurrencies are formed through a duplication of the national currencies treated as international 'objects' of payment, it becomes clear that they dissimulate a valueless capital whose appearance here is a sign of a serious monetary disorder.

If we take one last time the example of the payment of US net imports, we observe that the domestic income paid by US importers remains deposited with US banks. It is true that these deposits are now owned by foreign creditors (their banks), but it is also certain that these creditors fail to exert any purchasing power over US output (if they did, the US commercial balance would not be negative, which would be inconsistent both with the example under exam and with factual evidence). Thus, US banks can and do lend within the United States the deposits whose ownership had initially been transferred abroad. In the United States domestic output is therefore totally in the power of US banks' deposits. But if US output is still the real 'content' or 'object' of the dollars deposited with US banks, no real good or service can 'fill up' the dollars entered into the banking system of the creditor countries. US output cannot be simultaneously the real object of the dollars deposited in the United States and of their duplicates. Eurodollars are thus 'empty' of any real 'content'.

Because of the present system of international payments, the world is being invaded by a growing 'mass' of worthless eurocurrencies. The enormous amount of 'empty' or 'hollow' money created through duplication represents a purely nominal capital whose investment is of an essentially speculative nature. Banks operating on the euromarket are indeed increasingly aware of its destabilizing impact and have been trying to control the risks through diversification and innovation. It is only fair to recognize, however, that instability has not been sensibly reduced and that a world financial crisis is still around the corner. The presence of speculative, pathological capital is the source of major disturbances on the foreign exchange market as well as on the stock exchange market, where the discrepancy between the 'economic' and the nominal value of shares has often characterized its increasingly speculative aspect. It is therefore correct to claim that '[t]he development of the euromarkets and associated innovations have not been without risk, as many of the *financial crises* that have occurred since 1970 have been felt most acutely in these markets' (ibid.: 785). Indeed, euromarkets did not merely feel the financial crises of the 1970s, but have been the major cause of such crises and will continue to put a strain on monetary and financial markets as long as a reform is not implemented.

10 A macroeconomic cause for exchange rate fluctuations

Exchange rates as relative prices

As clearly stated by Eichengreen, the exchange rate is mainly conceived of as the price of a national currency as determined on the foreign exchange market. 'The most important lesson to be gleaned from recent research in international monetary economics is that the exchange rate is an asset price' (Eichengreen 1994: 1). From this quotation it is clear that currencies are identified with net assets whose prices are determined through their relative exchange much in the same way as market prices of tradable goods are supposed to be determined through their reciprocal exchange on the commodity market. 'After all, the exchange rate is merely the relative price of two currencies' (Obstfeld and Rogoff 1995: 79). Thus, consistent with their belief that the exchange rate is the relative price of a given currency with respect to others, mainstream economists maintain that the exchange rate is influenced by all the factors liable to modify the relationship between supply of and demand for the currency under consideration. Leaving, momentarily, aside the factors influencing speculation on the euromarket, it can immediately be observed that, within the mainstream theoretical framework, imports define a demand for foreign currencies, while exports entail a demand for domestic currency in terms of foreign currencies. Commercial imports, unilateral transfers, and capital exports (that is, imports of financial claims) define a demand for foreign currencies, whereas commercial and financial exports define a supply of foreign currencies and a demand for the exporting country's domestic money. When current and capital accounts are balanced, exchange rates are stable. When the balance of payments is momentarily out of balance – whatever this might mean – the supply of foreign currency can either be greater or lesser than the correspondent demand, which leads to a re-evaluation or to a devaluation of the domestic money's exchange rate. 'Trade and private service flows, government transactions and capital movements are subject to several disturbances – secular, cyclical, seasonal and random. Under a system of flexible exchange rates, the net current impact of all these disturbances would be manifest as changes in the exchange rates' (Kenen and Yudin 1965: 243).

The different theories endeavouring to explain exchange rate fluctuations are all founded on the assumption that currencies are positive assets traded on the foreign exchange market and subject to the law of supply and demand. These theories have been classified according to various criteria. For example, Isard (1995), an official of the International Monetary Fund, distinguishes the theories relating exchange rates to domestic price levels from those relating them to interest rates and to the balance of payments. Visser groups 'the various theories according to the period for which their explanation of the exchange rate is relevant' (Visser 1991: 116) and distinguishes between the very short, short, long, and very long period's theories, whereas the Italian economist Fiorentini (1990) classifies them according to whether exchange rates are thought of as relative equilibrium prices among domestic products or among financial assets of different countries. In order to emphasize the role played by international transactions within the traditional explanation of exchange rate fluctuations, we will adopt as a criterion the distinction between exchange rate fluctuations caused by capital flows, by current account imbalances, and by both capital and current account imbalances.

A short survey of the main theories attempting to explain exchange rate fluctuations

1. Current account models of exchange rate fluctuations

A first set of models explaining exchange rate changes refers to the very long period and to the belief that exchange rates are related to domestic price levels. The principle that is supposed to play a key role here is Cassel's concept of purchasing power parity (PPP). In 1918 the German economist argued that exchange rates deviate from parity 'in proportion to the inflation of each country' and claimed that 'at every moment the real parity between two countries is represented by this quotient between the purchasing power of the money in one country and the other. I propose to call this parity "the purchasing power parity"' (Cassel 1918: 413). According to the PPP postulate, exchange rates would be determined so as to allow national currencies to exert the same purchasing power within every single country. The exchange rate between two currencies would thus be established by the relationship existing between the level of domestic prices in the two countries involved.

Now, even according to its advocates, the theory of PPP, whether in its 'absolute' or 'relative' form, has limited validity, since it is capable of accounting for exchange rate determination only in relation to variations in the general level of prices.

Variations in relative prices do not allow for the application of PPP, which is strictly dependent on the most orthodox version of the quantity theory of money. The other conditions pertaining to its implementation are extremely restrictive: that products are homogeneous, international markets perfectly competitive and integrated, and that there are no transport costs are unlikely assumptions reducing considerably the significance of this approach. Moreover, as noted by Isard, 'direct evidence on the behaviour of real exchange rates strongly confirms that PPP is not a valid hypothesis about the relationship between nominal exchange rates and national price levels in the short run' (Isard 1995: 63). Contradicted by empirical evidence as an appropriate assumption about the reciprocal influence between exchange rates and domestic price levels in the short and medium period, the PPP hypothesis has been relegated to the very long period. As observed by Cannata, however, 'if the exchange rate shows a tendency to obey the PPP principle only in the very long-run, this theory appears to lose most of its relevance since it might provide some insight only with respect to secular exchange rate fluctuations' (Cannata 1996a: 107, our translation).

It is important to note here that, according to experts, rejection of PPP should not be understood to mean that 'nominal exchange rates do not respond systematically to the large imbalances of trade in goods and services that can result from divergent trends in the price-competitiveness of different countries' (Isard 1995: 72). It is thus made clear that, regardless of PPP's validity, international trade imbalances remain a major cause of exchange rate fluctuations. Indeed, early models emphasizing the interdependence between exchange rates and the balance of payments were essentially focusing on the role played by the current account, 'and usually simply the trade balance' (ibid.: 91). Consistently with the neoclassical paradigm 'the earliest models relating the current account to the exchange rate followed an "elasticities approach" in the Marshallian tradition of treating the exchange rate as a relative price that cleared a market with well-defined flow demand and supply curves' (ibid.: 92). The notion that exchange rates are relative prices whose fluctuation can equilibrate the supply of and demand for currencies generated by balance of payments transactions is at the core of the early models of current account, and can still be found – albeit under a different form – in the models developed as an extension of Keynesian economics to the open economy. In particular, models elaborated in the 1960s started including capital flows in their analysis of the balance of payments–exchange rate relationship, combining Hicks' *IS–LM* interpretation of Keynes's theory with international capital mobility. The way was thus opened for a new set of exchange rate models applying to the very short period and concerned with capital flows related to the supply of and demand for financial assets.

2. Asset equilibrium models of exchange rate fluctuations

Unlike what happens in the current account approach to the balance of payments, in the asset approach the supply of and demand for money are not derived from real transactions, but from financial activities carried out internationally. The monetary as well as the portfolio models assume that 'the international financial market is highly integrated and characterized by an almost perfect mobility of capitals' (Fiorentini 1990: 44, our translation). In this approach, the instruments required to analyse the exchange rate problem are those also used to study money market equilibrium and financial assets' price determination. Convinced of the need to replace the traditional analysis in terms of flow with an analysis in stock terms, specialists of the asset equilibrium approach distinguish between two sets of models according to whether foreign and domestic financial assets are perfect substitutes (*monetary models*) or imperfect substitutes (*portfolio models*). Thus, whereas for the advocates of the monetary approach exchange rates are determined by financial flows concerning money only, according to the experts of the portfolio approach their determination cannot ignore the supply of and demand for bonds (imperfect substitutes for money). Behind the various models typifying these two main approaches we find the idea that exchange rate variations must be ascribed to a disequilibrium between supply of and demand for money (whether it is meant in its strict or broad meaning). The direction and range of these variations depend on the assumptions of each model. In the monetary approach, for example, the flexibility or rigidity of prices leads to opposite results as far as the relationship between exchange rates and interest rates is concerned, while in the portfolio models the initial variation in exchange rates can generate the phenomenon of overshooting.

In conformity with the monetary models' hypothesis that domestic and foreign financial assets are perfectly interchangeable, it is assumed that 'economic agents are indifferent as to the shares of domestic and foreign titles in their portfolios, provided they yield the same return' (Visser 1991: 118). Exchange rate fluctuations are thus thought to account for the *uncovered* parity between domestic and foreign interest rates, that is, for the equality between the domestic interest rate and the foreign interest rate plus the expected profit from exchange rate movements. 'The hypothesis of uncovered interest parity (UIP) postulates that market forces equilibrate the return that investors expect to earn on the uncovered investment alternative to the return on the riskless option of converting into currency *A* initially' (Isard 1995: 76). Besides the UIP hypothesis, basic monetary models assume the mechanism of exchange rate determination to be influenced by changes in the supply of and demand for money, by variations in inflation rates, and by the possibility of satisfying the PPP principle. In order to briefly illustrate some characteristics of the best-known models, let us analyse a case in which money supply is suddenly increased. In the hypothesis of flexible prices and from the monetary approach point of view, the increase in the quantity of money generates an increase in domestic prices, which calls for a rise in nominal interest rates. The increase in prices and interest rates leads to a decrease in the domestic demand for money, and triggers off an adjustment mechanism that leads to a fall in the exchange rate and in the price level. Eventually, the new monetary equilibrium re-establishes the real exchange rate at its previous level, in compliance with the principles of a purchasing power parity whose validity is taken for granted both in the short and long run. The same result is obtained when the initial increase concerns the rate of interest, since it is presumed – as in the previous case – that this increase reduces the domestic demand for money, creating a positive gap between the quantity of money effectively supplied and the one desired by the public.

Even in the fixed price model the increase in money supply leads to an exchange rate deterioration, but this time the adjustment between supply of and demand for money does not involve a change in nominal prices and implies a different relationship between the change in interest rates and in exchange rates. Here, the increase in the quantity of money supposedly causes a reduction in interest rates and a consequent outflow of capital leading to an exchange rate devaluation. Once again, the variations in exchange rates are bound to be re-absorbed at the real level, although this time the hypothesis of purchasing power parity is retained only relative to the long term. In both analyses expectations play an important role, being in a position to hinder restoration of the initial equilibrium if monetary authorities' intervention is not up to the task of providing for the necessary coherence in the pursuit of a stable and predictable monetary policy (even though both theories assume that monetary policies tend to be neutral). Let us also observe that, while in the monetarist approach (flexible prices) the interest rate reflects expectations on inflation, in the 'Keynesian' approach (fixed prices) expectations can lead to exchange rate overshooting. In the case of monetary expansion, for example, exchange rate depreciation in the short run could be greater than required by the new long run equilibrium, which would lead to a further adjustment in the exchange rate obtained through its (relative) appreciation.

Let us now briefly consider the *portfolio models*. Since it is assumed that domestic and foreign financial assets are not perfect substitutes, exchange rate fluctuations are no longer determined by the equilibrium between the money stocks held by the various countries. Instead of the uncovered interest parity applying in the models of the monetary approach, it is the *covered interest parity* that represents the distinguishing feature of the portfolio approach. As clearly stated by Isard, the covered interest parity (CIP) condition 'provides an expression for the forward premium or discount [...] that merchants or investors would have to pay at time t to hedge or "cover" the exchange rate risk associated with a contract to receive or deliver foreign currency at time $t+1$' (ibid.: 76). The basic assumption of portfolio models is that economic agents are ready to accept risk only on condition that expected returns be higher than risk itself. Investments in foreign financial assets are determined by considering the expected variation in exchange and interest rates. In this theoretical framework, the fluctuation of exchange rate can be determined by variations in risk premiums. A decrease in risk premiums, for example, would in principle lead economic agents to raise their demand for foreign financial assets, thus inducing a rise in the exchange rate of foreign currencies. However, as recalled by Visser, empirical evidence and econometric estimation show that it is extremely difficult to find a clear relationship between variations in the asset composition and 'the actual fluctuations in real-returns differences' (Visser 1991: 135). The results of numerous, detailed investigations based on empirical evidence converge to the same conclusion: risk premiums and exchange rates are not functionally correlated. 'So one may arrive at the admittedly somewhat lame conclusion that there are interesting, but not conclusive, results from applying the risk approach to exchange-rate determination' (ibid.: 136). Analysis gets more complicated if foreign currencies are added to domestic and foreign financial assets in economic agents' portfolios, that is, if portfolio models are made to account also for the perfect substitution among national currencies. Even in this case, however, conclusions are not encouraging: '[e]mpirical research suggests that currency substitution is not a significant factor in exchange-rate movements between the currencies of the industrialized rich countries' (ibid.: 140).

Generally more complex than monetary models, portfolio models take into account both monetary and financial flows, and they consider the current account to play a role in the determination of long-term exchange rates. 'The demand for financial assets is made to depend on domestic and foreign interest rates, exchange rate expectations, and wealth, and it is precisely the inclusion of this last variable that allows the portfolio balance approach to get back into the analysis the real sector of the economy, represented by the current account' (Fiorentini 1990: 86, our translation). To illustrate a possible chain of events in a basic portfolio model assume the quantity of money to vary. This initial shock causes a series of adjustments whose importance is derived from its direct or indirect impact on interest rates, risk premiums, expected returns, exchange rate expectations, and wealth. Thus, if we suppose the variation in the money supply to decrease domestic interest rates, the ensuing reduction in exchange rates will depend on the increase in the demand for foreign exchange, which is itself influenced by expectations and preferences as to combinations of risk and expected returns. In its turn, the exchange rate depreciation encourages the rest of the world to increase its imports, provoking an accumulation of foreign securities and a current account surplus that leads to a revaluation in exchange rates, whose existence depends on numerous factors, among which expectations and the degree of substitutability of national and foreign bonds stand out.

3. 'Keynesian' models of exchange rate determination

As shown by Kenen, the early 1960s marked the shift from balance of payments models of exchange rate determination focused on current account transactions to models focused on both current and capital account transactions. 'Keynesian models of the closed economy were opened to trade and capital flows' (Kenen 1985: 673) and capital mobility was introduced 'into the theory of economic policy' (ibid.: 669). Fleming (1962) and Mundell (1961, 1963, 1969) are the authors who have mostly contributed to this change in perspective. In the Mundell–Fleming model 'a simple Keynesian model of the goods and money market for an open economy [is combined] with the assumption that net international capital flows into the economy depend positively on the home rate of interest' (Isard 1995: 9). Thus, for example, in his 1961 paper Mundell attempts to show that the international adjustment mechanism can be described 'in a sufficiently general way to incorporate as special cases the *price*-specie flow mechanism of HUME and the *income*-specie-flow mechanism of KEYNES' (Mundell 1961: 154). Taking over Hicks's standard *IS–LM* diagram, Mundell extends it to an open economy in which the trade balance depends on domestic income 'while the overall balance of payments also reflects the relationship of the capital account balance to the home interest rate' (Isard 1995: 99).

The aim of the Mundell–Fleming model is to show how internal and external balance can be achieved simultaneously, taking into account the impact of exchange rate fluctuations on both capital and current accounts. Hence, assuming perfect capital mobility, Mundell argues that a rise in the domestic money supply will tend to decrease the interest rate, depreciate the exchange rate, create a trade balance surplus and enhance domestic production and employment. 'The monetary expansion puts downward pressure on the interest rate and induces a capital outflow, further depreciating the exchange rate and creating an exports surplus, which in turn increases, through the multiplier effect, income and employment' (Mundell 1963: 478).

Other models of exchange rate determination have been proposed over the years which emphasize the role played by one or more of the variables considered by the basic models we have briefly surveyed. New assumptions concerning expectations, elasticities, substitution effects, behaviour, exogeneity, endogeneity, structural changes, temporal adjustments, and so on are almost endless. It thus becomes difficult to survey the constantly changing parade of models offered by today's experts. In the conclusion of their thorough survey of the analysis of high-frequency exchange rate data carried out by Goodhart and various collaborators, Goodhart and Payne state that 'in line with results from more coarse data samplings, the links between the inputs to standard macro-exchange rate models and exchange rates themselves are shown to be weak' (Goodhart and Payne 2000: 548). Visser was thus right in the concluding comments of his book when he claimed that '[i]n view of the bewildering variety of exchange-rate models, it is not surprising that *econometric testing has yielded disappointing results*. Indeed, had those results been more satisfactory, no such proliferation of models would have occurred in the first place' (Visser 1991: 157, our emphasis).

Now, while Visser's negative conclusion seems reasonable, his inference as to the causes of the hopeless proliferation of models attempting to explain exchange rate fluctuations derives from a specific, microeconomic approach to the problem. 'We must reconcile ourselves to the fact that human behaviour can only be imperfectly modelled, let alone satisfactory predicted' (ibid.: 157). If exchange rate fluctuations were determined by economic agents' decisions to invest in domestic or foreign financial assets and to import or export real goods and services, we would have to share in Visser's diagnosis and hope to find models that mimic best the economic behaviour of individual agents in different circumstances of an ever changing economic framework. This is, of course, the stance taken by most of today's economists. The search for appropriate microfoundations of macroeconomics and the 'aggregation approach' endorsed by Keynesian and new Keynesian economists is clear evidence of the widespread belief that individuals' decisions are the central element of economic theorizing. Yet, as we have repeatedly claimed, another, macroeconomic approach to macroeconomics is possible, one in which the laws governing the workings of the system as a whole are not affected by economic agents' behaviour. As we will show in the next section of this chapter, exchange rate fluctuations are one indirect manifestation of these laws or, more precisely, of the anomalies engendered by the pathological workings of a system that does not yet comply with these laws.

A macroeconomic analysis of exchange rate fluctuations

As we have seen in the first section of this chapter, economists have mainly answered the question why exchange rates fluctuate by emphasizing the role played either by interest rate differentials, inflation rate differentials, risk premiums, balance of payment variations, speculations, expectations, or by any combination of these and other factors. As observed by Visser, however, none of the analyses proposed to explain and predict exchange rate fluctuations have fulfilled their ambitious aim. From the balance of payment approach to the structural (asset) approach, from the speculative bubble to the random walk, we are offered a variety of formally sophisticated models that seem unable to get to the heart of the problem. Why is this so? Why have they failed?

In the first two subsections we will show that, contrary to what is often believed, both current account and capital account transactions leave exchange rate unaltered, while in the third and fourth subsections we will be dealing with the hypothetical influence of national monetary disorders (inflation and deflation) and of interest rates on exchange rates. Finally, in the fifth and last subsection we will argue that exchange rate fluctuations are essentially erratic manifestations of a pathology affecting the economic system taken as a whole.

Exchange rates are not influenced by commercial transactions

1. Trade balance equilibrium

Let us start with the simplest case, where commercial imports of country *A* are matched by an equivalent measure of commercial exports to country *R* (the rest of the world) (Figure 10.1).

It is clear that in this particular case no net demand for money A (MA) is exerted in money R (MR) or vice versa. There seems to be no reasons, therefore, for a variation in the exchange rate between the two currencies. Yet, it might be objected that the equilibrium between the supply of and demand for each currency in terms of the other is reached only once the payments of *A*'s commercial exports and imports have actually taken place. It seems possible to argue, then, that in the interval between these payments a net demand for, or a net supply of, money A occurs, which provokes a fluctuation in MA's exchange rate. If this were the case, exchange rate stability would be only the temporary result of the matching of opposite disequilibria, one of which leads to re-evaluation and the other to devaluation. In order to settle this question it is therefore necessary to analyse what happens to MA's exchange rate when country *A* pays for its net imports or gets paid for its net exports.

2. Trade balance surplus

Let us assume that country *A*'s net commercial exports are paid by the rest of the world in money R (a reserve currency). As is well known, the sum

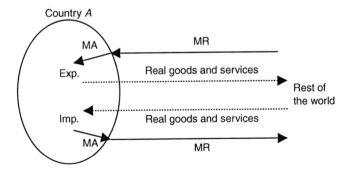

Figure 10.1 The trade balance equilibrium.

paid by R increases A's official reserves, while A's exporters are paid in money A (Figure 10.2).

At first sight, it seems that the payment of R's net imports increases the demand for money A and leads to a rise in MA's exchange rate relative to money R. This would indeed be the case if the supply of money A were not infinitely elastic. However, as banks' double-entry book-keeping shows, the amount of money with which country A's commercial exporters are credited is issued by their banking system as a counterpart of the amount of money R entered by banks on their assets side (Table 10.1).

Money A is literally 'created' on the basis of the new asset in money R earned by country A as a whole thanks to its net commercial exports. The credit on country R increases A's official reserves, and the newly issued amount of money A is paid to A's commercial exporters. The demand for money A exerted by R is thus immediately satisfied by the creation of an equivalent supply of money A by the banking system of country A. On these conditions, no net demand occurs that might cause a fluctuation in MA's exchange rate.

Do things change when country A is a net commercial importer?

3. Trade balance deficit

When commercial imports exceed commercial exports, and A's money is not accepted by the rest of the world as a key-currency, the payment of A's net purchases of goods and services implies the transfer of a positive amount of money R to the benefit of R (Figure 10.3).

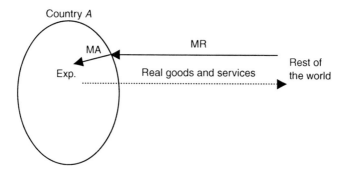

Figure 10.2 The trade balance surplus.

Table 10.1 The payment of net commercial exports

Banking system of country A		
Liabilities	*Assets*	
Banking system of exporters money A	Country R	money R

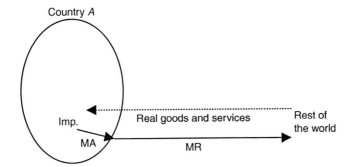

Figure 10.3 The trade balance deficit.

Does the payment of *A*'s net commercial imports imply a net demand for money R in terms of money A? If this were the case, the increased demand would devaluate the exchange rate of money A relative to money R. Yet, the necessity for country *A* to pay for its net external purchases in money R has further consequences. Country *A*'s payment, in fact, can only be financed through a decrease in *A*'s official reserves or via an increase in its external debt. In both cases, *A* pays for its net commercial imports by transferring to *R* an equivalent amount of *financial assets*. When official reserves are used, the whole transaction corresponds to a monetized exchange between the goods and services imported by *A* and the claims on *R*'s bank deposits obtained by *R*. When *A* resorts to an external loan in money R, the real payment is made up of the financial claims that *A* gives to *R* in exchange for its net commercial imports.

Whether *A* pays *R* by decreasing its credit (that is, by a reduction in its official reserves) or by increasing its debt (that is, through an external loan), the transaction between the two countries defines a reciprocal real exchange: goods and services against financial assets. On this condition, the money involved as a means of payment is used in a perfectly circular way, that is, with no consequences whatsoever on exchange rates.

A comparable result is obtained when it is assumed that country *A* has the possibility to pay for its net commercial imports by using its own money (which is thus accepted as a key-currency by the rest of the world). In this particular case – in which there is obviously no need for country *A* to demand money R – in exchange for its net imports of goods and services country *A* gives country *R* financial assets in the form of claims on *A*'s bank deposits (Figure 10.4).

It is important to observe that money A is *reflexively and circularly* used as a means of payment, the real object of the payment being the claims on *A*'s bank deposits transmitted from *A* to *R* by money A's circular flow. It is in the nature of bank money to flow instantaneously back to its point of origin. Because of double-entry book-keeping, in each payment carried

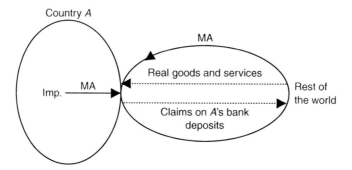

Figure 10.4 The payment of net commercial imports by a reserve currency country.

out by country *A* using its own currency, money A is immediately recovered by *A*'s banking system. Thus, in exchange for its net commercial exports country *R* gets, not a sum of money A, but the *ownership* over a bank deposit formed in country *A*.

The vehicular use of money A prevents any net demand for money R, and allows for the exchange rate stability of the two currencies. It is thus demonstrated that the monetary settlement of commercial transactions is never a cause of exchange rate fluctuations. Does the same conclusion apply also when payments concern the settlement of financial transactions?

Capital and financial account transactions leave exchange rates unchanged

As we have done before with commercial transactions, let us distinguish the case of net exports from that of net imports of financial assets.

1. Capital inflow

If *A*'s net sale of financial assets is matched by an equivalent purchase of goods and services, we revert to the case analysed in the previous section. The exchange between *A*'s financial claims and *R*'s goods and services implies the circular intervention of money A (or money R) so that no net demand occurs that could provoke a fluctuation in MA's (or MR's) exchange rate.

What happens, then, when *A*'s net exports of financial assets are not balanced by its net commercial imports? Let us assume, for example, that, in order to finance its public debt, the state of country *A* sells abroad part of its Treasury bonds, and that *A*'s commercial imports are entirely covered by its commercial exports. Does this lead to a net demand for money A in terms of money R and, therefore, to a devaluation of MR relative to MA? Once again the answer is imposed by the reciprocity of the exchanges occurring between *A* and *R* (Figure 10.5).

Money R, used by the rest of the world to pay *A* for its net sale of Treasury bonds, flows immediately back to *R*'s banking system, leaving *A* with a net credit that defines its ownership of an equivalent bank deposit formed in *R*. The terms of the reciprocal exchange between *A* and *R* are thus the Treasury bonds exported by *A* and those exported by *R* (in the form of claims on *R*'s bank deposits). The exchange being perfectly balanced, the circular use of money R holds good, and no force intervenes to upset MR's (MA's) exchange rate.

2. *Capital outflow*

The case of net imports of financial assets is merely the opposite of the one just analysed. Such a case applies to countries rich enough to be net exporters of capital and it may be viewed as their financing of the rest of the world's net commercial imports. It may also result from a net flow of investment from one key-currency country to another, in which case the import of financial assets is matched by an equivalent export of claims on the investor country's bank deposits. Now, as far as exchange rates are concerned the conclusion remains unchanged: their variation cannot be due to the payment of international (commercial or financial) transactions.

The alleged role of 'fundamentals' in exchange rate determination

For a long time economists have believed exchange rate fluctuations to be determined by variations in one or more of the economic variables considered fundamental by the main theories advocated in the leading schools of economic thought. Thus, interest rates, inflation rates, relative asset supplies, unemployment, real and money growth and the level of income are some of the variables that have been (and often still are)

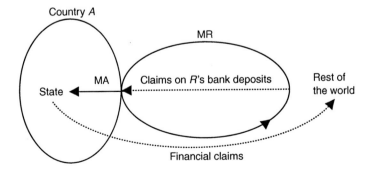

Figure 10.5 The reciprocity of exchanges between country *A* and the rest of the world.

expected to influence economic agents' decision to invest, import and export, and thus lead to a possible variation in exchange rates. Sadly and curiously, not only is it admitted that there is 'no general agreement about the fundamentals that ought to determine exchange rates' (Visser 1991: 159), but it is also recognized that 'certainly exchange rates can be out of line with fundamentals for considerable periods of time and capital flows allow exchange rates to be in some sort of equilibrium within a more or less wide range rather than at one unique value, given those fundamentals' (ibid.: 160). Experts of exchange rate economics are thus very sceptical about the possibility to tie exchange rate fluctuations to fundamentals: 'economists today still have limited information about the relationship between equilibrium exchange rates and macroeconomic fundamentals' (Isard 1995: 182). This is obviously bad news for the new classical approach and the advocates of rational expectations models, since 'it is hardly conceivable that rational market participants with complete information about macroeconomic fundamentals could use that information to form precise expectations about the future market-clearing levels of exchange rates' (ibid.: 182–3). Yet, as we will soon observe, the problem is not limited to the present incapacity of economists to establish when exchange rates fluctuate consistently or inconsistently with economic fundamentals, but extends to the very possibility of 'fundamentals' influencing exchange rates. *Can variations in the rate of inflation or in the rate of interest have any effect whatsoever on exchange rates?* This question has never been seriously asked by mainstream economists, who assume, axiomatically, that exchange rates are a matter of equilibrium and that whatever influences economic agents' behaviour has necessarily an impact on equilibrium and, hence, on interest rates. In what follows we will show that – however strange it may appear to the orthodox economist – this is not the case, at least as fundamentals have an impact on current and capital account transactions other than pure speculation.

1. Inflation

Economists have long believed that exchange rates fluctuate according to the differentials in inflation rates between countries. For example, the supporters of the asset market approach – particularly in its monetary versions of fixed and flexible prices – still maintain that exchange rates vary proportionally to inflation rates. Although numerous econometric studies have shown that there is no necessary connection between variations in inflation rates and in exchange rates, it may be of interest to investigate further the question of whether or not internal disequilibria such as inflation and deflation can determine fluctuations in exchange rates. Let us do it briefly, taking advantage of the results obtained so far.

Defined as the loss of purchasing power suffered by each single monetary unit, inflation is usually identified with an increase in the general price level (see Chapter 8). As our concern is exchange rates, we shall simply observe that, although inflation raises prices, the increase in prices may not necessarily be detected at the general price level. Since the increase is relative, it may simply raise the new prices up to the level of previous ones. What matters here, however, is that it can consistently be claimed that inflation raises the prices in country A relative to those in the rest of the world. Under these conditions, can inflation provoke a variation in the exchange rate of money A? The traditional argument runs as follows: inflation pushes prices up, the rise in domestic prices decreases A's commercial exports and increases its imports, the increased demand for R's goods and services implies a net increase in the demand for money R in terms of money A, the increased demand for money R leading to a devaluation of money A.

Hence, the assumed relationship between inflation and exchange rates passes through the variation in commercial transactions due to the rise in prices. To dispose of it once and for all, it is thus enough to recall the analysis relating to the payment of A's net commercial imports. If A is a key-currency country, the payment of its net commercial imports defines an exchange between the imported goods and services and the claims on its bank deposits transferred to R. *If A is not a key-currency country, the same payment defines either a decrease in A's official reserves or an increase in its external debt.* In every case, no net demand for money R is formed that might justify a devaluation of money A.

2. Deflation

Often defined as a decrease in the general level of prices, deflation seems apt to increase exports and lead, consequently, to a variation in exchange rates. This would indeed be the case if the payment of a country's net commercial exports were to provoke a net increase in the demand for its national currency, unmatched by an equivalent increase in supply. As we have seen, however, this is not what happens. In fact, double-entry bookkeeping features are such that for any positive amount of money R entered on the assets side of country A's banking system, an equivalent amount of money A is created that satisfies instantaneously its increased demand. Because of the infinite elasticity of money A's supply, the increase in demand that might result from a decrease in country A's general price level would have no effect whatsoever on the exchange rate of money A.

As the reader will observe, the same result is achieved when considering the fact that the payment of A's net commercial exports is perfectly consistent with the 'vehicular' use of money R. When the rest of the world pays A, R transfers to A an amount of financial claims (that is, claims on R's bank deposits) equivalent to the amount of commercial goods and services exported by A. The reciprocity of the exchange between the two countries is proof that the money used to carry out the transaction flows immediately back to its point of departure. *Being used in a circular flow, money R does not demand money A more than money A demands money R.* Supplies and demands are perfectly balanced and no variation occurs in the exchange rate between money A and money R.

Of course, the definition of deflation we have referred to is far too simple to provide a serious understanding of this anomaly and of its consequences (see Chapter 8). Yet, whatever the level reached by the analysis, it can easily be grasped that both inflation and deflation are national disorders that leave unaltered the 'inter-national' relationship between currencies. What inflation and deflation modify is the relationship between a country's money and its corresponding national output. In no case can a variation in this relationship have an effect outside the country and provoke a fluctuation of exchange rates.

3. Exchange rates and interest rates

As we have seen in the first section of this chapter, monetary and portfolio models consider exchange rates as the relative prices of national currencies and relate the supply of and the demand for money both to current and capital account transactions. The main difference between these two models of the assets approach is that, while monetary models assume that domestic and foreign securities are perfect substitutes, portfolio models consider them to be only partially exchangeable. From covered to uncovered interest rate parity, from rational expectations to risk premiums, a whole series of taken-for-granted assumptions are made by economists endeavouring to explain exchange rates fluctuations by relating them to capital movements and, in the case of portfolio models, to current account transactions.

Now, in so far as capital movements are considered as financial transactions taking place *between* countries, no causal relationship can be established between these transactions and the fluctuations of exchange rates. As we have shown, net imports (or net exports) of financial assets elicit a *reciprocal exchange* that guarantees the vehicular use of money and thus leaves exchange rates unaltered. The result is that, to the extent that they encourage or discourage capital flows between countries, variations in interest rates have no impact on exchange rates.

This conclusion should not come as a surprise to the attentive reader aware of the fact that exchange rates actually fluctuate irrespective of the evolution of the so-called 'economic fundamentals'. In light of this, let us note that the result just reached as to the independence of exchange rate fluctuations with respect to balance of payments transactions is confirmed by a critical analysis of the relative price conception of exchange rates. According to the neoclassical approach to relative price determination, supply of and demand for (real) output adjust through a variation in relative prices until they settle at a level allowing for markets to clear. Analogously to what is supposed to happen on the domestic commodity market, variations in *currencies'* relative prices are said to reduce temporary balance of payments disequilibria *before* transactions actually take place. In the same way as adjustment in relative prices takes place, through groping, before exchange actually occurs, exchange rates would fluctuate *ex ante*, through an adjustment between virtual or desired magnitudes that would make exchange rates to converge to their equilibrium point. How is it possible, however, to accept the idea that the foreign exchange market is controlled by an imaginary auctioneer and that exchange rates are thus determined through an equally imaginary adjustment process? Supply and demand could determine exchange rates only if they were real forces acting on the market. Yet, supply and demand can be valued only in relative terms, that is, by referring to the relationship existing between different currencies. The demand for money A is determined by the amount of money R it is exchanged for, and the demand for MR by the MA given in exchange for it. In order to be 'real', these two forces have to be referred back to a pre-determined exchange rate. Since such exchange rate would be only hypothetical or imaginary, supply and demand would also be merely imaginary, and could not help in any real adjustment process. Moreover, contrary to what is said to happen on domestic markets, decisions concerning imports and exports are reciprocally independent and there is no reason to believe that there are market forces driving them into balance.

To sum up, there are two different ways of conceiving of the relationship between exchange rate and the balance of payments. It may be claimed either that exchange rate variations allow for the (*ex ante*) solution of balance of payments' imbalances or that balance of payments' imbalances give rise to *ex post* variations in exchange rates. In the first case theorists are confronted with the annoying fact that balance of payments transactions do not reciprocally adjust in any market. In the second case they have to come to terms with the fact that neither current nor capital and financial account transactions are the cause of exchange rate fluctuations. Under these conditions it is not really surprising to find out that most experts have long applied a pragmatic approach to the problem, since theories have proved unreliable if not altogether erroneous. In particular, it is increasingly recognized today that erratic fluctuations of the exchange rates are mainly due to speculation. In the next subsection we will see that, the moment we move from the analysis of current, and capital and financial account transactions between countries to the analysis of the monetary transactions on the foreign exchange market, we can better grasp the reasons why exchange rates fluctuate despite the vehicular nature of bank money. It is to the increasingly widespread activity of speculation that we must turn our attention if we are to justify the belief that interest rates may influence the determination of exchange rates.

Exchange rates and speculation

While speculation sounds like a well-defined concept, it is not self-evident why it can have such a disruptive effect on exchange rates. Does any kind of speculative transaction have this effect? Of course not, since – as we have seen – sales and purchases of either goods and services or financial assets leave exchange rates unaltered. Whatever the reasons that push residents of country A to purchase or sell on the commodity market or on the financial market, payments are carried out through the intermediary of banks and imply the 'vehicular' use of money A (or money R). Hence, the only possibility left for speculation to influence exchange rates is through sales and purchases taking place on the foreign exchange market. Here again, however, it is not obvious why, for example, the purchase of foreign currencies is liable to modify the exchange rate of money A. Is it not true that to purchase money R means to purchase a bank deposit of country *R*? And is it not also true, therefore, that this transaction amounts to a purchase of financial claims, which has no effect on MA's exchange rate?

Now, the previous conclusion would be unavoidable if currencies were consistently used as *means* of payment. In reality, this is not always the case. Irrespective of their banking nature (which calls for their 'vehicular' use) currencies are considered *as if* they were (positive) assets, *objects* of trade on the foreign exchange market. At first this sounds perfectly plausible. Is it not true, after all, that as soon as it is associated with physical output money acquires a positive purchasing power and defines the net asset generated by production? Far from abdicating this state of affairs, what we want to highlight is that, because it is an asset only insofar as it specifies physical output, money itself cannot become an object of exchange *per se*. Money can be considered a positive asset only in the form of a financial claim whose object is current output. Thus, the purchase of money R should define the purchase of country *R*'s output in the form of a bank deposit and not the purchase of a sum of money R as such. If this is not what happens in reality, it is because money qua *numerical form* is erroneously taken to be an asset independently of its relationship with produced output. What has still to be explained, however, is how the misrecognition of money can lead to a series of anomalous transactions whose consequence is an unpredictable fluctuation of exchange rates.

The problem is as follows. Given that double-entry book-keeping affords the 'vehicular' use of currencies both at the national and international levels, how is it possible for some of them to survive their circular flow? Each time that a bank carries out a payment, money is simultaneously created and destroyed, since it defines an instantaneous flow from and to the bank at the very moment the latter debits the payer and credits the payee. The result of the payment is either the creation of a new bank deposit or the transfer of an old deposit, a stock (money income) and not a flow (money as such). Yet, nobody denies the fact that on the foreign exchange market currencies are sold and purchased as if they were real goods. How is it, then, that a currency – say money R – can be an object of trade on the foreign exchange market, when every time it is used in a payment it is instantaneously destroyed by the issuing bank?

As we have seen in Chapter 9, Rueff was the first economist to have addressed and resolved this apparent dilemma. Analysing the way payments of a key-currency country's net commercial imports are entered on the exporting country's book-keeping, he was able to show that today's system of international payments allows for a phenomenon of monetary *duplication*. 'Entering the credit system of the creditor country, but remaining in the debtor country, the claims representing the deficit are [...] doubled' (Rueff 1963: 324). Hence, the duplication arises from the fact that the same claims on the debtor country's bank deposits are simultaneously at the disposal of the debtor and the creditor countries. Since the national output defining the object of these claims is not itself doubled, only the claims circulating within the net importing country (R) have a real content, the others being mere duplicates. Now, while R's banking system lends within country R the totality of its deposits, the banking system of country A is free to lend its duplicates on the foreign exchange market. Known as eurocurrencies (though it would be preferable to use – as suggested by Machlup (1970, 1972) – the expression 'xeno-currencies'), these duplicates are considered as positive assets on their own and become proper objects of trade.

As it happens with real goods, 'xeno-currencies' are sold and purchased, and their market prices are determined through the adjustment of supply and demand. On the foreign exchange market, exchange rates are the price of the commodity-like currencies traded, and their variation is directly influenced by the demand exerted by investors and the offer supplied by the market.

It is true that this market is not automatically a speculative one, transactions being carried out for various purposes, including the financing of capital increases by private firms (through the emission of xeno-bonds), and of *LDCs*' external debt. Transactions on the xeno-market may thus be distinguished according to whether or not they are capable of provoking a variation in exchange rates. The purchase of a eurocurrency R on the euro or xeno-market, for example, defines an increase in the demand for money R in terms of the currency used by the buyer to finance his purchase (MA). Yet, an increase in demand is not enough to conclude that the price of money R will rise in terms of money A. The effect of the variation of the demand for MR depends, in fact, on the elasticity of the supply of money R. In our example, the supply of money R in the xeno-market is inelastic, that is, banks cannot instantaneously adjust their supply of MR to the variations in the demand for MR. This does not mean, however, that the demand for money R cannot be matched by an equivalent supply. If people (or institutions) who had previously invested in money R are now willing to replace their investment in money R with an investment in money A, xeno-banks would balance the new demand for MR with the new supply of MR and no side effects would be noticed on the foreign exchange market. On the contrary, if the new demand for money R defines a net increase in the demand for MR – as we have assumed in our example – the adjustment is carried out by a variation in prices. In fact, since the money R deposited with the xeno-banks is already entirely demanded – a direct consequence of double-entry book-keeping – the new demand exerted in terms of money A will lead to a re-evaluation of MR with respect to MA.

If the system of international payments were founded on the instantaneous circular use of an international money, no duplication would occur. In exchange for its net commercial imports a key-currency country would have to give up an equivalent amount of financial assets, so that the instantaneous flow of its currency would be explicitly recorded, thus avoiding the book-keeping duplication occurring today. If this were the case, currencies would no longer be denatured, that is, transformed into objects of trade. Things being what they are, in the present system of international payments the process of duplication described by Rueff feeds a speculative capital market, and the transactions taking place on this market inevitably lead to fluctuations in exchange rates.

From the moment currencies are sold and purchased as if they were (real) assets, exchange rates become the expression of their (relative) prices and are made to vary according to the interaction of supply and demand. Besides the reciprocal exchanges between countries that guarantee the 'vehicular' use of money and leave exchange rates unchanged, a market is created in which transactions define net sales and net purchases of currencies pathologically transformed into assets. Under these conditions it is not surprising to observe that speculation becomes the main cause of exchange rate fluctuations. As is clearly stated by one of the major experts in the field, 'there is enormous volume of very short-term position-taking, the basis of which is not well understood theoretically: but such very short-term position-taking is *not* based on a view about longer-term fundamentals' (Goodhart 1988: 438). Goodhart's opinion that short-term speculators act ignoring fundamentals is shared by Stiglitz (1989), who claims that, despite the fact that financial markets are intrinsically efficient, to actually achieve efficiency it is necessary to reduce the activity of irrational speculators, for example, by introducing a tax on all financial market transactions as proposed by Tobin (1978). Without entering here into Stiglitz's analysis in any detail, let us simply observe, as clearly argued by Davidson, that it is rather inconsistent to claim that financial markets are efficient – which implies that irrational traders will necessarily disappear or become rational through a learning-by-doing process – and that financial markets' volatility is caused by 'the persistent existence of foolish market participants' (Davidson 2002: 185). Stiglitz thus seems to miss the point that if the financial market is constantly characterized by the presence of irrational short-term traders whose activity is enough to make it highly volatile, the market is *de facto* inefficient. Now, the problem we are confronted with cannot be dealt with in terms of behaviour modification. Speculation may lead to more or less rational behaviour, may have more or less disruptive consequences, may be more or less justified or condemned. The central point is that speculation exists because it is fuelled by an ever increasing pathological capital.

What has to be clearly understood is that speculation has reached such an enormous extent because the xeno-market has been increasingly fed by the process of duplication described above. *Speculation is the effect and not the cause of speculative capital, and speculative capital is the direct result of currency duplication.* As soon as currencies are transformed from *means* into *objects* of exchange their exchange rates vary according to their sales and purchases, and speculation arises from the possibility of capital gains resulting from these variations. As observed by Schmitt (1984b), speculative transactions on the xeno-market can lead to an increasing rise or fall in the exchange rate of a given currency. For example, the inflow of foreign capitals demanding money R causes its re-evaluation on the foreign exchange market, while their subsequent outflow leaves money R's exchange rate unaffected since its amount is independent of the number or volume of transactions taking place on the xeno-market. In the foreign exchange market as well as in the stock exchange market things work out like in a newspaper competition:

> where each competitor has to pick, not those faces which he himself finds prettiest, but those which he thinks likeliest to catch the fancy of the other competitors, all of whom are looking at the problem from the same point of view. It is not a case of choosing those which, to the best of one's judgment, are really the prettiest, nor even those which average opinion genuinely thinks the prettiest. We have reached the third degree where we devote our intelligences to anticipating what average opinion expects the average opinion to be. And there are some, I believe, who practise the forth, fifth and higher degrees.
>
> (Keynes 1936/1973a: 156)

Needless to say, the variations in exchange rates caused by supply and demand do not affect only the currencies traded on the xeno-market. Any net purchase of money R in terms of money A affects both currencies, even if MR alone is a xeno-currency. Moreover, the fluctuation of a xeno-currency's exchange rate defines simultaneously the fluctuation of the national money of which the xeno-currency is a duplicate. Xeno-dollars, for example, are not practically distinguished from the US dollar so that a variation in the xeno-dollar's exchange rate defines also an equal variation in the US money's exchange rate.

Finally, let us note that information or expectations about the evolution of economic 'fundamentals' can indeed play a role in the process of exchange rate determination, albeit only in so far as they are one of the elements that may influence speculation. Other elements, which have sometimes very little to do with economics, may also play a part in this highly unpredictable game, whose consequences are potentially disruptive for the world as a whole as well as for its residents. It is easy to imagine a situation in which speculation leads to massive sales or purchases of one or a few currencies thus triggering a snowball process of re-evaluation or devaluation almost entirely unrelated with the way 'fundamentals' do actually perform. In 1992, for example, a currency crisis hit Europe and in just a few days the European Monetary System was wrecked by speculation. As long as speculation will be nurtured by an increasing pathological capital, the risk of ever more severe crises will rise and the monetary and financial systems will be increasingly put in jeopardy and will head for a generalized collapse. To avoid this worrying event it is necessary, first of all, to understand the origin and nature of speculation. In particular, it is important to realize that if currencies were not considered as if they were tradable goods and if the system of international payments did not allow for their duplication, speculation in the foreign exchange market would not even exist. Closely linked to the formation of international pathological capital, speculation is thus of a macroeconomic nature. Even though it is obviously true that speculation is carried out by individual speculators (single agents or groups), pathological speculative capital derives from an anomaly affecting the whole system of international payments. Duplication arises independently of economic agents' behaviour. Its origin is to be found in the lack of compliance between the present system of international payments and the 'vehicular' or flow nature of money. Speculation is thus the consequence of a macroeconomic disorder engendering pathological capital more than the result of microeconomic agents' decision to invest on the foreign exchange or the stock exchange markets. Caused by speculation, exchange rate erratic fluctuations are therefore also a consequence of the macroeconomic disorder hindering the present system of international payments.

11 The macroeconomic analysis of world monetary discrepancies

The balance of payments

As stated in the *Balance of Payments Manual* edited by the International Monetary Fund (IMF), the balance of payments is essentially 'a statistical statement that systematically summarizes, for a specific time period, the economic transactions of an economy with the rest of the world' (International Monetary Fund 1993: 6). A wider instrument than the simple record of foreign payments, the balance of payments is concerned with all sorts of international transactions, included those that do not involve any payment. Thus, '[d]espite the connotation, the balance of payments is not concerned with *payments*, as that term is generally understood, but with *transactions*' (ibid.: 8). According to the fifth edition of the IMF *Manual*, the standard components of the balance of payments are classified in two major accounts: the current account, and the capital and financial account (itself made up of a capital account and a financial account). Transactions entered into the current account relate to goods and services, income and current transfers. Exports and imports of real goods and services, compensation of employees, investment income (dividends, profits, reinvested earnings, and interests), workers' remittances, and gifts are among the transactions entered in the current account. The major components of the capital account are capital transfers (transfers of funds linked to, or conditional upon, acquisition or disposal of fixed assets), and acquisition/disposal of non-produced, non-financial assets (patented assets, leases or other transferable contracts, goodwill). Finally, transactions relating to direct, portfolio and other investments, and to reserve assets are entered into the financial account.

The balance of payments identity

Often referred to as the balance of international transactions, the balance of payments is a historical record of the transactions taking place between the *residents* of one country and the rest of the world, constructed according to the rule of double-entry book-keeping. 'The basic convention applied in constructing a balance of payments statement is that every recorded transaction is represented by two entries with equal values. One of these entries is designated a credit with a positive arithmetic sign; the other is designed a debit with a negative sign' (ibid.: 6). Generally speaking, it may be claimed that the necessary balance between debits and credits is obtained only at the global level (once all the accounts making up the balance of payments of a country have been taken into consideration), and not at the level of each single account. Thus, for example, 'the receipts and payments arising from merchandise and service exports and imports shown in the current account may have their counterpart debits or credits recorded in one or more of the remaining accounts. The balance of payments must accordingly be looked at as a whole rather than in terms of its individual parts' (Stern 1973: 2). The traditional textbook example of balance of payments double-entry refers to an export of commercial goods (recorded in the current account) being balanced by a (monetary) payment recorded in the capital account. This does not mean, however, that compliance with double-entry book-keeping is attained when only at least two different (though related) accounts are taken into consideration. The rules of double-entry book-keeping must be respected for each international transaction. In the case of a country's unilateral transfers, for example, the amount of capital transferred abroad is instantaneously balanced by an equivalent capital inflow defining the increase in foreign claims on the country's banking system. As claimed by Salvatore, a US unilateral transfer is a payment made to foreigners and '[t]he payment itself is the U.S. bank balance given to the government of the developing nation. This represents an increase in foreign claims on, or foreign assets in, the United States and is recorded as a capital inflow, or credit, in the U.S. balance of payments' (Salvatore 2001: 436).

The key principle is that '[e]*very international transaction automatically enters the balance of payments twice, once as a credit and once as a debit*' (Krugman and Obstfeld 2003: 314). This leads Krugman and Obstfeld to maintain that '[t]his principle of payments accounting holds true because every transaction has two sides: if you buy something from a foreigner you must pay him in some way, and the foreigner must then somehow spend or store your payment' (ibid.: 314). Superficially interpreted, this sentence means that the double-entry simply represents the obvious fact that transactions are two-sided, so the purchase of one country is the sale of another and vice versa. Looked at more closely, however, Krugman and Obstfeld's quote discloses the presence of a fundamental law guaranteeing the necessary duality between each resident's sales and purchases (see Schmitt 1975). In fact, if the foreigner from whom we buy *must* spend our payment – if he stores it, he spends it for the purchase of claims on bank deposits – this means that our purchase is necessarily matched by an equivalent sale and that, reciprocally, the sale of our foreign correspondent is balanced by a purchase of the same amount. Schmitt's Law does not state that our purchase is our foreign correspondent's sale (which is a truism), but that our purchase implies our own simultaneous sale, and his respective sale a simultaneous purchase for him. When Krugman and Obstfeld claim that the foreigner must spend our payment, they implicitly confirm the fact that each economic agent, nationally and internationally, is simultaneously a seller and a purchaser on the labour, product, and financial markets. It thus follows that, when referred to balance of payments transactions, double-entry book-keeping works in two distinct stages. First, it applies to every phase a single transaction, whether commercial or financial, can be subdivided into. Thus, for example, a commercial export is entered both as a debit (the decrease in domestic output available in the exporting country) and as a credit (the claim on the foreign importers). When the export is paid, there is another double-entry, defining an equivalent credit (a capital inflow) and debit (a capital outflow due to the increase in assets abroad deriving from the instantaneous deposit of the sum paid by the foreign importers). Second, it applies to the two phases of the transaction taken as a whole. In our example, the commercial export and its payment are entered as a debit in the current account (the outflow of goods) and as a credit in the capital and financial account (the inflow of claims on bank deposits held abroad).

As claimed by Stern, '[t]ransactions are recorded in principle on a double-entry bookkeeping basis. Each transaction entered in the accounts as a credit must have a corresponding debit and vice versa. [...] It follows from double-entry bookkeeping that the balance of payments must always balance: total debits equal total credits' (Stern 1973: 2). The necessary equality of total debits and credits is recognized as a central feature of the balance of payments both by IMF experts and by academic economists, even though they do not attribute the same heuristic significance to it. In fact, IMF experts are pragmatically inclined to consider the equality more as a theoretical possibility than as a logical, necessary requirement. 'In principle, the sum of all credit entries is identical to the sum of all debit entries, and the net balance of all entries in the statement is zero. In practice, however, the accounts frequently do not balance' (International Monetary Fund 1993: 6). At the other end of the spectrum, the most rigorous experts define the equality as the *fundamental balance of payments identity* and claim that the overall balance of the current, capital and financial accounts is the logical consequence of double-entry book-keeping. 'Because any international transaction automatically gives rise to two offsetting entries in the balance of payments, the current account balance, the financial account balance, and the capital account balance automatically add up to zero: Current account + financial account + capital account = 0' (Krugman and Obstfeld 2003: 310).

A neoclassical interpretation

According to the mainstream analysis of the balance of payments, the equation relating to the current account (CA) – that is, to exports (X), imports (M), and unilateral transfers (U) – can be associated with the identity defining national income as the sum of consumption (C), investment (I), and public expenditures (G) in order to express the value of national income in an open economy (Y). The resulting equation takes the following form:

$$Y = C + I + G + (X - M + U). \tag{1}$$

Since $CA = X - M + U$ and $Y - C = S$ (saving), equation (1) can be written as:

$$CA = S - I - G. \tag{2}$$

If we include public expenditures in C and I, equation (2) reduces to:

$$CA = S - I, \tag{3}$$

which states that the current account 'reflects the difference between national savings and national investment or the rate of change in the nation's holdings of foreign assets' (Cumby and Levich 1992: 114).

The aim of this exercise is to show that 'the *current account* balance mirrors the saving and investment behaviour of the domestic economy' (International Monetary Fund 1993: 158), that is, that the consumption, saving, and investment behaviour in one country is closely related to 'its payment balance versus the rest of the world' (Cumby and Levich 1992: 114–15). Thus, a current account surplus would define a net saving, while a current account deficit would reflect a net investment. At closer examination, however, it appears that no difference can ever be found between a country's saving – the difference between exports and imports – and a country's investment – its net (positive or negative) foreign lending, because every current account deficit is necessarily financed 'by borrowing from abroad or by running down [the country's] previously acquired stock of foreign assets' (ibid.: 114), whereas every current account surplus entails the financing of the rest of the world through a positive purchase of foreign assets. A country with a current account surplus saves part of its foreign income, it is true, but it also invests the very amount saved, through its net foreign lending. Analogously, a country whose net borrowings are positive – whose saving is negative – is a country benefiting from positive foreign investment and, therefore, whose own foreign investment is negative. Perfectly in line with the macroeconomic identity between national S and I discussed in Chapters 3 and 4, the necessary equality between a country's foreign saving and investment is the logical implication of the 'vehicular' nature of money and finds strong confirmation in the concept of the international investment position (*IIP*) adopted by the IMF. Defined as 'the balance sheet of the stock of external financial assets and liabilities' (International Monetary Fund 1993: 104), the *IIP* 'is a statistical statement of (i) the value and composition of the stock of an economy's financial assets, or the economy's claims on the rest of the world, and (ii) the value and composition of the stock of an economy's liabilities to the rest of the world' (ibid.: 6). Thus, a current account surplus defines an increase in the economy's claims on the rest of the world and is entered in the international investment position as a positive change in the value and composition of the stock of the economy's financial assets, that is, as an investment. Inversely, a current account deficit marks a decrease of the economy's net claims on the rest of the world and is entered in the *IIP* as an increase in the value and composition of the stock of the country's liabilities to the rest of the world, that is, as a negative investment.

The logical identity between a country's saving and a country's investment does not imply, of course, that current account transactions necessarily balance. The balancing of current account transactions is certainly not a requirement of the balance of payments, whose identity applies only at the global level, that is, for the whole of current, capital and financial account transactions. In accordance with double-entry book-keeping, each single current account transaction is entered twice in the balance of payments, but this does not mean that a current account credit (or debit) is necessarily matched by a current account debit (or credit). In fact, a current account imbalance is almost the rule in a highly diversified world benefiting from international trade and international capital flows. Now, this is not in the least hampered by the identity between a country's saving and investment. A country with a positive current account imbalance is a country whose net (inter)national saving is positive and is matched by an equivalent investment, while a country running a current account deficit is a country whose saving is negative and which benefits from a foreign investment of the same amount. '[A]ny current-account imbalance must be matched by borrowing and lending. A current-account deficit must coincide with an equal decline in net foreign assets and a current-account surplus must coincide with an equal increase in net foreign assets' (Cumby and Levich 1992: 116). Equation (3) is therefore both erroneous and misleading. It is erroneous because it suggests that a current account surplus could define a positive saving that is not necessarily invested (or that a current account deficit could not imply a positive borrowing), which is openly in contrast with the nature of money, the actual workings of the monetary and financial systems, and the principle behind the concept of the international investment position adopted by the IMF. It is misleading because it endorses the belief that current account balance is a matter of equilibrium between the residents' decision to save and to invest. Equation (3) is therefore also a clear example of the atavistic need to continue interpreting economic reality by referring to the concept of equilibrium derived from classical physics and introduced into economic theory by Walras, Menger, and Jevons.

A further example of the misguided influence exerted by general equilibrium analysis on international economics is given by the interpretation of the accounting identity between the sources and uses of funds in a properly defined balance of payments. According to Stern (1973), this identity would hold good only *ex post*, that is, only after prices and quantities have adjusted. As claimed in the IMF *Manual*, the balance of payments identity establishes the necessary equality (with sign reversed) between the current account balance (*CBA*) and 'the net capital and financial account balance [*NKA*] plus reserve asset transactions [*RT*]' (International Monetary Fund 1993: 160):

$$CAB = NKA + RT \tag{4}$$

According to the IMF experts '[t]his relationship shows that the net provision, as measured by the current account balance, of resources to or from the rest of the world must – by definition – be matched by a change in net claims on the rest of the world' (ibid.: 160). Now, according to the neoclassical paradigm and in the words of Cumby and Levich, this identity 'is another example of an *ex post* accounting identity; *ex ante* planned current-account and capital-account transactions might not have been consistent' (Cumby and Levich 1992: 114). But what is a *planned* current or capital and financial account transaction, and what adjustment can it engender *ex ante*? What kind of force can an export of real goods, that has not yet taken place, exert and on which market? Exporters do certainly not adjust their decisions to those of importers and, moreover, whatever the decisions actually taken by importers and exporters of goods, services and financial assets, honouring and obeying double-entry book-keeping does not allow for any divergence between current, and capital and financial account balances. An *ex ante* adjustment between an exporter's willingness to sell abroad a given amount of his production and a foreign importer's desire to purchase a different amount of it (or the same amount at a different price) is perfectly conceivable. Yet, before the transaction actually takes place, it would be meaningless to talk about a possible imbalance between current, and capital and financial accounts. Since neither the current nor the capital and financial account transaction has yet occurred, how is it possible for them to be inconsistent? A planned or desired transaction is not yet a transaction and can therefore not be inconsistent with another planned transaction that, like itself, is actually no transaction at all. It is only after a transaction has indeed occurred that it can be defined as such, and when this happens it is too late to find any adjustment between its entries in the current, and capital and financial accounts.

Despite this indisputable conclusion, most economists stick to a neo-classical interpretation of the balance of payments and keep considering the book-keeping identity

$CAB + NKA$ (official reserves excluded) $= 0$

as a condition of equilibrium in a system of free floating exchange rates, thus dogmatically endorsing the universal character of general equilibrium analysis. '[T]he measurement of payments equilibrium and the interpretation of balance-of-payments data are general equilibrium questions' (ibid.: 115). The microeconomic approach proper to GEA is generalized so as to include balance of payments analysis, and general equilibrium models of the balance of payments are construed in order to explain how economic shocks or policy changes may affect current and/or capital and financial accounts.

Once more we are confronted with the choice between a logical identity that does not allow for individual behaviour to play any equilibrating role at the global level, and a conditional equality in which a prominent role is reserved for an adjustment mechanism based on individual and aggregate decisions. Inherently macroeconomic, the first alternative emphasizes the structural aspect of the system of international payments and aims at explaining today's economic disorders by referring to the lack of alignment between the laws the present system should comply with and its actual working. The second alternative, on the contrary, is essentially microeconomic and it is implicitly centred on the idea that economic order is the momentary result of a process of adjustment taking place between opposite forces in a constantly renewed attempt to equilibrate more or less diverging forms of behaviour. Whereas, in a national context, GEA is put at bay by the logical impossibility to determine relative prices, in an international setting its irrelevance derives from the impossibility to adjust international transactions through '*tâtonnement*' (groping) as well as from the impossibility of treating the entire balance of payments as a system of independent equations whose simultaneous solution would determine the equilibrium level of international transactions and exchange rates.

Another related question is whether a balance of payments equilibrium is sustainable in the first place. This question has usually been asked in order to verify if the accounting balancing of current, capital, and financial accounts is compatible with a given level of national income, prices, saving, investment, and exchange rates, that is, whether a country's balance of payments 'can be sustained without intervention' (Kindleberger 1969: 874). The sustainability of balance of payments equilibrium is mainly analysed in terms of official reserve variations and the costs related to them. Without entering any detailed examination of the problem, let us observe that 'current-account imbalances might persist for periods of several years without signalling any disequilibrium provided that the imbalances are financed by voluntary capital flows' (Cumby and Levich 1992: 116). As correctly pointed out by Cumby and Levich, in fact, 'a country with a high private saving rate might experience persistent current-account surpluses that are accompanied by net private acquisition of foreign claims. A rapidly growing developing country might run persistent current-account deficits that are voluntarily financed by foreign residents' (ibid.: 116). If this were indeed the case, there would be no serious reasons to worry about current account imbalances, the overall equilibrium having been achieved without resorting to compensating transactions that leads to the adoption of trade restrictions or related measures likely to alter the autonomous balance of payments transactions.

As a matter of fact, Cumby and Levich's example refers to an ideal state of affairs that would suit particularly well the needs of industrialized countries, which would thus increase their exports of real goods and services and invest their capital at greater profit, and for developing countries, which could develop faster thanks to foreign investments and greater imports of foreign goods and services. Why does such a prospect sound utopian today? Is it only because of their internal difficulties, both at the economic and political level, that LDCs do not benefit from an inflow of foreign capitals sufficient to finance the imports they need to speed up their economic development and which would simultaneously favour an increase in production of highly industrialized countries? What if the system of international payments itself were a major source of disorder? One of the aims of a truly macroeconomic analysis of international transactions is precisely to provide a clear answer to this question. In this respect, the balance of payments represents a privileged conceptual framework for analysis. The search for reasons why the fundamental accounting identity of the balance of payments does not avoid the formation of major discrepancies both at the national and at the international levels will in fact open the way to a new understanding of what hampers today the development of poor countries as well as the economic growth of the rich nations.

Balance of payments discrepancies

The role of official reserves

A complement to the capital and financial account, the official reserves account measures the net change in a country's holding of foreign reserve assets. Essentially made up by monetary gold, special drawing rights, reserve positions at the IMF, and foreign exchange holdings, reserve assets 'consist of those external assets that are readily available to and controlled by monetary authorities for direct financing of payments imbalances, for indirectly regulating the magnitude of such imbalances through intervention in exchange markets to affect the currency exchange rate, and/or for other purposes' (International Monetary Fund 1993: 97).

Let us start our considerations from the balance of payments fundamental identity as represented in equation (4). Bearing in mind that transactions entered in the current account are opposite in sign with respect to those entered in the net capital and financial account and in the reserve assets account, equation (4) can be written as:

$$RT = CAB - NKA \qquad (5)$$

Equation (5) states that changes in reserve assets are equal to the difference between the two main accounts of the balance of payments, but it does not establish any causal relationship between its two terms. An economic interpretation is needed in order to explain whether a causal relationship exists, and, if so, in which direction it is exerted. The problem does not seem to pose any serious threat, since it is unanimously accepted that, measuring the net holdings of a country's foreign financial assets, official reserves are the result of the transactions entered in the current, capital and financial accounts. Thus, for example, a positive entry in the current account that is not matched by an increase in official or private claims on non-residents entered in the capital and financial account is balanced by the acquisition of reserve assets by monetary authorities. Does this mean that official reserves are what, following Meade (1952), economists call a compensating item?

According to IMF experts, the answer varies depending on whether the country's exchange rates are pegged or are free to float. In the case of pegged exchange rates, a difference between *CAB* and *NKA* would lead to a variation in reserve assets (owing to official intervention on the foreign exchange market), whereas in the case of pure float a variation in exchange rates would take place that would guarantee the perfect matching between current account and capital and financial account (*CAB* = *NKA*) without any need for intervention on the foreign exchange market and, therefore, without any change in official reserve assets. But what if – as we have shown in Chapter 10 – exchange rates did *not* fluctuate according to balance of payments transactions? In this case, would it still be possible to argue in favour of the compensating role played by official reserves? Equation (5) does not provide any answer, since it simply shows that reserve asset transactions are part of the balance of payments, which could at most suggest that reserve asset transactions may be themselves a cause of a balance of payments discrepancy. Besides, it seems self-contradictory to claim that '[c]hanges in official reserves are a highly visible part of international capital movements and, in principle, they should be among the most reliable and best-measured elements of capital flows' (International Monetary Fund 1992: 69), and, simultaneously, maintain that changes in official reserves can help reduce a balance of payments imbalance. If reserve asset transactions are among the most reliable and best-measured elements of capital flows, they are necessarily entered in a balanced way in the capital and financial account and can therefore not compensate for any imbalance.

Let us consider the case in which official reserves increase their assets through borrowing, and that in which the increase is financed by a current account surplus. The borrowing of reserve assets (for example foreign reserve currencies) is entered in the balance of payments as a credit (the sale of domestic securities, for example Treasury bonds) and as a debit (the inflow of reserve currencies) in the capital and financial account. The fact that foreign reserve currencies flow into the reserve asset component of the financial account does not alter the final result: the increase in official reserve assets obtained through borrowing is a self-compensatory transaction and does not contribute to the restoring of the overall equilibrium of the balance of payments. The same is true when reserve assets are acquired through a current account surplus. While the commercial surplus is entered as a credit in the current account, its payment is entered as a debit in the capital and financial account: the two entries balance and no compensating effect is exerted on the other balance of payments entries. Even if the reserve assets newly acquired by official reserves might be used in the future by monetary authorities, this is not enough to conclude that they exert a balancing effect from the outset. The 'availability for use' criterion adopted by the IMF to classify an asset controlled by monetary authorities as a reserve asset is not a sufficient condition to make of it a compensating item. This conclusion is in part implicitly admitted by the IMF experts themselves, who claim that '[t]he use or acquisition of *reserve assets*, therefore, does not necessarily reflect the degree or size of the payments imbalance of concern to the authorities. The authorities also may hold reserves for other motives – such as to maintain confidence in the currency of the economy, to satisfy domestic legal requirements, or to serve as a basis for foreign borrowing' (International Monetary Fund 1993: 97).

The official introduction by the IMF of a statistical coverage of the data reflecting the stocks of a country's international assets and liabilities – known as international investment position – has marked an important progress towards a new interpretation of the balance of payments. If a role for the official reserves account is to be found, it is in this direction that it must be looked for. The conceptual improvement made by IMF experts has to be matched by a new theoretical interpretation of official reserves, starting from a critical analysis of the impact of monetary authorities' intervention on the balance of payments equilibrium. If it were to be confirmed, for example, that exchange rate fluctuations are not determined by current or capital and financial account imbalances (Chapter 10), it would be clear that monetary authorities' interventions in the foreign exchange market has no compensating effect on the discrepancies inherent to the balance of payments itself. By reducing exchange rate fluctuations, the intervention – if successful – would avoid a worsening of the imbalance, but it would not affect the causes at the origin of the initial discrepancy. As statistical evidence shows, errors and omissions subsist and their variation is not correlated in any significant way with changes in official reserves (Table 11.1).

Conceived of as the account recording a country's external capital and financial transactions, the official reserves account would mimic the traditional capital and financial account of the balance of payments. This is not surprising, of course, since a country is implicitly involved in the transactions of its residents and the balance of payments is indeed meant to represent the country's involvement with its residents' external transactions. *It is worth observing here that, although the country itself does not carry out any transaction, the overall result – a net increase or decrease in reserve assets – concerns the country as such and not anyone of its specific residents.* A net increase in official reserves deriving from net commercial exports, for example, does not define the gain of any particular individual importer but that of the country itself, which, as the *set* of its residents, represents them all

Table 11.1 Errors and omissions, and official reserves of major industrialized countries (in billions of US dollars)

	1996	1997	1998	1999	2000	2001	2002
United States							
Net errors and omissions	−19.39	−90.45	129.63	59.16	−44.08	−20.77	−45.84
Official reserves	6.67	−1.01	−6.73	8.73	−0.29	−4.93	−3.69
Japan							
Net errors and omissions	0.65	34.31	4.36	16.97	16.87	3.72	0.39
Official reserves	−35.14	−6.57	6.16	−76.26	−48.95	−40.49	−46.13
Germany							
Net errors and omissions	−1.35	4.20	−2.33	37.87	−22.88	10.46	28.74
Official reserves	1.20	3.75	−4.02	14.11	5.22	5.47	1.98
France							
Net errors and omissions	1.08	4.26	9.94	1.30	10.14	6.85	3.83
Official reserves	−0.24	−5.94	−19.82	1.39	2.43	5.57	3.97
United Kingdom							
Net errors and omissions	3.66	9.79	6.68	−0.70	6.13	−6.14	0.39
Official reserves	0.65	3.90	0.26	1.04	−5.30	4.46	0.63
Canada							
Net errors and omissions	5.56	−2.98	4.55	6.73	−3.67	−5.90	−6.47
Official reserves	−5.49	2.39	−4.99	−5.93	−3.72	−2.17	0.18
Italy							
Net errors and omissions	−20.18	−15.81	−25.75	−1.71	−1.36	2.79	−2.02
Official reserves	−11.91	−13.15	21.47	8.05	−3.25	0.59	−3.17

Source: Data elaborated from IMF, *Balance of Payments Statistics Yearbook*, Vol. 54, Part 1, 2003.

indistinctly. The function of the official reserves account would thus be 'isotopic' to that of the international investment position. What would then be the specific advantage of this new arrangement? As we will see in some detail in Part IV, it amounts to an explicit recognition of the economic existence of countries, which results from the creation of each country's own account. The shift from international monetary disorder to order will require a reform of the present system of international payments, and the introduction of each country as a book-keeping subject accountable for accordingly.

To conclude this short analysis of reserve asset transactions, let us observe that, from a logical point of view, official reserves could be so conceived as to be implicated in every current, capital and financial account transaction. A commercial export, for example, would be matched by a foreign exchange inflow that would be entered in the country's official reserves, while a commercial import would be balanced by a financial outflow that would reduce the country's official reserves. Every transaction recorded in the balance of payments concerns the country as such and modifies its credit or debit situation *vis-à-vis* the rest of the world. It would therefore be perfectly consistent to construe the official reserves account as the account of the country itself and have it involved in the external transactions carried out by its residents (government included). This would give the term *official reserves* its full meaning and help in clarifying the problem of the role reserve assets can play. If official reserves are to represent the country's external position, they cannot be affected by only a restricted number of transactions carried out by its monetary authorities. This means that a fully significant official reserves account would have to be construed along the same lines as the international investment position or, to be more precise, as the flow version of the *IIP*. The net result of the flows entered into the official reserves account during a given period of time would thus correspond to the net international investment position and define the external financial position of the country, that is, its net stock of financial assets and liabilities.

Net errors and omissions

As we have seen, IMF experts maintain that the balance of payments identity holds good only *in principle*, while *in practice* 'the accounts frequently do not balance' (International Monetary Fund 1993: 6). Giving little, if any, consideration to the contradiction implicit in the assumption that an identity might be verified only under favourable circumstances (when it is unanimously recognized by logicians that an identity is an equality that holds under any circumstances), experts claim that, 'because data for balance of payments entries often are derived independently from different sources, implementation of the double-entry recording system is not perfect' (ibid.: 160). In order for the sum of all international transactions

for each single country to be equal to zero, it becomes necessary to introduce a compensating entry known as *net errors and omissions.*

> In balance of payments statements, the standard practice is to show a
> separate item for net errors and omissions. Labelled by some com-
> pilers as a balancing item or statistical discrepancy, that item is
> intended as an offset to the overstatement or understatement of the
> recorded components. Thus, if the balance of those components is a
> credit, the item for net errors and omissions will be shown as a debit
> of equal value, and vice versa.
>
> (ibid.: 38)

Now, the quantitative relevance of errors and omissions can hardly be
denied. As a source of concern for balance of payments analysts, it led –
among other initiatives – to the creation by the IMF of a Working Party
charged to 'evaluate statistical practices relating to the measurement of
international capital flows and, in particular, investigate the principal
sources of discrepancy in the components categories of the capital
account' (International Monetary Fund 1992: xi).

World balance of payments discrepancies

The first anomaly tackled by IMF experts was that concerning the current
account balance of the world taken as a whole. Consistently with the fact
that one country's purchases are the rest of the world's sales, the world
current accounts should necessarily add up to zero.

> Because the world as a whole is a closed economy, world saving must
> equal world investment and world spending must equal world output.
> Individual countries can run current account surpluses or deficits to
> invest or borrow abroad. Because one country's lending is another
> country's borrowing, however, the sum of all these individual current
> account imbalances necessarily equals zero. Or does it?
>
> (Krugman and Obstfeld 2003: 314)

In fact, as was already clearly pointed out by the IMF *Report on the World
Current Account Discrepancy* published September 1987, 'after 1979, the
available statistics on the world current account began to show a large
negative discrepancy, indicating that either the deficits of some countries
and areas were being overstated, or that surpluses were being understated'
(International Monetary Fund 1987: 1). As Table 11.2 shows, despite
remarkable improvements in statistical data collection and compilation,
the world current account is still significantly out of balance.

As we have already anticipated, the world current account discrepancy
is not the only global discrepancy detected by balance of payments

Table 11.2 World current account's evolution (in billions of US dollars)

	1996	1997	1998	1999	2000	2001	2002
World current account	−32.3	29.9	−48.7	−80.0	−102.7	−117.8	−76.0

Source: Data elaborated from IMF, *Balance of Payments Statistics Yearbook*, Vol. 54, Part 2, 2003.

compilers. The members of the Working Party set up in 1992 to investigate international capital flows identified a discrepancy in the global capital account deriving from a substantial difference between global capital inflows and outflows. Logically, the capital and financial transactions of one country should be mirrored by those of other countries so that, on the whole, the world capital and financial account should always and necessarily balance. Table 11.3 shows that this has not been the case even after the adjustments suggested by the two IMF working parties were implemented.

Up to this point, if we were to summarize we would say that there are two sorts of global discrepancies: one regarding the world current account; and one affecting the world capital and financial account. Now, a priori, there seems to be no reason to rule out the fact that these discrepancies may well add up to one another. 'In principle, the current and capital accounts should be mirror images, and for the world as a whole each should sum to zero. However, it can be seen that over the years the consistency of both sets of accounts has deteriorated, generating large cumulative debits and credits' (ibid.: 12). If the causes of the imbalances were disparate and if they were potentially at work in any of the numerous items of the balance of payments, how could it be claimed that, in reality, these discrepancies are two expressions of just one imbalance? This would indeed be the case only if it were possible to show that they are the joint effect of one and the same cause. Figures, as they appear in Tables 11.2 and 11.3, do not provide any explanation of the discrepancies they measure. On one end, 'positive and negative errors cancel out in the summation leading to the global figures' (Krugman and Obstfeld 2003: 314), so that discrepancies are only inaccurately measured. On the other end, without the support of a conceptual analysis it is impossible to know whether the discrepancies are due to misreported debits or credits, to deficits being overstated or surpluses being understated, to insufficient

Table 11.3 The evolution of the world capital and financial account (in billions of US dollars)

	1996	1997	1998	1999	2000	2001	2002
World capital and financial account	110.8	93.3	−24.9	24.7	228.3	166.8	101.3

Source: Data elaborated from IMF, *Balance of Payments Statistics Yearbook*, Vol. 54, Part 2, 2003.

outflows or to exuberant inflows. It is to the analytical efforts of academic economists and IMF experts that we must therefore turn our attention in order to verify if any satisfactory explanation of world balance of payments discrepancies has been provided so far and, if not, which direction analysis should take in the future.

Attempts at explanation

Let us distinguish the certainly wrong-headed from the more insightful attempts.

From statistical coverage to capital flight

The most common and plain explanation of world balance of payments discrepancies consists in identifying their cause in the lack of statistical accuracy and reliability of data entering the balances of payments. A well-known difficulty, for example, arises from the necessity to respect the uniqueness of time recording. 'In the double-entry system of the balance of payments, two entries must be recorded simultaneously for each transaction. Simultaneous recording ensures that both entries show the transaction occurring at the same time, that is, on the same date' (International Monetary Fund 1993: 30). As clearly stated by IMF experts, '[i]n practice, however, the two entries for a transaction often are derived independently from different sources and accounting records, and conventions for time of recording for the participants in that transaction may differ. Consequently, simultaneous recording of the two sides may not be achieved' (ibid.: 30). The problem is twofold: agree on a unique rule as to the time of recording of balance of payments transactions, and implement worldwide the operational structure required in order to stick to it. Be that as it may, it is clear that the lack of uniformity in the timing of data collection is a source of statistical discrepancies. It is also true, however, that the importance of this cause of statistical discrepancy is very limited both because of constant technical improvements, and because over the long run the differences in timing compensate. It is thus enough to include a time-lag in the computation of statistical data to avoid introducing this particular cause for discrepancies.

Apart from other minor causes of statistical errors and omissions, another serious problem is represented by the anomalous outflow of capital known as *capital flight*. Although it is not a clear-cut concept, capital flight is usually meant to represent an illegal outflow of capital carried out in order to evade taxation or exchange controls, for fear of confiscation, or to avoid legal prosecution. 'The primary motivation for certain current account transactions may be the evasion of tariffs, quotas, or laws regarding trade in illegal drugs or other activities, and these transactions necessarily generate a capital account dimension' (Cumby and

Levich 1987: 30). IMF experts distinguish between capital flight proper and capital outflows associated with drug trafficking and other illegal activities. Yet, they agree that the two are deliberately hidden, illegal capital outflows that may lead to imbalances in world capital and financial accounts. 'Discrepancies in the global data arise when haven countries record increases in foreign liabilities that are not compiled as assets in the exporting country's accounts' (International Monetary Fund 1992: 95). Now, even if this occurrence cannot be entirely ruled out, it has to be kept in mind that the most common device through which capitals are surreptitiously 'transferred' abroad is by over-pricing imports and under-pricing exports. The consequent variation in the current account balance – a smaller surplus or a larger deficit – is in fact statistically 'equivalent to the omission of a capital outflow' (ibid.: 90) and clearly shows that capital flight can take place even if there is 'no direct evidence in the reported capital account that an outflow has occurred' (ibid.: 90). This is also a further confirmation of the fact (analysed in Chapter 10) that capitals never really flow out of their country of origin. A capital flight does not define the transfer of a capital that abandons its country to increase the capital accumulated in the rest of the world. Through under-invoicing exports and over-invoicing imports a resident of country A can hide part of his capital from fiscal authorities but cannot reduce the amount of domestic capital available within A's banking system. If it is through under-invoicing exports that a capital flight occurs, it is immediately clear that the resident of A becomes the holder of a foreign bank deposit corresponding to the difference between the price at which he actually sells his exports to the rest of the world (R) and the price he declares to his domestic fiscal authorities, and that no capital flows from A to R. If it is by overpricing his imports that A's resident evades taxation, he does so either by converting part of his domestic capital into a foreign bank deposit in money R or by transferring abroad the claims on part of his domestic capital still deposited in A's banking system. In both cases, A's domestic capital is not reduced by capital flight, whose negative effect is beyond dispute but confined, in our example, to tax evasion.

IMF experts are aware of the difficulties inherent in the analysis and in the measurement of capital flight. In particular, they seem to endorse the idea that 'illegal capital flows' are unlikely to provide an adequate explanation of a country's errors and omissions: 'the essential point is that a concealed capital outflow may not be evident at all in a country's balance of payments accounts' (ibid.: 90). Since abnormal capital outflows are essentially illegal, they are very difficult to track down. If successful, capital flight goes unrecorded and it is obvious that '[i]n such a case the country's balance of payments accounts will also show no errors and omissions associated with the missing transactions' (ibid.: 90, n. 141). For the same reasons, it is not at all clear why capital flight could help explaining world balance of payments discrepancies. If an illegal transaction goes unrecorded in a country, very likely it will remain hidden also from the rest of the world. If the sale of drugs to foreigners leaves no traces in the balance of payments, it does so with respect to the current *and* the capital and financial accounts of both the selling and the purchasing country. Being deliberately concealed from national authorities and compilers, illegal capital outflows resulting from outright capital flight or from other illegal activities define at most two missing entries and therefore can hardly be considered as the main cause of world statistical discrepancies.

Although errors are still widespread at the various levels of statistical data collection, it would be simplistic to take them to be the main cause of balance of payments discrepancies. Moreover, as we have seen, omissions are often two sided, in which case transactions that get unrecorded in one country escape detection also in the rest of the world. It is thus clear that the analysis must go beyond a mechanical interpretation of statistical data if it is to provide a satisfactory explanation of what has come to be defined as the *mystery* of balance of payments discrepancies. Let us once again follow the trail of world experts in their search for new insights into this difficult problem.

The search for a common cause

Let us start from the world current account discrepancy. Even though, in principle, this discrepancy might be due to current account deficits being systematically overstated or surpluses understated, IMF experts have come to the conclusion that it is best described as the result of a surplus going unrecorded. Identified with a *missing surplus*, this discrepancy has mainly been attributed to the misreporting of international investment income transactions. In its *Report*, the 1987 IMF Working Party went in a long and detailed analysis of the various investment income items – direct investment income, portfolio income, 'shipment' and 'other transportation', unrequited transfers and 'offshore financial centres and financial innovation'. Since our aim is to investigate if it is possible to isolate, *conceptually*, a common cause of national and world discrepancies, we will not enter any further discussion about IMF technicalities, but simply retain the idea that the world current account discrepancy is essentially generated by a global under-recording in the investment income position.

As far as the world capital and financial account discrepancy is concerned, members of the IMF 1992 Working Party were unanimous in identifying it with a mysterious unrecorded capital outflow even if, in principle, the discrepancy could also have been imputed to a general overstatement of capital inflows. 'The global capital flow discrepancy indicates that recorded capital outflows have been relatively understated' (International Monetary Fund 1992: 10). In line with the view that 'the countries that receive cross-border financing via financial intermediaries most often remain able to collect information on these capital inflows, while the capital outflows are more erratically recorded by the authorities of the countries in which the capital exporters reside' (International Monetary Fund 1987: 30), the understatement of capital outflows mirrors the current account imbalance caused by a greater reported amount of investment income paid than income received. Since a current account deficit is balanced by a capital and financial account surplus and vice versa, it is clear in fact that the entry of the capital and financial account balance corresponding to a negative entry of the current account (the excess of investment income paid over investment income received) is necessarily referred to a positive capital outflow. IMF experts seem therefore justified to conclude that the understatement of capital outflows 'is consistent with the earlier findings of the Working Party on the Statistical Discrepancy in World Current Account Balances as to the major sources of the discrepancy in the measurement of investment income' (International Monetary Fund 1992: 10).

Up to this point the IMF analysis has led us to conclude that the global current account discrepancy is a question of a missing surplus deriving from the understatement of payments related to investment income, and that the global capital and financial account discrepancy is due to unrecorded capital outflows, that is, to the current account investment income understatement. The connection is clear; yet it is still too broad to allow for the determination of a precise common cause of world accounts discrepancies. A further step is needed, and this time it is the World Bank that provides additional insight into the problem.

On capital flight again

Instead of being limited to the illegal outflows of capital, the concept of capital flight can be given the meaning of an unrecorded capital outflow, that is, of a capital lost by some countries without being recorded in the balance of payments of the rest of the world. This seems to be the first meaning given to capital flight by the World Bank, by which it refers to the increase in external debt and, at least implicitly, to the payment of interests. According to the *World Development Report*, in fact, capital flight is measured as the difference between capital inflows – as determined by the increase in external debt and net foreign investment – and capital outflows – as determined by current account deficits and variations in official reserves.

Let us consider the set of indebted countries in their relationship with the rest of the world. In the last 24 years, from 1978 to 2002, these countries have benefited from a capital inflow measured by the sum of net foreign direct investment + portfolio equity flows + grants (2,428,975), plus the amount of net flows on debt (1,537,667), that is 3,966,642 million dollars (Table 11.4).

Table 11.4 The measure of capital flight (all developing countries, in millions of US dollars)

	1			2	3	4
	Net foreign direct investment	Portfolio equity flows	Grants	Net flows on debt	Current account deficit	Variation in reserves
1977	–	–	–	–	–	117,713
1978	8,130	1	8,459	55,008	38,379	–
1979	7,493	–1	10,527	67,240	11,912	–
1980	6,279	–1	12,821	94,953	7,885	–
1981	20,376	130	11,424	97,671	50,707	–
1982	23,050	–4	10,644	83,912	66,724	–
1983	14,999	–1	10,130	43,798	54,955	–
1984	14,384	–2	12,341	42,434	38,879	–
1985	12,274	46	13,436	38,427	42,366	–
1986	10,904	225	15,736	36,545	64,065	–
1987	9,394	282	16,714	50,657	31,409	–
1988	17,654	719	18,086	44,902	40,387	–
1989	21,312	3,291	18,982	46,373	41,919	–
1990	24,033	3,004	27,737	54,822	15,815	–
1991	33,106	6,541	33,928	65,344	68,568	–
1992	45,399	12,991	30,104	94,090	82,135	–
1993	68,060	42,444	27,669	108,746	127,417	–
1994	89,894	35,810	31,700	71,999	80,139	–
1995	105,303	17,320	31,590	151,252	101,512	–
1996	127,598	32,884	26,799	116,468	88,725	–
1997	171,095	22,594	25,290	105,307	93,851	–
1998	175,563	6,586	26,719	57,618	109,342	–
1999	181,722	12,640	28,519	13,807	9,777	–
2000	162,170	12,634	28,705	–9,821	–51,173	–
2001	175,035	4,397	27,899	–1,226	–14,445	–
2002	147,086	4,945	31,228	7,341	–74,708	996,900
	–	–	2,428,975	1,537,667	1,126,542	879,187
Total	(1 + 2)	–	–	3,966,642	(3 + 4)	2,005,729

Source: Data elaborated from The World Bank, Global Development Finance Online, January 2004.

During the same period of time, the indebted countries have financed their net current account deficit (1,126,542) and their net increase in official reserves (879,187) for an amount total of 2,005,729 million dollars defining their capital outflows. Thus, statistical data show that indebted countries' capital inflows exceeded by 1,960,913 million dollars their recorded capital outflows. The difference, which the World Bank calls a capital flight, is the amount lost by the indebted countries, that is, the amount mysteriously missing from their official reserves. What this insight into capital flight suggests is that world balance of payments discrepancies derive from *a loss of capital suffered by indebted countries and that this loss is closely related to the payment of their current account deficits.* Furthermore, if we take into consideration the fact that current account deficits are mostly due to interest payments, we arrive at the conclusion that *the payment of interest on external debt is the most likely common cause of world accounting discrepancies.* 'A more plausible hypothesis links the missing surplus to one specific cause of accounting discrepancies at the national level, the systematic unreporting of international interest income flows' (Krugman and Obstfeld 2003: 314).

Global current account and global capital and financial account discrepancies: a simple or a multiple effect?

Our understanding of national and global discrepancies is still very inadequate. The identification of their cause with the payment of interest on external debt is little more than a hypothesis and too many questions have yet to be answered. However, the World Bank suggestion as to the nature of unreported capital flows is very promising and, as we will see in the next chapter, Schmitt's analysis of external debt is apt to provide strong support to the idea that external debt servicing is the common cause of the anomaly affecting world balance of payments accounts. A complete analysis of world discrepancies along these conceptual lines would require an investigation of each country's indebted position and net interest payments. However, even if such a detailed analysis is still in the future, it is already possible to apply the principles of the pathological servicing of external debt to the set of net indebted countries. In particular, it is possible to present a very simplified version of the effects produced on the global balance of payments accounts by the anomalous payment of interests. Let us assume the net payment of interest carried out by indebted countries – the 138 countries considered in the World Bank's *Global Development Finance* – to be equal to ten units (equivalent to *x* million dollars). As implied by the World Bank definition of capital flight and by Krugman and Obstfeld's hypothesis (itself resulting from the IMF experts' suggestion as to the central role played by the investment income position), the interest payment of ten units will cause a whole series of discrepancies, namely, between the current accounts of creditor and debtor countries and between the capital and financial accounts of the two sets of countries. If we suppose the whole payment of interest to have these effects, we can synthetically represent them as follows (Table 11.5).

Table 11.5 Global current account, and capital and financial account discrepancies

Debtor countries	CA	interest	10 (debit)	KFA	Capital inflow	10
Creditor countries	CA	interest	0	KFA	Capital outflow	0
Global discrepancies	CA		10	KFA		10

As can easily be seen, the payment of interest gives rise to:

1   ten units of capital outflows in the debtor countries – defining a missing increase in official reserves;
2   a global current account discrepancy of ten units – corresponding to the current account's missing surplus; and
3   a global capital and financial account discrepancy also of ten units – defining the global unreported capital outflow.

It is important to observe here that the analysis developed so far seems to corroborate the idea that both the 'missing surplus' and the 'missing capital outflow' exist because the payment of interest fails to be recorded in both the current account and in the capital and financial account of creditor countries. If this were the case, then world discrepancies could be blamed on statistical inaccuracy, misreporting, or inadequacy of data recording and not as the mark of a serious structural disorder of the system of international payments. This is indeed the simplest interpretation of the message conveyed by the choice of the adjective 'missing'. The world current account discrepancy would thus pose the problem of tracing down the payment of interest in order to enter it to the benefit of creditor countries. Debtor countries pay what they have to pay as interest and creditor countries are paid their due, yet the amount paid gets unrecorded in the current account of creditor countries; this seems to be the way IMF experts conceive of the 'missing surplus'. 'The IMF has recently examined this problem and concluded that most of the missing surplus represents unreported interest income earned abroad. Interest income earned abroad is often credited directly into foreign bank accounts without even crossing national boundaries, and thus it is difficult to detect' (Salvatore 2001: 457). Despite its apparent absurdity, another possibility cannot be ruled out a priori, namely that the payment of interest elicits a second, pathological payment of net debtor countries' current account. In this case, Table 11.5 would refer to the second payment of interest, that is, to an over-expenditure carried out by the indebted countries and unrecorded by creditor countries. Instead of looking for the 'missing surplus' in order to transform it into a recorded payment, the problem would then be avoiding the overpayment of interest in the first place. The choice between these two alternatives – only partial un-recording of a single versus a double payment of interest – requires a careful and thorough analysis of international interest payments (see Chapter 12). For the time being, let us simply note that interest payment has been almost unanimously pinpointed as a highly original transaction and as the likeliest source of balance of payments discrepancies, which is a good enough reason to investigate it further with the explicit aim to throw some new light on what might be dubbed the puzzle of world balance of payments imbalance.

As we shall see in the next chapter, statistical evidence confirms the result of conceptual analysis: the payment of interest on external debt is indeed the cause of an international disorder leading to balance of payments discrepancies, its effect being felt both at the national and at the global level. Yet, this does not mean that global current account discrepancies and global capital and financial account discrepancies are added to one another. As IMF experts seem also to suggest, they are twin effects of the same cause.

The International Investment Position and the reconciliation of stocks and flows

National and global discrepancies are concerned with the transactions entered into the balance of payments. They are thus the sign of a disorder deriving from the recording of *flows*. In order to better understand the cause and nature of this disorder, IMF experts resort to a comparative analysis between the flow data of the balance of payments and the *stock* data of the international investment position, that is, of 'the balance sheet of the stock of external financial assets and liabilities' (International Monetary Fund 1993: 104). Experts believe, in fact, that 'statistics on international assets and liabilities can serve as a check on the capital *flow* data that enter the balance of payments accounts' (International Monetary Fund 1992: 96). *Indeed, it is important to observe that the discrepancies investigated by the IMF manifest themselves in a divergence between stock and flow accounting data.* The problem of stocks–flows reconciliation is correctly seen as a major obstacle towards sound and reliable statistical coverage, and it is generally thought that the reduction of the stocks–flows divergence (as well as the cutback in balance of payments discrepancies) can be achieved through 'consistent classification'. 'Because stock levels often are utilized in the determination of investment income receipts and payments in balance of payments accounts, consistent classification throughout the income category of the current account, the financial account, and the position components is essential for reconciliation of stocks and flows' (International Monetary Fund 1993: 104).

What is crucial here is to determine what a consistent classification would look like. Is this only meant to describe an improvement in statistical coverage or does it extend to a conceptual understanding of what causes the present disorder to exist *independently* of inaccurate statistical coverage? Is the discrepancy originating in the investment income account and defining the 'missing surplus' the result of a 'technical shortcoming' or does it represent the unavoidable consequence of a logical inconsistency characterizing today's system of international payments? If it could be confirmed that interest payments are at the origin of an excess expenditure causing a divergence between current account, and capital and financial account flows (a net capital inflow, as in Table 11.5), it would then be possible to show that the disparity between stock and flows is the effect of a structural disorder of the system of payments. The payments of interest made by the current account correspond to a transfer to the creditor countries of part of the debtor countries' domestic output: a stock. If two flows were necessary for the transfer of this unique stock, a discrepancy would appear that could not be considered merely the side effect of imperfect data collection.

The current IMF position seems to endorse a more pragmatic and technical explanation. 'The links between investment income in the balance of payments accounts and the international investment position – particularly those between net investment income and the net position – are complex and underline the importance of consistent classification of transactions and stocks and of viewing the two as an integrated set of accounts' (ibid.: 106). The most obvious interpretation of this sentence is that discrepancies and divergences can be successfully dealt with through a constant adjustment and improvement in data collection. Such an interpretation, however, *is not* corroborated by statistical evidence. IMF experts are well aware of the fact that 'in all recent years except 1997, the global *current account* shows an increasing negative imbalance, that is, a continuously widening excess of recorded debits over recorded credits' (International Monetary Fund 2003: 3). It is thus justified to infer that the problem, though clearly exposed by the IMF, remains an 'unresolved mystery'. In fact, the mystery of the 'missing surplus' is even more staggering today than it was when it was first investigated two decades ago. Could this not be a sign that its origin has to be tracked down to an anomaly far more fundamental than the inadequate reporting of statistical data?

As will be shown in the last chapter of Part III, this is precisely the case. Irrespective of individuals or governments' behaviour, the present system of international payments is so structured as to impose on indebted countries a double payment of interests. Two equivalent flows are required to convey the real payment of net interests between countries. In conformity with the IMF experts' intuition, the payment of net interests gives thus rise to an unreported capital outflow defining a net loss for the indebted countries' official reserves. It is this unaccounted loss that explains the mystery of the 'missing surplus'. To understand it thoroughly it is necessary to unveil another little understood phenomenon: the macroeconomic servicing of external debt.

12 External debt servicing
A striking example of macroeconomic disorder

The macroeconomic concept of nation

What does it mean to claim that countries or nations are distinct macro-economic entities not only from a political, geographical, juridical and lin-guistic standpoint, but also from an economic point of view? Is this expression to be interpreted so as to mean that a nation is the result of the aggregation of a country's residents (state included), or is it the set-theoretic description of a country's residents? Let us start by considering the latter alternative. If a nation were the simple aggregate of its residents, the implication for international transactions would merely reflect what already happens at a microeconomic level. Thus, if no domestic resident were currently indebted to foreign residents or institutions, the country itself would also not be indebted to the rest of the world (R). Likewise, if residents were paid for the totality of their current net foreign sales of goods, services and financial assets, not one of them or their country would be a creditor with respect to R. Within this framework it seems plausible to maintain that a country can be a debtor or a creditor irrespec-tive of the position of its residents only if the nation is thought erro-neously as coextensive with the state. As soon as it is realized that the state is also a resident – albeit a very important one – it becomes clear that, on the assumption that the nation be identified with the sum of its residents, in no circumstances can the nation as such be involved in international transactions beyond the involvement of its residents.

Now, even a quick look at the balance of payments accounts is enough to see how inappropriate it is to identify the nation with the sum of its residents. The official reserves account, in fact, is not the account of any particular resident but it reflects the reserve position of the country taken as a whole. For example, an increase in official reserves resulting from a current account surplus defines an international gain for the country itself: neither its formation nor its ownership can be attributed to anyone of A's residents. A similar result applies to the international investment position. The IIP reflects the country's financial position, and is clearly concerned with the global situation of the nation taken into consideration. At this point it could be objected that the fact that official reserves and *IIP* apply at the global level is not necessarily in contrast with the choice to represent the nation as the aggregate of its residents. Superficially, the sum of a country's residents seems to be as encompassing as that of the set of a country's residents, and then it is not obvious, for example, why an increase in official reserves could not be interpreted as a gain for the aggregate. To counter this objection it is enough to observe that if the official reserves were an account for the sum of residents, some residents would necessarily be entitled to it. To illustrate this, let us take again the example of a current account surplus increasing a country's official reserves. Suppose country *A*'s exports to be greater than its imports, the difference being equal to ten million dollars. Since *A* is defined as being the sum of its residents, the ten million dollars that flow into *A*'s official reserves account are the very amount of dollars earned by some of *A*'s exporters. Only two logical possibilities appear open to us. Either we claim that the increase in official reserves is entirely made up of the amount earned by our exporters, or we maintain that the exporters are paid by their commercial banks and that the dollars transferred into the official reserves account are owned by the country as the set of its residents. The first possibility would lead us to the conclusion that official reserves are in reality owned by some residents, which is openly in contrast with the very conception of *official* reserves (country's reserves as opposed to private reserves) as well as with the way exporters are actually paid by their banking system. In fact, as shown in Table 12.1, the ten million dollars entered into *A*'s official reserves are converted into an equivalent amount of money A by *A*'s central bank, which thus backs the payment of the exporters carried out by commercial banks.

The example of *A*'s net commercial exports is particularly useful, since it clearly shows that a nation can be a creditor independently of the creditor position of its residents. As we have already pointed out in Chapter 9, once they have been paid by their banks, *A*'s exporters no longer own any credit on their foreign correspondents and yet country *A* is a net creditor, since the ten million dollars increasing its official

Table 12.1 The formation of official reserves

A's central bank			
Liabilities		*Assets*	
Commercial banks (equivalent in MA of 10 million dollars)	*x* MA	Official reserves	10 million dollars
A's commercial banks			
Liabilities		*Assets*	
Exporters	*x* MA	Central bank	*x* MA

reserves define precisely its credit with respect to the rest of the world. Reciprocally, even though R's importers have entirely paid their foreign purchases, so that not one of them is still indebted to A's residents, their country run a debit to country A, defined by the amount of dollars (R's acknowledgement of debt) entered in A's official reserves. Finally, the existence of national currencies is the best proof of the existence of nations themselves. Being an acknowledgement of debt spontaneously issued by a country's banking system, national money is what gives nations their own economic identity and specificity. Now, since nations cannot be reduced to the sum of their residents, their necessary involvement in the foreign payments of their residents has to be carefully analysed in order to verify if it is perfectly neutral or whether it leads to a major monetary disorder. In particular it must be investigated whether in some particular case the payment of a nation – which is the necessary companion to the payment of its residents – is not compensated by the reciprocal payment of the rest of the world. In other words, the problem we have to deal with is not that of establishing whether or not nations are additionally made to carry out their residents' foreign payments, but that of determining if there are cases in which the two payments clearly add up to one another.

In many cases, the involvement of nations is two-sided and leads to a compensation, so that the analysis can be limited to the payment carried out by the residents. Now, the involvement of nations in the external payments of their residents is a direct implication of the macroeconomic aspect of international economics. It derives straightforwardly from the necessity to convey between countries the foreign payments of their residents, that is, from the need to convert domestic into international payments. When transactions are reciprocal this result is obtained without negative side effects. Yet, when transactions are unilateral a problem arises. The only case of unilateral transfer concerns the external debt servicing, and is the main subject of the present chapter. Does the conversion of money A into money R required by the servicing of A's external debt entail a pathological payment by country A? In order to introduce the problem, let us start from Keynes's analysis of the difficulty faced by Germany in the payment of its war debt.

Keynes and the German transfer problem

As claimed by Keynes in a famous paper published in the March 1929 issue of the *Economic Journal*, after World War I Germany was confronted with the need of both 'extracting the necessary sums of money out of the pockets of the German people' (Keynes 1929a: 1) and 'converting the German money so received into foreign currency' (ibid.: 1). The second of these problems – called by Keynes the *transfer problem* – was at the origin of an animated controversy between the author of the *General Theory*,

Ohlin, and Rueff that led to a series of papers also published in the *Economic Journal*. Essentially, the debate concentrated on whether the priority should have been given to the increase of Germany's exports or to the payment of war reparations. On one side, Keynes claimed that in order to pay for its external debt Germany had first to increase its exports; on the other side, Ohlin and Rueff maintained that it had first to increase its financial flows by decreasing its borrowing and pay more in war reparations. According to Rueff and Ohlin, German exports would have risen as a consequence of Germany's external debt servicing, whereas for Keynes the payment of Germany's external debt required the previous increase in German exports.

Now, Keynes went much further in his analysis maintaining that the earning of foreign currencies through increased commercial exports would not have been enough for Germany to service its external debt. As the following quotation clearly shows, the famous British economist was well aware of the fact that the conversion by Germany of the external payment of reparations carried out by the German government entailed an additional, macroeconomic cost of the same amount as the sum paid to the Allies.

> For I hold that the process of paying the debt has the effect of causing the money in which the debt is expressed to be worth a larger quantity of German-produced goods than it was before or would have been apart from the payment of the debt; so that the population of the debtor State suffers a loss of purchasing power greater than the original equivalent of the amount of the debt.
>
> (Keynes 1929b: 405)

Keynes's argument can be explained as follows. The payment of reparations fell to the German government and, through it, to German residents, who had ultimately to pay for it. This is the precise meaning of the '*Budgetary* Problem of extracting the necessary sum of money out of the pockets of the German people and paying them to the account of the Agent-General' (Keynes 1929: 1). However, the payment of the German government had to be converted on the foreign exchange market in order to be transferred to Germany's creditors (the transfer problem). Keynes realized that, even if Germany had succeeded in earning the necessary amount of foreign exchange *by increasing its commercial exports and reducing its imports, the German government would have had to buy it; such a purchase would have multiplied by two the total cost of Germany's external debt servicing.* The net increase in the demand of foreign exchange, in fact, would have led to a devaluation of Germany's domestic currency 'causing the money in which the debit is expressed to be worth a larger quantity of German-produced goods than it was before' (Keynes 1929b: 405). Because of the excess demand exerted by the German government, the relative prices of foreign currencies in terms of German money would have increased, thus provoking a loss of Germany's foreign purchasing power equivalent to the amount paid to the Allies.

Of course, Germany would not have been able to become a net exporter without unbearable sacrifices by its population. The assumption on which Keynes's argument is based is therefore purely theoretical. However, the case-study of German war reparations has the merit to show that external debt servicing raises a particular and difficult problem. In the present system of international payments, the existence of a lack of symmetry between reserve and non-reserve currency countries, as well as the use of national currencies as 'objects' of international payments, have a direct consequence on the involvement of nations in the external payments of their residents. In the absence of monetary coherence, indebted countries have to shoulder the cost of conveying, or converting, internationally the external debt servicing of their residents. Keynes was able to spot this problem in the case of German war reparations, yet his analysis is not developed enough to account for the whole of it. It is only when the problem is extended to the payment of *net interests* on the external debt that it acquires its full significance and that it can be appropriately accounted for.

The problem concerning the payment of net interests on a country's external debt

The peculiarity of net interest payments

What distinguishes the net payment of interests from the payment of commercial and financial imports is the fact that it defines a unilateral transfer of national resources. As we have already seen, the payment of country A's foreign purchases of real goods, services, and financial assets implies a reciprocal transaction between the rest of the world and A. In fact, the transfer of A's national resources defined by A's payment is balanced by the reciprocal transfer of R's national resources, in the form of present or future real goods and services. Things are different when A pays for its net interests on debt. This time A does not get any present or future foreign output in exchange for its transfer of domestic resources. The counterpart of its payment is indeed the writing off of a debt and not a real transfer from R.

The unilateral transfer defining the payment of interests is a direct consequence of the fact that interests are the compensation due to the lender of capital. The investment in A of a capital initially lent by R is supposed to allow A to increase its national output. Being due to the investment of a foreign capital, this increase has to be in part transferred abroad in the form of interest. It is to conform to economic practice to ask for the payment of interests, and it is irreproachable as long as the interest rate is set at a level allowing for the fair distribution of the gains deriving from the investment of capital. Yet a problem arises when (and it has always been the case up to now) the specificity of this payment is not taken into account by the existing system of international payments. Because of today's system of international payments, the payment of interests amounts to a unilateral transfer from the debtor to the creditor country. Under these conditions, the involvement of the nation in the payments of its residents cannot be *neutral.* On the contrary, as we will show in the following pages, the nation is forced to carry out an interest payment on top of that of its residents, which doubles since it duplicates the overall charge of net interest payments carried out by non-reserve currency countries.

As we have seen at the outset of this chapter, nations are always implicated in the international transactions of their residents. In the case at stake, it is perfectly consistent with the very nature of international payments to maintain that interest payments on the external debt have to be carried out both by the indebted residents and by their country. This does not imply, however, the necessary addition of the two payments. In an orderly system, in fact, the payment made by the indebted residents would be made to their country, which would then, it alone, be charged with paying off the foreign creditor country (Figure 12.1).

As shown in Figure 12.1, interests are paid both by A's residents and by the country as a whole. Yet, instead of being credited to R, the payment of A's residents benefits their own country, which is thus credited with an amount of domestic resources equivalent to the amount of foreign exchange transferred to R. Figure 12.1 depicts the proper state of affairs in which country A acts *as an intermediary* between its indebted residents and their foreign creditors. The payments of A and of its residents cannot add up, so the total charge of interest payment is single. Country A and its residents pay only once the net interests on their foreign debt and, reciprocally, country R and its residents benefit from a single payment relative to their initial investment of capital in A. Another possibility can however

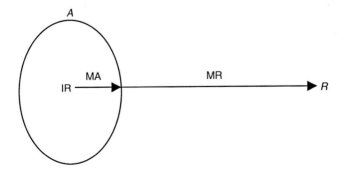

Figure 12.1 The 'orderly' payment of interests.

not be discarded a priori. In a disorderly system, interests could indeed be paid according to Figure 12.2.

As in Figure 12.1, interests are paid here both by *A* and by its residents. Yet, this time the payment of *A*'s indebted residents is not carried out to the benefit of their country. *A*'s foreign creditors (residents of *R*) *and* their country taken as a whole are thus *both* credited as a consequence of the payment of *A*'s net interests on debt.

Which one of the two scenarios shown in Figures 12.1 and 12.2 applies in today's system of international payments? Book-keeping evidence does not leave room for controversy: since the central banks of all those countries that are net interest payers do not enter any positive amount of domestic income derived from the payment of indebted residents, it is the scenario represented in Figure 12.2 that applies in today's real world. The implication that the payment of say *x* million dollars of net interests involves a total charge of twice this amount – that is, 2*x* million dollars – for the indebted countries sounds at first so preposterous that our inference has to be backed by further statistical and theoretical evidence if it is to convince the sceptical reader. Let us start with a concise statistical analysis.

Statistical evidence confirms the existence of a problem related to the net payment of interests on external debt

Let us summarize in a table the principal entries concerned with the payment of interests carried out by the 138 less developed countries (*LDCs*) examined by World Bank's experts during a period of 24 years, from 1978 to 2002 (Table 12.2).

The negative balance of the first two columns describes the net total expenditure incurred by *LDCs* from 1980 to 2003, while columns 4 and 5 give the amount of *LDCs*' total receipts deriving from foreign direct investment, portfolio equity flows, grants and net borrowing (net flows on debt). The last two columns show the amounts (long-term and total) paid

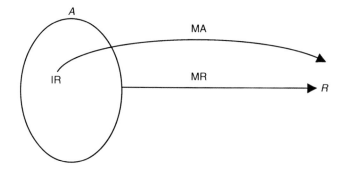

Figure 12.2 The 'disorderly' payment of interests.

Table 12.2 The payment of LDCs' interests on debt and related entries, 1978–2002 (all developing countries, in millions of US dollars)

	1	2	3			4	5	6	7
	Current account deficit	Current account surplus	Net foreign direct investment	Portfolio equity flows	Grants	Net flows on debt	Variation in reserves	Interest payments total long-term	Interest payments total
1977	–	–	–	–	–	–	117,713	–	–
1978	38,379	–	8,130	1	8,459	55,008	–	14,307	16,308
1979	11,912	–	7,493	–1	10,527	67,240	–	21,166	24,530
1980	7,885	–	6,279	–1	12,821	94,953	–	30,633	44,991
1981	50,707	–	20,376	130	11,424	97,671	–	37,930	57,552
1982	66,724	–	23,050	–4	10,644	83,912	–	44,634	64,490
1983	54,955	–	14,999	–1	10,130	43,798	–	43,555	61,045
1984	38,879	–	14,384	–2	12,341	42,434	–	49,502	65,464
1985	42,366	–	12,274	46	13,436	38,427	–	51,504	66,890
1986	64,065	–	10,904	225	15,736	36,545	–	49,229	61,997
1987	31,409	–	9,394	282	16,714	50,657	–	50,379	61,801
1988	40,387	–	17,654	719	18,086	44,902	–	57,990	70,888
1989	41,919	–	21,312	3,291	18,982	46,373	–	52,551	67,249
1990	15,815	–	24,033	3,004	27,737	54,822	–	51,523	65,346
1991	68,568	–	33,106	6,541	33,928	65,344	–	51,985	67,736
1992	82,135	–	45,399	12,991	30,104	94,090	–	50,892	64,067
1993	127,417	–	68,060	42,444	27,669	108,746	–	48,993	63,971
1994	80,139	–	89,894	35,810	31,700	71,999	–	57,039	72,924
1995	101,512	–	105,303	17,320	31,590	151,252	–	73,033	92,425
1996	88,725	–	127,598	32,884	26,799	116,468	–	76,704	97,081
1997	93,851	–	171,095	22,594	25,290	105,307	–	82,006	103,241
1998	109,342	–	175,563	6,586	26,719	57,618	–	90,745	110,850
1999	9,777	–	181,722	12,640	28,519	13,807	–	95,732	115,181
2000	–	51,173	162,170	12,634	28,705	–9,821	–	101,001	121,772
2001	–	14,445	175,035	4,397	27,899	–1,226	–	101,753	117,287
2002	–	74,708	147,086	4,945	31,228	7,341	996,900	83,756	96,241
	1,266,868	140,326			2,428,975	1,537,667	879,187	1,468,542	1,851,327

Source: Data elaborated from The World Bank, Global Development Finance Online., January 2004.

as interest to the rest of the world. Now, the difference between *LDCs'* total receipts, 3,966,642 million dollars, and their total expenditures, 1,126,868 million dollars, represents the expected increase in official reserves for the whole of *LDCs* and for the 24-year period considered by Table 12.2. Statistical evidence shows, however, that instead of increasing by 2,840,100 million dollars, *LDCs'* international reserves have actually risen by 879,187 million dollars only. The difference between the expected and the actual increase in *LDCs'* international reserves is nothing other than the 'missing surplus' denounced by IMF experts, the mysterious discrepancy whose origin has essentially been imputed to investment income recording. If we compare the amount of the unjustified decrease in official reserves, 1,960,913 million dollars, with that of the interests paid by *LDCs*, 1,851,327 million dollars, we immediately note that they are significantly similar. This strongly suggests that the payment of interests has the undesirable side-effect of decreasing *LDCs'* official reserves by an amount equivalent to that already paid by *LDCs'* current accounts.

As Schmitt pointed out (2000a, 2000b, 2003, 2004), statistical evidence itself indicates that interests have been paid twice, once by an increase in *LDCs'* external debt, and again by the decrease in their official reserves. If the small amount of current account surplus realized in the 24-year

Table 12.3 Global balance of payments discrepancies and *LDCs'* interest payments (in billions of US dollars)

	Global current account discrepancies	Global capital and financial account discrepancies	Interest payments total long-term	Interest payments total
1989	−94.9	63.8	52.6	67.2
1990	−127.8	113.8	51.5	65.3
1991	−120.0	163.1	52.0	67.7
1992	−114.1	146.4	50.9	64.1
1993	−80.4	88.5	49.0	64.0
1994	−78.8	95.8	57.0	72.9
1995	−82.4	80.2	73.0	92.4
1996	−32.3	110.8	76.7	97.1
1997	29.9	93.3	82.0	103.2
1998	−48.7	−24.9	90.7	110.9
1999	−80.0	24.7	95.7	115.2
2000	−102.7	228.3	101.0	121.8
2001	−117.8	166.8	101.8	117.3
2002	−76.0	101.3	83.8	96.2
Total	−1,126.0	1,451.9	1,017.7	1,255.4

Source: Data elaborated from IMF, *Balance of Payments Statistics Yearbook*, Vol. 47, Part 2, 1996 and Vol. 54, Part 2, 2003 and from The World Bank, Global Development Finance Online, January 2004.

period is added to official reserves, it is clear in fact that the payment of interest has been the cause of a deficit of *LDCs*' current account. Now, statistical data show that in order to cover this deficit *LDCs* have incurred a new foreign debt of 1,537,667 million dollars. In a logically consistent framework, this increase in external debt would be the only cost entailed by the payment of *LDCs*' net interest. Yet, this is not the message conveyed by statistical evidence, which shows that *LDCs* have been submitted to a second charge that takes the form of an unjustified decrease in official reserves equal to 1,960,913 million dollars. Referencing to Schmitt's latest publications, let us present a synthetic version of the theory of external debt servicing developed by the French economist during the last 25 years.

Let us take the example suggested by Schmitt as it appears in an unpublished working paper presented at a seminar held in April 2003 at the University of Lugano, Switzerland, and consider the case in which the indebted countries' commercial account is balanced, that is, their imports of real goods and services are equal to their exports. It is enough to observe that a commercial surplus can always be analysed as an increase in official reserves to realize, in fact, that the case under examination covers all the other alternatives. Let us therefore suppose commercial imports and exports to be equal to 40 units (millions of US dollars) respectively. If net interests paid by the indebted countries (*A*) to their creditors (countries *R*) are supposed to equal ten units, *A* will have to finance its current account deficit through an external loan of ten units. Now, it is very important to note at this point that *A*'s borrowing required to cover the current account deficit caused by the net payment of interest is only *indirectly* related to this payment. In other words, interest is not paid out of *A*'s foreign loan, which is part of *A*'s capital and financial account. As every economist knows, interest payments and receipts are part of a country's current account, which clearly means that the payment of net interest is financed by *A*'s commercial exports. Hence, given that ten of the 40 units obtained through commercial exports are being used to pay *A*'s interest on debt, a new loan of an equal amount is necessary to finance the commercial imports that are no longer covered by *A*'s commercial exports: the current account deficit caused by the payment of interest must be matched by a surplus of the capital and financial account. The *direct* payment of interest by the current account, which implies the transfer to *R* of part of *A*'s domestic output, is thus coupled with an *indirect* payment corresponding to the imports of the goods and services (*im$_i$*) that paying the interest leaves un-financed.

The additive nature of the direct and indirect payments of interest

As argued by Schmitt, the *direct* and the *indirect* payments of interest are two separate payments carried out by the economy *A* and the country as a whole, and it is only when they have both been covered that interest is actually paid. 'It is only through the payment of im_i, that is, through the *second*, indirect payment of i that A's interest debt is finally settled. If we consider the payment of i only, without taking the payment of im_i into account, the payment of the interest debt would still have to be completed' (Schmitt 2003: 5, our translation). Let us compare what happens when interest is paid – as it actually is – by a transfer of domestic output, and what would happen if it were paid through a new loan. In the first case, country A is confronted with three different flows, namely, the payment of interest itself, i, the new loan obtained from R, l_i, and the payment of imports no longer covered by the exports because of the payment of interest, im_i (Figure 12.3).

As shown in Figure 12.3, A has to face up with two different outflows, i and im_i, while benefiting from only one inflow, l_i. For country A, the payment of interest (ten units) entails therefore a global outflow of 20 units, of which only ten are covered by a corresponding inflow. If interest were directly paid through a new loan, l_i, the pertinent flows would be reduced to two and the N-shaped scheme of Figure 12.3 would have to be replaced by the V-shaped scheme of Figure 12.4.

In this case, and in this case only, the payment of interest would be 'simple', the sum flowing into A being of exactly the same amount as the sum flowing out of it. In actual facts, economies are not free to choose between the cases depicted in Figures 12.3 and 12.4. The V-shaped scheme does not represent an alternative to the N-shaped scheme, and this is so for the compulsory reason that 'the payment of interest is the transfer of an income or an output *of A* – and *not of R*' (ibid.: 6, our translation). If l_i paid i – as in Figure 12.4 – the interest would be paid by

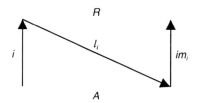

Figure 12.3 The N-shaped scheme of interest payment 1.

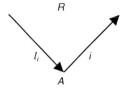

Figure 12.4 The V-shaped scheme of interest payment.

a domestic income of R lent to A. Thus, interest being necessarily paid by the current account, it is the N-shaped scheme that applies, which confirms Schmitt's claim about the double charge of external debt servicing.

The macroeconomic cause of the second, pathological payment of interest

The first payment of interest is carried out by the domestic economy of A. Since interest is the remuneration of the capital imported by A, its payment implies the transfer to R of part of A's national output. Invested in A, the capital lent by R is supposed to increase A's output and this is what justifies the payment of interest and what explains why this payment has necessarily to be imputed to A's current account. 'The received orthodoxy acknowledges the fact that the real payment of interests is debited in the current account; there is no need to challenge this common wisdom; on the contrary it would be seriously erroneous to claim that interests are a direct burden on the capital account' (Schmitt 2004: 25). The second payment is a consequence of the first, a side-effect due to the difference created at the macroeconomic level between A's total expenditures and receipts. In fact, A's expenditures amount to:

$$40 \text{ (imports)} + 10 \text{ (interest)} + 10 \ (im_i) = 60, \tag{1}$$

while its total receipts are only equal to:

$$40 \text{ (exports)} + 10 \text{ (new loan)} = 50. \tag{2}$$

This is explained by the fact that the net financial resources obtained by A through its sale of financial claims (R's new loan) are necessarily spent to cover A's current account deficit generated by the payment of i. 'When the interest payments are taken out of the balanced trade account, an equal deficit is generated in the current account, a deficit that can only be met by the expenditure of equivalent financial resources' (ibid.: 35). The difference between A's total expenditures and its total receipts, ten units, justifies the case for the second payment of interest. The total cost of interest payment is thus equal to 20 units, ten corresponding to the direct payment of interest and ten to the amount required to back up A's net expenditures.

The double charge of interest payment is such an absurd result that the reader will very likely remain puzzled despite ample factual and theoretical evidence. This is why, anticipating a possible objection to the latest argument that we have just summarized, Schmitt gives an alternative proof of the fact that A's total expenditures amount indeed to 60 units. At first sight it might in fact be difficult to understand that, since it defines an additional cost generated by the payment of interest, the payment of im_i must add up to that of imports and interest. It might thus be claimed that the payment of im_i (10) is already included in the payment of A's total imports (40), which would reduce A's total expenditures to 50, the exact amount of its receipts. Yet, this is not so, because if im_i were included in A's imports, an additional expenditure of ten would be accounted for, which corresponds to the repayment of the loan obtained by A in order to cover its current account deficit and finance im_i. Once the repayment of A's new debt (rl_i) is taken into account, A's total expenditures are as follows:

$$40 \text{ (imports, } im_i \text{ included)} + 10 \text{ (interest)} + 10 \ (rl_i) = 60. \tag{3}$$

Once again the difference between A*'s total expenditures and total receipts is equal to the amount paid as interest, which confirms that, in order to pay an interest of ten,* A *has to run a total cost of 20 units. Whether* im_i *is included or not in the amount of* A*'s imports, the current account deficit caused by the payment of interest is covered by a new loan that finances the amount of imports that are no longer covered by* A*'s exports.* This means that A has to account for both the payment of interest and the payment of the cost generated by im_i. If this cost is identified with im_i, Figure 12.3 applies and the sum of A's total expenditures is given by relation (1). If it is represented by the repayment of the new loan (rl_i), it is relation (3) that sets the total amount of A's expenditures and the N-shaped scheme of Figure 12.3 is replaced by the N-shaped scheme of Figure 12.5.

Two important points have to be emphasized here. The first point is that the second payment of interest is carried out by A's current account even though its cost is taken over by A's capital and financial account. Both the payment of interest and of im_i are in fact entered in A's current account since they imply the transfer to R of part of A's domestic output. This is clearly true for the payment of i, since interest is the income paid to R for an investment of capital in A. Part of the output generated by this investment is due to R, which precisely means that A pays its due by transferring part of its domestic resources to R. As for im_i, it is likewise clear that its payment originates in A's current account, since it is this account that is debited for all of A's imports, including those which cannot be

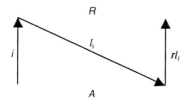

Figure 12.5 The N-shaped scheme of interest payment 2.

financed by A's exports. This extra payment leads to a deficit of A's current account, which is covered through a new loan obtained through the capital and financial account: it is precisely because im_i is paid by the current account that a deficit is formed and so a new loan is required to finance it. The second point we would like to emphasize is that *the difference between* A's *total expenditures and total receipts shows the macroeconomic nature of the second payment of interest. It would be vain, in fact, to look for the second payment at the microeconomic level.* A's indebted residents pay only once the interest on their foreign debt. Thus, it is on the nation as a whole that the second interest payment is inflicted. It is the entire set of A's residents that has to cover the second cost of interest payment, and it does so through a decrease in A's official reserves.

The payment of im_i does not replace that of i

As observed by Schmitt, if i and im_i were substitutes, the payments of interest and of im_i would be single transactions. In fact, if this were the case, A's current account would pay for i, while the payment of im_i would be directly carried out by the capital and financial account. A would transfer only an amount of its domestic output equal to i, the payment of im_i being financed by an income of R. But this would mean that A's current account could have equally well paid for A's total imports (im_i included), leaving to A's capital and financial account the task to pay (directly) for i. It is clear, therefore, that in this case the interest would have been paid only once, either by the current account or by the capital and financial account. Now, this is not what happens today, for the compulsory reason that i and im_i are not substitutes of each other. Schmitt shows, in fact, that i and im_i are magnitudes of opposite algebraic sign, which means that their payment is a double expenditure. This is clearly shown by the fact that A's payment of interest entails the loss of a positive asset, whereas the payment of im_i gives rise to a net debt, which defines the formation of a net liability. Being derived from a capital invested in A, interest is necessarily paid through a transfer to R of part of A's own output. It thus immediately follows that, by paying for i, A loses part of its domestic assets to the benefit of R. The payment of ten units in interest reduces to zero a positive asset of ten units (Figure 12.6).

On the other hand, the payment of im_i is financed by the new

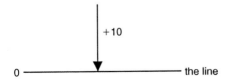

Figure 12.6 The interest payment as the loss of a positive asset.

loan obtained by *A* in order to cover for the deficit of its current account, generated by the payment of *i*. The expenditure of the sum borrowed from *R* leaves *A* with a *net* debt, that is, with a net liability represented by a negative magnitude of the same amount as the sum spent (Figure 12.7).

Both payments, of *i* and *im_i*, are necessary for the payment of *A*'s net interest on debt to be completed. A priori this does not imply that, in order to pay for ten units of interest, *A* has to face a total expenditure of 20 units. Indeed, the cost would only be of ten units if *i* and *im_i* were merely interchangeable aspects of the same payment, that is, as we have previously put it, if they were perfect substitutes. Yet, this is not the case. Whereas to pay for *i* amounts to reducing a positive asset – the part of *A*'s domestic output that the debtor country has to transfer to its creditors – to zero, the payment of *im_i* takes *A* under 'the line', in the realm of negative magnitudes (net liabilities). In the words of Schmitt, the payment of *i* and *im_i* are *two distinct flows*, since it is formally impossible for two flows of equal value to converge into a single or unique expenditure if one stands for a decrease in assets and the other for an increase in liabilities. As shown in Figure 12.8, the payment of interest (equal to ten units) implies both a flow reducing *A*'s assets from +10 to zero and a flow pushing *A* into negative numbers (defining an increase in its liabilities), from zero to −10.

On the whole, the direct and indirect payments of interest entail a cost total of 20 units, the exact measure of the 'distance' separating +10 from −10. If *i* did not reduce *A*'s assets, the payment of interest would corres-

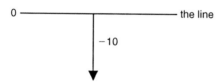

Figure 12.7 The payment of *im_i* as the formation of a net liability.

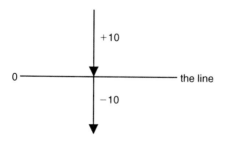

Figure 12.8 The two flows implied by the payment of interest.

pond to the payment of im_i. The two payments would cover the same increase in A's liabilities (the interest falling due) so that they could *de facto* as well as theoretically be substituted for one another. If this were the case, i and im_i would be arithmetically and algebraically equal and the payment of A's net interest would be reduced to either of them. As we have seen, this would indeed be the case only if i were paid by a domestic output of R lent to A. Now, the loan obtained by A in order to cover its current account deficit does not give A any net claim on R's output (or income). As far as this loan is concerned, A is in fact both a debtor (the amount it owes to R) and a creditor (the amount it gets from R), which is a further confirmation of the fact that A pays i by transferring to R part of its own (A's) domestic income. It thus necessarily follows that the payment of i implies a reduction of A's domestic resources, that is, a decrease in its assets. Since assets and liabilities are opposite in sign, the increase in liabilities and the decrease in assets that define the payment of im_i and i are algebraically opposite transactions, which explains why they add up to one another, multiplying thus by two the total cost of A's external debt servicing.

The necessary distinction between the two flows relating to the payment of interest is all important. Let us therefore repeat, once again, that it rests on the unanimously recognized fact that interest is paid by the current account, that is, by a transfer of current domestic resources. Being financed by an export, the payment of interest leaves an equivalent import of A (im_i) uncovered. *The necessity to pay for* im$_i$ *is thus generated by the very payment of* i. *Both the payment of* i *and of* im$_i$ *are therefore constitutive parts of the payment of* A*'s net interest.* The problem of the double cost of interest payment does not derive from the fact that A must pay for both i and im_i, but from the fact that these two payments as distinct add up to one another. This is so because the decrease of an asset (the payment of i by A's internal resources) cannot be assimilated to the increase of a liability (the payment of im_i, financed by the sum borrowed from R), or, alternatively said, because flow i is the payment of a liability (the debt incurred by A when interest falls due) while flow im_i is the payment of an asset (the goods imported by A that are not covered by A's exports). Thus, the interest debt – a liability – is paid by the decrease of an asset, while the payment of im_i – a real asset – engenders an increase in A's net liabilities. All in all, two distinct flows of ten units are required for A to pay its interest on debt (equal to ten units): the payment of an interest of ten units costs A a sum total of 20 units. The pathology of the present system of international payments is such that each time an indebted country pays x units of net interest it suffers a total loss of resources equal to $2x$ units.

Again on the double payment of net interests

The payment of net interest: a unilateral transfer

What distinguishes the payment of net interest from any other payment carried out by country *A* is that the transfer of a domestic income to cover for *A*'s net interest is the only case in which a country pays the rest of the world without benefiting from a reciprocal payment. Reciprocity is obviously realized when a country pays for its imports and gets paid for its exports in a situation of a perfectly balanced trade account. The same is true if our country (*A*) spends a sum borrowed from *R* to finance its net commercial imports. In this case the payment made to the benefit of *R* is the reciprocal of the payment made by *R* for the purchase of *A*'s financial claims, that is, for the purchase of *A*'s future output. *Things are entirely different, however, when* A *pays* R *for the net interest on its external debt.* This time *A* will never be able to compensate its payment with an equivalent import of *R*'s output. In fact, the payment of *A*'s net interest is financed by an export of *A*'s domestic output, which means that the sum borrowed from *R* will simply restore the level of *A*'s imports to the level of its exports. In Schmitt's stylized numerical example *A*'s imports and exports are equal to 40 units. The payment of interest (ten units) by the current account reduces to 30 units the amount of foreign exchange available for the financing of *A*'s imports. The new loan granted by *R* will therefore be used to settle *A*'s current account deficit and thus finance the imports of ten units that the payment of interest left un-financed. *Used up to restore its trade balance,* A*'s financial surplus will never be matched by an equivalent increase in commercial imports.* When *A* spends the amount of foreign exchange obtained from *R* to finance a new import, it compensates its sale of (future) domestic output with a purchase of an extra amount of *R*'s domestic product. *A*'s commercial imports are thus increased from 40 to 50 units, which is also the total amount of *A*'s exports of real and financial assets. In the case of interest, such compensation never occurs. Since *A* spends the sum obtained from its net sale of financial assets to cover its current account deficit, it will forever be deprived of the counterpart to its (future) commercial surplus.

As observed by Schmitt, the reader unfamiliar with the problem might think it right for country *A* to be deprived of the possibility to ever compensate its net sale of financial assets, since it spends the sum obtained through its sale to finance the payment of its net interest. Yet, this would be true only if interest were directly paid by the capital and financial account, a hypothesis that is rejected both by theory and practice. As unanimously agreed by economists and experts all over the world, interest is paid by the current account. This means that, having already been covered through a transfer of *A*'s domestic resources, the payment of interest should not entail, on top of it, the loss of a future import. The direct payment of interest by A's current account should imply a total cost of ten units, corresponding to the real goods and services produced by A's economy and transferred to R. It is thus clear that if A has also to give up the counterpart of its financial surplus (ten units), the cost total of the direct and indirect payments of interest increases from ten to 20 units.

As we have already seen, the redoubled charge is the unavoidable consequence of the fact that, in the present system of international payments, the direct and the indirect payment of interest add up. If one could be substituted for the other, the payment would be 'simple'. But this cannot be the case, since the direct payment (i) defines a decrease in A's assets, while the indirect payment (im_i) implies an increase in A's liabilities. The argument introduced in this section shows that the indirect payment of interest amounts to the loss suffered by A since it will never be allowed to obtain any positive counterpart to the financial surplus absorbed in the payment of im_i.

Interest payment and official reserves

Let us compare the payment of interest with the payment of a supplementary amount of imports of real goods and services. If A were to spend the amount earned through the sale of financial assets to increase its commercial imports, its situation would be the following:

Exports of real goods and services	40
Exports of financial claims	10
Imports of real goods and services	50
Increase in external debt	10

A's commercial imports would thus be balanced by A's exports of its present and future output, which explains – A's future income being advanced by R – the increase in A's external debt. If, instead of increasing its imports, A were to pay the interest on its foreign debt, the state of affairs would be as follows:

Exports of real goods and services	40
Exports of financial claims	10
Imports of real goods and services	40
Payment of interest	10
Increase in foreign debt	10

This time, the sum obtained through the financial surplus being absorbed in the indirect payment of interest, the increase in A's external debt is not matched by an increase in its commercial imports. Whereas in the case of additional commercial imports A's payments in favour of R are compensated by R's payments in favour of A, the payment of interest defines a unilateral transfer from A to R. It is true that, in exchange for the transfer to R of A's domestic output, A's interest debt is cancelled. Yet, this cancellation is obtained at the price of a new foreign loan, the proceeds of which, being spent to cover the current account deficit caused by the payment of interest, will never be compensated by a transfer of R's domestic resources to the benefit of A. As the distinction between the two cases shows, the payment of interest implies the double loss of A's domestic output and of its claim over R's output.

Now, the second loss incurred by A is a supplementary expenditure, necessary for A to restore the level of its domestic resources to its initial level. As shown by Schmitt, in fact, while the first decrease in the amount of A's internal resources is made good by the new loan making up for A's current account deficit, the second charge of interest payment implies a further decrease in domestic resources, which can be restored at their previous level only through a new expenditure carried out by A. Following Schmitt, let us suppose A's domestic resources to be initially equal to 300 units. The payment of interest reduces them to 290 units. Their level is then restored to 300 units by the loan obtained from R. It is here that the problem of interest payment arises. Instead of transferring to A part of R's output, the new loan only allows A to recover its own domestic resources. This means that the indirect payment of interest (im_i) reduces again A's domestic resources, whose initial level can be restored only by the expenditure of an equal amount of reserves. Since both i and im_i are paid by the current account, it is clear that both the payment of i and of im_i reduce the total amount of A's domestic resources. The new loan allows A to recover half of it, the complement being recovered only at the expense of a transfer of foreign exchange.

The decrease in official reserves caused by the second, pathological payment of interest 'fills' the 'black hole' brought to the fore by the analysis of the statistical data referring to the set of indebted countries considered in the *Global Development Finance* compendium.

Let us refer back to Table 12.1. Given the amount of *LDCs*' total receipts, 3,966,642 million dollars – obtained by the sum: current account surplus + foreign direct investment + portfolio equity flows + grants + net flows on debt – and the total amount of their expenditures, 1,126,542 million dollars (their cumulated current account deficits), their official reserves should have grown by 2,840,100 million dollars, that is, by the difference between total receipts and total expenditures. In reality, for the whole 24-year period, from 1978 to 2002, *LDCs*' official reserves increased only by 879,187 million dollars. The difference between the expected and the actual increase in official reserves defines the 'missing capital outflow' of *LDCs*, their 'black hole' (1,960,913 million dollars). At this point it is enough to compare the amount of the anomalous decrease in official reserves with that of the interest paid by *LDCs* to verify that the former is indeed the consequence of the latter. Statistical evidence confirms thus the result of theoretical analysis: interest is paid *twice* by *LDCs*, which finance the second payment by a decrease in official reserves.

The second payment of interest as the cause of world current account, and capital and financial account discrepancies

At the end of Chapter 11 we reached the conclusion that world current account and world capital and financial account discrepancies might well be the effect of a single cause that experts tend to explain away alleging an imperfection in recording the sum of investment income.

> The report of the Working Party on the Measurement of International Capital Flows addressed the problems in measuring international capital flows, and, in that connection, compared the data on debt flows produced by the World Bank with data covering approximately the same category in the national balance of payments statistics. It was hoped the detailed database on external debt would help explain and reduce the discrepancies observed in balance of payments reporting.
>
> (BIS, IMF, OECD, WB 1994: 11)

The analysis introduced here shows that the flawed payment of interests is indeed the common cause of world current account and capital and financial account discrepancies. The direct (i) and the indirect (im_i) payments of interest are both carried out by *LDCs'* current account, yet foreign creditors within R are paid only once. The 'missing surplus' is thus explained by the fact that only one receipt entered by R's current account corresponds to the two expenditures entered by *LDCs'* current account. One of the two expenditures entailed by the payment of interest is carried out by *LDCs'* indebted residents, the other is taken over by the countries themselves, which have to cover for the imports (im_i) that – because of the payment of i – are unfinanced by the exports. Now, while the first expenditure is entered as a receipt in R's current account, the second gets unrecorded into R's current account. This is so because, as far as R's current account is concerned, the payment of im_i is not recorded on top of R's receipts derived from its commercial exports. In Schmitt's numerical example, R's exports amount to a total of 40 units and are not increased by A's payment of im_i. The fact is that the second payment carried out by A's current account does not accrue to any exporter of R, but to the whole of country R. The first payment of interest benefits *LDCs'* creditors, residents of R, and is recorded both in A's and in R's current accounts. Yet, while the second, indirect, payment of interest is also recorded in A's current account – because it implies the transfer of a positive amount of A's domestic resources – its counterpart remains unrecorded in R's balance of payments – since it amounts to a gain obtained by country R considered as a whole. If we look at the global current accounts of A and R, we can thus easily verify that, only half of the payments entered by A's current account are recorded in R's current account, and a global deficit arises whose amount is determined by the indirect payment of A's net interest on its external debt.

The very same amount of interest is transferred twice by *LDCs*. The second flow, payment of im_i, is thus at the origin of the gap between debtor and creditor countries' current accounts known as the 'missing surplus'. As statistical data show, from 1989 to 2002, the world current account discrepancy (1,126,000 million dollars) is entirely accounted for by *LDCs*' net interest payment (1,255,400 million dollars). Because of a lack of published data, we cannot provide any statistical evidence of the impact of external debt servicing among countries R. Yet, data concerning the 138 *LDCs* analysed by the World Bank are enough to show that the payment of net interest is indeed at the origin of the 'missing surplus' making up for the world current account discrepancy.

The case of the 'missing capital outflow' can also be correlated with the double charge of interest payment. The second payment of interest carried out by A's current account is in fact taken over by A's capital and financial account. As the mirror image of A's current account, A's capital and financial account shows a pathological decrease in A's official reserves, which is entered as a positive capital inflow into A's balance of payments. *This explains why statistical data referring to the world balance of capital and financial account show a net surplus very close to the amount of the 'missing surplus' corresponding to the world current account discrepancy.* Statistical evidence confirms also the common source of the world current account and the world capital and financial account discrepancies, which are almost entirely accounted for by the amount of net interest paid by *LDCs*. In fact, if we compare the amount of interest paid by our 138 *LDCs* from 1989 to 2002 (1,255,400 million dollars) with the amount of the world capital and financial account discrepancy for the same 14-years period (1,451,900 million dollars), we can easily verify that the payment of interest by *LDCs* explains a substantial part of this discrepancy. The remaining quantitative difference between the two global discrepancies can be attributed to errors and omissions and does not modify the general conclusion that both discrepancies are clear evidence of the double payment of interest to which debtor countries are compelled by the present system of international payments.

Let us briefly show how the existing direct connection between world current account and capital and financial account discrepancies, and net interest payments can be substantiated by the distinction of stocks and flows.

Stocks and flows and the payment of interest

The growing importance experts have been attributing to the international investment position reflects their belief in the possibility to explain away statistical world discrepancies through a reconciliation of stocks and flows. In particular, in the explicit attempt to clarify 'the ways in which stock data enter into the analysis of the flow of external resources between creditor and debtor countries' (BIS, IMF, OECD, WB 1994: 5), experts of the Bank for International Settlements, the International Monetary Fund, the Organisation for Economic Co-operation and Development, and the World Bank issued a report on *Debt Stocks, Debt Flows and the Balance of Payments* whose main objective was the reconciliation between debt stock and debt flow data, as well as the reconciliation of 'the data in the World Bank's Debtor Reporting System with those in the Fund's balance of payments statistics' (ibid.: 80). Two of the aims behind this exercise is that data collected in the international investment position may 'serve to verify and improve the quality of the flow data' (ibid.: 74), and that reliable data on external debt may 'help explain and reduce the discrepancies observed in balance of payments reporting' (ibid.: 11).

As the analysis of interest payment shows, world current and capital account discrepancies are indeed caused by an over-expenditure resulting in the lack of correspondence between stock and flow data. Yet, this is not to say that global discrepancies are statistical flaws that can be successfully dealt with by improving the system of data collection through a stock and flow reconciliation. World discrepancies do not arise from the mere fact that interest payment is badly recorded, but from the way this payment is necessarily carried out in the present system of international payments. Let us go back to Schmitt's analysis. The double payment of net interest lays on the indebted countries' current account at first. Two distinct flows of ten units each are therefore necessary to convey to R's residents ten units of A's domestic resources. The comparison between stocks and flows reveals the existence of a discrepancy between A's expenditures (flows), equal to 20 units, and the stock of domestic output (A's commercial exports) transferred to R's residents. The reason for this particular discrepancy is not easy to grasp and requires a clear perception of the nature of interest payment. First of all, it is necessary to understand that, being carried out by the current account, the payment of interest is financed by A's commercial exports. The first payment of interest is the transfer to A's creditors of a sum of foreign exchange earned by A through its exports of real goods and services. This first flow of ten units out of A's current account is matched by an equivalent flow into R's current account and corresponds to a stock of equal amount: the real resources transferred from A to R. In our previous example, A's internal resources decrease from 300 to 290 units. Now, it is important to understand that the payment of interest by the current account leaves an equivalent amount of A's imports uncovered, im_i. The second flow out of A's current account is thus the payment of im_i. Because of this payment, then, A's current account incurs a deficit that has to be financed through a new loan obtained from R. This means that the second transfer to R of A's domestic resources – defined by the second payment of interest (im_i) made by A's current account – is matched by an opposite transfer from R to A. Through the new loan, the level of A's domestic resources, reduced from 290 to 280 units by the payment of im_i, is re-established at 290 units. It is thus confirmed that *two flows* of ten units are necessary to transfer ten units of A's domestic output to R. It also appears that the two payments carried out by A's current account, for a total of 20 units, are offset only to the extent of ten units entered into R's current account. The difference between the stocks and flows created by the payment of A's interest is the actual reason for the difference between A and R's current account balances and, therefore, the 'mystery of the missing surplus'.

Analysed with respect to capital flows, the second payment of interest defines a decrease in A's official reserves. Taken over by the capital and financial account, the second payment allows for A's domestic resources to be re-established at their initial level – 300 units – at the expense of a capital flow decreasing A's international reserves. On the whole, A's capital and financial account is subjected to two capital flows of ten units each, corresponding to the new loan obtained from R and covering A's current account deficit, and to the fall in official reserves allowing A to recover its domestic resources lost in the payment of im_i. Since the two flows compensate, A's capital and financial account shows no net capital outflow that would match the entry of ten units recorded into R's capital and financial account because of the loan disbursements granted to A. The difference between R's and A's capital and financial account balances explains the 'mystery of the missing capital outflow'.

The macroeconomic nature of the second payment of interest

We have already seen that the double payment of interest is a consequence of the fact that each country is the set and not the sum of its residents. At the beginning of the chapter we have shown that countries are necessarily implicated in the payments carried out by their residents, and we have maintained that, in the case of a unilateral transfer such as the payment of net interests, it is the nation itself that has to provide the resources required to cover the double charge of the payment. In light of Schmitt's analysis it is now possible to clarify the idea that, having first being paid by country A's residents, interests entail a second charge for the country itself.

First, it is important to note that a country's external debt is first incurred by its residents and not by the country itself. Likewise, interests on a country's external debt are paid out by the country's indebted residents. Furthermore, it is also certain that interests are paid only once by the indebted residents of the debtor country and that creditors – residents of the creditor countries – receive a single payment. The double payment of i does not derive from the (absurd) hypothesis that a country's external debt adds up to the debt incurred by its residents, and does not imply the double payment to foreign creditors. Yet, this does not mean that countries themselves are not involved in the payment of their residents, and in particular that the payment of interest carried out by the residents cannot entail an equivalent charge for their country. The microeconomic payment of i – a transfer of domestic resources entered on the current account – is carried out by the indebted residents. Now, precisely because of this unilateral transfer, the indebted country (A) suffers a second loss of domestic resources resulting from the payment of im_i (see Figure 12.3). Thus, while the first deficit is compensated by a new loan and entails an increase in A's external debt, the second is matched by a reduction in A's official reserves, which is the unmistakable mark of a macroeconomic payment of i that adds up to the microeconomic payment carried out by A's residents. 'The severe pathology that we have brought to light breaks out exclusively on the *macro-level*, between the debtor country taken *as a whole*, namely the set of residents [...] and the *set of all agents* residing in the domestic economies of the rest of the world' (Schmitt 2004: 46).

As clearly stated by Schmitt, variations in official reserves are macroeconomic flows, since they concern the country taken as a whole. If interests were settled by a single flow, A's official reserves would remain unaffected. As we have attempted to show, this would indeed be the case if i were paid by the transfer to R (the creditor countries) of a domestic income of R. If the new loan obtained by A to cover its current account deficit gave A a positive purchasing power over R's output, i would be paid only once, since im_i – the imports that remain unpaid for because of the payment of i by the current account – would immediately be compensated by the new loan. Under these conditions, i and im_i would be perfect substitutes, and the payment of interest would eventually be taken over by the capital and financial account. However, the new loan granted by R does *not* give A any positive purchasing power over R's domestic output. This is so because, by lending part of its domestic income to A, R is simultaneously a creditor and a debtor to A, which means that A's credit over R is matched by an equivalent debit to R. It thus follows, consistently with what is unanimously claimed by economists, that *interest must be paid by the current account and that this payment cannot be financed by the new loan entered on the capital and financial account*. As a consequence, the domestic income paid in interest by A's current account is not compensated by an external income obtained from R: the transfer of A's domestic resources to R is net or '*unrequited*'. The deficit of A's current account resulting from this net transfer is then paid for by the new loan obtained from R. But if A spends its credit to cover its current account deficit, what remains of the new loan is a *net* debit. It is clear, in fact, that, through the new loan, *A* obtains simultaneously an asset – a credit over *R*'s banking system – and a liability – a debit to *R*'s banking system – and that the expenditure of the asset leaves *A* with a *net liability*. In order to cover this new, net debt, *A* must again transfer to *R* a portion of its domestic resources. The dynamics of events is as follows. *A* pays *i* from its current account receipts, that is, by transferring to *R* part of its domestic output. *A*'s internal resources are then restored by *R*'s loan, whose object is precisely the domestic product initially transferred by *A*. Finally, the net debt resulting from the expenditure of *R*'s loan is reimbursed through another transfer of *A*'s domestic resources. As an end result, the payment of interest requires two distinct outflows of *A*'s domestic resources, one corresponding to the direct payment of *i* and the other corresponding to the reimbursement of *A*'s net debt. Now, while the first loss of domestic output is neutralized by the expenditure of the new loan obtained from *R*, the second loss can be balanced only by a decrease in *A*'s official reserves. The first compensation – achieved through an increase in *A*'s external debt – is a direct consequence of the microeconomic payment of *i*; the second – implying a decrease in *A*'s official reserves – corresponds to the macroeconomic payment of *i*. 'These two transactions, which take place concurrently, are not linked by the conjunction *or* but by the conjunction *and*: they *add up one to the other*, with the result that the interest payment is unfailingly redoubled' (Schmitt 2000b: 15).

In the present system of international payments, countries are involved in the payments carried out by their residents. In the case of net interest payments, this has the devastating consequence of multiplying by two the total charge of the transaction carried out by *LDCs*. The fundamental reason for this is that the transfer of domestic resources required for the microeconomic payment of *i* is *unilateral*, which means that for *LDCs* the monetary cost of interest payment adds up to the real cost. It is clear, in fact, given the transfer of domestic resources – that is, the direct payment of *i* by the current account – taking place through a monetary payment, that only two responses are a priori possible: (a) the international monetary system provides *free of charge* the monetary 'vehicle' required to convey *LDCs*' real payment to their creditors; or (b) *LDCs* are forced to purchase this 'vehicle' on the foreign exchange market. When transactions are reciprocal, no monetary cost adds up to their real cost, since the reciprocity of payments guarantees the vehicular use of money. In the case of interest payments, this does unfortunately not happen. The unilateralism of the payment does not allow *LDCs* to benefit from a monetary intermediation, so that the total cost of the transaction is made up by the real plus the monetary payment of interest. Finally, the real cost is covered by a new loan that increases *LDCs*' external debt, while the monetary cost is covered by a reduction in *LDCs*' official reserves.

Let us conclude this brief sketch of Schmitt's theory of the redoubling of *LDCs*' payment of their net interests on debt by observing that it is precisely because of its macroeconomic status that the second payment of *i* went unnoticed so far. In fact, no economic agent – resident of the indebted countries – carries out the second payment, and no resident of the creditor countries gets paid twice. As stated by Schmitt, the second payment of interest depletes *LDCs*' official reserves, and, while it does not provide *R* with an additional capital, it allows *R* to avoid spending its domestic saving in order to finance part of its imports. Since official reserves define a country's savings, the double payment of interest amounts to the expenditure of a saving by *LDCs* and to the saving of an expenditure by *R*. The mark of a true capital flight suffered by *LDCs*, the increase in *R*'s capital inflows caused by the second payment of *LDCs*' current account defines a macroeconomic gain obtained by the whole of country *R* in the form of a saving. Thus *LDCs* finance part of *R*'s commercial imports. The saving of its own domestic resources by *R* is what is really 'missing' in *R*'s balance of payments. Yet, what has to be done in order to definitively dispose of the 'missing surplus' and of the 'missing capital outflow' is to remove the only true cause of global balance of payment discrepancies: the double payment of net interest by indebted countries.

Statistical data confirm our analytical results. From 1989 to 2002 world current account discrepancies reached the total amount of 1,126,000 million dollars, and world financial and capital account discrepancies the total amount of 1,451,900 million dollars. Since global discrepancies are partly due to payments carried out between developed countries, it is clear that statistical data concerning *LDCs* cannot account for the whole of these discrepancies. Yet, *LDCs*' net interest payments are the greatest part of global interest payments. In order to confirm our previous analysis statistically it is thus necessary to find significant convergence between the amounts of the 'missing surplus' and of the 'missing capital outflow', and the amount of net interests paid by *LDCs*. Now, from 1989 to 2002 *LDCs* paid interest on their external debt in the sum total of 1,255,400 million dollars. It thus appears that the second payment of net interest by indebted countries can indeed explain away the global discrepancies affecting both the world current account and the world capital and financial account.

Part IV

Conclusions and prospects

13 The laws of macroeconomics

As clearly stated by Robbins, at the beginning of the last century the majority of economists believed the nature of economic analysis to consist 'of deductions from a series of postulates, the chief of which are almost universal facts of experience present whenever human activity has an economic aspect, the rest being assumptions of a more limited nature based upon the general features of particular situations or types of situations which the theory is to be used to explain' (Robbins 1932: 99–100). Today, mainstream economists still share Robbins's definition. What he called 'postulates' are nowadays called axioms, but their meaning has remained the same. 'Axioms [...] constitute claims about this world so widely agreed as to make further argument unnecessary' (Hahn 1985: 5). And unchanged remains the belief that economic theories essentially consist of logical deductions from axioms and assumptions. Now, the deductive method followed by mainstream economics is based on the premise that events are causally correlated. Following Hume's conception of causality, the great majority of economists believe that a meaningful theory must look for event regularities (of a deterministic or a probabilistic kind) starting from a more or less extended set of axioms and assumptions. 'This conception of laws is formulated in terms of constant conjunctions of events or states of affairs. It is an interpretation of laws as, or as dependent upon, constant relations connecting outcomes at the level of the actual cause of events or states of affairs' (Lawson 1997: 17).

As a matter of fact, this is not entirely true as far as the theoretical core of mainstream economics is concerned. The more or less explicit aim of each major theory is to provide a coherent set of laws universally valid and capable to explain any possible cause of economic events. Logical analysis progresses from axioms to fundamental laws, and then from hypotheses to empirical regularities. Hence, were the empirical findings of mainstream economics rejected on account of the unrealistic assumptions on which they rest, the theories themselves remain untouched in their 'hard core' unless it is proven that their axioms and their fundamental laws are also logically flawed. One of the aims of this book has been precisely that of showing that Keynesian, monetarist, new classical, new Keynesian, and real business cycle theories share a common logical shortcoming and therefore fail to provide a satisfactory foundation for modern macroeconomics. The reliance on a microeconomic foundation for macroeconomics, which all these theories share, derives from their acceptance either of the general equilibrium framework or of the neoclassical interpretation of Keynes's analysis. Now, both GEA and Keynesian economics (in its original or in its new Keynesian version) consider individuals' behaviour as central, try to represent it and its consequences through mathematical formalism, and elaborate their models in terms of equilibrium. Unfortunately, none of these approaches is really appropriate since none of them can explain how prices are formed and how an actual monetary system of production in fact works. This is inevitable given that such mainstream axioms – like, for example, Debreu's that physical goods can be taken to be pure numbers – are incoherent statements about the real world. Furthermore, the general laws endorsed by the major theories are derived from a reductive physicalist interpretation of economics rather than from economic analysis proper. What is lacking today is a *sui generis* economic perspective allowing for the development of economics into a science based on its own structures and logical laws. Lawson has it right when he observes that 'if the aim of science is to illuminate structures that govern surface phenomena then *laws* or *law-statements* are [...] precisely statements elucidating structures and their characteristic models of activity' (ibid.: 24).

A true economic theory should not be influenced by the ideological predilections of its advocates. Economic pathologies must be explained on scientific grounds and not just attributed to the behaviour of one or more categories of agents singled out for their specific, social, or political role. This was the objective of all the great economists of the past and should be the sole end of today's research. In order to fulfil this ambitious task, it is necessary to put aside the still dominant idea that macroeconomics is the outcome of individual choices. If macroeconomics were behaviour driven, its foundations would necessarily be microeconomic, and we would have to choose between demand-side and supply-side theories. On the contrary, if macroeconomics is logically independent of individual behaviour, every distinction between demand-side and supply-side economics has to be rejected and replaced by a unified theory founded on structural laws instead of behavioural occurrences.

Let us consider, for example, the new classical economics' attempt to reduce macro to microeconomics. As observed by Vercelli, the microfoundations of macroeconomics postulated by new classical economists 'are by now far from satisfactory. They rely on the heroic assumption that the decision-makers of the models are representative agents, whose behaviour fairly well approximates the aggregate behaviour of the economy' (Vercelli 1991: 235). Now, Vercelli's own criticism is itself far from satisfactory since it still envisages the possibility for macroeconomics to be based on sound micro-foundations. As is claimed by the Italian economist, his rejection of Lucas's analysis rests on the consideration that the representative agents' assumption 'surreptitiously eliminates the main object that should be studied by macroeconomics: aggregation problems and failures of coordination between the behaviour of individuals' (ibid.: 235). It is thus clear that, as the great majority of today's economists, Vercelli still believes macroeconomics to be a matter of aggregation and coordination of individuals' behaviour. As we have attempted to show, however, the true problem is neither behaviour nor aggregation. This is not to say, of course, that individual or collective behaviour is altogether irrelevant. It is clear, for example, that consumers and producers' preferences as to present and future output have a direct impact on the economy. Yet, individual or collective decisions cannot modify the nature of the laws governing our economic systems, since not one of them is based on or influenced by economics agents' behaviour. Macroeconomic laws derive from the double-entry book-keeping nature of money and are concerned with the logical structure of payments relating to production and exchange. Far from being influenced by individual or collective behaviour, these laws set the structural framework within which economic agents are free to take their decisions and model their society in accordance with a set of ethical, juridical, sociological, and political rules that go far beyond the field of economics proper.

Once it is understood that macroeconomic laws are not of a behavioural kind, it becomes also easier to see that macroeconomic magnitudes do not derive from aggregation. Production is the clearest example of an economic event whose result is immediately macroeconomic, irrespective of the number of agents involved (and, therefore, regardless of aggregation). The production of a single economic agent is in fact of an equal macroeconomic nature as that of any group of agents, since it too engenders a net increase in national output, which entails a change, not just for the singular economic agent, but also for the society as a whole, of which he is a member.

Common-sense beliefs are difficult to eradicate. It is therefore not surprising to find that even an author so sympathetic to Keynes's macroeconomic analysis of production as Arena is unable to distinguish the economic act of production proper (an instantaneous event allowing for the absolute exchange between physical output and its monetary form) from the process accounting for entrepreneurs' decisions. Thus, according to Arena (1988), the macroeconomic theory of the circuit also advocated by quantum analysis does not take into account the existence of microeconomic phenomena that play an important role in the determination of production and circulation. In particular, he points out that firms' decisions are influenced by the productive techniques at their disposal and by their financial situation, so that production cannot be reduced to a process involving firms and workers alone and can therefore not be identified with the payment of wages. Yet, nobody has ever denied that various factors may enter the process of decision adopted by firms nor has the need for a microeconomic analysis ever been straight away dismissed. Of course, technology is important and so is the credit policy of banks and firms. What the quantum theory of emissions maintains is not that microeconomics has no right of citizenship in economic analysis, but that it is of no help in explaining or deriving the laws of macroeconomics. The distinction between micro and macroeconomics is not a question of relative number or size, which is one of the reasons why the two categories are not functionally correlated. Macroeconomics is concerned with the logical structure of what we may call the monetary organization of the economy. Microeconomics, on the contrary, deals with the way agents decide to act once this structural setting is in place. If the laws of monetary economics could be influenced by economic agents' behaviour, the analytic separation between micro and macroeconomics would no longer hold. Since this is not the case, macroeconomics can stand on its own and provide the necessary infrastructure for a sound microeconomic analysis.

To conclude this series of analytical remarks on the macroeconomic nature of the laws governing the monetary structure of our economic systems, let us consider a last argument in favour of the behaviourist conception of economic principles. Having observed that human nature and the society must be understood as an open system, Chick and Dow maintain that economic theories must change following changes in institutions, so no immutable laws become possible in the realm of economics. In the absence of true laws, concepts themselves have only a temporary validity since they 'actually have different meaning in different contexts' (Chick and Dow 2001: 6). Now, Chick and Dow's analysis would be correct only if economics were a social theory concerned with human habit. If this were indeed the case, economics should be based on micro-foundations and macroeconomics would not warrant its specific irreducible status. Yet, as the new quantum theoretical approach shows, economics is the sort of science that pertains simultaneously to the realm of the social sciences and to the realm of the exact sciences. And it is as a new science in Vico's sense that macroeconomics finds its profound *raison d'être*. Economics is not only the study of human behaviour with respect to economic activities; it is also the study of the laws governing the monetary structure, which is the *sine qua non* for an economic system to exist. Chick and Dow are apparently not aware of the peculiar nature of money and of the Janus Face of economics. In fact, they consider the concept of human culture and the concept of money on the same footing, maintaining that the meaning of both concepts changes as society changes – or that, in the case of money, the notion 'may have different meanings simultaneously' (ibid.: 7).

Whether it is claimed that the concept of money varies in time or that its meaning is constant while 'its real-world counterpart is unidentifiable' (ibid.: 7), Chick and Dow are convinced that in an open, evolving and complex system as the actual economy, money itself is evolving in form and nature (that is, conceptually). Nobody denies, of course, that important changes have occurred in the material form assumed by money or in the way payments are materially carried out. But, unless we make the error of identifying money with what has been historically used to represent it, the changes in the material form of money cannot be taken as a proof of the variation in its own nature and in the laws governing it. Even if we accept the idea that economies are part of a 'process of interdependent evolutionary change, a process which itself evolves' (ibid.: 11), this does not imply that this evolutionary change does not allow for the existence of a unique system of coherent laws circumscribing the domain of economics proper. In this context, the evolutionary argument made by Chick and Dow would not stand for a change in the meaning of concepts, but for an increasing degree of conformity between the working of the economic system and the laws that engender it. More precisely, a positive evolution can occur only if the practical structure of the (monetary) economic system is made to comply with the set of laws implicit in the banking nature of money and its relationship with production.

The identity between macroeconomic supply and macroeconomic demand

Let us start by clarifying, once again, what shall be meant by macroeconomic supply and macroeconomic demand.

It is current output that makes up the supply of a given economy in a given period of time. As the reader will remember, economic production is an instantaneous event through which physical output is given a monetary form. The measure of current supply is thus given by that of current production. The bundle of heterogeneous goods and services resulting from the physical process of transformation taking place in continuous time becomes a homogeneous economic output as soon as it is associated with money. If physical output were not 'integrated' into money, it could not be measured by any common standard and macroeconomic supply would remain an abstract concept of little, if any, use. As a matter of fact, in the absence of a common, numerical standard, the economic system itself would be a pure figment of one's imagination, and no economic theorizing would be possible. As the indeterminacy of relative prices shows, no numerical standard can be derived from relative exchange, which confirms the Classics' intuition that goods and services must be measured by production. Macroeconomic supply is therefore the result of a (instantaneous) process through which physical output acquires its numerical expression. As we know, it is through the payment of the costs of production that physical output is transformed into economic output, the very definition of current, macroeconomic supply. Now, the costs of production that really matter here are only those referring to the costs incurred by the economic system as a whole. In other words, the measure of current supply coincides with the numerical expression of the macro-economic costs of production of current output.

The numerical determination of current supply is closely related to that of the macroeconomic value of current output, one of the most difficult problems of economic analysis. In this book we have followed the traditional approach of assimilating value to the cost of the macroeconomic factors of production. The identification of these macroeconomic factors with labour has led us to the conclusion that value is determined by the total amount of (direct and indirect) wages. It thus follows that current, macroeconomic supply is unambiguously expressed by the total amount of wages paid, directly or indirectly, to all the workers whose activity is socially recognized as being productive. What really matters in this context is not the social classification of human activities with respect to their productive role – a problem worth investigating in its own right – but simply the fact that money wages provide the homogeneous standard required to express current supply in a common unit of measure. This is what Keynes's wage units stand for: a monetary standard through which physical output acquires its numerical form.

As for the determination of macroeconomic demand, it is necessary to point out straightaway that, from an economic point of view, a positive demand can actually be exerted only if it is backed by a positive income. Neither necessity nor desire is a sufficient condition for economic demand to exist. At the same time, the very existence of a positive income is enough to define a positive economic demand, irrespective of the needs or desires of income holders. This may sound strange to those who are inattentive to the nature of money and the principles of double-entry book-keeping. The reader who has followed us in our analysis of monetary economics, on the contrary, is well acquainted with the fact that savings exist in the form of bank deposits and that, as such, they are necessarily lent in order to finance an equivalent demand. What distinguishes macro from microeconomics in this respect is that, in macroeconomics, demand is independent of economic agents' behaviour. Whether income holders are more or less willing to spend their deposits in a longer or shorter period of time is irrelevant for the determination of current demand. What is saved by income holders can be spent by other economic agents in their stead, and if nobody is willing to borrow their initial deposits, these are nevertheless lent, double-entry book-keeping forcing banks to match their liabilities with their assets. Income holders' deposits – entered on the liabilities side of bank accounts – are necessarily balanced by the debt incurred to banks by firms at large – entered on the assets side of bank accounts. Now, firms are indebted to banks precisely because they have benefited from a loan. And what is the object banks lend to firms if not the very object income holders lend to banks? Thus, savings do not reduce current demand; they merely distribute it, firms themselves exerting part of it on behalf of the final purchasers of current output.

Current demand is therefore determined by the amount of income available in a given economy, that is, by the amount of its bank deposits. This leads us straight to the question of how macroeconomic income is itself determined. The answer is now well known by the reader: it is through production that macroeconomic income is formed. When money and output become one and the same thing a positive income is formed, which defines the very result of economic production: the 'product-in-the-money'. The double-entry recorded by banks shows this very clearly (Table 13.1).

Physical output, entered on the assets side, is the very object of income holders' credit to the bank. Assets and liabilities form a duality expressed through the bank's double-entry book-keeping. Likewise, income – deposited on the bank's liabilities side – and output – deposited on the bank's assets side – are the two complementary parts of production. One of the greatest and most frequent mistakes of mainstream economic analysis is to consider income and output as two distinct objects, each separately determined by monetary authorities and production managers respectively. Such a dichotomous and erroneous conception is overtly rejected by the unanimous recognition that national income and national output are not two separate and additive parts of a country's wealth. Indeed, national income and national output are the two terms of an identity, the two aspects of one and the same reality. It thus necessarily follows that current global supply – national output – and current global demand – national income – can never be different.

The identity between macroeconomic demand and supply is a direct consequence of the fact that they are the twin effect of a single act. Production creates simultaneously the product and its monetary form. Supply and demand are not two separate entities, but the two faces that jointly define the unique result of production. Hence, to produce is to create both a supply – macroeconomic output – and its own demand – macroeconomic income. The reader at home with the history of economic thought will immediately recognize the familiar formulation of Say's Law, according to which supply creates its own demand. Rejected by mainstream and post-Keynesian economics, this law finds a new *raison d'être* in the quantum theoretical approach advocated here. It is the macroeconomic analysis of production that provides final evidence of the validity of Say's Law. Supply

Table 13.1 The formation of macroeconomic income

Bank			
Liabilities		*Assets*	
Income holders	x	Firms (output)	x

is determined by production and is expressed in wage units. Likewise, demand is determined by nothing else but the amount of income generated by production. The unicity of the macroeconomic factors of production leaves no room for any other conclusion: the amount of (direct and indirect) wages gives simultaneously the economic measure of current supply and that of the income feeding macroeconomic demand.

The reason that pushed mainstream economists to reject Say's Law was its apparent inconsistency with situations in which demand is manifestly greater than supply – inflation – or in which supply is greater than demand – deflation. Now, although it is true that Say did not provide any appropriate explanation of inflation and deflation, it can be shown that his law is in fact perfectly consistent with the existence of these two kinds of imbalance. Indeed, the very meaning of an excess demand (supply) would be missed if the (numerical) inequality between supply and demand could not be referred to the fundamental identity between these two terms. As shown in Chapter 8, inflation is actually better represented by the expression

$$D\,(120) \equiv S\,(100) \tag{1}$$

than by the usual expression

$$D\,(120) > S\,(100). \tag{2}$$

Inequality (2) does not tell us much, apart from the obvious fact that 120 units are different from 100 units. Equality (1), on the contrary, tells us that, although demand is still equal to supply in value terms (100), it is now conveyed by an increased number (120) of monetary units. But this is precisely what inflation stands for: a decrease in purchasing power suffered by each monetary unit. Far from being an obstacle in the understanding of inflation, the identity between macroeconomic supply and demand is also a necessary point of reference in the analysis of deflation (and, therefore, of unemployment). Like inflation, deflation cannot be reduced to a simple inequality of the type

$$S\,(120) > D\,(100). \tag{3}$$

What information can we derive from inequality (3)? Is it supply that is too great with respect to demand or is it demand that is not great enough? A meaningful answer can only stem out of equality (4):

$$S\,(120) \equiv D\,(100). \tag{4}$$

The identity between current supply and demand allows us to conclude, in fact, that – given the amount of income formed through the payment of wages (100) – it is supply that has been pathologically (numerically) increased by deflation.

As the reader will remember, in Chapter 3 we considered Keynes's fundamental identity between Y and $C + I$, where Y stands for national income and $C + I$ for the final demand for consumption and investment goods. This means that $Y \equiv C + I$ can be interpreted as stating the necessary equality between the amount of available income and its final expenditure. Briefly, Keynes's identity can be taken to establish the fact that the totality of national income is necessarily spent for the purchase of both consumption and investment goods. Thus, it is only if national income derives from national production that it follows that the final purchase of produced output is always equal to the monetary expression of this same output, that is, that national supply is always necessarily equal to national demand. Keynes's identity between global supply and global demand is therefore the result of his monetary analysis of production and of his identification of national income with national output. Quantum monetary analysis confirms Keynes's intuition and shows that the necessary equality between supply and demand does not hold only at the global level, but is true for any single production since, independently of its size, production is a macroeconomic event, a creation whose result increases the amount of income available within the economic system considered as a whole. Furthermore, quantum analysis shows also that the identity between macroeconomic demand and supply results directly from production, since macroeconomic output and macroeconomic income are its twin outcome. The identity $S \equiv D$ applies even before income is distributed between C and I, and is therefore the very foundation of monetary macroeconomics.

The identity between supply and demand is a macroeconomic law in that it derives from the very nature of monetary production and is totally independent of economic agents' behaviour. It specifies the logical framework within which economic activity takes place but does not in any way limit economic agents' freedom to take the decisions they find best suited to fulfil their interest. When a conflict arises, one must look for the disparity between this macroeconomic law and the accounting structure of monetary payments. Hence, a pathology such as inflation or deflation cannot result from economic agents' behaviour being at odds with the identity $S \equiv D$, but derives from the implementation of an accounting structure for payments that is not honouring this identity. The macroeconomic law establishing the necessary equality of supply and demand is therefore not sufficient to avoid any numerical discrepancy between these two terms. The identity holds in all circumstances, in principle, but it cannot prevent a monetary disorder if it is not matched by a system of payments whose double-entry mechanism is in compliance with it. In the next chapter we will deal with the problem of conforming normative to positive analysis. For the time being, let us consider the second law of macroeconomics, which establishes the necessary equality of each agent's sales and its own purchases.

The identity between each agent's sales and purchases

First introduced by Schmitt in 1975, this law is the building block of the macroeconomic analysis of the circuit and applies both at the national and international levels. Let us consider the national circuit first. According to Schmitt's Law any single economic agent, A, can finance his purchases only through contemporaneous sales and, vice versa, each time he sells he must simultaneously purchase. This appears clearly as soon as it is realized that the identity between A's sales and purchases must be referred to the transactions that this single agent carries out on the commodity, labour and financial markets. Thus, A can finance its net purchases on the commodity market only if he is a net seller of labour services or securities. It is obvious, in fact, that A can find the income required to finance his net purchases of goods and services only by selling his productive services on the labour market or by getting indebted, that is, through the sale of securities on the financial market. What is less straightforward is the fact that A's purchases are necessarily matched by his *simultaneous* sales. Indeed it would be weird to maintain that A's sales on the labour or on the financial market are immediately balanced by his purchases of real goods and services. Most likely, A will in fact spend the income earned or borrowed only after a positive period of time. How it is, then, that A's sales are nevertheless simultaneous with his purchases?

The answer to our previous question requires a deeper understanding of the nature of money and of its 'circulation'. If money were an asset, it could be used as a *medium of exchange*, which would split direct exchange into two non-concomitant transactions: a sale and a purchase. This is the point of view advocated by neoclassical analysis. Money is considered to be essentially a commodity-money so that the relative direct exchange between commodity *a* and commodity *b* is split into two relative exchanges, one between commodity *a* and money and the other between money and commodity *b*. The relative exchange of *a* against a given sum of money is a sale for the owner of commodity *a* and a purchase for the owner of the commodity-money, but not a sale and a purchase for both of them. Money being also considered as a simple *veil*, the seller will later become a purchaser, yet sale and purchase will be equivalent only at equilibrium (which is but one possible outcome of economic agents' behaviour), and they will remain two chronologically distinct events.

However, as claimed by Schmitt and as we have endeavoured to show in this and other books, money is fundamentally a flow. Thus, money exists only at the very instant a payment takes place, and defines a circular flow from and to the issuing bank. For example, issued by the bank in order to allow agent A to pay for his purchase from agent B, money is simply an immaterial (numerical) means of payment and not the object – the real 'content' – of *A*'s payment. This is so because bank money is neither a commodity nor a positive asset. As confirmed by double-entry book-keeping, money as such can never be the term of a relative exchange. But if money is an instantaneous and circular flow, this necessarily implies that both *A* and *B* are simultaneously credited and debited for the same amount of money. This is indeed what happens when the bank pays *B* on behalf of *A*: the bank credits *A* with a sum of money that is immediately credited to *B* who, instantaneously, deposits it back to the bank. Now, if *A* and *B* are simultaneously credited and debited for the same amount of money by the bank, it immediately follows that they are both sellers and purchasers alike.

Let us suppose *A* to own a positive bank deposit prior to his purchase of *B*'s commodity. When *A* is credited by his bank with a positive amount of money (needed to convey his payment to *B*), his deposit is simultaneously debited for the same amount. *A*'s purchase of commodity *b* requires in fact the presence of both a vehicular money – provided by the circular emission of the bank – and a positive amount of money income – obtained by *A* through the sale of his bank deposit. The instantaneous flow of money necessary to convey *A*'s payment is thus associated with a circuit of money income. Now, the simultaneous presence of a monetary and a financial circuit is verified in every transaction. In our example, *A* finances his commercial purchases through a sale of claims (on his bank deposits) in the financial market. Yet, in order to own a positive bank deposit agent *A* must be a seller on the labour and/or on the financial markets. The identity of *A*'s sales and purchases is thus verified when he purchases commodity *b* as well as when he sold labour services and/or financial claims. While *A*'s sale of labour services and/or securities was immediately matched by an equivalent purchase of a bank deposit, his purchase of commodity *b* is balanced by the sale of this same bank deposit.

Banks carry out, simultaneously, a monetary and a financial intermediation and this is why the instantaneous flow defining money entails the necessary equality between each agent's sales and purchases. If this law did not apply, no monetary circuit would exist, which means that money itself would not exist. The fact that monetary systems are a reality is a substantial evidence that Schmitt's identity is indeed a cornerstone of macroeconomic analysis. This is so much so that sales and purchases are always necessarily equal even at the international level.

As the set of its residents, a country can be considered as a single macroeconomic agent acting on the commodity and financial markets. Hence, in the same way as any single resident can finance his purchases only through equivalent sales, a country can finance its commercial and financial imports only through equivalent sales of goods, services, and financial assets. This would indeed appear with the greatest clarity if a proper system of international payments existed, in which an international bank were charged to act as a monetary and financial intermediary. In this case, the instantaneous and circular flow defining international money would be matched by the simultaneous sales and purchases of the countries involved in international transactions. The presence of an international bank and the existence of a true system of international payments would establish a perfect correspondence between Schmitt's Law and the way transactions are actually settled (see Chapter 14). Now, the law of the necessary equality of each country's sales and purchases applies also when the structure of international payments does not comply with it. The alternative is not that between accepting or rejecting the law, but between conforming to it or suffering from a monetary disorder. Derived from the very nature of money and income, Schmitt's Law specifies the logical framework within which countries carry out their transactions. If the system of international payments chosen to settle these transactions conforms to Schmitt's Law no harm is done. But if this law is not explicitly respected by the way international payments are actually carried out, it is the law that in spite of this triumphs. In the first case the system is sound, in the second case it is unsound and the source of a pathology leading eventually to monetary instability (see Part II).

In order to substantiate the latest conclusion let us consider the symptomatic example of the payment of a reserve currency country's net commercial imports. Let us call it country A. Because of the particular status recognized to its domestic currency by the present system of international payments, A pays for its net purchases of goods and services by transferring a given amount of money A to its foreign creditors. Thus, country A's net commercial purchases are apparently not matched by any equivalent sale. Yet, once again appearances prove to be misleading. In fact, double-entry book-keeping does not allow defining A's payment as a net transfer of money A to the benefit of the rest of the world, R. Carried out by its banking system, A's payment implies necessarily the circular flow of money A, which thus flows immediately back to its point of departure (Table 13.2).

As entry (1) shows, A's payment does not reduce in the least the amount of A's bank deposits. The entire amount of MA is immediately

Table 13.2 The payment of a reserve currency country's net imports

A's banking system		
Liabilities		*Assets*
1. R's banking system	x MA	Importers	x MA

R's banking system		
Liabilities		*Assets*
2. Exporters	y MR	A's banking system	x MA

recovered by A's banking system so that no true transfer of money ever occurs. What the rest of the world obtains from A is *not a positive amount of money A*, but rather a claim on A's bank deposits. Through its circular flow, MA conveys a financial claim to R and an equivalent amount of R's domestic output to A. This clearly means that A's purchase of R's goods and services is instantaneously balanced by its sale of a sum of claims on its bank deposits.

If the law of the necessary equality of sales and purchases were explicitly implemented by the system of international payments, entry (2) would never be interpreted as defining the positive inflow of a sum of money A into the assets side of R's banking system. This not being the case, entry (2) is misperceived. Instead of leading to the explicit import of a positive amount of A's securities, the sum entered on R's banking system is given the status of an autonomous monetary asset and is invested as such in what is known as the euromarket (see Chapter 9). The duplication of money A is thus the pathological result of the lack of conformity between the macroeconomic law of the monetary circuit and the system of payments adopted internationally. This shows, once again, that the nature of macroeconomic laws is entirely different from that of microeconomic norms. While the latter are subject to and representative of economic agents' behaviour, the former are entirely independent of it. The nature of macroeconomic laws is such that they are not only totally independent of human behaviour, but also transcend any specific structure of national and international payments. Yet, while human behaviour is not directly influenced by any of these laws – which simply set the logical framework within which economic agents are free to make their decisions – lack of proper implementation by the monetary system inevitably leads to a monetary disorder.

The two macroeconomic laws that we have examined so far derive both from the flow nature of money and are therefore perfectly consistent with one another. Hence, for example, the law of the identity between each agent's sales and purchases is well in line with the law of the necessary equality between macroeconomic supply and demand. Let us illustrate this by means of two examples, one referring to national production and the other to international exchange. As we have seen, production defines both supply – macroeconomic output – and its corresponding demand – macroeconomic income. This is so because money and output form a unique object; they are the two faces of the unique result of economic production: the product-in-the-money. Actually, economic production is nothing other than the payment of the macroeconomic costs of production – the very transaction allowing output to acquire its monetary form. As the reader knows, the unicity of the macroeconomic factors of production – labour – reduces economic production to the payment of wages. Thus, it is through the payment of wages that macroeconomic supply and macroeconomic demand are jointly formed. Now, the payment of wages defines the instantaneous sale and purchase of both firms and wage earners. Firms sell financial claims to the bank that carries out the payment on their behalf and purchase labour services, while wage earners sell their labour services and purchase financial claims in the form of claims on bank deposits. The instantaneous and circular flow of money implied in the payment of wages does not leave room for any other interpretation: firms and wage earners are simultaneously credited and debited by the bank through whose intermediation output becomes the object of firms' negative bank deposit – the financial debt incurred to the bank – and of wage earners' positive bank deposit.

Things work differently at the international level for the simple reason that no direct production is involved here. The international economy is an exchange economy, so that the concepts of macroeconomic supply and demand cannot have the same meaning they have within a national economy. What country A sells abroad is part of its domestic output, while what it purchases is part of the rest of the world's domestic output. This is so even when A's commercial purchases are net, since the corresponding net financial sales required to finance the current account deficit define the sale of a claim on A's future output. It thus seems possible to maintain that the necessary equality of A's sales and purchases implies the equality between A's supply of its domestic output and its demand of R's domestic output. Now, the relationship between A's supply and demand can be verified also with respect of a single output and thus related to the macroeconomic identity of national supply and demand. To show this, let us consider the case of A's commercial purchases being matched by its sales of financial claims. The goods and services purchased by A are part of R's domestic output and make up its international supply. In order to finance its commercial deficit, A sells an equivalent amount of financial claims to R. Through this sale A is credited by R with the amount of income necessary to purchase R's output. Hence, through the intermediation of the financial market, R gives A part of its national output in the form of money. In other words, R gives A both part of its physical output – defining the supply side of its corresponding national production – and the income required for its purchase – defining the demand side of its corresponding national production. The identity between supply and demand is therefore verified as far as R's international transactions are concerned. Unsurprisingly, this is also the case for A's transactions, since they are reciprocal with respect to R's. In fact, it is R itself that supplies its output and demands it (on behalf of A). Reciprocally, A demands R's output (in its physical form) and offers it back (in its monetary form). Likewise, A's sale of financial claims implies that, sometime in the future, A will supply part of its output and will demand it on behalf of R (by giving R the necessary income).

The identity between saving and investment

At first sight, the identity between saving and investment seems to follow directly from that between macroeconomic supply and demand. Is it not true, in fact, that, for Keynes, Y (global supply) is equal to $C + I$ (global demand) and that, saving being defined as that part of national income that is not spent for the purchase of consumption goods (C), the identity $I \equiv S$ is a direct consequence of I being equal to $C + I$? Indeed, it is hard to deny that in the *General Theory* Keynes defines both saving and investment as the difference between Y and C, so that the identity between saving and investment appears to be given by definition rather than established by conceptual analysis. Yet, this is not the whole story. Despite appearances to the contrary, identity $S \equiv I$ is not a simple matter of *nominal* attribution. The relationship between saving and investment results from an analytical process leading to the *conceptual* definitions of S and I, which has nothing to do with the arbitrariness of nominal definitions. It is macroeconomic analysis that shows that saving is determined by investment so that S is always necessarily equal to I.

In Chapters 2, 3 and 4, we have shown why $S = I$ is in fact an identity and not a simple condition of equilibrium as maintained by generations of economists influenced by neoclassical analysis and by Hicks's interpretation of Keynes's *General Theory*. In this first chapter of our concluding part we will reiterate the argument that macroeconomic saving and macroeconomic investment form a unity and emphasize the implications that this identity has on the analysis of capital.

To start with, it might be useful to remind the reader that a clear distinction has to be made between microeconomic and macroeconomic saving. That part of current income that is not directly spent by income earners but is lent by banks to other economic agents who spend it in their stead defines a simple microeconomic saving. Now, this conclusion would apply even if nobody were borrowing from the bank in order to finance his purchases of consumption goods. The sum saved by income earners would be lent even in this case – a necessary consequence of double-entry bookkeeping – and would be spent by firms to cover the costs of production of current output. If it is spent for the final purchase of current output by households, the income initially saved by income earners is destroyed, and savers will recover their due only when borrowers will become income earners in their turn. The transfer of current income from income earners to borrowers and the reverse transfer of future income from borrowers to lenders are two microeconomic transfers that do not alter the situation of the economy considered as a whole. If the amount saved is spent by firms to cover their costs of production, no final destruction of current income occurs. Momentarily transformed into capital (capital-time), the income saved can always recover its initial form later in time and be finally spent on the commodity market. Since the transformation of current income into capital-time is perfectly reversible, no true macroeconomic saving can derive from it. Capital-time simply allows for the final expenditure of current income to be postponed, but does not entail the formation of any macroeconomic saving. The criterion of demarcation between micro and macroeconomic saving is thus very simple indeed: if the sum currently saved is spent – today or in the future – for the purchase of current output, saving is microeconomic; if it is never to be spent for the purchase of current output, saving is macroeconomic.

How is it possible for a given amount of income to be preserved from any final expenditure? The only conceivable answer is: through its investment in the production of fixed capital goods. In order to understand this properly, it is necessary to establish what has to be meant by investment, of course. Yet, this should not present any serious difficulty since, following Keynes, economists all around the world agree in defining macroeconomic investment as the production of investment goods. The term 'investment' can, problematically, be given a much wider meaning by referring it to the total financing of production (of both consumption and investment goods) by firms, and to the transactions carried out by investors on the financial, foreign-exchange or stock-exchange markets. Thus conceived, however, investment has little to do with Keynes's use of the term, which is confined to the production and the purchase of investment goods, that is, of fixed capital goods (also denominated instrumental goods or produced means of production). It is in this restricted and more precise meaning that macroeconomic investment has to be conceived of. To invest is therefore to expand production from the initial category of consumption goods to that of fixed capital goods. It is through the process of capitalization that an economy can grow and improve the quality and quantity of its physical output. Macroeconomic investment is precisely what allows this process to take place.

The determinant step here is the shift from capital-time to fixed capital. The amount of current income initially saved in the form of capital-time has to be transformed into a sum of irreversible, macroeconomic capital. The reader who has followed us so far is already well acquainted with the idea that it is through the investment of profits that macroeconomic capital is formed. Profits are in fact the source of the capital-time that firms can invest in the production of fixed capital goods. The income earned by firms as a profit is, by definition, an income that has not been spent for the final purchase of consumption goods. In this sense, profit is a saved-up income transferred to firms, and which immediately takes up the form of capital-time. To the extent that profit will later be redistributed by firms – as interest or dividend – capital-time will recover its initial form of current income and be spent as such. The final transformation of capital-time into a macroeconomic saving will concern only that part of profit that is invested in a new production. It is only in this case, in fact, that the income saved as a profit is irreversibly transformed into a macroeconomic capital. Then, it is precisely because investment into fixed capital transforms current income into a macroeconomic saving that S and I are the terms of an identity, $S \equiv I$.

As we have shown in Chapter 8, the investment of profit is today at the origin of a serious anomaly leading to inflation and deflation. Once again the disorder is due to an incongruity between a macroeconomic law and the way the present system of payments is structured. In the case in point, the law refers to the necessary equality of S and I, and the inadequacy of the present system is shown by the fact that the sum invested is reproduced through its expenditure on the labour market instead of being converted into an amount of fixed capital and be conserved as such in an appropriate department of the banking system. According to Keynes's macroeconomic law, the income invested in the production of fixed capital goods is necessarily transformed into a macroeconomic saving. This sounds perfectly coherent: *the profit transformed into macroeconomic capital is an income definitively saved by the entire economy, whose sacrifice in income terms is balanced by a gain in capital terms.* If the current system worked in compliance with the necessary equality between the sum invested (macroeconomic investment) and the sum saved (macroeconomic saving), not even a fraction of the profit invested could be spent on the labour market. Transferred to the fixed capital department of banks, invested profit would never be available on the financial market, thus respecting the obvious principle according to which an income macroeconomically saved and invested (that is, transformed into macroeconomic capital) cannot finance any positive expenditure on the commodity, labour or financial markets. Unfortunately, this is not what happens today. Given the lack of a structural differentiation between monetary, financial, and fixed capital departments, profit is spent on the labour market and is thus converted into a sum of wages immediately deposited with the banking system. Instead of being preserved in a specific department of the banking system, invested profit is spent for the direct purchase of labour services, which leads to the birth of pathological capital, fixed capital goods being definitively owned by 'depersonalized' firms.

As it happens with the other macroeconomic laws, the law of the identity between macroeconomic saving and investment must necessarily be complied with. If this is done by structuring the system of payments in accordance with the conceptual distinction between money, income, and fixed capital, the law applies without any negative side effects. On the contrary, if the system of payments does not respect this threefold conceptual distinction, the law applies at the expense of a monetary anomaly leading to inflation and unemployment. What has to be clearly understood, in this respect, is that monetary disorders do not arise from the macroeconomic laws themselves, or from what is known as economic agents' behaviour, but from the inadequate structure of the present accounting system of payments, which does not adequately conform to these laws.

Before considering the normative implications of this positive analysis, let us observe that the identity between S and I is also verified at the international level, provided we interpret the concepts of saving and investment bearing in mind that at this level we are necessarily dealing with an exchange economy. Thus, country A's saving defines that part of its external receipts obtained through a current account surplus. Country A's external income can also have its source in the capital and financial account, through a sale of financial claims and direct investment, but in this case it would be *lent* to A by R, and would therefore still define part of R's own income. Let us consider, for example, the case in which A's external receipts are due to a surplus of its commercial balance. If A sells more goods and services than it purchases, its saving is positive and equal to the difference between its commercial exports and its commercial imports. At the international level, investment acquires also a slightly different meaning, since it cannot define an international production of capital goods. What is saved by country A is actually invested, yet A's investment takes place in the rest of the world. Thus, it is R that benefits from A's investment, which amounts to the external financing of R's commercial deficit. As the reader will remember, A's net commercial sales entail, necessarily, an equivalent purchase of R's financial assets. This means that A invests its saving by purchasing R's financial assets and by doing so, it finances R's net commercial purchases.

The entire amount paid by R flows immediately back to R's banking system, either through an explicit purchase by A of R's securities, or through an implicit transfer to A of an equivalent amount of claims on R's bank deposits. In the first case, the identity $I \equiv S$ is fully respected and A's saving corresponds to the lending to R of part of A's domestic capital. Part of A's capital-time is thus used by R to finance its net commercial purchases and flows therefore back to A, where it recovers its initial income form and is used-up in the covering of the costs of production of A's exported goods. Country A's saving – defined here by A's external earnings generated by its commercial surplus – is therefore immediately matched by A's investment, that is, by the instantaneous lending to R of A's external earnings. Consistent with the necessary equality of each agent's sales and purchases, the amount of A's external income that is not spent for the purchase of imported goods and services – that is, the amount saved by country A in its international transactions – is invested by A in the purchase of R's financial assets. In the second case, that is, if the system of international payments is such that reserve currency countries can pay for their commercial imports by crediting, in their own monies, exporting country A, identity $I \equiv S$ implies the balancing of A's net commercial exports with an equivalent amount of R's bank deposits. Hence, what distinguishes a disorderly situation – in which the system of international payments does not respect the 'vehicular' nature of bank money – from a situation in which payments are carried out consistently with the laws of monetary macroeconomics is the fact that in the latter case A's saving is invested in R, whereas in the former it acquires the form of a monetary duplicate – eurocurrency – and is invested on the euromarket.

In the same way as the discrepancy between the structure of national payments and the identity $S \equiv I$ leads to the formation of a domestic pathological capital, the discrepancy occurring between the present structure of international payments and the necessary equality of saving and investment causes the formation of an international pathological capital. In both cases a duplication occurs, which is essentially due to the misconception of how bank money works. The idea that money is fundamentally a positive asset is still deeply anchored in the way economists think of a monetary economy and seriously conditions the structure of our monetary systems, both nationally and internationally. At the origin of this misconception we find the neoclassical belief that money is not integral to the existence of an economic system. According to *GEA*, a pure economic system can dispose of money, relative exchange being enough to determine prices and equilibrium. This leads us to a further consequence of monetary macroeconomics: the shift from relative to absolute prices.

From relative to absolute exchange

The principle of absolute exchange is what characterizes best the new paradigm of quantum macroeconomics. A direct corollary of the flow nature of money, this principle implies the unequivocal rejection of the theorem of relative exchange on which the dichotomy of the neoclassical paradigm rests. Incapable of determining relative prices, the neoclassical conception of relative exchange has to be replaced by the idea that, in economics, exchanges are necessarily *absolute*. This can be easily understood only if money is introduced as a true *means* of exchange. As long as money is conceived of as a positive asset, exchanges can only be perceived as relative transactions between two distinct objects, each of them taking the place of the other. Yet, this is an outdated expression of economic reality, which contrasts both with theory – given the logical indeterminacy of relative prices – and practice – because of double-entry book-keeping. It is only once money starts to be conceived of as a numerical form or as a numerical vehicle or flow that absolute exchange becomes a meaningful concept.

Macroeconomic production is the first example of absolute exchange. At the precise instant productive services are paid, physical output is exchanged against itself through the intermediation of money and banks. Deposited on the assets side of the bank's balance sheet, output relinquishes momentarily its physical form to acquire a monetary form: it changes itself into an amount of money income deposited on the liabilities side of the bank's balance sheet. Figure 13.1 shows the absolute exchange current output goes through at the moment of its monetary emission – payment of wages.

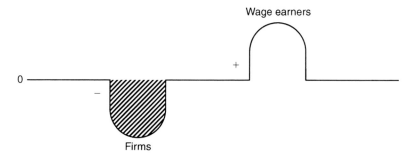

Figure 13.1 The absolute exchange defining production.

Another example of absolute exchange is given by macroeconomic consumption. The final purchase of current output by income holders entails, in fact, the absolute exchange of current output, which gives up its monetary form and recovers its physical form. Literally destroyed by its final expenditure, income disappears – firms' debits and credits cancel out – and physical output ceases to be the object of a negative bank deposit. Expulsed from its monetary form, current output is no longer an economic commodity – what the Classics called a 'value in exchange' – but a physical good or service – a 'use value' – that can be physically enjoyed by its final owners. Thus, while in the absolute exchange of production current output is changed into a sum of money income, in the absolute exchange defining macroeconomic consumption, current output is changed back into physical goods and services.

The principle of absolute exchange is the cornerstone of Schmitt's quantum theoretical approach to macroeconomics, and rests on the flow nature of bank money and on the necessary equality between each agent's sales and purchases. Thus, in the example of production, wage earners are simultaneously credited and debited by their bank because of the circular flow of money implied in the payment of wages. At the same time, wage earners are sellers and purchasers of the same object: current output. Through the payment of wages, wage earners give up the physical outcome of their productive services and receive in exchange for it a claim on a bank deposit whose object is an amount of money income: they exchange current output in its physical form against this same output in its monetary form.

As the reader can easily guess, the concept of absolute exchange is not confined to national transactions, but applies also to international exchange. In particular, it concerns the exchange between currencies, which, in the absence of any international production, replaces the exchange between produced goods and services. The central problem here is analogous to the one discussed above: do currencies exchange according to the neoclassical axiom of relative exchange or according to the principle of absolute exchange? If the neoclassical paradigm applied, the exchange rate would be a relative price determined through the direct exchange of distinct currencies supplied and demanded on the foreign exchange market. Yet, as much as mainstream economists would like it to be the case, analysis shows that relative exchange leaves exchange rates totally undetermined. This is so because relative exchange is a two-sided transaction and can therefore not determine the common and unique standard necessary to solve the heterogeneity problem. In the absence of such a standard, currencies are bound to remain heterogeneous and exchange rates unexplained. The only possible way to avoid this dead end is to switch from relative to absolute exchange rates, that is, to conceive of international transactions as instantaneous events through which each national currency is changed against itself, albeit through the intermediation of a common standard.

Let us be straightforward. No absolute exchange rate regime exists as yet. In the present system of international payments, currencies are considered as if they were real goods and exchange rates are subject to erratic fluctuations essentially due to speculative transactions made possible by the presence of an ever growing pathological capital. In this context, exchange rates elude any rational determination, and are symptomatic of the disorder caused by the divergence between conceptual consistency and structure of payments. As we will show it again in our concluding chapter, the shift from relative to absolute exchange rates requires international payments to be carried out in conformity with the flow nature of money and with the law of the identity between each country's sales and purchases. A reform is therefore needed in order for the systems of national and international payments to be structured according to the laws and principles of monetary macroeconomics. It is to the basic steps entailed by this normative reform that we will now turn our attention.

14 Positive and normative analysis
The national level

While positive analysis is concerned both with the laws underlying the structure of the economic system and with the actual working of the system (in compliance to or in discord with these laws), normative analysis refers to the way the system should work in order to achieve a given result, the norm. Now, economics can be considered as an exact science only to the extent that its laws are logical-conceptual as opposed to hypothetical–empirical. This is precisely what we have been claiming throughout this book, attempting to show that macroeconomic identities are the logical framework of analysis of economic events. The existence of logical identities that cannot be empirically disproved is however not a sufficient condition for the system to work consistently with the principles of positive analysis. If the system fails to comply with the logical rules of positive analysis, a pathology arises, leading to monetary disorder. Broadly speaking, the norm derives from the need for the system to work in an orderly way so as to avoid generating such anomalies as inflation, deflation, exchange rates erratic fluctuations, and external debt crises. Having established its objective, normative analysis must then refer again to positive analysis, whose task is to determine the principles of the reform needed to create a perfect correspondence between theory and practice. Normative analysis is thus assigned the twofold goal of establishing the norm – that is, a required standard that has to be complied with or reached – and determining the structural changes required for the objective fixed by the norm to be achieved. Now, while the first goal can be simply enunciated as the need for a sound economic system free of monetary pathological disturbances, the second objective of normative analysis can only be achieved with the backing of positive analysis. It is positive analysis, in fact, that, once the laws of economics successfully determined, can diagnose the pathological working of the system and suggest the structural remedies apt to eradicate its causes. In economics, normative analysis is therefore essentially a branch of positive analysis, whose task is to transform today's pathological system through a reform allowing for its accounting structure to be in line with the conceptual laws discovered by positive analysis itself. The norm being easily agreed on, and defined as the absence of monetary disorders, the present and the following chapter will be essentially devoted to the analysis of the changes that have been introduced so far in order to achieve monetary stability as well as to the reform deriving from the macroeconomic approach to monetary economics advocated in this book. Because of important differences, let us start by considering the improvements that have been introduced, namely those suggested by mainstream economists and those required by positive quantum analysis, at the national level.

The building-up of the present system of national payments

From double-entry book-keeping to interbank clearing

The first, incisive step in the instituting of a modern monetary system was the introduction of double-entry book-keeping. Made possible by the discovery of negative numbers – attributed to the Indian mathematician Brahmagupta in the seventh century – double-entry book-keeping was developed only much later (in the thirteenth century) by Italian traders, who took advantage both of Arabic numerals and of the Indian concept of zero. It is to Indian mathematicians, in fact, that we owe the knowledge that zero has a definite numerical value of its own, that it is an even number – the integer that precedes one – and that it separates positive from negative numbers. Italian merchants were the first to realize that positive and negative numbers could be used to represent the dualistic character of commercial transactions as well as to allow for the activity of newly born intermediaries that became the ancestors of today's banks. Bank money is the most striking result of double-entry book-keeping. Its introduction fostered both the development of economy and banking that western societies have benefited from in the last centuries. Unfortunately, this process has not been a smooth one. Slumps and crises have too often marked it, and populations all over the world have seriously suffered from its setbacks. Yet, none of them can be attributed to money itself or to double-entry book-keeping. Their true cause is not to be looked for in bank money *per se*, but rather in our inadequate conception of its inherent link to double-entry book-keeping, and in our imperfect understanding of the latter.

Since the birth of modern banking in the Renaissance, economists have endeavoured to unveil its logical rules and to suggest improvements more or less apt to reduce the risks of involuntary mismanagement. Among the authors who have most contributed to our understanding of bank money, Ricardo is at the forefront. His monetary writings are an outstanding example of rigorous and creative analysis, and his suggestion to structure the Bank of England by distinguishing between a monetary and a financial department still deserves all our admiration and attention. In a period when money was almost unanimously identified with gold, it was not at all easy to realize that money and money income must conceptually be separated and that transactions must be recorded so as to avoid monetary and financial intermediations getting erroneously mixed-up. Ricardo had the great merit of showing that the emission of money does not amount to the creation of a positive purchasing power, and that monetary stability requires the emission of money to be backed by a financial intermediation allowing for the transformation of nominal into real money.

In two of his last contributions – *Proposals for an Economical and Secure Currency* (1816) and *Plan for the Establishment of a National Bank* (1824) – Ricardo endeavoured to show that neither the Bank of England nor any other banking or governmental institution should be endorsed with the faculty of issuing money beyond the limits set by production.

> In the present state of the law, they [central bankers] have the power, without any control whatsoever, of increasing or reducing the circulation in any degree they may think proper; a power which should neither be entrusted to the state itself, nor to any body in it; as there can be no security for the uniformity in the value of the currency, when its augmentation or diminution depends solely on the will of the issuers.
>
> (Ricardo 1951, Vol. IV: 69)

Indeed Ricardo was perfectly aware of the fact that a monetary over-emission would have inevitably led to inflation, and this is one of the reasons why he was so vehemently against the possibility for the Bank of England to increase its profits through money creation. Issued at almost zero cost, nominal money has no intrinsic value whatsoever. It would therefore have been gravely mistaken to allow the Bank of England to finance its transactions or those of the state by a simple stroke of the pen. Ricardo's analysis is crystal clear: government spending must be financed out of the real money (income) generated by production and not through money creation. 'If Government wanted money, it should be obliged to raise it in the legitimate way; by taxing the people; by the issue and sale of exchequer bills, by funded loans, or by borrowing from any of the numerous banks which might exist in the country; but in no case should it be allowed to borrow from those, who have the power of creating money' (ibid.: 283).

Money creation and financial intermediation are two distinct functions. Nominal money is created in order to provide the economy with a numerical standard, whereas it is only after it is transformed into income that money becomes the object of financial intermediation. While nominal money is literally created, real money (income) derives from production, which is why credit must be backed by a financial intermediation instead of being wrongly identified with money creation. 'The Bank of England performs two operations of banking, which are quite distinct, and have no necessary connection with each other: it issues a paper currency as a sub-stitute for a metallic one; and it advances money in the way of loan, to merchants and others' (ibid.: 276). If monetary stability is to be achieved, the emission of money must not be greater than what is required by the financial intermediation carried out by banks on behalf of the real economy: this is the central message conveyed by Ricardo's analysis. In order to avoid the inflationary increase of money, every monetary emis-sion must be related to a financial intermediation, since it is only under these conditions that bank loans are not financed out of a purely nominal money but out of a positive income generated by production. Ricardo's positive analysis leads thus to the enunciation of a norm and to the search of a strategy allowing us to respect it. The list of the 16 rules that, accord-ing to the Anglo-Portuguese economist, was to make for the establishment of a national bank, was essentially concerned with the attempt to decen-tralize the emission of money, thus depriving the Bank of England of the unlimited power to create money at will. Properly understood, Ricardo's remedy to the risks of monetary instability caused by a Bank of England's over-emission consisted in a reform leading to the creation of a new banking system operating in such a way as to guarantee the immanent determination of money by the economy. Thus, regional banks were to take over money creation from the Bank of England and act as monetary and financial intermediaries between firms and wage earners, producers and consumers, savers and investors. Money creation would then be determined by the needs of the real economy and would be constrained by the financial intermediation generated, directly and indirectly, *qua* production.

As the historical development of our banking systems shows, Ricardo's suggestions have eventually been implemented. Decentralization is a fact, and the political independence of central banks is a barrier against financ-ing public deficits through money creation. Even if Ricardo's claim for the perfect correspondence between money creation and financial intermedi-ation has not entirely been understood yet, bankers themselves have greatly contributed to the improvement of their banking systems, substan-tially reducing the risk of a pathological over-emission due to the still imperfect structure of national payments. One of the fundamental contri-butions that has to be mentioned here is the introduction of the inter-bank clearing system. Initially based on bilateral settlement agreements, the system moved to a multilateral type of arrangements with the intro-duction – which set off in the United Kingdom towards the end of the eighteenth century – of banks acting as clearinghouses. As stressed by Rossi in his 1997 book on central banking, a substantial improvement was then achieved with the emission of clearinghouse certificates, the first form of what was to become an inter-bank currency (central bank money) issued by a national central bank acting as the clearinghouse of the entire system of national payments (Rossi 1997: 242). The risk of a systemic breakdown owing to a bank failing to carry out its net payments at the end of the day, has recently led to switching from a net settlement system to a gross, real time settlement system where each single payment has to be compensated, that is, where each paying order has to be financially backed in order for the central bank to be authorized to carry it out.

The result of a series of practical improvements introduced by bankers for optimizing doing business, the present system of inter-bank clearing is also the mark of the substantial convergence between theory and practice advocated by Ricardo. The intervention of the central bank as a monetary and financial intermediary between commercial banks is a clear confirmation of the theoretical principles according to which nobody pays by getting indebted, and nobody is a purchaser without being a seller and vice versa. Commercial banks pay each other through the intermediation of the central bank, that is, by using a central bank money and not their own IOUs. Furthermore, inter-bank payments are carried out only if they are compensated, which means that each commercial bank can be a payer (on behalf of its clients) only if it is simultaneously paid (for the benefit of its clients), that is, only if it is simultaneously a purchaser and a seller on the commodity and financial markets.

It seems fair to claim that, after Ricardo, the most noticeable improvements in the field of national money and banking have been more the doing of practitioners than of academic economists. To some extent, Keynes's is a notable exception. His contribution to the macroeconomic analysis of income is outstanding, yet still greatly misunderstood. The monetary policy implications of his theory have too often been reduced to the claim for a change in income distribution based on the belief that an increase in national income has to be matched – through the consumption function – by an increase in demand that, given the propensity to consume, depends on the way income is distributed among the different categories of economic agents. Keynes's fundamental identities have mostly been ignored by his followers, as has his distinction between money, income, and capital. This explains why Keynes's monetary analysis did not lead to the final rejection of general equilibrium analysis and was mostly superseded by the modern version of the quantity theory of money and by its 'Keynesian' interpretations. Given the historical importance of the monetarist approach to monetary policy, let us briefly comment on some of its problematic assumptions.

Monetarist policies and monetary disorders

The importance of monetary policy as a means to achieve price stability, high employment, and economic growth is closely related to the theoretical choices of its advocates or its detractors. Thus, for example, while some of Keynes's followers believed interest rates to have little impact on investment and consumption – so that monetary measures would be of a little use in stimulating investment and undermining thriftiness – Friedman maintained that changes in the quantity of money are most likely to affect total spending even when Keynes's liquidity preference is absolute. In his 1968 article on the role of monetary policy, Friedman shows how in the past economists have often changed their mind as to the relevance of monetary policy and claims that 'there is major disagreement about criteria of policy, varying from emphasis on money market conditions, interest rates, and the quantity of money to the belief that the state of employment itself should be the proximate criterion of policy' (Friedman 1968: 5). Let us analyse some of Friedman's own criteria for the role of monetary policy.

Friedman's considerations as to the hypothetical relationship existing between interest rates and money supply is another clear example of the way economists have essentially been thinking of money in literally physicalist terms. According to the influential American scholar, interest rates vary because of changes in the money supply, high and rising nominal interest rates being 'associated with rapid growth in the quantity of money' (Friedman 1968: 6–7), while low and falling interest rates are 'associated with slow growth in the quantity of money' (ibid.: 7). Friedman's chain of causality is well known. An increase in the growth of the money supply will initially stimulate consumption and investment, thus rising prices, the liquidity preference schedule and the demand for loans, which will induce a rise in market interest rates. In the case of a falling rate of growth of the money supply, the chain of events will simply go the opposite direction. Spending will fall, thus inducing a fall in prices, in the liquidity preference schedule, and in the demand for loans that will bring about a reduction in interest rates. This is the kind of relationship that is still today supposed to exist between interest rates and the rate of change in the quantity of money. In particular, it is still widely believed that the most efficient way to fight against inflation and deflation is through a monetary policy affecting interest rates.

The idea that inflation can be brought down by a reduction in spending obtained by rising interest rates and that deflation can be checked by an increase in spending brought about by falling interest rates is so prevalent among economists that it might be taken to represent a kind of axiom of monetary analysis. In reality, it could aspire to this status only if monetary economics were fundamentally grounded on microeconomic foundations. It is only in such case that interest rates could, through their impact on spending, modify the relationship between supply and demand so as to reduce inflation or stimulate economic growth. Yet, a rigorous analysis of the way money is issued by banks and associated to physical output through production shows that, despite appearances to the contrary, Friedman's microeconomic conception is highly problematic and misleading.

First of all, the very idea of money being a stock is in contrast with the a-dimensional nature of bank money, which is literally created by banks and is nothing more than an asset–liability of no intrinsic value. By defining money as a positive asset, Friedman rejects the teaching of the Classics. In particular, he shows to have entirely missed the deep meaning of Smith's and Ricardo's distinction between nominal money (money proper) and real money (money income). Second, the American economist fails to understand the nature of economic production and the role it plays in the determination of money's purchasing power. His conception of production is essentially of a physicalist kind and so is his take on money. The level of prices is therefore derived from the relationship between two 'masses' or 'quantities' – that of money and that of output – and its fluctuations are determined by the interplay of these two distinct and autonomous stocks.

Friedman's conception of inflation and deflation does not come as a surprise, nor does his monetary policy, whose main role is said to consist in avoiding too sharp a fluctuation of one stock with respect to the other. A more rigorous investigation of economic production shows, however, that money and output form a unity. It thus appears that inflation and deflation cannot result from a divergence between supply and demand induced by changes in economic agents' behaviour. In fact, production establishes the identity between supply (current output) and demand (current income), a logical relationship that is at work independently of behaviour. This clearly means that neither inflation nor deflation can be tackled by adopting a monetary policy aiming at modifying economic agents' behaviour. Friedman's claim for a control of the rate of growth of the money supply entirely misses the point, both because monetary authorities have no direct control over the 'quantity of money', and because interest rates are not influenced by the money supply but by the process of capital accumulation.

Wicksell's concept of 'natural interest rate' is totally misunderstood in Friedman's analysis and so are Marx, Böhm-Bawerk, and Keynes's investigations over the nature of capital. As a matter of fact, Wicksell's analysis is not entirely alien to Friedman, who claims that '[t]hanks to Wicksell, we are all acquainted with the concept of a "natural" rate of interest and the possibility of a discrepancy between the "natural" and the "market" rate' (ibid.: 7). Yet, in Friedman's analysis Wicksell's distinction is interpreted so as to fit with the American economist's own distinction between real and monetary variables. In short, Friedman identifies Wicksell's natural interest rate with the neoclassical concept of 'real' interest rate, so that the discrepancy between natural and market rates becomes a discrepancy between the rate of interest determined according to the principle of general equilibrium analysis – that is, by the sole interplay of 'real' factors – and the rate of interest determined by purely nominal or monetary factors. 'I use the term "natural" for the same reason Wicksell did – to try to separate the real forces from monetary forces' (ibid.: 9). Now, Wicksell's natural rate proves to be a far richer concept than Friedman's real rate provided it is interpreted outside a general equilibrium theoretical framework. Thus, in a context in which the neoclassical dichotomy is finally disposed of, Wicksell's natural rate appears to be the ratio between the amount of interest produced in a given economy and the amount of capital accumulated in the same economy. Were Friedman able to acknowledge that it is precisely because money 'is so pervasive' (ibid.: 12) that the neoclassical paradigm has to be rejected, he would have a broader understanding of Wicksell's contribution and be able to conceive of monetary policy in an entirely new way.

As shown by the quantum theoretical approach to monetary macroeconomics, Wicksell's natural interest rate tends to fall and line up with the market rate of interest because of the pathological process of capital accumulation characterizing today's advanced economies. Monetary authorities' intervention has to be considered in such a context. A direct intervention on the natural rate of interest is obviously not an option, since central banks cannot directly influence capital accumulation. Monetary authorities can therefore play a role only through an indirect intervention aiming at modifying the structure of national payments so as to keep it in line with the laws of monetary economics. This allows capital accumulation to occur in an orderly way, thus avoiding the pathological shrinking of the natural interest rate. As long as a reform is not implemented, monetary authorities can at most postpone the fatal moment when no positive margin will subsist between natural and market rates of interest. They can do this through the only means under their control: a variation in the market interest rate below the level of the natural rate of interest. It is clear, however, that such a manoeuvre can take place only in so far as the market rate of interest is higher than zero. The more it approaches to zero, the fewer the possibilities remaining to lower it further. Unless the system is reformed, its struggle for survival is doomed to failure since, the market interest rate being forced to remain positive, the gap between natural and market interest rates is bound to disappear, leaving no room for capitalization to go on expanding at the same rate as before. Once it reaches this limit, the system will enter a crisis that will inevitably increase involuntary unemployment and drastically reduce the standard of living of the population.

As a neoclassical economist at heart, if not mind, Friedman is caught between two antithetical conceptions of money. According to the first, money is essentially a commodity, whereas according to the second it is merely a 'veil'. In both cases, the priority rests with real goods, and the system is based on relative exchange. Even though he explicitly claims that money matters, Friedman has never rejected the neoclassical paradigm and its homogeneity postulate. Now, this postulate establishes the fundamental neutrality of money. It is therefore not entirely surprising to find out that Friedman's attempt to reconcile his belief in the neutrality of money with the logical implications of general equilibrium analysis fails.

What his analysis is essentially lacking in, is a correct conception of money, which is neither a positive asset (or a commodity) nor a 'veil'. Friedman's main mistake is to believe that it is enough to add money to a system of general equilibrium to work out a satisfactory model of the monetary economy. In reality, money cannot simply be added but must pervade the entire system, which is thus 'monetary' from the outset. Failing to see that money is so closely associated with output as to be its twin aspect, Friedman thinks of money as an external element whose 'quantity' has to be controlled by monetary authorities in order to avoid too great a discrepancy between nominal and real magnitudes. His vision of the economic world is still dichotomous, and his analysis of monetary policy remains strongly influenced by it. The relationship established by Friedman between the quantity of money and the level of interest rates is far too simplistic to give a correct idea of the way interest rates are correlated to production and capital accumulation, and to provide the foundations of a sound and effective monetary policy.

Answering to the question of what monetary policy can actually do, Friedman claims 'that monetary policy can prevent money itself from being a major source of economic disturbance' (ibid.: 12), and he then adds that the 'second thing monetary policy can do is provide a stable background for the economy' (ibid.: 13). There will hardly be an economist who will disagree with these broad aims of monetary policy. It is clear that our economic systems would work better if economic agents could take their decisions with full confidence in future monetary stability. Yet, this is not the same as saying that the working of our economic system is subject to economic agents' behaviour. In fact, in contrast with Friedman's point of view, it can be shown that monetary disturbances cannot be imputed to the behaviour of any economic agent. As we have repeatedly argued, these arise instead from the incompatibility of today's system of payments with the laws of monetary macroeconomics. In order to fulfil the twofold task of preventing money from being a major source of economic disturbance and to provide a stable background for the economy, monetary authorities have therefore to reform the present system of payments, a structural change that has nothing to do with Friedman's attempt to control the rate of growth of the money supply. If it is true, as claimed by Friedman, that 'the monetary authority should guide itself by magnitudes that it can control, not by ones it cannot control' (ibid.: 14), then how is it possible to maintain that 'the most appealing guides for policy are exchange rates, the price level as defined by some index, and the quantity of a monetary total' (ibid.: 15)? How can as canny an economist as Friedman really believe monetary authorities to be able to control any one of these three magnitudes? Exchange rates fluctuate mainly according to speculation and no central bank can pretend to have direct control over them. Prices are also essentially beyond the control of monetary authorities, which could influence their level only if the quantity of money *could* be modified through monetary policy. As for the monetary total itself, it is nowadays widely recognized that monetary authorities have no *direct* control over the commercial bank deposits' component of the quantity of money and their power to determine the monetary basis is further limited by the needs of commercial banks and their clients.

As observed by Wray, in the United States '[t]he attempt to target nonborrowed reserves effectively ended in 1982; the attempt to hit M1 growth targets was abandoned in 1986; and the attempt to target growth of broader money aggregates finally came to an official end in 1993' (Wray 1998: 101). Generally speaking, central bankers themselves no longer consider the control of the quantity of money as a feasible objective of their monetary policy, which substantiates the claim that '[t]he central bank never has controlled, nor could it ever control, the quantity of money' (ibid.: 98). Now, in his 1998 book on the understanding of modern money Wray shows that the idea that the central bank can *indirectly* control the money supply through its intervention on commercial bank reserves is also seriously undermined by empirical evidence, and that monetary authorities are forced to adapt their intervention to the need of the system instead of trying to force the system to adjust to the requirements of the central bank. The supposed impact of reserves requirement on the quantity of money is traditionally explained by referring to a credit or money multiplier. Change in the official reserves ratio is thus said to cause a change in the money supply via the credit banks can grant in compliance with the new reserve requirements. Once again, Wray provides empirical evidence to dismiss 'the myth of the money multiplier'.

> In the real world banks make loans independent of reserve position, then borrow reserves to meet requirements. Bank managers generally neither know nor care about the aggregate level of reserves in the banking system. Certainly, no loan officer ever checks the bank's reserve position before approving a loan. Bank lending decisions are affected by the price of reserves and expected returns, not by reserve positions.
>
> (ibid.: 107)

Wray's conclusion is confirmed by the quantum theoretical approach to money and credit. Being a numerical 'vehicle', a nominal flow, money proper is instantaneously created and destroyed in each payment carried out by a bank. Fundamentally distinct from credit money, vehicular money has no positive value whatsoever and can be freely issued by banks any time they are asked to act as monetary intermediaries. Since money as such flows immediately back to its point of emission, banks can never suffer from any loss because of their monetary intermediation, so that they can satisfy the needs of their clients without having to worry about the level of their reserves. In very simple words, vehicular money stands for the faculty of banks to use their own IOU as a means of payment, that is, as a 'carrier' to convey payments from the payer to the payee. What is all important here is to avoid confusing the *means* with the *object* of payments, nominal or vehicular money with credit money or income. While vehicular money can be supplied costless and without any need for financial backing, credit money can be purveyed only if a positive bank deposit exists that 'feeds' bank loans. Unlike money proper, money income is not a simple numerical form, but results from the association of this numerical form with produced output. Income is thus not created by banks, which can lend to their clients only the amount that has been deposited with them.

Since bank deposits have their origin in current production, national income represents the theoretical limit to credit. Practically, this limit can then be reduced to account for the risk involved in the financial intermediation banks carry out to the benefit of their clients. It is thus immediately clear that the concept of credit multiplier is ill-founded. In fact, banks have to comply with the rule that loans must be financed by deposits, which greatly limits the risk for any single bank to lend more than the income generated by production. It is true that this risk would entirely be avoided only if a distinction were made between a monetary and a financial department, yet the principles followed today by banks seem enough to prevent a cumulative inflationist expansion of credit. The result of production, income cannot be multiplied by being repeatedly lent by banks. To believe the contrary amounts to mixing up macro and microeconomic events such as production and financial transfers. Production gives rise to a macroeconomic income that can be spent only once for the final purchase of produced output. In this sense, a given income can finance only one equivalent macroeconomic credit. This same income can however be transferred a number of times before being finally spent. For example, the income earned by A can be first lent to C, spent by C for the purchase of a second-hand car sold by D, deposited by D and then lent a second time to E. The two loans and the four transfers of the income initially deposited by A do not multiply its amount, they are microeconomic transactions that leave national income unchanged. Finally, the idea of the credit multiplier is logically inconsistent with the nature of income even as the present system of national payments does not entirely exclude the possibility of an over-emission of credit. When this happens, the result is not a multiplication of income but an inflationary increase of nominal money with respect to real money. If it is admitted that monetary authorities must now intervene, it will have to be not through useless monetary policies, but by implementing a monetary reform that aligns the structure of our monetary system with the logical and practical distinction between money, income, and capital.

Friedman is correct in claiming that there is 'a positive and important task for the monetary authority – to suggest improvements in the machine [the monetary system] that will reduce the chances that it will get out of order, and to use its own powers so as to keep the machine in good working order' (Friedman 1968: 13). Yet, it is not through an intervention on the rate of money growth or on interest rates that this can be done. The price stability advocated by Friedman is neither a necessary nor a desirable requirement for economic growth. What is important instead, is to provide a monetary framework that cannot give rise to structural disturbances such as inflation and deflation. The point is not to grant just 'a limited amount of flexibility in prices and wages' (ibid.: 13) by controlling the money supply, but to purvey a sound monetary structure via which money is made to play its role in conformity with its own (banking) nature. Let us show how this can be achieved by means of an analytical distinction, to be structurally enacted by banks, now organized in distinct monetary, financial and fixed capital departments.

The reform of the system of national payments

The monetary and financial departments

The structural distinction between the first two departments is the logical consequence of the difference distinguishing money from income. As quantum macroeconomics shows, money as such is a flow, while money income is a stock; money is a valueless, numerical vehicle, income is a positive bank deposit; money is a simple numerical form with no proper object, income is the monetary definition of current output. Every payment implies both a monetary and a financial intermediation and should therefore be recorded in two distinct departments. The monetary department (I) is the one concerned with vehicular money, whereas income bank deposits are recorded in the financial department (II). Let us consider, for example, the payment of wages and represent how it would be recorded in the two departments (Table 14.1).

Table 14.1 The payment of wages as recorded by the monetary and financial departments

Monetary department (I)			
Liabilities		*Assets*	
1. Wage earners	*x*	Firm	*x*
2. Department II	*x*	Wage earners	*x*
Department II	*x*	Firm	*x*

Financial department (II)			
Liabilities		*Assets*	
2. Wage earners	*x*	Department I	*x*

Entry (1) shows that the payment of wages implies a circular flow of money. On behalf of firms, the first department credits wage earners with a sum of money that is immediately recovered by the bank. Entries (2) show that wage earners are finally credited with a sum of income entered in the second department. Being at the origin of current output, wage earners are the initial owners of a positive income deposited with the bank's financial department.

Whereas, in principle, money is an instantaneous flow and therefore does not survive beyond the instant in which a payment is carried out, practically, the destruction of money in the first department can be postponed to the end of the accounting day. Since banks close their accounts daily, this is the period of time that can practically be chosen as a reference. The decision to start paying interest on bank deposits the day after their formation is one among other possibilities more or less justifiable on empirical grounds. Once taken, this decision sets the limit to the period entries in the first department cancel out. At the end of the accounting day, whatever is still deposited in the first department is transferred to the second, which means that the whole amount of money created during the day is destroyed within this same period of time, the sum deposited in the financial department defining the amount of income still available for the purchase of current output. In our example, the necessary daily balancing of department I would lead to the entries recorded in Table 14.2.

Finally, once it is taken over by the second department, the payment of wages defines a positive credit of wage earners and an equivalent debit of firms entered, respectively, as a liability and as an asset in the accounting system of the financial department.

At this stage of the analysis a question may arise as to the need for a distinction that leads to the same result as is currently reached by entering the payment of wages directly into the financial department. The answer lies in the risk, incurred by a system based on a single department, of banks ending up lending more than the amount of income generated by

Table 14.2 The end of the day balancing of department I

Monetary department (I)			
Liabilities		*Assets*	
Department II	x	Firm	x
1. Firm	x	Department II	x

Financial department (II)			
Liabilities		*Assets*	
Wage earners	x	Department I	x
1. Department I	x	Firm	x
Wage earners	x	Firm	x

current production. In the absence of a clear and operational distinction between monetary and financial departments, bankers have no precise information as to the amount of credit they can grant during the day. Logically, they should lend only up to the amount of the income deposited with their banks. In practice, they simply respect the principle requiring loans to be backed by equivalent deposits without being aware of the fact that some of these deposits might be made up of money instead of income, that is, they might result from money creation instead of production. As done by Schmitt in his 1984 book, let us suppose bank *B* to pay a sum of 100 money wages on behalf of firm *F*. Furthermore, let us suppose bank's officers to grant a total credit of 110 units to customers who spend their loans for the purchase of goods and services sold by *F*. At the end of the day the situation would be as shown in Table 14.3.

Entry (2) respects the principle of the necessary equality between loans and deposits, but is clearly inflationary since the amount lent is ten units greater than the amount of income available within the system and defined by entry (1). *Today, bank managers have no means of knowing the amount of income they can actually lend.* They have to worry about the price of reserves and the expected returns on their loans and this could well reduce the risk of over-emission, it is true, yet it is also the case that under these conditions monetary stability would be achieved only by chance. If the risk of credit inflation is to be avoided, loan officers have to be provided with a rigorous and simple instrument telling them in real time the exact amount they can lend without financing their loans through money creation. This is precisely the great merit of Schmitt's distinction between monetary and financial departments and what makes its implementation a necessary step towards the achievement of monetary stability. Thanks to this distinction, bankers will in fact know at once to what extent they can satisfy the needs of their clients through an actual or a future loan. To this effect, loan officers will simply have to verify the existence of a positive balance between the two departments and limit their loans to its amount. In our example, the payment of wages creates a balance of 100 units between the monetary and the financial department, which defines the maximum amount of loans the bank can grant to its clients. 'At every instant the "loanable" savings are precisely defined by the *total amount of the claims of the first department over the second*' (Schmitt 1984a: 310, our translation). If by the end of the day nobody asks for a loan, entries in the

Table 14.3 Inflationary lending

		B		
Liabilities			*Assets*	
1. Wage earners	100		Firm	100
2. Firm	110		Clients	110

first department *are cancelled out* and firm *F* becomes the beneficiary of the loan derived from the transformation of its monetary debt to the first department into a financial debt to the second department.

The fixed capital department

The reason for the introduction of a third department lies in the conceptual and factual distinction existing between income and fixed capital. If only capital-time existed, there would be no need for a third department, since capital would only be the form taken by income between the moment it is formed and the moment it is spent for the final purchase of produced output. Saving would merely finance consumption and the financial intermediation of banks would be all is needed to shorten the period during which income is conserved as capital-time. In fact, economic reality is far more complex and fixed capital is an important part of it. As we have already seen, part of current savings is transformed into macroeconomic saving through its investment in the production of fixed capital goods. Extremely important at enhancing economic development, fixed capital accumulation can however become itself the source of economic instability if the investment of saving – channelled through profit – implies its expenditure on the labour market. *Defining a macroeconomic saving – that is, an income that will never be spent by anyone – fixed capital cannot be lent on the financial market.* This is a straightforward result of our positive analysis. Yet, invested on the labour market, profit gives rise to a new bank deposit and, therefore, to a new loan by the financial department of banks. *Practice being inconsistent with the conceptual principles of positive analysis, a pathology arises, which brings about the monetary disorders of inflation and deflation.* Now, positive analysis does not only tell us what the principles of monetary economics are, but points the way leading to the structural reform that will allow practice to conform to logic, that is, leading to normative analysis. Thus conceived, normative analysis is a direct consequence of positive analysis: it tells us how the system should work in order to avoid monetary instability. In the case at stake, it tells us how fixed capital accumulation can take place without causing inflation and deflation.

What has to be avoided is the possibility for invested profits to remain available on the financial market. This means that, initially entered on the second department of banks, profits have to be transferred to what Schmitt calls their fixed capital department. In principle, it might be thought that only those profits that have been invested in the production of capital goods should be entered in the third department. Yet, *it must not be forgotten that saved-up income is immediately transformed into capital-time, independently of whether or not it will later give rise to a positive fixed capital.* Hence, while only invested profits will remain deposited in the third department, the entire amount of saved-up profits (those that will be invested as well as those that will be redistributed as interests and dividends) is initially transferred to the fixed capital department. Practically, at the end of the accounting day whatever amount of income is still deposited in department II is transferred to department III, according to the principle that saved-up income is conserved as capital. If we suppose wage earners to spend the totality of their current income and firms to realize a profit of *y* units, at the end of the day entries between the second and third departments will be as shown in Table 14.4.

Profits formed in day 1 and recorded as in entry (1) are transferred from the second to the third department, entries (2), where they are recorded as a sum of capital. If part of the profits saved in the form of capital is later to be distributed by firms to income holders, an opposite transfer between the two departments will take place. Part of the capital deposited in department III will recover its initial form of income and will finally be spent on the commodity market. What remains deposited in the third department represents the profits invested by firms in the production of instrumental goods and defines the amount of fixed capital formed in the economy. Thus, instead of being spent on the labour market, profits are deposited in the fixed capital department, while the payment of wages is recorded in the monetary and financial departments of banks. If we join departments I and II together, the investment of profits will be represented as in entry (1) (Table 14.5).

Table 14.4 The transfer of profits to the third department

Financial department (II)			
Liabilities		*Assets*	
1. Firms	*y*	Output	*y*
2. Department III	*y*	Firms	*y*

Fixed capital department (III)			
Liabilities		*Assets*	
2. Firms	*y*	Department II	*y*

Table 14.5 The investment of profit in the reformed system of national payments

Financial department (II)			
Liabilities		*Assets*	
Department III	*y*	Output	*y*
1. Fixed capital goods	*y*	Firms	*y*

Fixed capital department (III)			
Liabilities		*Assets*	
1. Firms	*y*	Department II	*y*

The rationale for the introduction of the third department lies in the need to avoid profits being spent on the labour market, since this would inevitably lead to the fixed capital being appropriated by what we have called, following Schmitt, 'depersonalized' firms. In other words, the structural reform advocated here will prevent the dual expenditure of the income transformed into fixed capital through the investment of profit. In fact, if profits are spent within the payment of wages, their investment gives rise to a new bank deposit. Despite having already being spent by firms for the purchase of fixed capital goods on the labour market, invested profits are thus still available on the financial market, where they 'finance' a second expenditure. At the origin of the process that, through fixed capital formation and amortization, leads to inflation and unemployment, we find therefore the fact that, in the present structure of national payments, profits are invested through their expenditure on the labour market. The role of the third department is precisely to prevent this from happening. Transferred to the fixed capital department, profits will no longer 'feed' the payment of wages, which – in conformity with the fact that it is the payment of wages that generates a positive income – will be simply 'conveyed' by a purely numerical money. The very formation of pathological capital being once and for all avoided by the transfer of profits to the third department, inflation and involuntary unemployment will be prevented from the outset, and economies will finally benefit from a monetary stability that has so far been beyond their reach.

15 Positive and normative analysis
The international level

Once again it is positive analysis that sets the principles normative analysis has to comply with in order for the system of international payments to allow for monetary stability. According to the theory they privilege, economists have advocated a whole series of measures that in their view should have reduced, if not altogether eradicated, the erratic fluctuations in exchange rates that so often characterize today's foreign exchange market. Let us consider some of these measures as well as a new proposal for world monetary reform derived from the principles of monetary macroeconomics introduced in this book.

From free exchange rate fluctuation to monetary unification

Soft pegged exchange rates

Countries choosing to peg their currency to a 'strong' foreign currency or to a basket of currencies commit themselves to limit (or even reduce to zero as in the case of currency boards) the extent of fluctuation of exchange rates. Several possibilities are open to them, from managed floats to currency boards, passing through adjustable and crawling pegs, adjustable and crawling bands, and fixed pegs. In the case of soft pegged exchange rates, it has been claimed that they are not particularly well equipped to suit those countries highly involved with international capital markets. '[S]oft peg systems have not proved viable over any lengthy period, especially for countries integrated or integrating into the international capital markets' (Fischer 2001: 9–10). It is not difficult to see, in fact, that pegged exchange rates of countries involved in capital markets are easily subjected to speculative pressures, which may be contrasted only through monetary policies that put a strain on their domestic economy as well as on their financial system. 'Countries that are not adequately prepared to withstand the potential strains of exchange rate defense should beware of slipping into exchange rate pegs that may later foster serious economic and financial crises' (Mussa et al. 2000: 34).

In a regime of pegged exchange rates, monetary authorities must be prepared to intervene both on the foreign exchange market and on the financial market to defend the external stability of their currency. This particular regime seems therefore to require a low involvement in the international capital market of the country implementing it, a flexibility of its fiscal policy and of its labour market, a close connection of its economy and of its financial system with those of the country with which it is pegged, and a high level of international reserves. IMF experts and economists are certainly right in observing that pegged exchange rates are not suited to emerging economies with strong links to global financial markets. Recent crises – the Mexican, Asian, Russian, and Brazilian crises – have shown that these economies are more sensitive than others to speculative pressures on their exchange rates, and that those which had pegged their currency suffered the most from the fluctuations on the capital markets. As noted by Fischer, '[i]n several countries, extensive damage has been caused by the collapses of pegged rate regimes that lasted for some time, and enjoyed some credibility. The belief that the exchange rate will not change removes the need to hedge, and reduces perceptions of the risk of borrowing in foreign currencies. This makes any crisis that does strike exceptionally damaging in its effects on banking systems, corporations, and government finances' (Fischer 2001: 10).

At this point a critical reader might ask whether there is any good reason to keep considering a system of soft-peg exchange rates as a viable regime at all. Most experts would answer that countries respecting the conditions listed above are likely to benefit from such a regime in so far as it would grant their currencies greater stability on the foreign exchange market. Others would go for a free floating system, arguing that in the present system of international payments free exchange rate fluctuations are the best balancing mechanism available to countries. All would probably agree that solutions vary according to the country and the period of time considered. Now, while most of these observations are a matter of common sense, some of them rest on the assumption that exchange rates are bound to fluctuate more or less erratically unless a country commits itself to supporting the costs of a monetary policy capable of reducing the destabilizing pressures on the foreign exchange market. 'If currencies are floating, they can fluctuate widely. If the authorities attempt to peg them, the costs of doing so, measured by reserve losses or interest-rate increases, can be extremely high. Even a government otherwise prepared to maintain a pegged exchange rate may be unwilling or unable to do so when attacked by the markets and forced to raise interest rates to astronomical heights' (Eichengreen *et al.* 1995: 162).

A rigorous analysis of the way the present system of international payments works shows that this is indeed the case today. In this respect, it is worth noting that experts such as Fischer, Mussa, Masson, Swoboda, Obstfeld, Eichengreen, Isard and many others tend to recognize that exchange rate fluctuations are mostly erratic and due to speculative capital movements rather than to fundamentals. In a system where currencies are considered as if they were real goods, exchange rates are defined as their relative prices and their variation is directly influenced by supply and demand on the foreign exchange market. Attempts to reduce or control exchange rate fluctuations through a soft peg are therefore bound to failure in the medium or long term, since their cost can hardly be supported for long by any country, let alone by a developing country. While it is indisputable that exchange rate stability is to be preferred to erratic fluctuations, it seems hopeless to pursue this aim through a regime requiring national monetary authorities to contrast erratic fluctuations provoked by international speculative capital movements.

Currency boards

As shown by Fischer (2001), in the last ten years an increasing number of countries has opted for a system of hard peg known as 'currency board', in which the government is institutionally committed to converting its national money into a foreign currency (usually the US dollar) at a fixed exchange rate. Argentina is the emblematic example of this kind of exchange rate regime. The high level of inflation suffered by the peso led Argentina's monetary authorities to enter a currency board in 1991.

The risks of using the exchange rate as a nominal anchor are usually identified by the fact that 'interest rates become completely independent of the will of the domestic monetary authorities [because they] are closely linked to those of the anchor currency' (Mussa *et al.* 2000: 26). In a currency board regime, in fact, monetary policy is subordinated to the maintaining of fixed exchange rates and convertibility so that fluctuations in domestic interest rates 'are determined by foreign exchange inflows and outflows' (ibid.: 25). On the other hand, benefits would derive from exchange rate stability, an increased control over fiscal policy and the credibility of the economic policy regime.

While entering a currency board a country does not give up its monetary sovereignty, it is clear that its commitment to guarantee convertibility seriously reduces its autonomy. This may prove useful in so far as it forces the country's monetary authorities to avoid inflationary over-emissions, but it might dangerously limit the process of capital accumulation within the country. The rigidity of the system is due to the fact that a currency board 'must hold foreign reserves at least equal to its total monetary liabilities' (ibid.: 26), and that, in its pure form, it 'severely limits the ability of the authorities to extend domestic credit' (Chang and Velasco 2000: 72). Hence, if it seems indisputable that modern currency boards have been successful in enhancing credibility of countries coming out of a period of high- or hyper-inflation, there is also evidence that '[e]ach of the major international capital market-related crises since 1994 [...] has in some way involved a fixed or pegged exchange rate regime' (Fischer 2001: 3).

The arguments against currency board arrangements range from the claim that nominal exchange rate invariability slows down adjustment to external or internal shocks, to the claim that countries entering a currency board must give up their seigniorage as well as the lender of last resort function of their central banks. Now, while the loss of seigniorage is a fallacy deriving from a poor understanding of modern banking, and the lender of last resort function of central banks can be 'compensated for by the creation [...] of a banking sector stabilization fund' (ibid.: 17) and by other measures of supervision, control and collaboration, the strain put on the domestic economy of a country entering a currency board is a serious shortcoming calling for renewed efforts to find a viable alternative solution.

Even though currency board and flexible exchange rate regimes are likely to suffer from the same disadvantages owing to a substantial increase in the US dollar exchange rate, the case against the hard-peg system is strengthened by the fact that a country implementing a currency board has no degree of freedom as to its own monetary emission. The commitment to redeeming its monetary liabilities at a fixed exchange rate forces a currency board country to hold foreign reserves at least equal to its total domestic currency. In the case of Argentina, this implied that banks' monetary emission of pesos was limited by the amount of US dollars recorded within the Argentinian banking system. Needless to say, this dangerously limited the capacity of the banking system to respond to the demand for monetary intermediation coming from Argentina's productive sector. In other words, Argentina's productive capacity could not expand beyond the limits posed by the availability of US dollars. Hence, if Argentina wanted to increase its domestic output, it had to increase its reserves of US dollars, which it might have done either by exporting more or by contracting a new external debt. In both cases, the growth in domestic production would have cost Argentina twice its price. To the cost of production proper, Argentina would in fact have had to add the cost of the goods, services, and financial claims it has had to sell in exchange for the US dollars required as guarantee to the monetary emission of its banks.

In order to gain credibility for its monetary policy, Argentina chose to peg its currency so hard as to lose, de facto, a great part of its monetary sovereignty. The price it had to pay was not balanced by the advantages it derived from exchange rate stability. In fact, Argentina's economic system needed to be backed by an autonomous banking system capable of monetizing, without any arbitrary restriction, the whole of its productive activity. This cannot happen within a currency board regime, whose advantages are henceforth compromised by the restraints imposed to the economic activity of the countries that choose it.

Dollarization

Some authors have recently argued in favour of dollarization, a process that has spread mainly in Central America, where Ecuador and El Salvador have just joined Panama among the group of countries that have replaced their domestic currency with the US dollar. The advantages of dollarization as compared to currency board regimes are said to lie 'in the reduction in spreads and the strengthening of the financial system' (Fischer 2001: 17). The obvious difference between the two systems is that through dollarization a country does away with its national currency. Exchange rate problems with the US currency are also definitively dealt with, of course. In its 'strong' sense dollarization or full dollarization expresses 'the idea that some countries should completely give up issuing their own money and adopt a foreign currency' (Calvo 1996: 168). In fact, exchange rate problems are literally suppressed together with the suppression of domestic money. Identified with the US dollar, the currency of these countries floats jointly with the floating of the US currency. Now, the shortcomings related to currency board regimes become even more evident in the case of dollarization. In particular, countries that choose this radical solution against their monetary instability must confine the credit activity of their banking systems to the amount of US dollars deposited with them. In contrast with what happens in the United States, these countries' banks are not allowed to issue new dollars, either to monetize their domestic production or to pay for their country's net commercial imports. What they can do is merely to lend the dollars they own as deposits. Of course, a central bank may increase its reserve of US dollars by incurring a new foreign debt. But this means that the countries that have dollarized their monetary systems must run into debt in order to be able to monetize their own production. Hence, either they cut production or they pay twice its new costs – once by getting indebted and once by covering the cost of their productive services. In both cases the price of dollarization is so high that it is hard to understand how it can be imposed on a population.

Things would be different if banks of 'dollarized' countries were allowed to issue their own dollars. However, in this case only two scenarios may be envisaged. Either the US government could agree to accept these countries as new States of the Union, or it would force their banks to change the denomination of their currencies. The first scenario is not likely to draw much favour, and would also have drastic consequences politically and culturally. The second solution would restore the situation existing before dollarization, since it would bring out the substantial difference existing between the US dollar in the United States and the dollar as used within other countries.

Economists seem to be aware of the consequences of dollarization, even though they do not always have a clear grasp of all of them. For example, Fischer claims that '[f]or a small economy, heavily dependent in its trade and capital account transactions on a particular large economy, it *may* well make sense to adopt the currency of that country, particularly if provision can be made for the transfer of seigniorage' (Fischer 2001: 17). Now, if it is true that such an economy should be allowed to issue the currency it needs in order to monetize its production (and it is in this sense that Fischer's use of the concept of seigniorage is interpreted), we should not forget to analyse the implications for the US monetary system. If the Federal Reserve were not prepared to control the banking system of the 'dollarized' country and to include it in its clearing system, the dollars issued in that country would become a source of instability. In particular, if the central bank were to abuse its lender of last resort function (which still happens to a worrying extent in numerous *LDCs*), the inflationary increase of dollars can have negative consequences in all the dollar areas. Besides, the 'dollarized' country would be able to pay in newly issued dollars for its net purchases of goods and services. Thus, the amount of dollars held abroad would increase and define the net debt of the 'dollarized' area as a whole, independently of the geographical location of the banks carrying out the payments.

In conclusion, this extreme solution does not seem to be appropriate, either for the *LDCs* inclined to adopt it, or for the United States. The loss of monetary sovereignty has a host of negative side-effects when it is unilateral. What happens when monetary sovereignty is given up simultaneously by a group of countries deciding to create a monetary union instead?

Currency unions

Another solution to exchange rate instability implying the loss of monetary sovereignty is the creation of a currency union among independent countries. Although it is not the first case of monetary unification, the creation of a European monetary area is the most significant example of such a solution. Unlike what happens for the CFA zone, the European project has led to the actual replacement of national currencies with an entirely new currency – the euro – and to the birth of a new monetary area – Euroland. Of course, the introduction of the euro has removed any risk of exchange rate fluctuations among the 12 currencies replaced by the single European currency. Abandoning monetary sovereignty, on the other hand, will require an increased macroeconomic co-ordination ranging from common monetary and fiscal policies to a greater integration of labour and commodity markets. Co-operation and regional solidarity will also prove essential in the process, and it is to be feared that this might prove to be more difficult to obtain than generally recognized. Worries come from the observation that the criteria for the successful implementation of a single currency area were not entirely satisfied by EU countries. It is no mystery that a whole variety of 'public accounting fiddles' (Dafflon and Rossi 1999: 63) have occurred during 1997, the year chosen to assess if countries complied with the convergence criteria imposed by the Maastricht Treaty. Things have not drastically improved since, and there are signs that disparities are far from going away. In this context, one feels entitled to ask whether monetary unification is indeed going to benefit EU countries; in other words, whether the advantages will outweigh disadvantages.

In order to answer this question we have to consider the full implications of free capital mobility that the euro makes possible within the new European monetary area. As noted by Obstfeld, 'this [capital mobility] is a very relevant issue. Here, I think the question of whether capital mobility enhances the gains from a single currency or not depends very much *on the type of capital flow* that is being considered' (Mundell *et al.* 2000: 4, our emphasis). Let us dwell briefly on this matter.

The concept of capital flight has often been taken to mean – literally – that capitals may leave the country in which they originate, to be 'hidden' or invested abroad. Now, while it is true that capitals may be illegally concealed from fiscal authorities by being transferred to a foreign banking system, it is mistaken to believe that by doing so they also escape their original banking system. If a resident of country *A* manages to hide his capital by transferring it to a foreign bank (of country *B*), he causes his national fiscal authorities a net loss; it is a fact. However, this does not entail an equivalent loss for his domestic banking system. Double-entry book-keeping prevents such loss. In reality, the entire amount 'transferred' abroad remains deposited with *A*'s banking system, the fraudulent resident exchanging it for an equivalent deposit with *B*'s banking system. This means that national monetary boundaries are natural barriers against capital movements, free capital flows being possible only within a single monetary area.

Logically, even investment between countries does not modify the amount of capital initially available in each of them. Of course, the logical impossibility for capital to ever leave a country's banking system does not mean that capitals cannot be *invested* from one country to another; in this sense, capital mobility would not be hampered. By transferring their capitals to country *B*, *A*'s residents actually convert them into an equivalent capital formed in *B*. Their investment does not reduce the amount of capital available in *A*, the whole amount of which is thus liable to be invested – either directly or indirectly – in this same country. If capital is lent to firms in *A*, the investment is direct; if it is lent to country *B* it becomes part of *B*'s foreign transactions and finances its imports from country *A*, thus defining an indirect investment in *A*. In both cases, it is correct to claim that, whatever the decision taken by *A*'s residents, their external financial transactions do not decrease the amount of capital that may be invested in *A*. It is double-entry book-keeping that brings about this result, which will hold good as long as countries do not give up their monetary sovereignty.

By adhering to monetary union, EU countries have de facto created an area within which capitals move as freely as they do within each national monetary system. It is precisely this free capital movement in the euro area that is likely to bring about the most serious troubles for the European Union. It is a well-known fact that capitals move from the regions of lesser to those of higher productivity, which, in the last decades, means from South to North. This would mean that, in the euro area, capital will 'flee' from the Southern to the Northern part of Europe, thus increasing disparities among countries of the two 'regions'. In particular, it is not exaggerated to forecast that unemployment will grow dramatically in the regions suffering from capital outflow and that public transfers will prove insufficient to match its negative effects.

It is true, of course, that the financial structure of the capital accumulated so far in each country will play an important role in determining the way capital will move within the European Union. For example, if the capital accumulated by firms of a given Southern country in, say, the last ten years has been obtained by selling medium- to long-term bonds, monetary unification will put them at a disadvantage with respect to their Northern competitors. *The cost of capital accumulated in the Southern countries is in fact higher than that accumulated in the Northern countries. Disparities in the gross rate of profit and reduced costs of production have allowed Southern firms to remain competitive prior and up until the adoption of the euro.* Monetary unification, however, will raise their current costs – direct and indirect wages, fiscal harmonization, environmental safeguard, and so on – without reducing the cost of the capital accumulated prior to the introduction of the euro. Under these conditions it is very likely that even firms of the most productive regions of the South will be forced to accelerate their restructuring process drastically. Mergers with Northern firms will probably increase and employment will be the first to suffer from the measures adopted in order to avoid shut down.

This might be thought to be the very pessimistic scenario of a eurosceptic. It is not. If the European unification project is to have a real chance of success, difficulties must be faced and discussed openly and not kept hidden from the public. If this is not done, Europeans could well refuse to pay the price of unification and force their countries to return to their prior state of monetary and political sovereignty. The question has to be dealt with: can European countries afford a drastic increase in capital movements? In other words, will there be an efficient network of adjustments capable to counter its negative effects? The limited mobility of workers, the lack of fiscal redistribution mechanisms of some efficacy, and the structural rigidity of numerous economies seem to speak against it. If this is indeed the case, would it not be better to think again about giving up monetary sovereignty? An answer will be closely related to the aim of achieving monetary stability without adopting a common and unique currency. Is exchange rate stability an outcome that necessarily implies monetary unification? Apparently, yes. As we have seen, neither 'soft' nor 'hard' pegs are viable solutions, and free floating is, by definition, a system where exchange rates are intrinsically unstable. Yet, despite the problems apparent, a new structure of accounting payments can be devised, which ensures the automatic stability of exchange rates between the countries adopting it, and which is perfectly euro-compatible. Let us expound the main principles on which such a system would rest.

The reform of the system of international payments

Towards a new regime of stable exchange rates compatible with safeguarding monetary sovereignty

Let us be upfront. *Today's exchange rate regimes belong to the category of relative exchanges, for currencies are considered as if they were real goods, and exchange rates are defined as their relative prices, that is, as the price of each of them expressed in terms of one or the other with which it is exchanged on a foreign exchange market.* By close analogy with what is supposed to happen on the commodity market – at least according to the neoclassical point of view – exchange rates are thus made to depend on supply and demand, and their determination becomes an issue of equilibrium. To avoid the instability inherent in every conception of equilibrium it is necessary to move from a regime in which exchange rates are identified with relative prices to a new regime in which currencies are no longer objects of trade *per se*, and the exchange rate does not define the price of one currency in terms of another. Does such an aspiration sound unrealistic to the modern reader? We think not. Rather, the oddity is in the fact that in the twenty-first century there are still economists who believe that money is stuff of the physical world. Modern banking, e-money, and speculative financial transactions ought to have disabused them of atavistically identifying money with its tokens. How is it possible to claim that a simple, numerical means of exchange can be itself treated as an ordinary object of exchange? If it is true, as shown by Rueff and definitively confirmed by double-entry book-keeping, that national currencies may enter a foreign banking system only as mere *duplicates* (see Chapter 10), how can it be maintained that, once abroad, national currencies are transformed into a stock of autonomous material-like assets? However, once recognized and affirmed that money is an undimensional means of payment and not an object of exchange, it should be clear that our payment systems must be structured in a manner that complies with the vehicular nature of money. This can be done if today's regime of relative exchange rates *is replaced by a system of absolute exchange rates in which each currency is exchanged against itself* (albeit through another currency or through a common standard such as the euro).

During a panel discussion at a conference held at Princeton, in April 1993, McKinnon pleaded for the adoption of *a common monetary standard* instead of a common currency. 'A common monetary standard that keeps national central banks and national currencies in place is preferable to a common currency' (McKinnon 1995: 97). What McKinnon calls a common monetary standard is a set of convergence requirements that, if fulfilled, would allow a group of countries to fix par values and narrow exchange rate bands for their currencies. Although McKinnon's pledge is perfectly in line with the analysis advocated here, his solution cannot be accepted, since it would not be up to the task of guaranteeing monetary stability. His 1988 proposal to anchor the yen, dollar, and D-mark exchange rates to a common price level allowing for purchasing power parity requires monetary authorities to adjust their policies according to this precise target, independently of the cost that these policies may have for their economies. But what is by far more worrying is that in McKinnon's plan nothing is said about the role played by the system of international payments. In this respect, his analysis does not substantially differ from that of mainstream experts of international economics. Their common belief is that exchange rates vary according to supply and demand, and that their stability can be reached only through a continuous adjustment between these two forces. Is there any need to stress how far all this is from Keynes's proposal for the institution of an international clearing union? As suggested by Keynes's plan, what is needed is a common monetary standard inserted within a structure of international payments allowing for the implementation of a system of absolute exchange rates, and not a complicated set of costly monetary policies that might well hamper economic growth without achieving exchange rate stability.

Let us take the European example. Our idea is that exchange rate stability can be achieved without EU member countries giving up their monetary sovereignty. Still, the euro will play an essential role in the new system, as will the European Central Bank (ECB). In order to avoid duplication as well as exchange rate fluctuations, transactions among EU countries and between them and the rest of the world will have to be carried out in euros. It is the ECB that will be called upon to issue the euro according to the same principles of double-entry book-keeping adopted at the national level. As already observed by Keynes in his plan of reform presented at Bretton Woods in 1944, the necessary balance between liabilities and assets will be enough to prevent any liquidity problem. This means that double-entry book-keeping is all the ECB needs in order to provide the EU countries with the amount of vehicular euros required to monetize their external transactions. However, if we were to stop here, the system would not be viable, for it would leave us with the problem of how countries are to finance their unsettled transactions. It is again the ECB that must intervene by acting as a financial intermediary. What is required in order to give a real content to the payments in euros is a system of inter-European clearing. The principle is well known. Adopting a real-time gross settlement system, the ECB will carry out payments between member countries only if each of them provides for its financial backing. In simple terms, this means that a country must finance its net commercial imports by an equivalent amount of exports of goods, services, or securities.

It is not difficult to show that if external payments are carried out through the monetary and financial *intermediation* of the ECB, each national currency is instantaneously exchanged against itself through the euro. Put in more familiar terms, each currency is simultaneously offered against and demanded by the euro, which obviously leaves its exchange rate unaltered. Together with the central banks of the member countries, the ECB will thus be the hub of the new system. Thanks to the new structure of external payments, European countries will be allowed to benefit from their monetary sovereignty until it proves necessary. In the meantime, the ECB will create a common monetary area that, besides guaranteeing exchange rate stability, will provide a strong link among member countries, and make of the euro the European currency *vis-à-vis* the rest of the world. Far from being a 'second best' solution, the new system will allow a better new start to the process of European unification without hampering it with the negative consequences of the sudden loss of monetary sovereignty.

As already noted, the reform is based both on the vehicular use of the euro and on a system of inter-European clearing managed by the ECB. As such, it will allow co-operation among member countries to be strengthened, particularly at the level of monetary and economic policies, yet at the pace and to the extent better suited to a harmonious process of economic and political convergence. Although the main purpose of the ECB will be that of providing EU member countries with an orderly payment system, nothing will prevent it from playing a more active role, both in order to promote new forms of co-operation among national central banks and to widen its field of intervention. For example, we may well imagine a scenario in which the ECB could intervene on the European financial markets to sell its own securities. Through its active financial *intermediation*, less developed countries of the euro area – which might easily be extended to incorporate other European countries now on the EU waiting list – could thus find new resources, besides those invested directly by their fellow countries, to accelerate their economic recovery. Well managed, this instrument could prove extremely helpful in reducing today's discrepancies between rich and poor countries, thus reinforcing solidarity among EU countries.

As just mentioned, another advantage of the new regime of absolute exchange rates would be to greatly facilitate the extension of the euro area to other European countries. Since countries will no longer be asked to give up their monetary sovereignties and thus be transformed into regions of one sole new country, requirements for adhering to the new European system of payments will be easily met by would-be member countries. In fact, conditions for membership would be limited to one's pledge to comply with the rules of the system. Each new country applying for membership should simply be prepared to have its central bank collaborate with the ECB and adopt the euro and the European clearing system for the settlement of its external transactions. Hence, while the new system of external payments will allow each new member country to benefit from a regime of exchange rate stability, the collaboration with the ECB will favour the implementation of all the reforms needed to guarantee the orderly working of their domestic monetary system. This is not to say that the ECB will exert any direct control whatsoever over any member country's monetary system. Let us repeat it with no room for ambiguity: each member country will retain its monetary sovereignty and will be free to choose the fiscal and monetary policies best suited to its needs. Yet, monetary sovereignty is not enough to guarantee monetary order. Collaboration with the ECB should precisely help less advanced countries to organize their banking system in such a way as to avoid anomalies.

Let us also observe that the maintenance of monetary sovereignty and the use of the euro as a means of international payment (both between European countries and between them and the rest of the world) will not stop European residents from using euro-banknotes for their payments. Domestic transactions will be settled in domestic currencies, but it is neither unreal nor wrong to imagine that some of them may be settled by using euro-banknotes. Tourism is the most obvious example. Polish residents might well spend their holidays in Italy and pay for them in euro-banknotes obtained in exchange for zloties. The ECB will also be involved in the operation, for it is through its *intermediation* that Polish banks can provide their clients with euro-banknotes, and that these same banknotes will give Italy a credit in its clearing account. The euro-banknotes earned by Italian residents, in fact, will be transferred to the ECB (through the intermediary of the Bank of Italy), where they will be credited on the Italian clearing deposit. Not surprisingly, services sold to Polish tourists are part of Italy's exports, increasing its capacity to import goods, services, and securities from Poland (or from other EU countries). If, for political reasons, related to the symbolism inherent in euro-banknotes, the use of European notes were encouraged, the new system would naturally adjust, to everybody's satisfaction.

In conclusion, the shift from a regime of relative to one of absolute exchange rates would mark a radical change for the European monetary system. Without depriving EU countries of their monetary sovereignty, the new structure of payments will gather the different countries together in a common area where transactions will all be settled by the use of a common currency: the euro. While protecting themselves from exchange rate instability EU countries will, in the meantime, create the sound premises for fostering economic integration. Once again, this would be achieved through the monetary and financial *intermediation* of the ECB, and would invest the ECB with the tasks of creating the euro as a European vehicular money, managing the system of inter-European (gross) settlements, and providing extra investments to less developed countries.

In Appendix IV of the *IMF Occasional Paper* No. 193, devoted to exchange rate regimes in an increasingly integrated world, we read: 'it must be recognized that while so far economic science has developed a number of criteria that seem relevant for the choice of exchange rate regime, there is no agreement on how precisely to quantify the various criteria or, to the extent that they conflict, on how to decide which should take priority' (Mussa *et al.* 2000: 48). This is indeed the present state of the art as far as exchange rate regimes are concerned. We maintain that the main cause for most economists' discomfort and disagreement is the lack of distinction between relative and absolute exchange rates. In particular, a clear step forward towards monetary stability will be achieved when payments are carried out without entailing any duplication, that is, by respecting the vehicular nature of money. The European attempt to create a common monetary area is of a great interest, for it goes a long way in the right direction. If it fails, it would be a disaster that will weigh heavily on all the people who believed in European integration and in monetary stability. This is why it is necessary to face and thoroughly analyse all the problems related to monetary unification. The loss of monetary sovereignty caused by the adoption of the euro as a unique currency has had a negative impact on capital movements, which has arguably been underestimated. Given the past and present economic situation of EU member countries, monetary unification is a great threat to employment in the South and a cause of increasing social turmoil in the North. These should be good enough reasons to push ECB's experts to look afresh at the role of the euro. As recent analysis shows, in fact, the very objective of monetary unification – exchange rate stability – may be reached while allowing countries to maintain their national sovereignty.

In these few pages we have summarized the principles on which the new European payments system should rest. Our aim is mainly to raise the reader's interest in a reform that could rapidly and easily be enforced at the EU level. The necessary institutions are already in place, and the ECB could well take the lead in devising for Europe a sound and stable payment system between its sovereign countries. Let us hope that the European experts will not immolate scientific analysis on the altar of politics, and that they will join after Schmitt's example in a concerted effort to give Europe and the world a real chance to achieve monetary stability.

If the 'impossible' lives in Utopia, it is certainly not utopian to suppose that, once achieved, scientific progress may take hold of people's mind, especially if the well-being of whole populations depends on it. In our field, advancement of learning is [twofold].

Bank money is a *means* of payment and not a net *asset* (bank money is an object of *mediation* and not a *final* product); European monetary union requires the creation of a common currency *qua* European *countries* and not a single currency for their residents.

(Schmitt 1988: 173, our translation)

The present structure of the ECB and of the electronic Trans-European Automated Real-time Gross-settlement Express Transfer system (TARGET) will make it extremely easy to implement a regime of absolute exchange rates at the European level. What about the world level then? How may exchange rate stability be achieved world-wide?

What future for the world monetary system?

At the Economic Forum held at the IMF, November 8, 2000, the main item on the agenda concerned the possibility of transforming the world into a unique currency area. All the participants agreed on the unrealistic character of such a proposal if by world currency union it is meant the introduction of one single world currency. Can things change radically if – as Mundell does – we define a currency area as a zone of fixed exchange rates? Is it not reasonable to suggest that all the countries of the world should enter a single currency area by fixing the exchange rates of their national currencies to a unique standard (a currency or a basket of currencies)? Certainly not if the model proposed were that of a currency board or of dollarization. As we have shown, each of these solutions will seriously hamper economic development and soon becomes untenable. A much better model would be that of the euro area, where 12 national currencies form part of a system in which each of them could be exchanged against any other albeit at a fixed exchange rate. Yet, such a fixed exchange rate system can be viable only in the short term. If it is not rapidly replaced by monetary unification – which was precisely what these EU countries were committed to do – destabilizing pressures will unavoidably grow and force countries to abandon the system in order to recover monetary sovereignty. If it is true, as Mundell observes, that fixed and irrevocable exchange rates are bound to completely abolish speculative capital movements (Mundell *et al.* 2000), it is equally certain that if the present structure of international payments is not modified, settlement of international transactions will go on increasing the amount of speculative capital available internationally (see Chapter 9). Irrevocably fixing exchange rates will thus not be enough to introduce monetary order world-wide. Besides, disparities among countries are so great, that it is foolish to believe that the conditions for the creation of a world currency area will be met in the foreseeable future.

Today, experts seem unanimous in forecasting the formation of two or three big currency areas toward which all the existing national currencies might gradually converge. '[T]he advent of the euro and the move of a number of countries toward euro- or dollar-based pegs (possibly as a precursor to full monetary union or dollarization) indicates a trend movement toward a bi- or tri-polar system of major currency areas' (Mussa *et al.* 2000: 36). Hence, while it is difficult to foresee the creation of other currency areas in the near future, the primacy of the dollar, the euro and the yen seems sufficiently well established to make a tripolar system the most likely substitute for the present dollar-standard system. Now, the majority of experts seem to endorse the idea that a regime of floating exchange rates will be best suited to deal with fluctuations among the three major currencies than any pegged exchange rate regime. Given the great volatility shown by these three currencies, the costs of managing a system of pegged exchange rates would be too high and its results too hazardous for it to be a viable alternative to free floating. It is generally believed, therefore, that exchange rates between the dollar, the euro, and the yen will continue to exhibit a high degree of volatility and that in order to limit their fluctuations monetary authorities need simply turn to an informal or loose system of co-ordinated foreign exchange market interventions.

In this respect, Mundell's is a voice that stands out against the orthodoxy. He claims, in fact, that a system of fixed exchange rates among the three major currency areas is perfectly conceivable today and would greatly benefit monetary stability (Mundell *et al.* 2000). According to Mundell, exchange rates between the dollar, the euro and the yen should be 'locked', replicating what was done in Europe in 1999. What he proposes is a three-currency monetary union in which speculative capital movements would be abolished by the simple fact that exchange rates would remain irrevocably fixed. As we have already noted, however, the decision of irrevocably fixing exchange rates is not enough to avoid the accumulation of international speculative capital. Duplication would still occur, and exchange rate stability itself would be continuously threatened by speculation. Transactions on the foreign exchange market, in fact, would put the three major currencies under a destabilizing pressure, which, instead of leading to exchange rate fluctuation, would provoke disruptive variations in interest rates, inflation rates, employment, capital accumulation, and so on. The conditions required for the implementation of a currency area would no longer be fulfilled and a return to free or partially managed floating becomes unavoidable.

Yet, Mundell's proposal deserves serious consideration. A system of stable exchange rates extended to the dollar, the euro, and the yen would indeed mark a clear progress towards international monetary order. Now, the main obstacle to this end is the fact that today currencies are traded on the foreign exchange market and that the exchange rates reflect their relative prices. As long as this is the case, any attempt to fix exchange rates is bound to fail. As we have seen in the euro case, true exchange rate stability can be achieved – without giving up monetary sovereignty – only by moving from the present regime of relative exchange rates to a new regime of *absolute exchange rates*. If this were done for the dollar, the euro and the yen, their exchange rates would acquire a much greater stability, for they would no longer contribute to the increase of speculative capital. It is true, of course, that complete stability could be reached only if the currencies already present on the foreign exchange market were no longer objects of trade. But it is also true that once the principles of absolute exchange rates are sufficiently understood, the logic of monetary payments points unambiguously to the solution. More specifically, the new system will allow experts to work out a plan to avoid speculative trading on the foreign exchange market and to gradually reabsorb (for example, through a capital-equity programme) the speculative capital formed so far.

As for the three-currency area envisaged by Mundell, its realization will require the institution of an international central bank responsible for issuing a currency that will become the common standard for the dollar, the euro and the yen, and that will be used to carry out payments among countries of the three currency areas. The new central bank will also have to act as a clearing house in connection with the central banks of the three areas. What is needed for the whole system to work is therefore that (a) within each currency area payments among countries be carried out through the *intermediation* of their central banks and of a central bank of central banks, and that (b) between currency areas an international central bank acts as the central bank of their central banks (Figure 15.1).

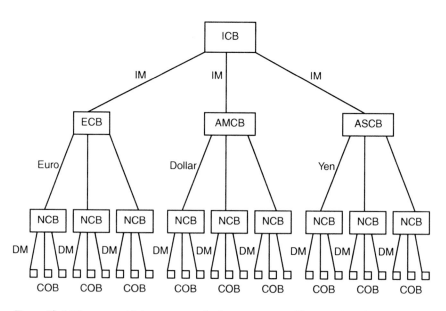

Figure 15.1 The pyramidal structure of a future system of international payments.

Figure 15.1 depicts the pyramidal structure of the new system. On the bottom line we find the commercial banks (COB) operating in each single country of the three currency areas. Their transactions are carried out in domestic currencies, for countries maintain their monetary sovereignty. The second line represents the national central banks (NCB). They act as clearing institutions for commercial banks and guarantee national monetary homogeneity. At the third level we have the central banks of the euro, dollar and yen currency areas. They guarantee monetary homogeneity in each area through the emission of a monetary standard used as vehicular currency by member countries in all of their reciprocal payments. They also provide a mechanism for the financial settlement of transactions by operating a system of clearing in collaboration with national central banks. Then, at the top of Figure 15.1, we have represented the international central bank (ICB), which brings the European central bank (ECB), the American central bank (AMCB) and the Asian central bank (ASCB) together into a system of international clearing based, like the national clearings, on the principles of real-time gross-settlement transfers. Finally, DM stands for the domestic money used by each country; the euro, the dollar, and the yen are the currencies used within each currency area when payments between member countries are involved; and the international money (IM) is the new means of payment used to 'vehiculate' transactions among the three currency areas members and between them and the rest of the world.

What future awaits LDCs?

The solution consisting in creating three or more world currency areas can obviously be extended to *LDCs*, and it is easy to imagine African and South American countries adhering to one of the currency areas proposed by Mundell or form distinct African and South American currency areas. However, this project is still far from realization so that *LDCs* will have to wait long before benefiting from an orderly system of international payments. Does this mean that they will also have to go on enduring a system in which they have to pay twice the interests on their external debt? Fortunately not: positive analysis has shown that, when paying their net interests on debt, *LDCs* suffer both from an increase in their external debt *and* from an equivalent reduction in their official reserves. This allows to work out the principles of a reform that, if implemented, would protect *LDCs* from the iniquity of the present system. The interesting thing here is that each single *LDC* can adopt the reform, independent of the system followed by the rest of the world and without reducing the amount of interest paid to its foreign creditors. What such reform manages to avoid concerns the second, *macroeconomic* payment of interest, and not the microeconomic payment of the indebted country's foreign creditors. Specifically, the aim of the reform is to avoid adding the two

payments to one another. Indeed every payment of interest between countries implies both a micro and a macroeconomic payment. Yet, these two
payments should not add up, the payment of foreign creditors being
theoretically enough to free both the indebted residents and their country
from any further obligation. In actuality, this is not what happens today,
the system being such that the payment of the indebted residents generates the additional payment of their country (the loss of official reserves).
The reform will radically modify this state of affairs. Foreign creditors,
residents of *R*, will be paid once by *LDCs*' indebted residents, but their
countries will no longer benefit from the additional payment of interest
carried out by *LDCs*. This will be obtained through a new structural platform for external payments that will allow *LDCs* to immediately recover
the amount of foreign exchange lost because of the decrease in official
reserves induced by the payment of interest, *i*.

Let us briefly recall the nature of today's double payment of *i*. The first
monetary flow corresponds to the transfer of foreign exchange from the
indebted residents of *LDCs* to their foreign creditors. This outflow of
foreign exchange is then converted into an outflow of real resources,
since the amount of foreign exchange earned by *R* is spent to finance an
equivalent amount of its imports from *LDCs*. The first payment of *i* entails
therefore the transfer to *R* of a positive amount of *LDCs*' domestic
resources. Being included in the payment of *LDCs*' exports, the conversion of interest by *R* does obviously not increase *LDCs*' total inflow of
foreign exchange. Increased by the payment of interest, *LDCs*' total
expenditures are thus greater than their total receipts, the difference
being made up for by a decrease in official reserves. On the whole, the
payment of *i* entails therefore *both* a real transfer of domestic output and a
transfer of foreign exchange. In order to pay *x* million (of US dollars) as
interest on their accumulated external debt, *LDCs* must face a double
charge, real and monetary. Now, the loss of domestic resources calls for a
new foreign loan allowing *LDCs* to re-establish their level of real resources,
so that the payment of *x i* gives finally rise to an increase of *LDCs*' foreign
debt equal to *x* million dollars, and to a decrease of the same amount of
dollars in their official reserves, leading to a total charge of twice the
amount of *x* million dollars.

The reform will be aimed at converting the second payment – carried
out by the macro-economy of *LDCs* to the benefit of the macro-economy
of *R* – into a transfer from the macro-economy of *LDCs* to the macro-
economy of these same countries, that is, to the benefit of their Trea-
suries. The first payment will not be substantially modified: foreign
creditors will be paid by *LDCs*' indebted residents, the monetary payment
of *i* will be converted into a real payment, and *LDCs*' current account
deficit will be financed by a new foreign loan. It is the second payment of *i*
that will be affected by the reform. Instead of being lost to the benefit of
R's macro-economy, *LDCs*' official reserves will flow back to their banking

system, where they will be recorded as a macroeconomic resource by their central banks. The new platform of *LDCs'* external payments will be totally neutral as far as creditor countries are concerned. *LDCs'* indebted residents will go on paying their due to their foreign creditors, who remain entirely unaffected by the reform. It is at the macroeconomic level that such reform manifests its effect. The pathological, unjustifiable loss of million of dollars suffered by *LDCs'* official reserves will in fact be immediately made up for by the new system guaranteeing its daily reflux into *LDCs'* central banks.

The very reason of the double charge suffered by *LDCs* lies in the fact that the payment of *i* is a unilateral ('unrequited') transfer. An orderly monetary system requires every payment to define a reciprocal transaction. It is only in this case that money is used 'vehicularly', as a pure means of payment, and that the monetary payment of *i* does not add to its real payment. The correct use of money requires the implementation of a new system of payments conforming to the principles advocated by Keynes in his proposals for the institution of an International Clearing Union. Waiting for this world reform to be achieved, *LDCs* can meanwhile autonomously protect themselves from the double charge of interest payment. Each of them can right away implement a system allowing for the reciprocity of its transactions, thus halving the total cost of today's interest payment. The outline of the reform is rather simple. Each single *LDC's* external payment of interest will have to be carried out by its central bank on behalf of the country's indebted residents. A specific department of the central bank will act as an intermediary between indebted residents and foreign creditors. Since no world central bank exists as yet, it will also be necessary to ask a foreign private bank to be an interface for the country's central bank, so as to guarantee that the second payment of *i* flows back to it. Payments will thus have to be entered in such a way that the central bank that conveys them will be credited with the amount of foreign exchange that today is definitively lost by the country's official reserves.

Even though *LDCs* are often heavily dependent on international institutions such as the IMF, they can enjoy a high degree of autonomy and sovereignty as long as their decisions do not unfairly disadvantage their foreign creditors. Furthermore, the IMF itself is an institution aiming at improving the economic and financial performance of its member countries. By avoiding the double charge of interest payment, the reform sketched here will actually provide *LDCs* with an amount of financial resources that will sensibly foster their economic development, thereby creating new advantageous opportunities for their richer partner countries as well. Generalized economic growth can be achieved only if the present, disorderly 'non-system' of international payments is replaced by an orderly system enabling the effective and unique payment of each and every transaction. Let us hope that the joint effort of economists, bankers, and politicians will soon make it possible.

Bibliography

Akerlof, G.A. (1979) 'The case against conservative macroeconomics', *Economica*, 27 (4): 596–625.

Akerlof, G.A. and Yellen, J. (1985) 'A near-rational model of the business cycle with wage and price inertia', *Quarterly Journal of Economics*, 100 (5): 823–38.

Alesina, A. and Barro, R. (eds) (2001) *Currency Unions*, Stanford: Hoover Institution Press.

Arena, R. (1988) 'Moneta, capitale e circolazione: problemi e un tentativo di articolazione teorica', in M. Messori (ed.) *Moneta e produzione*, Torino: Einaudi, 191–213.

—— (1996) 'Investment decision in circuit and post Keynesian approaches: a comparison', in G. Deleplace and E.J. Nell (eds) *Money in Motion. The Post Keynesian and Circulation Approaches*, Basingstoke and New York: Macmillan and St. Martin's Press, 417–33.

Arestis, P., Palma, G. and Sawyer, M. (eds) (1997) *Capital Controversy, Post-Keynesian Economics and the History of Economics*, London and New York: Routledge.

Argy, V. (1994) *International Macroeconomics. Theory and Policy*, London and New York: Routledge.

Arrow, K.J. (1964) 'The role of securities in the optimal allocation of risk-bearing', *Review of Economic Studies*, 31 (2): 91–6.

Backhouse, R. (1995) *Interpreting Macroeconomics. Explorations in the History of Economic Thought*, London and New York: Routledge.

Baliño, T., Enoch, C., Ize, A., Santiprabhob, V. and Stella, P. (1997) 'Currency board arrangements: issues and experiences', *IMF Occasional Paper*, No. 151.

Ball, L. and Mankiw, N.G. (1995) 'Relative-price change as aggregate supply shocks', *NBER Working Paper*, No. 4168.

Ball, L. and Romer, D. (1990) 'Real rigidities and the non-neutrality of money', *Review of Economic Studies*, 57 (2): 183–203.

—— (1991) 'Sticky prices as coordination failure', *American Economic Review*, 81 (3): 539–52.

Bank for International Settlements, International Monetary Fund, Organisation for Economic Co-operation and Development, World Bank (1994) *Debt-Stocks, Debt Flows and the Balance of Payments*, Paris: OCDE.

Baranzini, M. (ed.) (1982) *Advances in Economic Theory*, Oxford: Blackwell.

Baranzini, M. and Scazzieri, R. (eds) (1986) *Foundations of Economics. Structure of Inquiry and Economic Theory*, Oxford: Blackwell.

—— (eds) (1990) *The Economic Theory of Structure and Change*, Cambridge and New York: Cambridge University Press.

Barro, R.J. (1984) *Macroeconomics*, New York: Wiley.

Barro, R.J. and Grilli, V. (1994) *European Macroeconomics*, London: Macmillan.

Barro, R.J. and Grossman, H.I. (1971) 'A general disequilibrium model of income and employment', *American Economic Review*, 61 (1): 82–93.

Benassi, C., Chirco, A. and Colombo, C. (1994) *The New Keynesian Economics*, Oxford: Blackwell.

Benassy, J.-P. (1982) *The Economics of Market Disequilibrium*, New York: Academic Press.

Bilson, J.F.O. and Marston, R.C. (eds) (1984) *Exchange Rate Theory and Practice*, Chicago: University of Chicago Press.

Blinder, A.S. (1988) 'The fall and rise of Keynesian economics', *Economic Record*, 64 (187): 278–94.

Bliss, C.J. (1975) *Capital Theory and the Distribution of Income*, Amsterdam: North-Holland.

Blundell-Wignall, A. (ed.) (1993) *The Exchange Rate, International Trade and the Balance of Payments*, Sidney: Reserve Bank of Australia.

Böhm-Bawerk, E. (1959) *Capital and Interest*, South Holland: Libertarian Press, 3 vols (first published 1884–1909).

Boland, L.A. (1986) *Methodology for a New Microeconomics*, Boston: Allen & Unwin.

Braasch, B. and Hesse, H. (1998) 'Global capital movements, exchange rates and monetary policy', in K.-J. Koch and K. Jaeger (eds) *Trade, Growth and Economic Policy in Open Economies. Essays in Honour of Hans-Jürgen Vosgerau*, Frankfurt: Springer-Verlag, 249–68.

Bradley, X. (2003) 'Involuntary unemployment and investment', in L.-P. Rochon and S. Rossi (eds) *Modern Theories of Money. The Nature and Role of Money in Capitalist Economies*, Cheltenham and Northampton: Edward Elgar, 384–408.

Branson, W.H., Frenkel, J.A. and Goldstein, M. (eds) (1990) *International Policy Coordination and Exchange Rate Fluctuations*, Chicago: University of Chicago Press.

Brunner, K. and Meltzer, A.H. (eds) (1984) *Essays on Macroeconomic Implications of Financial and Labour Markets and Political Processes*, Amsterdam: North-Holland.

Buiter, W.H. (1980) 'The macroeconomics of Dr Pangloss: a critical survey of the neoclassical macroeconomics', *Economic Journal*, 90 (357): 34–50.

Bunge, M. (1963) *Causality*, Cambridge, MA: Harvard University Press.

Calvo, G. (1996) *Money, Exchange Rates, and Output*, Cambridge, MA: The MIT Press.

Calvo, G. and Reinhart, C.M. (2000) 'Fear of floating', *NBER Working Paper*, No. 7993.

Cannata, F. (1996a) 'Tassi di cambio e mercati finanziari internazionali: una rassegna', *Rivista bancaria*, 52 (3): 75–94.

—— (1996b) 'Tassi di cambio e mercati finanziari internazionali: una rassegna', *Rivista bancaria*, 52 (4): 79–116.

Capie, F. and Wood, G. (eds) (1989) *Monetary Economics in the 1980s*, London: Macmillan.

Cassel, G. (1918) 'Abnormal deviations in international exchanges', *Economic Journal*, 28 (112): 413–15.

—— (1922) *Money and Foreign Exchange after 1914*, New York: Constable & Co.

Cencini, A. (1982) 'The logical indeterminacy of relative prices', in M. Baranzini (ed.) *Advances in Economic Theory*, Oxford: Blackwell, 126–36.

—— (1984) *Time and the Macroeconomic Analysis of Income*, London and New York: Pinter Publishers and St. Martin's Press.

—— (1988) *Money, Income and Time*, London and New York: Pinter Publishers.

—— (1996) 'Inflation and deflation: the two faces of the same reality', in A. Cencini and M. Baranzini (eds) *Inflation and Unemployment. Contributions to a New Macroenomic Approach*, London and New York: Routledge, 17–60.

—— (1997) *Monetary Theory, National and International*, London and New York: Routledge.

—— (2000) 'World monetary disorders: exchange rate erratic fluctuations', *Quaderno di ricerca No. 2*, Lugano-Vezia: Research Laboratory of Monetary Economics.

—— (2001) *Monetary Macroeconomics. A New Approach*, London and New York: Routledge.

—— (2003a) 'IS–LM: a final rejection', in L.-P. Rochon and S. Rossi (eds) *Modern Theories of Money. The Nature and Role of Money in Capitalist Economies*. Cheltenham and Northampton: Elgar, 295–321.

—— (2003b) 'Micro, macro et l'analyse du circuit', in P. Piégay and L.-P. Rochon (eds) *Théories monétaires post Keynésiennes*, Paris: Economica, 209–25.

Cencini, A. and Baranzini, M. (eds) (1996) *Inflation and Unemployment. Contributions to a New Macroeconomic Approach*, London and New York: Routledge.

Cencini, A. and Schmitt, B. (1976) *La pensée de Karl Marx. Critique et synthèse*, Vol. I *La valeur*, Albeuve: Castella.

—— (1992) 'Per la creazione di uno spazio monetario europeo garante della sovranità di ogni singolo paese', in AA.VV. *Europa '93! E la piazza finanziaria svizzera?*, Lugano: Centro di Studi Bancari/Meta Edizioni, 99–136.

Chang, R. and Velasco, A. (2000) 'Exchange rate policy for developing countries', *American Economic Review*, 90 (2): 71–5.

Chick, V. and Dow, S.C. (2001) 'Formalism, logic and reality: a Keynesian analysis', *Cambridge Journal of Economics*, 25 (6): 705–21.

Chrystal, K.A. and Price, S. (1994) *Controversies in Macroeconomics*, London and New York: Harvester-Wheatsheaf.

Clark, J.B. (1899) *The Distribution of Wealth*, Reprints of Economic Classics, New York: Kelley (1965).

Cline, W.R. (1984) *International Debt. System Risk and Policy Response*, Washington: Institute for International Economics.

—— (1995) *International Debt Reexamined*, Washington: Institute for International Economics.

Clower, R.W. (ed.) (1969) *Monetary Theory. Selected Readings*, Harmondsworth: Penguin.

—— (1997) 'Effective demand revisited', in G.C. Harcourt and P.A. Riach (eds) *A 'Second Edition' of the General Theory*, London and New York: Routledge, Vol. I, 28–51.

Coddington, A. (1976) 'Keynesian economics: the search for first principles', *Journal of Economic Literature*, 14 (4): 1258–73.

Cohen, A.J., Hagemann, H. and Smithin, J. (eds) (1997) *Money, Financial Institutions and Macroeconomics*, Boston, Dordrecht, London: Kluwer Academic Publishers.

Corti, M. (1989) *Esogeneità e causalità. Epistemologia dei modelli in scienza economica*, Fribourg: Editions Universitaires.

Cottarelli, C. and Giannini, C. (1997) 'Credibility without rules? Monetary frameworks in the post-Bretton Woods era', *IMF Occasional Paper*, No. 154.

Cross, R. (ed.) (1995) *The Natural Rate of Unemployment. Reflections on 25 Years of the Hypothesis*, Cambridge: Cambridge University Press.

Cuddington, J.T. (1986) 'Capital flight: estimates, issues, and explanations', *Princeton Studies in International Finance*, No. 58, Princeton: Princeton University Press.

Cumby, R. and Levich, R. (1987) 'On the definition and magnitude of recent capital flight', in J. Williamson and D.R. Lessard (eds) *Capital Flight and Third World Debt*, Washington: Institute for International Economics, 27–51.

—— (1992) 'Balance of payments', in P. Newman, M. Milgate and J. Eatwell (eds) *The New Palgrave Dictionary of Money & Finance*, Vol. I, London and Basingstoke: Macmillan, 113–19.

Dafflon, B. and Rossi, S. (1999) 'Public accounting fudges towards EMU: a first empirical survey and some public choice considerations', *Public Choice*, 101 (1–2): 59–84.

Davidson, P. (1987–88) 'A modest set of proposals for solving the international debt crisis', *Journal of Post Keynesian Economics*, 10 (2): 323–38.

—— (1994) *Post Keynesian Macroeconomic Theory*, Aldershot and Brookfield: Edward Elgar.

—— (2002) *Financial Markets, Money and the Real World*, Cheltenham and Northampton: Edward Elgar.

Davis, E.P. (1992) 'Euromarkets', in P. Newman, M. Milgate and J. Eatwell (eds) *The New Palgrave Dictionary of Money & Finance*, Vol. I, London and Basingstoke: Macmillan, 783–5.

Debreu, G. (1959) *Theory of Value. An Axiomatic Analysis of Economic Equilibrium*, New Haven: Yale University Press.

De Grauwe, P. (1992) *The Economics of Monetary Integration*, Oxford: Oxford University Press.

Deleplace, G. and Nell, E.J. (eds) (1996) *Money in Motion. The Post Keynesian and Circulation Approaches*, Basingstoke and New York: Macmillan and St. Martin's Press.

Dell, S. (1989) 'The future of the international monetary system', in O.F. Hamouda, R. Rowley and B.M. Wolf (eds) *The Future of the International Monetary System*, Aldershot and Brookfield: Edward Elgar, 89–116.

De Vroey, M. (1984) 'Inflation: a non-monetarist monetary interpretation', *Cambridge Journal of Economics*, 8 (3): 381–99.

Dooley, M.P. and Isard, P. (1983) 'The portfolio-balance model of exchange rates and some structural estimates of the risk premium', *IMF Staff Papers*, 30 (4): 683–702.

Dornbusch, R. (1976) 'Expectations and exchange rate dynamics', *Journal of Political Economy*, 84 (6): 1161–76.

—— (1980) *Open Economy Macroeconomics*, New York: Basic Books.

—— (1986) *Dollars, Debts and Deficits*, Cambridge, MA: The MIT Press.

Dornbusch, R. and Fischer, S. (1980) 'Exchange rates and the current account', *American Economic Review*, 70 (5): 960–71.

Dow, S.C. (1996) *The Methodology of Macroeconomic Thought*, Cheltenham and Brookfield: Edward Elgar.

Eatwell, J., Milgate, M. and Newman, P. (eds) (1988) *The New Palgrave. A Dictionary of Economics*, London and Basingstoke: Macmillan.

Eichengreen, B. (1994) *International Monetary Arrangements for the Twenty-First Century*, Washington: Brookings Institution.

—— (1998) 'European monetary unification', *Oxford Review of Economic Policy,* 14 (3): 24–40.

Eichengreen, B. and Hausmann, R. (1999) 'Exchange rates and financial fragility', *NBER Working Paper,* No. 7418.

Eichengreen, B., Tobin, J. and Wyplosz, C. (1995) 'Two cases for sand in the wheels of international finance', *Economic Journal,* 105 (428): 162–72.

Erbe, S. (1985) 'The flight of capital from developing countries', *Intereconomics,* 20 (6): 268–75.

Feldstein, M. and Horioka, C. (1980) 'Domestic savings and international capital flows', *Economic Journal,* 90 (358): 314–29.

Fiorentini, R. (1990) *I tassi di cambio flessibili, teorie e verifiche,* Padova: CEDAM.

Fischer, S. (2001) 'Exchange rate regimes: is the bipolar view correct?', *Journal of Economic Perspectives,* 15 (2): 3–24.

Fisher, F.M. (1969) 'Causation and specification in economic theory and econometrics', *Synthese,* 20: 489–500.

Fitoussi, J.-P. (ed.) (1983) *Modern Macroeconomic Theory. An Overview,* Oxford: Blackwell.

Fitzgibbons, A. (2000) *The Nature of Macroeconomics,* Cheltenham and Northampton: Edward Elgar.

Fleming, J.M. (1962) 'Domestic financial policies under fixed and under floating exchange rates', *IMF Staff Papers,* 9 (3): 369–79.

Fontana, G. (2000) 'Post Keynesians and Circuitists on money and uncertainty: an attempt at generality', *Journal of Post Keynesian Economics,* 23 (1): 27–48.

Frankel, J.A. (1984) 'Tests of monetary and portfolio balance models of exchange rate determination', in J.F.O. Bilson and R.C. Marston (eds) *Exchange Rate Theory and Practice,* Chicago: University of Chicago Press, 239–60.

—— (1996) 'Recent exchange-rate experience and proposals for reform', *American Economic Review,* 86 (2): 153–8.

Frankel, J.A. and Rose, A.K. (1995) 'Empirical research on nominal exchange rates', in G. Grossman and K. Rogoff (eds) *Handbook of International Economics,* Vol. III, Amsterdam: North-Holland, 1689–720.

Frege, G. (1950) *Foundations of Arithmetic. A Logico-Mathematical Enquiry into the Concept of Number,* Oxford: Blackwell.

—— (1984) *Collected Papers on Mathematics, Logic, and Philosophy,* edited by B. McGuinness, Oxford and New York: Blackwell.

Frenkel, J.A. (1976) 'A monetary approach to the exchange rate: doctrinal aspects and empirical evidence', *Scandinavian Journal of Economics,* 78 (29): 200–24.

—— (ed.) (1983) *Exchange Rates and International Macroeconomics,* Chicago: University of Chicago Press.

Frenkel, J.A. and Johnson, H.G. (eds) (1976) *The Monetary Approach to the Balance of Payments,* London: Allen & Unwin.

Frenkel, J.A. and Mussa, M.L. (1985) 'Asset markets, exchange rates and the balance of payments', in R. Jones and P.B. Kenen (eds) *Handbook of International Economics,* Vol. II, Amsterdam: North-Holland, 679–740.

Friedman, B.M. and Hahn, F.H. (eds) (1990) *Handbook of Monetary Economics,* Amsterdam and New York: Elsevier, 2 vols.

Friedman, M. (ed.) (1956) *Studies in the Quantity Theory of Money,* Chicago: Chicago University Press.

—— (1968) 'The role of monetary policy', *American Economic Review,* 58 (1): 1–17.

—— (1970) 'A theoretical framework for monetary analysis', *Journal of Political Economy*, 78 (2): 193–238.

Gerrard, B. (1996) 'Review article: competing schools of thought in macroeconomics – an ever-emerging consensus?', *Journal of Economic Studies*, 23 (1): 53–69.

Ghosh, A.R., Gulde, A.-M. and Wolf, H.C. (2000) 'Currency boards: more than a quick fix?', *Economic Policy. A European Forum*, 0 (31): 270–335.

Gnos, C. and Rasera, J.-B. (1985) 'Circuit et circulation: une fausse analogie', in *Production et monnaie, Cahier de la Revue d'économie politique*, Paris: Sirey, 41–57.

Goldstein, M. (1977) *The Case for an International Banking Standard*, Washington: Institute for International Economics.

Goodhart, C.A.E. (1977) 'The role, functions and definition of money', in G.C. Harcourt (ed.) *The Microeconomic Foundations of Macroeconomics*, London and Basingstoke: Macmillan, 205–27.

—— (1988) 'The foreign exchange market: a random walk with a dragging anchor', *Economica*, 55 (220): 437–60.

—— (1994) 'What should central banks do? What should be their macroeconomic objectives and operations?', *Economic Journal*, 104 (427): 1424–36.

Goodhart, C.A.E. and Payne, R. (2000) *The Foreign Exchange Market*, London and Basingstoke: Macmillan.

Goodhart, C.A.E. and Schoenmaker, D. (1995) 'Should the functions of monetary policy and bank supervisor be separated?', *Oxford Economic Papers*, 47 (4): 539–60.

Gordon, R.J. (ed.) (1974) *Milton Friedman's Monetary Framework*, Chicago and London: University of Chicago Press.

—— (1990) 'What is new Keynesian economics?', *Journal of Economic Literature*, 28 (3): 1115–71.

Grandmont, J.-M. (1983) *Money and Value. A Reconsideration of Classical and Neoclassical Monetary Theories*, Cambridge: Cambridge University Press.

Graziani, A. (1988) 'Il circuito monetario', in M. Messori (ed.) *Moneta e produzione*, Torino: Einaudi, xi–xliii.

—— (1990) 'The theory of the monetary circuit', *Economies et Sociétés*, 24 (6): 7–36.

—— (1996) *La teoria del circuito monetario*, Milano: Jaca Book.

—— (2003) *The Monetary Theory of Production*, Cambridge: Cambridge University Press.

Greenaway, D. (ed.) (1989) *Current Issues in Macroeconomics*, London and Basingstoke: Macmillan.

Greenwald, B.C. and Stiglitz, J.E. (1987) 'Keynesian, new Keynesian and new classical economics', *Oxford Economic Papers*, 39 (1): 119–33.

—— (1993) 'New and old Keynesians', *Journal of Economic Perspectives*, 7 (1): 23–44.

Grossman, G. and Rogoff, K. (eds) (1995) *Handbook of International Economics*, Vol. III, Amsterdam: North-Holland.

Grubel, H.G. (ed.) (1963) *World Monetary Reform. Plans and Issues*, Stanford and London: Stanford University Press and Oxford University Press.

Hahn, F. (1984) *Equilibrium and Macroeconomics*, Oxford: Blackwell.

—— (1985) 'In praise of economic theory', *The Jevons Memorial Fund Lecture*, London: University College.

Hahn, F. and Solow, R. (1995) *A Critical Essay on Modern Macroeconomic Theory*, Oxford: Blackwell.

Hammond, J.D. (1996) *Theory and Measurement. Causality Issues in Milton Friedman's Monetary Economics*, Cambridge: Cambridge University Press.

Hamouda, O.F., Rowley, R. and Wolf, B.M. (eds) (1989) *The Future of the International Monetary System: Change, Coordination or Instability*, Aldershot and Brookfield: Edward Elgar.

Handa, J. (2000) *Monetary Economics*, London and New York: Routledge.

Hansen, A.H. (1938) *Full Recovery or Stagnation?*, New York: Norton.

—— (1949) *Monetary Theory and Fiscal Policy*, New York: McGraw-Hill.

Harcourt, G.C. (ed.) (1977) *The Microeconomic Foundations of Macroeconomics*, London and Basingstoke: Macmillan.

Harcourt, G.C. and Riach, P.A. (eds) (1997) *A 'Second Edition' of the General Theory*, London and New York: Routledge, 2 vols.

Hargreaves-Heap, S. (1988) 'Unemployment', in J. Eatwell, M. Milgate, and P. Newman (eds) *The New Palgrave. A Dictionary of Economics*, Vol. IV, London and Basingstoke: Macmillan, 745–9.

Harrod, R.F. (1937) 'Mr. Keynes and traditional theory', *Econometrica*, 5 (1): 74–86.

Hicks, J.R. (1937) 'Mr. Keynes and the "classics": a suggested interpretation', *Econometrica*, 5 (2): 147–59. Reprinted in J.R. Hicks (1982), *Money, Interest and Wages: Collected Essays on Economic Theory*, Vol. II, Oxford: Blackwell, 100–15.

—— (1980–81) 'IS–LM: an explanation', *Journal of Post Keynesian Economics*, 3 (2): 139–54. Reprinted in J.R. Hicks (1982), *Money, Interest and Wages. Collected Essays on Economic Theory*, Vol. II, Oxford: Blackwell, 318–31.

—— (1982) *Money, Interest and Wages. Collected Essays on Economic Theory*, Vol. II, Oxford: Blackwell.

—— (1983) *Classics and Neoclassics. Collected Essays on Economic Theory*, Vol. III, Oxford: Blackwell.

Hood, W.C. and Koopmans, T.J. (eds) (1953) *Studies in Econometric Method*, New York: Wiley.

Hoover, K.D. (1988) *The New Classical Macroeconomics. A Sceptical Inquiry*, Oxford: Blackwell.

—— (2001) *Causality in Macroeconomics*, Cambridge: Cambridge University Press.

Howard, M.C. (1979) *Modern Theories of Income Distribution*, London and Basingstoke: Macmillan.

Howitt, P.W. (1992) 'Macroeconomics: relations with microeconomics', in P. Newman, M. Milgate and J. Eatwell (eds) *The New Palgrave Dictionary of Money & Finance*, Vol. II, London and Basingstoke: Macmillan, 632–5.

International Monetary Fund (1987) *Report on the World Current Account Discrepancy*, Washington: International Monetary Fund.

—— (1992) *Report on the Measurement of International Capital Flows*, Washington: International Monetary Fund.

—— (1993) *The Balance of Payments Manual*, Washington: International Monetary Fund.

—— (1982–2004) *Balance of Payments Statistics Yearbook*, Washington: International Monetary Fund.

Isard, P. (1995) *Exchange Rate Economics*, Cambridge and New York: Cambridge University Press.

Isard, P. and Faruqee, H. (eds) (1998) 'Exchange rate assessment. Extensions of the macroeconomic balance approach', *IMF Occasional Paper*, No. 167.

Jevons, W.S. (1871) *The Theory of Political Economy*, London: Macmillan.

—— (1875) *Money and the Mechanism of Exchange*, London: Appleton & Co.

Johnson, H.G. (1958) *International Trade and Economic Growth*, London: Allen & Unwin.

—— (1972a) *Further Essays in Monetary Theory*, London: Allen & Unwin.

—— (1972b) *Macroeconomics and Monetary Theory*, New York: Aldine Publishing Company.

Jones, R. and Kenen, P.B. (eds) (1985) *Handbook of International Economics*, Vol. II, Amsterdam: North-Holland.

Kahn, R. (1984) *The Making of Keynes's Theory*, Cambridge: Cambridge University Press.

Kahneman, D. and Tversky, A. (1979) 'A prospect theory: an analysis of decision under risk', *Econometrica*, 47 (2): 263–91.

—— (eds) (2000) *Choices, Values and Frames*, Cambridge, New York and Melbourne: Cambridge University Press; New York: Russell Sage Foundation.

Kalecki, M. (1939) *Essays on the Theory of Economic Fluctuations*, London: Allen & Unwin.

Kenen, P.B. (1985) 'Macroeconomic theory and policy: how the closed economy was opened', in R.W. Jones and P.B. Kenen (eds) *Handbook of International Economics*, Vol. II, Amsterdam: North-Holland, 625–77.

—— (ed.) (1995) *Understanding Interdependence. The Macroeconomics of the Open Economy*, Princeton: Princeton University Press.

Kenen, P.B. and Yudin, E.B. (1965) 'The demand for international reserves', *Review of Economics and Statistics*, 47 (3): 242–50.

Keynes, J.M. (1929a) 'The German transfer problem', *Economic Journal*, 39 (153): 1–7.

—— (1929b) 'Mr. Keynes's views on the transfer problem: a reply by Mr. Keynes', *Economic Journal*, 39 (155): 388–408.

—— (1930/1971) *A Treatise on Money*, Vol. V and VI of *The Collected Writings of John Maynard Keynes*, London and Basingstoke: Macmillan.

—— (1936/1973a) *The General Theory of Employment, Interest and Money*, London: Macmillan. Reprinted in *The Collected Writings of John Maynard Keynes*, Vol. VII, London and Basingstoke: Macmillan.

—— (1937) 'Alternative theories of the rate of interest', *Economic Journal*, 47 (186): 241–52. Reprinted in *The Collected Writings of John Maynard Keynes*, Vol. XIV, London and Basingstoke: Macmillan.

—— (1973b) *The Collected Writings of John Maynard Keynes*, Vol. XIII *The General Theory and After: Part I, Preparation*, London and Basingstoke: Macmillan.

—— (1973c) *The Collected Writings of John Maynard Keynes*, Vol. XIV *The General Theory and After: Part II, Defence and Development*, London and Basingstoke: Macmillan.

Kindleberger, C.P. (1969) 'Measuring equilibrium in the balance of payments', *Journal of Political Economy*, 77 (6): 873–91.

—— (1981) *International Money. A Collection of Essays*, London: Allen & Unwin.

King, R.G. and Plosser, C.I. (1984) 'Money, credit and prices in a real business cycle', *American Economic Review*, 74 (39): 363–80.

Knight, F. (1934) 'Capital, time and the interest rate', *Economica*, 1 (3): 257–86.

Koch, K.-J. and Jaeger, K. (eds) (1998) *Trade, Growth and Economic Policy in Open Economies. Essays in Honour of Hans-Jürgen Vosgerau*, Frankfurt: Springer–Verlag.

Koopmans, T.J. (1957) *Three Essays on the State of Economic Science*, New York: McGraw-Hill.

Kregel, J.A. (1992) 'Effective demand', in P. Newman, M. Milgate and J. Eatwell (eds) *The New Palgrave. A Dictionary of Economics*, Vol. II, London and Basingstoke: Macmillan, 99–102.

Krugman, P.R. (1979) 'A model of balance-of-payments crises', *Journal of Money, Credit and Banking*, 11 (3): 311–25.

—— (1989) *Exchange Rate Instability*, Cambridge, MA: The MIT Press.

—— (1991) 'Target zones and exchange rate dynamics', *Quarterly Journal of Economics*, 106 (3): 669–82.

—— (1992) *Currencies and Crises*, Cambridge, MA and London: The MIT Press.

Krugman, P.R. and Obstfeld, M. (2003) *International Economics. Theory and Policy*, Reading, MA: Addison-Wesley.

Kurz, H.D. and Salvadori, N. (1995) *Theory of Production*, Cambridge and New York: Cambridge University Press.

Laidler, D. (1981) 'Monetarism: an interpretation and an assessment', *Economic Journal*, 91 (361): 1–28.

—— (1997) 'The new classical contribution to macroeconomics', in B. Snowdon and H.R. Vane (eds) *A Macroeconomic Reader*, London and New York: Routledge, originally published in *Banca Nazionale del Lavoro Quarterly Review*, 39 (1): 27–55.

—— (ed.) (1999) *The Foundations of Monetary Economics*, Cheltenham and Northampton: Edward Elgar, 3 vols.

Laidler, D. and Parkin, M. (1975) 'Inflation: a survey', *Economic Journal*, 85 (340): 741–809.

Lange, O. (1938) 'The rate of interest and the optimum propensity to consume', *Economica*, 5 (17): 12–32.

Lavoie, M. (1992) *Foundations of Post-Keynesian Economic Analysis*, Aldershot and Brookfield: Edward Elgar.

Lawson, T. (1997) *Economics and Reality*, London and New York: Routledge.

Leijonhufvud, A. (1967) 'Keynes and the Keynesians: a suggested interpretation', *American Economic Review*, 57 (2): 401–10.

—— (1992) 'Keynesian economics: past confusion, future prospects', in A. Vercelli and N. Dimitri (eds) *Macroeconomics. A Survey of Research Strategies*, Oxford: Oxford University Press, 16–37.

Leontief, W. (1966) *Essays in Economics*, Oxford: Blackwell.

—— (1982) 'Letter', *Science*, 217: 104–7.

Lerner, A.P. (1947) 'Money as a creature of the state', *American Economic Review*, 37 (2): 312–17.

—— (1983) 'What was the matter with IS–LM?' in J.-P. Fitoussi (ed.) *Modern Macroeconomic Theory*, Oxford: Blackwell, 64–90.

—— (1984) 'Hicks on time and money', *Oxford Economic Papers*, 36 (supplement): 26–46.

Levitt, K. (1989) 'Some reflections on the *LDC* debt crisis', in O.F. Hamouda, R. Rowley and B.M. Wolf (eds) *The Future of the International Monetary System*, Aldershot and Brookfield: Edward Elgar, 131–48.

Lucas, R.E. Jr. (1972) 'Expectations and the neutrality of money', *Journal of Economic Theory*, 4 (2): 103–24.

—— (1973) 'Some international evidence of output–inflation tradeoffs', *American Economic Review*, 63 (3): 326–34.

—— (1980) 'Methods and problems in business cycle theory', *Journal of Money, Credit and Banking*, 12 (4): 696–715.

—— (1987) *Models of Business Cycle*, Oxford: Blackwell.

Lucas, R.E. Jr. and Sargent T.J. (eds) (1981) *Rational Expectations and Econometric Practice*, London: Allen & Unwin.

—— (1997) 'After Keynesian macroeconomics', in B. Snowdon and H.R. Vane (eds) *A Macroeconomics Reader*, London and New York: Routledge, 270–92.

Machlup, F. (1970) 'Euro-dollar creation: a mystery story', *Banca Nazionale del Lavoro Quarterly Review*, 0 (94): 219–60.

—— (1972) 'Euro-dollars, once again', *Banca Nazionale del Lavoro Quarterly Review*, 0 (1721): 119–37.

Magnan de Bornier, J. (1990) 'Vertical integration, growth and sequential change', in M. Baranzini and R. Scazzieri (eds) *The Economic Theory of Structure and Change*, Cambridge and New York: Cambridge University Press, 122–39.

Malinvaud, E. (1991) *Voies de la recherche macroéconomique*, Paris: Editions Odile Jacob.

Malinvaud, E. and Younès, Y. (1977) 'Some new concepts for the microeconomic foundations of macroeconomics', in G.C. Harcourt (ed.) *The Microeconomic Foundations of Macroeconomics*, London and Basingstoke: Macmillan, 62–85.

Mankiw, N.G. (1990) 'A quick refresher course in macroeconomics', *Journal of Economic Literature*, 28 (4): 1645–60.

—— (1992) 'The reincarnation of Keynesian economics', *European Economic Review*, 36 (2–3): 559–65.

—— (1997) 'An interview', in B. Snowdon and H.R. Vane (eds) *A Macroeconomics Reader*, London and New York: Routledge, 454–70.

Mankiw, N.G. and Romer, D. (eds) (1991) *New Keynesian Economics*, Cambridge, MA: The MIT Press, 2 vols.

Marshall, A. (1950) *Principles of Economics*, London: Macmillan (first published 1890).

Marx, K. (1973) *Grundrisse*, Harmondsworth: Penguin (first published 1839).

—— (1976) *Capital, Vol. I*, Harmondsworth: Penguin (first published 1867).

—— (1978) *Capital, Vol. II*, Harmondsworth: Penguin (first published 1885).

—— (1981) *Capital, Vol. III*, Harmondsworth: Penguin (first published 1894).

Masson, P.R., Krueger, T.H. and Turtelboom, B.G. (eds) (1997) *EMU and the International Monetary System*, Washington: International Monetary Fund.

Mayer, T. (1975) 'The structure of monetarism', *Kredit und Kapital*, 8 (2): 191–215, 292–313.

—— (1990) *Monetarism and Macroeconomic Policy*, Aldershot and Brookfield: Edward Elgar.

McCallum, B.T. (1990) 'Inflation: theory and evidence', in B.M. Friedman and F.H. Hahn (eds) *Handbook of Monetary Economics*, Vol. II, Amsterdam and New York: Elsevier, 963–1012.

MacDonald, R. and Taylor, M.P. (1992) 'Exchange rate economics', *IMF Staff Papers*, 39 (1): 1–27.

McKenzie, G. (1992) 'Eurocurrency markets', in P. Newman, M. Milgate and J. Eatwell (eds) *The New Palgrave Dictionary of Money & Finance*, Vol. I, London and Basingstoke: Macmillan, 780–3.

McKinnon, R.I. (1988) 'Monetary and exchange rate policies for international financial stability: a proposal', *Journal of Economic Perspectives*, 2 (1): 83–104.

—— (1990) 'Interest rate volatility and exchange rate risk: new rules for a common monetary standard', *Contemporary Policy Issues*, 8 (2): 1–17.

—— (1995) 'One money for how many?', in P.B. Kenen (ed.) *Understanding Interdependence. The Macroeconomics of the Open Economy*, Princeton: Princeton University Press, 88–97.

—— (ed.) (1996) *The Rules of the Game. International Money and Exchange Rates*, Cambridge, MA: The MIT Press.

Meade, J.E. (1937) 'A simplified model of Mr. Keynes' system', *Review of Economic Studies*, 4 (2): 98–107.

—— (1952) *The Balance of Payments*, London, New York and Toronto: Oxford University Press.

Messori, M. (ed.) (1988) *Moneta e produzione*, Torino: Einaudi.

Metzler, L.A. *et al.* (1948) *Income, Employment and Public Policy. Essays in Honor of Alvin H. Hansen*, New York: Norton.

Minsky, H.P. (1986) *Stabilizing an Unstable Economy*, New Haven: Yale University Press.

Mirowski, P. and Cook, P. (1990) 'Walras's "Economics and Mechanics": translation, commentary, content', in W.J. Samuels (ed.) *Economics as Discourse. An Analysis of the Language of Economics*, Dordrecht and Boston: Kluwer Academic Publishers, 189–224.

Mizen, P. (ed.) (2003a) *Central Banking, Monetary Theory and Practice*, Cheltenham and Northampton: Edward Elgar.

—— (ed.) (2003b) *Monetary History, Exchange Rates and Financial Markets*, Cheltenham and Northampton: Edward Elgar.

Modigliani, F. (1944) 'Liquidity preference and the theory of interest and money', *Econometrica*, 12 (1): 45–88.

—— (1988) 'The monetarist controversy revisited', *Contemporary Policy Issues*, 6 (1): 3–18.

Moore, B.J. (1988) *Horizontalists and Verticalists. The Macroeconomics of Credit Money*, Cambridge: Cambridge University Press.

Mullineux, A. (1987) *International Money and Banking. The Creation of a New Order*, Brighton: Wheatsheaf.

Mundell, R.A. (1961) 'The international disequilibrium system', *Kyklos*, 14 (2): 153–72.

—— (1963) 'Capital mobility and stabilization policy under fixed and flexible exchange rates', *Canadian Journal of Economics and Political Science*, 29 (4): 475–85.

—— (1969) 'Problems of the international monetary system', in R.A. Mundell and A.K. Swoboda (eds) *Monetary Problems of the International Economy*, Chicago: University of Chicago Press, 21–38.

Mundell, R.A. and Swoboda, A.K. (eds) (1969) *Monetary Problems of the International Economy*, Chicago: University of Chicago Press.

Mundell, R.A. and Zak, P.J. (eds) (2002) *Monetary Stability and Economic Growth*, Cheltenham and Northampton: Edward Elgar.

Mundell, R.A., Masson, P., Obstfeld, M. and Swoboda, A.K. (2000) 'One world, one currency: destination or delusion?', Transcript of the *Economic Forum* held at the International Monetary Fund, November 8, Washington: International Monetary Fund.

Mussa, M. (1990) 'Exchange rate in theory and reality', *Essays in International Finance*, No. 179, Princeton: Princeton University.

Mussa, M., Goldstein, M., Clark, P.B., Mathieson, D.J. and T. Bayoumi (1994)

'Improving the international monetary system: constraints and possibilities', *IMF Occasional Paper*, No. 116.

Mussa, M., Boughton, J.M. and Isard, P. (eds) (1996) *The Future of the SDR in Light of Changes in the International Monetary System*, Washington: International Monetary Fund.

Mussa, M., Masson, P., Swoboda, A., Jadresic, E., Mauro, P. and Berg. A (2000) 'Exchange rate regimes in an increasingly integrated world economy', *IMF Occasional Paper*, No. 193.

Muth, J.F. (1981) 'Rational expectations and the theory of price movements', in R.E. Lucas and T.J. Sargent (eds) *Rational Expectations and Econometric Practice*, London: Allen & Unwin, 3–22 (first published 1961).

Nell, E.J. (1988) 'Accumulation of capital', in J. Eatwell, M. Milgate and P. Newman (eds) *The New Palgrave. A Dictionary of Economics*, Vol. I, London and Basingstoke: Macmillan, 14–18.

Newman, P., Milgate, M. and Eatwell, J. (eds) (1992) *The New Palgrave Dictionary of Money and Finance*, London and Basingstoke: Macmillan.

Niehans, J. and Hewson, J. (1976) 'The eurodollar market and monetary theory', *Journal of Money, Credit and Banking*, 8 (1): 1–27.

Obstfeld, M. (1995) 'International capital mobility in the 1990s', in P.B. Kenen (ed.) *Understanding Interdependence. The Macroeconomics of the Open Economy*, Princeton: Princeton University Press, 201–61.

Obstfeld, M. and Rogoff, K. (1995) 'The mirage of fixed exchange rates', *Journal of Economic Perspectives*, 9 (4): 73–96.

Ohlin, B. (1937) 'Some notes on the Stockholm theory of savings and investment', *Economic Journal*, 47 (185): 53–69.

Pareto, V. (1974) *Manuale di economia politica. Con una introduzione alla scienza sociale*, Padova: CEDAM.

Parguez, A. (1996) 'Beyond scarcity: a reappraisal of the theory of the monetary circuit', in G. Deleplace and E.J. Nell (eds) *Money in Motion. The Post Keynesian and Circulation Approaches*, London and New York: Macmillan and St. Martin's Press, 139–54.

Parguez, A. and Seccareccia, M. (2000) 'The credit theory of money: the monetary circuit approach', in J. Smithin (ed.) *What is Money?*, London and New York: Routledge, 101–23.

Pasinetti, L.L. (1974) *Growth and Income Distribution*, Cambridge: Cambridge University Press.

—— (1983) 'Comment on Leijonhufvud', in D. Worswick and J.A. Trevithick (eds) *Keynes and the Modern World*, Cambridge: Cambridge University Press, 205–11.

—— (1997) 'The principle of effective demand', in G.C. Harcourt and P.A. Riach (eds) *A 'Second Edition' of the General Theory*, Vol. I, London and New York: Routledge, 93–104.

—— (2000) 'Critique of the neoclassical theory of growth and distribution', *Banca Nazionale del Lavoro Quarterly Review*, 53 (215): 383–431.

Patinkin, D. (1990a) 'In defense of IS–LM', *Banca Nazionale del Lavoro Quarterly Review*, 0 (172): 119–34.

—— (1990b) 'On different interpretations of the *General Theory*', *Journal of Monetary Economics*, 26 (2): 205–43.

Phelps, E.S. (1990) *Seven Schools of Macroeconomic Thought*, Oxford: Oxford University Press.

Quesnay, F. (1966) *Scritti economici*, edited by R. Zangheri, Bologna: Forni edizioni.

Reddaway, W.B. (1936) 'Irrationality in consumers' demand', *Economic Journal*, 46 (183): 419–23.

—— (1937) 'Special obstacles to full employment in a wealthy community', *Economic Journal*, 47 (186): 297–307.

Ricardo, D. (1951) *On the Principles of Political Economy and Taxation*, Cambridge: Cambridge University Press (first published 1817).

—— (1951–55) *The Works and Correspondence of David Ricardo*, edited by P. Sraffa, Cambridge: Cambridge University Press.

Robbins, L. (1932) *An Essay on the Nature and Significance of Economic Science*, London: Macmillan.

Robertson, D. (1933) 'Saving and hoarding', *Economic Journal*, 43 (171): 399–413.

Rochon, L.-P. and Piégay, P. (eds) (2003) *Théories monétaires post Keynésiennes*, Paris: Economica.

Rochon, L.-P. and Rossi, S. (eds) (2003) *Modern Theories of Money. The Nature and Role of Money in Capitalist Economies*, Cheltenham and Northampton: Edward Elgar.

Romer, D. (1993) 'The new Keynesian synthesis', *Journal of Economic Perspectives*, 7 (1): 5–22.

—— (2001) *Advanced Macroeconomics*, New York: McGraw-Hill.

Romer, P.M. (1994) 'The origins of endogenous growth', *Journal of Economic Perspectives*, 8 (1): 3–22.

Rossi, S. (1997) *Modalités d'institution et de fonctionnement d'une banque centrale supranationale, le cas de la Banque Centrale Européenne*, Berne: Peter Lang.

—— (2001) *Money and Inflation. A New Macroeconomics Analysis*, Cheltenham and Northampton: Edward Elgar.

Rueff, J. (1963) 'Gold exchange standard: a danger to the west', in H.G. Grubel (ed.) *World Monetary Reform. Plans and Issues*, Stanford and London: Stanford University Press and Oxford University Press, 320–8.

—— (1980) *Oeuvres complètes*, Paris: Plon.

Sachs, J.D. (1989) *Developing Country Debt and the World Economy*, Chicago: Chicago University Press.

Salvatore, D. (2001) *International Economics*, New York: John Wiley & Sons.

Samuels, W.J. (ed.) (1990) *Economics as Discourse. An Analysis of the Language of Economics*, Dordrecht and Boston: Kluwer Academic Publishers.

Samuelson, P.A. (1948) 'The simple mathematics of income determination', in L.A. Metzler *et al. Income, Employment and Public Policy. Essays in Honor of Alvin H. Hansen*, New York: Norton, 133–55.

—— (1955) *Economics*, New York: McGraw-Hill.

Sarno, L. and Taylor, M.P. (2001) *International Economics*, New York: John Wiley & Sons.

—— (eds) (2002) *New Developments in Exchange Rate Economics*, Cheltenham and Northampton: Edward Elgar.

Say, J.-B. (1817) *Catechism of Political Economy*, Philadelphia: M. Carey & Son.

—— (1821) *A Treatise on Political Economy*, London: Longman, Hurst, Rees, Orme and Brown.

—— (2003) *Oeuvres complètes*, Paris: Economica.

Scazzieri, R. (1993) *A Theory of Production*, Oxford: Clarendon Press.

Schmitt, B. (1966) *Monnaie, salaires et profits*, Paris: Presses Universitaires de France.

—— (1972) *Macroeconomic Theory. A Fundamental Revision*, Albeuve: Castella.

—— (1973) *New Proposals for World Monetary Reform*, Albeuve: Castella.

—— (1975) *Théorie unitaire de la monnaie, nationale et internationale*, Albeuve: Castella.

—— (1977) *La monnaie européenne*, Paris: Presses Universitaires de France.

—— (1984a) *Inflation, chômage et malformations du capital*, Paris and Albeuve: Economica and Castella.

—— (1984b) *La France souveraine de sa monnaie*, Paris and Albeuve: Economica and Castella.

—— (1988) *L'ECU et les souverainetés nationales en Europe*, Paris: Dunod.

—— (1996a) 'A new paradigm for the determination of money prices', in G. Deleplace and E.J. Nell (eds) *Money in Motion. The Post Keynesian and Circulation Approaches*, London and New York: Macmillan and St. Martin's Press, 104–38.

—— (1996b) *Cours de théorie monétaire*, Fribourg: University of Fribourg, mimeograph.

—— (2000a) 'The double charge of external debt servicing', *Quaderno di ricerca No. 1*, Lugano-Vezia: Research Laboratory of Monetary Economics.

—— (2000b) 'Why the net interest on external debt weighs double on *LDCs*', *Quaderno di ricerca No. 3*, Lugano-Vezia: Research Laboratory of Monetary Economics.

—— (2003) 'Le paiement des intérêts par les PVD est *double*, les statistiques de la Banque mondiale ainsi que l'analyse le prouvent', Lugano: University of Lugano, mimeograph.

—— (2004) 'Between nations, the interest multiplier is equal to 2', *Quaderno di ricerca No. 12*, Lugano-Vezia: Research Laboratory of Monetary Economics.

Schmitt, B. and De Gottardi, C. (2003) 'An internal critique of general equilibrium theory', in L.-P. Rochon and S. Rossi (eds) *Modern Theories of Money. The Nature and Role of Money in Capitalist Economies*, Cheltenham and Northampton: Edward Elgar, 265–94.

Setterfield, M. (2002) 'Inflation: alternative theories of', in B. Snowdon and H.R. Vane (eds) *An Encyclopedia of Macroeconomics*, Cheltenham and Northampton: Edward Elgar, 345–50.

Sims, C.A. (1980) 'Macroeconomics and reality', *Econometrica*, 48 (1): 1–48.

Sinclair, P.J.N. (1983) *The Foundations of Macroeconomic and Monetary Theory*, Oxford: Oxford University Press.

Smith, A. (1776/1991) *The Wealth of Nations*, New York and Toronto: Everyman's Library.

Smithin, J. (ed.) (2000) *What is Money?*, London and New York: Routledge.

Snowdon, B. and Vane, H.R. (1996) 'The development of modern macroeconomics: reflections in the light of Johnson's analysis after twenty-five years', *Journal of Macroeconomics*, 18 (3): 381–401.

—— (1997a) *A Macroeconomics Reader*, London and New York: Routledge.

—— (eds) (1997b) *Reflections on the Development of Modern Macroeconomics*, Cheltenham and Brookfield: Edward Elgar.

—— (eds) (2002) *An Encyclopedia of Macroeconomics*, Cheltenham and Northampton: Edward Elgar.

Snowdon, B., Vane, H.R. and Wynarczyk, P. (eds) (1994) *A Modern Guide to Macroeconomics*, Aldershot and Brookfield: Edward Elgar.

Solomon, R. (1977) 'A perspective on the debt of developing countries', *Brookings Papers on Economic Activity*, 2: 479–501.

—— (1981) 'The debt of developing countries. Another look', *Brookings Papers on Economic Activity*, 2: 593–607.

—— (1999) *Money on the Move*, Princeton: Princeton University Press.

Solow, R.M. (1963) *Capital Theory and the Rate of Return*, Amsterdam: North-Holland.

—— (1984) 'Mr. Hicks and the classics', *Oxford Economic Papers*, 36 (supplement): 13–25.

—— (1994) 'Perspectives on growth theory', *Journal of Economic Perspectives*, 8 (1): 45–54.

Sraffa, P. (1960) *Production of Commodities by Means of Commodities*, Cambridge: Cambridge University Press.

Stadler, G.W. (1944) 'Real business cycles', *Journal of Economic Literature*, 32 (4): 1750–83.

Starr, R.M. (ed.) (1989) *General Equilibrium Models of Monetary Economies*, San Diego: Academic Press.

Stern, R.M. (1973) *The Balance of Payments. Theory and Economic Policy*, London and Basingstoke: Macmillan.

Stiglitz, J.E. (1989) 'Using tax policy to curb speculative short-term trading', *Journal of Financial Services Research*, 3 (2–3): 101–15.

—— (1992) 'Methodological issues and the new Keynesian economics', in A. Vercelli and N. Dimitri (eds) *Macroeconomics. A Survey of Research Strategies*, Oxford: Oxford University Press, 38–86.

Stoll, H.R. (ed.) (1990) *International Finance and Financial Policy*, Westport, Conn.: Quorum Books.

Summers, L.H. (2000) 'International financial crises: causes, prevention and cures', *American Economic Review*, 90 (2): 1–16.

Taylor, J.B. (1989) 'The evolution of ideas in macroeconomics', *Economic Record*, 65 (189): 185–9.

Taylor, M.P. (1990) *The Balance of Payments. New Perspectives in Open Economy Macroeconomics*, Aldershot and Brookfield: Edward Elgar.

—— (1995) 'The economics of exchange rates', *Journal of Economic Literature*, 33 (1): 13–47.

Tobin, J. (1978) 'A proposal for international monetary reform', *Eastern Economic Journal*, 4 (3–4): 153–9.

—— (1992) 'An old Keynesian counterattacks', *Eastern Economic Journal*, 18 (4): 387–400.

—— (1993) 'Price flexibility and output stability. An old Keynesian view', *Journal of Economic Perspectives*, 7 (1): 45–65.

—— (1995) 'The natural rate as new classical economics', in R. Cross (ed.) *The Natural Rate of Unemployment. Reflections on 25 years of the Hypothesis*, Cambridge: Cambridge University Press, 32–42.

—— (2003) 'A proposal for monetary reform', *Eastern Economic Journal*, 29 (4): 519–26.

Trautwein, H.-M. (1997) 'The uses of pure credit economy', in A.J. Cohen, H. Hagemann and J. Smithin (eds) *Money, Financial Institutions and Macroeconomics*, Boston, Dordrecht, London: Kluwer Academic Publishers, 3–16.

Trevithick, J.A. (1992) *Involuntary Unemployment. Macroeconomics from a Keynesian Perspective*, London and New York: Harvester-Wheatsheaf.

Ugur, M. (ed.) (2002) *An Open Economy Macroeconomics Reader*, London and New York: Routledge.

Uzan, M. (ed.) (2004) *The Future of the International Monetary System*, Cheltenham and Northampton: Edward Elgar.

Van Els, P.J.A. (1995) 'Real business cycle models and money: a survey of theories and evidence', *Weltwirtschaftliches Archiv*, 131 (2): 223–64.

Vane, H.R. and Thompson, J.L. (1992) *Current Controversies in Macroeconomics*, Aldershot and Brookfield: Edward Elgar.

Vercelli, A. (1991) *Methodological Foundations of Macroeconomics. Keynes and Lucas*, Cambridge and New York: Cambridge University Press.

Vercelli, A. and Dimitri, N. (eds) (1992) *Alternative Approaches to Macroeconomics*, Oxford: Oxford University Press.

Visser, H. (1991) *Modern Monetary Theory*, Aldershot and Brookfield: Edward Elgar.

Walras, L. (1984) *Elements of Pure Economics*, London: Allen & Unwin (first published 1874).

—— (1909) 'Economique et mécanique', *Bulletin de la Société Vaudoise de Sciences Naturelles*, 45: 313–25; reprinted in *Metroeconomica* (1960), 12 (1): 3–13.

—— (1909/1990) 'Economics and mechanics', in W.J. Samuels (ed.) *Economics as Discourse. An Analysis of the Language of Economists*, Dordrecht and Boston: Kluwer Academic Publishers, 189–224.

Weintraub, E.R. (1979) *Microfoundations*, Cambridge: Cambridge University Press.

—— (1984) *Elements of Pure Economics*, London: Allen & Unwin (first published 1874).

Weintraub, S. (1957) 'The micro-foundations of aggregate demand and supply', *Economic Journal*, 67 (267): 455–70.

Wicksell, K. (1934) *Lectures on Political Economy*, London: Routledge.

—— (1954) *Value, Capital and Rent*, London: Allen & Unwin.

—— (1965) *Interest and Prices*, New York: Kelly (first published 1898).

—— (1997) *Selected Essays in Economics*, edited by B. Sandelin, London and New York: Routledge (first published 1912).

Williamson, J. (1992–93) 'On designing an international monetary system', *Journal of Post Keynesian Economics*, 15 (2): 181–92.

—— (ed.) (1994) *Estimating Equilibrium Exchange Rates*, Washington: Institute for International Economics.

—— (1995) *What Role for Currency Boards?*, Washington: Institute for International Economics.

Williamson, J. and Lessard, D.R. (1987) *Capital Flight and Third World Debt*, Washington: Institute for International Economics.

Winters, A. (1992) *International Economics*, London and New York: Routledge.

World Bank (1982–2004), *Global Development Finance*, Washington: World Bank.

—— (1985) *World Development Report*, Washington: World Bank.

Worswick, D. and Trevithick, J.A. (eds) (1983) *Keynes and the Modern World*, Cambridge: Cambridge University Press.

Wray, L.R. (1996) 'Money in the circular flow', in G. Deleplace and E.J. Nell (eds) *Money in Motion. The Post Keynesian and Circulation Approaches*, London and New York: Macmillan and St. Martin's Press, 440–64.

—— (1998) *Understanding Modern Money. The Key to Full Employment and Price Stability*, Cheltenham and Northampton: Edward Elgar.

Young, W. (1987) *Interpreting Mr. Keynes. The IS-LM Enigma*, Cambridge: Polity Press.

Author index

Subject index

Printed in the United States
200486BV00013B/5/A